The Politics of Uneven Development

Why do some middle-income countries diversify their economies but fail to upgrade – to produce world-class products based on local inputs and technological capacities? Why have the "little tigers" of Southeast Asia, such as Thailand, continued to lag behind the Newly Industrializing Countries of East Asia? Richard F. Doner goes beyond "political will" by emphasizing institutional capacities and political pressures: Development challenges vary. Upgrading poses tough challenges that require robust institutional capacities. Such strengths are political in origin. They reflect pressures, such as security threats and resource constraints, which motivate political leaders to focus on efficiency more than clientelist payoffs. Such pressures help to explain the political institutions – "veto players" – through which leaders operate. Doner assesses this argument by analyzing Thai development historically, in three sectors (sugar, textiles, and autos) and in comparison with both weaker and stronger competitors (Philippines, Indonesia, Taiwan, Brazil, and South Korea).

Richard F. Doner received his Ph.D. in Political Science from the University of California, Berkeley, and is currently Associate Professor of Political Science at Emory University. His previous books include *Driving a Bargain: Automobile Industrialization and Japanese Firms in Southeast Asia* (1991) and (with David McKendrick and Stephan Haggard) *From Silicon Valley to Singapore: Location and Competitive Advantages in the Disk Drive Industry* (2000). He coedited (with Frederick Deyo and Eric Hershberg) *Economic Governance and the Challenge of Flexibility in East Asia* (2001). He has published numerous book chapters and articles in journals including *International Organization, World Politics, Studies in Comparative and International Development, World Development, Journal of East Asian Studies, Journal of Asian Studies, Review of Policy Research, Business and Politics,* and *Journal of Asian Business.* He has also consulted for several corporations and the World Bank on issues having to do with economic development in Southeast Asia.

The Politics of Uneven Development

Thailand's Economic Growth in Comparative Perspective

RICHARD F. DONER

Emory University

CAMBRIDGE
UNIVERSITY PRESS

CAMBRIDGE UNIVERSITY PRESS
Cambridge, New York, Melbourne, Madrid, Cape Town, Singapore, São Paulo, Delhi

Cambridge University Press
32 Avenue of the Americas, New York, NY 10013-2473, USA

www.cambridge.org
Information on this title: www.cambridge.org/9780521736114

First published 2009

Printed in the United States of America

A catalog record for this publication is available from the British Library.

Library of Congress Cataloging in Publication data
Doner, Richard F.
    The politics of uneven development : Thailand's economic growth in comparative
    perspective / Richard F. Doner.
        p.   cm.
    Includes bibliographical references and index.
    ISBN 978-0-521-51612-9 (hardback) – ISBN 978-0-521-73611-4 (pbk.)   1. Economic
    development–Thailand.   2. Thailand–Economic policy.   3. Industries–Thailand.
    I. Title.
    HC445.D65 2009
    338.9593–dc22   2008043671

ISBN 978-0-521-51612-9 hardback
ISBN 978-0-521-73611-4 paperback

Contents

Tables and Figures

Acknowledgments

Work on this book began, an embarrassingly long time ago, as an effort to make sense of Southeast Asian growth in light of new approaches to political economy. I had completed a study of Southeast Asian automotive industries in which I initially adopted a dependency-influenced view of developing country capitalists as something akin to compradors for foreign capital. Fieldwork in Thailand, Indonesia, Malaysia, and the Philippines quickly disabused me of that notion while alerting me to the important role of local business associations. That awareness in turn stimulated an interest in the broader role of institutions, private as well as public, in development. This interest was further inspired by the growing scholarship on the developmental state and on new institutional economics. These two literatures differ in important ways; and like any important line of thinking, each has its own weaknesses. But for me they combined to offer several important lessons: the centrality of collective action problems and institutional responses; the importance of distinguishing stages of development; the need to explore multiple influences on leaders' motivations; and the benefits of exploring such issues in the contexts of particular economic sectors.

At this point, I had the good fortune to become acquainted with the work of Ansil Ramsay, another scholar who also took seriously sectors, collective action, and Thailand. Ansil's pioneering work on Thai sugar stimulated a collaboration and friendship of more than two decades. This relationship is reflected not only in Ansil's co-authoring the sugar and textile chapters of this book, but also in seven co-authored articles and book chapters. Equally important, our ongoing discussions and joint fieldwork have been central to the elaboration of this book's overall framework.

The author of any serious scholarship depends on the advice and knowledge of others, but two features of this study have expanded such contributions. First, my theoretical approach has evolved in response to both newly emerging empirical puzzles and advances in the political economy of development. This evolution has benefited from discussions with colleagues from political science, economics, and sociology. Foremost among these have been Dan Breznitz, Cliff Carrubba, Scott Christensen, Gary Gereffi, Steph Haggard, Mark Hallerberg, Eric Hershberg, Allen Hicken, Tomas Larsson, Greg Noble, John Ravenhill, Tom Remington, Bryan Ritchie, Ben Schneider, Andrew Schrank, Dan Slater, and Robert Wade. My special thanks to Randy Strahan for scholarly insight and friendship over the years.

Second, as readers will soon discover, I place great evidentiary value on theoretically informed narratives of sectoral transformations. Although some information for such narratives comes from secondary sources, much of it requires access to knowledgeable participants and observers. In addition to the interviewees, listed anonymously at the back of this book, these include a number of other Thailand-based researchers, firm managers, and government officials who gave most generously of their time. Peter Brimble has been a source of friendship and wisdom about both Thailand and economic development issues for more than 20 years. Kevin Hewison has been generous in sharing his encyclopedic knowledge of Thai political economy. Patarapong Intarakumnerd has provided astute perspectives on the evolution of Thailand's science and technology structure. Anek Laothamatas was a valued collaborator in research on Thailand's experience in the 1980s. Pichai Kanivichaporn devoted innumerable hours to educating Ansil and me on the evolution and intricacies of Thailand's fascinating sugar industry. Prani Obhasanond offered an important and unique understanding of the collective action challenges facing Thai textile producers. Ammar Siamwalla, a man who read my first book about the auto industries of Southeast Asia while trapped in Bangkok traffic, has shared with Ansil and me his wisdom as the best kind of economist: one whose theoretical evolution is informed by the real-world politics of market failures as well as government failures. Nipon Paopongsakorn has been similarly generous with his expertise and wisdom. Rochana Kosiyanon, Suphat Suphachalasai, and Pichai Uttamapinat gave generously their time and knowledge in guiding us through the complexities of Thailand's textile industry. Sutham Vanichseri has been a consistent and thoughtful source of insight about the trials and tribulations of upgrading in Thailand. Over many years, Yeap Swee Chuan, one of Thailand's industrial pioneers, has demonstrated his belief in the importance of innovation through learning by sharing his experience and questions with me and other colleagues. Finally, Laurids Lauridsen's superb scholarship on Thailand has been both inspiration and guide for this project.

Having the opportunity to talk with these individuals and other interviewees has been a special privilege that only those conducting fieldwork in the developing world usually appreciate. It has provided insight into real-world development efforts. Some of these have not succeeded, usually due to the institutional and political factors outlined in this book. But most, if not all, were motivated by a commitment to Thai development, a commitment that too often goes unnoticed amidst Thailand's lively politics and vibrant entrepreneurial activity.

In researching and writing this book, I also benefited from a Social Science Research Council Grant for Advanced International Research in 1989, an Emory University Research Grant in 1996, a Research Fellowship at Stanford University's Asia-Pacific Research SSRC Fellowship in 1999, and an Emory University associate professor completion leave in 2007.

With very good reason, it is customary to express appreciation for the support of family and friends. Because this book took so long to complete (spanning numerous family changes, including the birth of several grandchildren to both Ansil and me), my debt is especially great. Thus, special thanks to my wife Susan for her patience laced with insightful humor.

Abbreviations

ADB	Asian Development Bank
ADC	Automobile Development Committee
AFTA	ASEAN Free Trade Area
AHDRP	Automotive Human Resources Development Project
AICO	ASEAN Industrial Cooperation
ASEAN	Association of Southeast Asian Nations
ASPL	Agricultural Sector Program Loan
ATDP	Association of Thai Textile Bleaching, Dyeing, Printing, and Finishing Industries
ATI	Association of Thai Industries
BAAC	Bank for Agriculture and Cooperatives
BDS	Business Development Services
BFC	Bangkok Fashion City
BIBF	Bangkok International Banking Facility
BOI	Board of Investment
BOT	Bank of Thailand
BUILD	BOI Unit for Industrial Linkage Development
CBU	Completely Built-Up
CCS	Commercial Cane System
CITA	Clothing Industry Training Authority
CKD	Completely Knocked-Down
CP	Charoen Phopkand
CPT	Communist Party of Thailand
CTAP	Cluster of Thai Automotive Parts
CTC	Canavieira Technology Center
DFT	Department of Foreign Trade

ESB	Eastern Seaboard
FDI	Foreign Direct Investment
FTA	Free Trade Agreement
FTI	Federation of Thai Industries
GBAP	Garment Business Association of the Philippines
GTEB	Garment and Textile Export Board
HCI	Heavy and Chemical Industrialization project
IAA	Instituto do Acucar e do Alcoool (Portuguese [Brazil])
IPM	Integrated Pest Management
IRP	Industrial Restructuring Program
ISI	Import Substitution
JPPCC	Joint Public and Private Sector Consultative Committee
KMT	Kuomintang
LC	Local Content
LDCs	Less Developed Countries
LIUP	Local Industry Upgrading Program
LTA	Long-Term Agreement
MFA	Multi-Fiber Arrangement
MITI	Ministry of International Trade and Industry
MOA	Ministry of Agriculture
MOF	Ministry of Finance
MOI	Ministry of Industry
MP	Member of Parliament
MTI	Ministry of Trade and Industry
NAC	National Agricultural Council
NAIC	Newly Agro-Industrializing Country
NESDB	National Economic and Social Development Board
NFTTI	National Federation of Thai Textile Industries
NICs	Newly Industrialized Countries
NIE	New Institutional Economics
NPA	New People's Army
NPLs	Nonperforming Loans
OBM	Original Brand Manufacturing
ODM	Original Design Manufacturing
OEM	Original Equipment Manufacturing
OIE	Office of Industrial Economics
PAP	People's Action Party
R&D	Research and Development
REM	Replacement Market
RESCOM	Restructuring Committee

S&T	Science and Technology
SAP	Social Action Party
SDA	Skills Development Act
SET	Stock Exchange of Thailand
SMEs	Small and Medium Enterprises
SNF	Siam Nawaloha Foundry
SRA	Sugar Regulatory Administration
TAI	Thai Automotive Institute
TAPMA	Thai Automotive Parts Manufacturers' Association
TAT	Tourism Authority of Thailand
TBA	Thai Bankers' Association
TCSA	Taiwan Cotton Spinners' Association
TFP	Total Factor Productivity
TGDF	Thai Garment Development Fund
TGMA	Thai Garment Manufacturers Association
ThTI	Thai Textile Institute
TID	Textile Industry Division
TIDC	Textile Industry Development Committee
TMAP	Textile Mills Association of the Philippines
TRT	Thai Rak Thai
TSC	Thai Sugar Corporation
TSTC	Thai Sugar Trading Corporation
TTMA	Thai Textiles Manufacturers Association
VAT	Value-Added Tax
VER	Voluntary Export Restriction

I

The Challenge of Uneven Development

I. DEVELOPMENT PUZZLES

Students of economic development have commonly focused on the question
of why some countries grow and others stagnate, and with good reason.
Empirically, the spectacular income gap separating the world's rich and
poor nations has become "the central economic fact of our time."[1] This
gap, moreover, now extends beyond the industrialized vs. developing
worlds to stark differences among developers.[2] The rich–poor gap has
defied easy theoretical explanations. Cultural explanations, for example,
foundered on the unexpected success of East Asian countries whose Con-
fucian ethic had previously been identified as an obstacle to growth.[3] Initial
endowments of assets such as human resources or manufacturing experience failed to explain the disappointing performance of countries such as
the Philippines.[4] Regime type – democracy or authoritarianism – failed to

---

[1] Rodrik (2003, 1). The ratio of differences in per capita incomes between the richest and
poorest countries rose from 3 to 1 in 1820 to 71 to 1 in 1992 (Milanovic 2005, 46). This
inequality reflects growth by some and stagnation by many, not simply the rich growing
more than others (Ibid. 131–133).

[2] The starkest difference, between East Asia and Africa, is epitomized by the fact that GDP
per capita were roughly the same for South Korea and Mozambique in 1960 but diverged
to $7,000 vs. $700 respectively by 1992 (Pritchett 2003, 127). Differences have also
emerged within regions, as reflected in the poor performance of the Philippines, relative to,
Taiwan, or sustained growth rates in Mauritius and Botswana in contrast to Africa's
overall stagnation (Acemoglu, Johnson, and Robinson 2001, 79; Submanian and Roy
2003).

[3] On the changing perceptions of Confucianism, see e.g. Morawetz (1980).

[4] Booth (1999).

correlate with variation in development outcomes.[5] Postwar development economists' belief that large, state-led projects could liberate entrepreneurs from traditional practices and other rigidities ran up against Latin America's state-led stagnation and Africa's institutional bloat.[6] Finally, the fact that global income levels exhibit not convergence but "Divergence, Big Time,"[7] has undermined the claims of neoclassical economists. As one long-time practitioner notes,

we economists have tried to find the precious object, the key that would enable the poor tropics to become rich. We thought we had found the elixir many different times. The precious objects we offered ranged from foreign aid to investment in machines, from fostering education to controlling population growth, from giving loans conditional on reforms to giving debt relief conditional on reforms. None has delivered as promised.[8]

While empirically and theoretically compelling, this emphasis on the "poor tropics" implies that little growth has occurred in the developing world. In so doing, it neglects the growth puzzle addressed in this book – namely, divergence among (and in some cases within) more successful developing countries. Although the poorest countries fared much worse than the rich, there has been growth among non-OECD countries, with some developing countries growing more than others.[9] As Alice Amsden has argued, "a handful of countries outside the North Atlantic – a group she labels 'the rest' – rose to the ranks of world-class competitors in a wide range of mid-technology industries."[10]

Within "the rest," countries such as Brazil, Argentina, Mexico, Turkey, Malaysia, Chile, and Thailand, have reached significant, albeit still constrained levels of development. They have increased the role of manufacturing in their economies, expanded the range of goods they produce, moved into more technology-intensive areas, and broadened their range of exports. Such "structural change" is a significant achievement. It has involved greater specialization, promoted new skills, and reduced vulnerability to product- or

---

[5] Przeworski and Limongi (1993).
[6] For example, Woo (1990).
[7] Pritchett (1997, 3).
[8] Easterly (2002, x).
[9] On growing disparities, see Easterly (2002, 60); Milanovic (2005, 49); and Collier (2007). Variation among developing countries is captured, but only partially, by the World Bank categories of "lower-middle-income economies," which includes countries ranging from Algeria to Brazil, to Ecuador, to Indonesia, and "upper-middle-income," whose members range from Argentina, to Equatorial Guinea to Argentina, to Malaysia (http://web.worldbank.org/WBSITE/EXTERNAL/DATASTATISTICS/0,contentMDK:2- accessed Dec. 18, 2006).
[10] Amsden (2001, 1).

sector-specific shocks.[11] However, these countries have had a harder time "upgrading" their economies – moving into higher value-added products, at high levels of efficiency, with local inputs.[12] As I discuss later, it is precisely such upgrading that has distinguished three of the East Asian newly industrialized countries (NICs) – Singapore, Taiwan and South Korea from other members of "the rest."

Accounting for these differences among successful developers is empirically important and theoretically challenging. Understanding why some countries have a hard time moving beyond sectoral diversification bears on the ability of middle-income developing countries to sustain growth in the face of new globalization pressures. Liberalized trade, new competitors, more volatile markets, and new technologies have shortened the period of time in which countries can grow on the basis of low costs, low skills, and high volumes.[13] The difficulties of moving beyond diversification also pose theoretical challenges equal to those raised in the rich vs. poor puzzle discussed earlier. Indeed, the performance of these "middle cases" is undertheorized. I suspect this reflects the fact that much of the otherwise valuable upgrading-related literature on innovation lumps these mixed performers into existing categories of success or failure.[14] Equally important, it ignores the institutional and political basis of mixed performance.[15]

Several scholars have begun to address these shortcomings. Amsden, for example, has argued that the limitations of otherwise impressive developers lie in their institutional weaknesses. These countries have emphasized macroeconomic stability rather than creating mechanisms through which their workers and firms develop the capacity to absorb and build on modern technology. They have, in other words, focused on "getting the prices 'right' and buying skills," as opposed to the NICs' strategies of "getting the institutions 'right' and building skills."[16] In a similar vein, Natasha Hamilton-Hart has argued that economic sustainability is less a function of policy choice than of "consistent implementation ..."[17] Implementation requires institutional capacity, but "getting the institutions right "is not

---

[11] Montobbio and Rampa (2005, 542); and Imbs and Wacziarg (2003, 62) who use the term "structural change" to describe sectoral diversification (82).

[12] On the distinction between structural change and upgrading, see Waldner (1999); Amsden (2001); Weiss (1998); Gibbon (2001); Ernst (2004).

[13] For example, Tewari (2006).

[14] For example, Mathews and Cho (2000).

[15] For example, Kim and Nelson (2000).

[16] Amsden (2001, 293).

[17] Hamilton-Hart (2002, 6).

easy. Atul Kohli has emphasized institutional strength as a key to the success of countries such as South Korea, noting that such capacities "are difficult to construct, even more difficult to institutionalize, and are not found in abundance in the developing world."[18] Robert Bates[19] has argued that while institutions are critical for development, they typically emerge not as efficient responses to new market conditions but out of the rough and tumble of politics.

In this book, I build on these insights by specifying the kinds of institutional capacities demanded by different development tasks and the conditions under which political elites will attempt to build such capacities. My hope is that this analysis will advance the transition from specifying what governments should do to the "economics and politics of how to accomplish the 'what'."[20] My core arguments, outlined later in this chapter and fleshed out more fully in Chapter 3, can be summarized as follows:

Different levels of development require *goodness of fit* between the tasks involved and the capacities of institutions – the norms, rules, and organizations that "govern" economic activities.[21] This "demand-side" account builds on a core contention of new institutional economics (NIE) – namely, that "the appropriate institutions of governance" depend on the attributes of the problem to be addressed.[22] We extend and apply this insight by specifying the attributes – the difficulties – of development problems and requisite institutions of governance. As suggested by Hamilton-Hart's question about types of growth – "Capacities for What?"[23] – economic development is not of a piece. Different levels of development involve tasks – understood as collective action problems – that vary in difficulty. Specifically, while structural change poses important challenges involved in mobilizing and investing funds in new activities, the difficulties of upgrading, involving learning and linkages, are even greater. Put differently, the interdependencies inherent in upgrading are particularly complex. Managing or "governing" such interdependencies in turn requires different,

[18] Kohli (2004, 382).

[19] Bates (1988; 1995).

[20] Pritchett and Woolcock (2004, 192).

[21] On defining institutions to include organizations, see the review in Doner and Schneider (2000). We equate institutions with "governance" mechanisms. By "governance" we mean the process through which economic and political institutions manage their interdependencies by coordinating their diverging interests. For an overview, see Ahrens (2002, 119–132). The core of this definition comes from Williamson, for whom governance structures refer to modes of organizing transactions (e.g., 1985).

[22] Ahrens (2002, 125); see also Aron (2000, 14).

[23] Hamilton-Hart (2002, 7).

indeed greater, institutional capacities.[24] Countries facing the same collective action problems with different institutional capacities will differ in their development outcomes.[25]

Turning to the "supply side," *why* would national leaders spend valuable time and resources to build institutional capacities appropriate for upgrading rather than buying off clients with side payments?[26] My answer is that they will only do so when faced with severe security and popular pressures on the one hand, and scarce resources with which to satisfy these pressures on the other. Such pressures serve both to motivate political leaders to construct growth-promoting, economic institutions and to concentrate the political structures through which elites operate. It is largely because such pressures are unusual that upgrading is so infrequent. In sum, I argue that (1) particular sets of institutional capacities and arrangements promote some levels of growth and not others, and (2) institutional capacities vary with pressures on political elites.

I assess these arguments through comparative – historical, cross-sectoral, and cross-national – analysis of growth in Thailand. Described as a "vexingly 'hybrid' image of both success and failure,"[27] Thailand has achieved stunning GDP growth rates *and* has diversified out of a small number of agricultural products to become a global export leader in a wide range of agricultural and industrial goods. Its performance made it one of the World Bank's "High Performing Asian Economies,"[28] an "Economic Miracle,"[29] and a probable *Fifth Tiger.*[30] Yet this impressive performance has been due largely to the efficient accumulation and mobilization of factor inputs "... rather than improvements in productivity."[31] These weaknesses emerged in the mid-to-late 1990s when the country's labor-intensive exports plunged, the stock market dropped, and Thailand became the first victim of the 1997 Asian economic crisis. The crisis transformed the country from "a miracle to needing one,"[32] forcing the authors of the popular *Thailand's*

[24] Weiss (1998).
[25] Waldner (1999, 153).
[26] Geddes (1994).
[27] Glassman (2004a, 1).
[28] World Bank (1993).
[29] Warr (1993b).
[30] Muscat (1994).
[31] Paopongsakorn and Somkiat (2001, 118). This pattern is similar to what the preeminent observer of early Thai economic change, described in 1955: "Thailand has been a sort of passive entity, adapting to changes and market influences originating in the world economy. Few innovations have originated within ..." (Ingram 1955, 217).
[32] Warr (1997; 1998).

Boom! to change the title of their revised edition to *Thailand's Boom and
Bust.*[33] The country's postcrisis growth rates have recovered, but as
described later in this book, its productivity problems remain. Indeed,
neoclassical economists' skepticism that East Asia's miracle growth reflected more "perspiration than inspiration" – more factor accumulation,
characteristic of structural change, than innovation, characteristic of
upgrading – may apply more to Thailand than to Singapore, South Korea,
or Taiwan.[34] In this study, I aim to shed light on the bases of this difference.

I do so first by establishing the core puzzles. Chapter 2 begins by
reviewing the Thai economy's impressive achievements and persistent
weaknesses. It then draws on Thai and other national experiences to
demonstrate the shortcomings of alternative explanations, such as education and political regime type, and to suggest the value of an account that
combines institutional capacities with political considerations. My own
approach, presented in Chapter 3, constitutes the basis for the comparative,
empirical analyses. Chapter 4 traces the postwar evolution of Thai institutions in the face of shifting political constraints. This serves both as an
initial test of our supply-side arguments and as country-level background
for the sectoral cases that follow.

Chapters 5–7 analyze Thai growth in three sectors – sugar, textiles/
garments, and automobiles.[35] Each chapter also compares Thai sectoral
performance with two national "shadow cases" – one a stronger performer,
the other a weaker one. As described at the end of this chapter, these
analyses provide opportunities to assess our arguments within and across
both sectors that pose different sets of challenges to developing country
firms and countries that provide different institutional and political contexts
in which firms operate. Taken together, they allow me to explain, for
example, (1) why the Philippines sugar industry deteriorated even as
Thailand sugar exports grew, while Brazil ascended to global sugar dominance by resolving productivity problems that continue to plague the Thais;
(2) why Thailand has been so successful at promoting investments in the
textile industry but has failed to develop the midstream and upstream
expertise, such as in dyeing and printing, so important to Taiwan's textile

---

[33] Pasuk and Baker (1996; 1998).
[34] For skeptical views, see e.g., Young (1994); and Kim and Lau (1994). For a critical
response, see Haggard and Kim (1997).
[35] Sectors are used here in the sense of "the sequence of activities required to make a product
or provide a service" (Schmitz 2005, 4), and thus involving "the design, production and
marketing of a good or service" (Gereffi 2005). See also Kaplinsky (2005, Ch. 5).

success; and (3) why Thailand has become a center of global pickup truck assembly but is increasingly devoid of indigenous auto parts producers.

The rest of this chapter lays groundwork for the subsequent analysis. The following two sections explain my focus on different growth challenges. Section II establishes the distinction between structural change and upgrading, especially as it is expressed in East Asia. Section III then addresses the "so what" question: How does upgrading influence a country's inequality and its ability to sustain growth? Section IV briefly introduces our explanation for such uneven performance (to be fleshed out in Chapter 3). Section V presents the benefits of examining Thailand in comparative perspective and outlines the book's design for doing so.

II. DEVELOPMENT DISTINCTIONS

In the last decade, several scholars have gone beyond rich vs. poor distinctions to provide a more variegated image of development stages. Drawing on multiple case studies, Dani Rodrik,[36] for example, has argued that the "transition from a low-income equilibrium to a state of rapid growth" may be qualitatively different from "the process of reigniting or sustaining growth for a middle-income country." Peter Evans has more squarely addressed the challenges of middle-income developers by distinguishing among (1) static efficiency, (2) the process of "ensconcing new entrepreneurial groups in a promising sector," and (3) the "full transformative job" in which "local firms ... continually respond to global changes in technology and market."[37] These last two challenges correspond to our understanding of structural change and upgrading, a distinction David Waldner labels "Gerschenkronian" and "Kaldorian" respectively. The former connotes the collective dilemmas involved in "capital accumulation and its subsequent socially productive investment in new industrial enterprises."[38] The challenges of structural change involve both mobilizing scarce capital and deploying such assets "in productive assets in the face of tremendous risks."[39] Upgrading, on the other hand, involves efforts to improve productivity or innovate in new products by

---

[36] Rodrik (2003, 15–17).
[37] Evans (1995, 80). Static efficiency involves "finding optimal combinations of given resources and factors of production ...," whereas dynamic efficiency typically involves mobilizing capacities and resources that are "hidden, scattered, or badly utilised," (Hirschman 1958, 5). In this sense, structural change and upgrading are both instances of dynamic efficiency.
[38] Waldner (1999, 167).
[39] Ibid.

"making existing factories more efficient and ... moving up the product cycle."[40] Gary Gereffi adds an important global dimension by defining upgrading as "the process by which economic actors – nations, firms, and actors – move from low-value to relatively high value activities – in global production networks."[41]

I draw from these authors three components necessary for upgrading: (1) shifting from lower-value to higher-value economic activities in processes, products, functions, and/or sectors; (2) increasing inputs, both material and technological, from local, that is, "indigenous" firms; and (3) producing at levels of price, quality, and delivery demanded by global value chains. Despite operating in new sectors, such as steel, local firms may be unable to meet global requirements of price, quality, or delivery.[42] Alternately, new, globally competitive sectors may be dominated by foreign producers operating largely in isolation from indigenous inputs. Neither of these scenarios – inefficient protectionism or denationalized, enclave-like

---

[40] Ibid. (170).

[41] Gereffi (2004, 171).

[42] For example, D'Costa (1999). Note that I am interested in degrees of or movement toward upgrading, since I do not presume a dichotomous distinction between structural change and upgrading in the real world. Structural change, as in the construction of a steel mill new to a country, clearly involves some increased use of local inputs and value added. And, as in innovation itself (Hobday 2000, 131), upgrading is a long-term process rather than a one-time event. An industry might rely on foreign goods for certain key inputs but be upgrading in the sense of constantly increasing its percentage of locally sourced inputs (e.g., Kim [1984] on Mitsubishi's early development). It might gradually move to exports. Or it might increase value added in particular areas. For example, it might move from original equipment manufacturing (OEM), in which a local firm produces a product according to the precise specification of a buyer (or multinational), to original design manufacturing (ODM) in which the supplier provides the design, to original brand manufacturing (OBM) in which the local firm designs and markets the product under its own name (Gereffi 2005). This progression might overlap with specific areas of technology development and innovation. These include (1) *Process upgrading*, in which inputs are transformed "into outputs more efficiently by reorganizing the production system or introducing superior technology" (e.g., improved engineering of assembly lines to cope with frequent model shifts, to reduce throughput and work-in-process); (2) *Product upgrading*, in which firms move into products with increased unit values, e.g., from un-dyed, cotton T-shirts sold in local markets to fancy shirts sold in the U.S.; (3) *Functional upgrading*, in which firms acquire new functions, such as computer-assisted design to increase the overall skill content of their production, or the use of computer-run filtration devices to ensure better quality of agricultural grain exports; and (4) *Intersectoral upgrading*, in which groups of firms move into new productive activities, e.g., the knowledge acquired in making TVs is used to produce computer equipment (Humphrey and Schmitz 2002, 1020). With regard to primary commodities, Gibbon (2001, 353–354) identifies three types of upgrading: moving up the quality grade ladder (e.g., higher quality sugar cane); producing new forms of existing commodities (e.g., gene-manipulated good crops, more differentiated types of an existing commodity); and localizing processing.

competitiveness – involves the dynamic exports based on increasing local value added that characterize upgrading.

Upgrading, not structural change, distinguishes the East Asian NICs from the Southeast Asian "little tigers" or, as some have labeled them, the ASEAN-4: Indonesia, Malaysia, the Philippines, and Thailand.[43] Table 1.1 shows that while the ASEAN-4 have not reached the levels of the NICs, they have made substantial progress in overall growth rates, the shift from agriculture to manufacturing, expansion and diversification of manu-factured exports, and levels of medium–high-tech exports. But the two groups differ with regard to local linkages and local technological capaci-ties. Foreign firms operating in the ASEAN-4 have moved into higher value-added products, but local producers account for little of this value. In contrast to South Korea, Taiwan, as well as Singapore, the ASEAN-4 economies tend to be dualistic, with foreign firms dominating high-tech exports as assemblers, exhibiting few linkages to domestic producers of intermediate and capital goods. This absence of linkages is reflected in the high trade deficits characteristic of mid- and high-tech industries through-out the ASEAN-4.[44]

This lack of indigenous inputs is strikingly illustrated by Malaysia's semiconductor industry. Although this industry has grown to become the second largest exporter of semiconductors to the United States,[45] the industry "has remained relatively stuck at the same downstream stages of production as 25 years ago, still doing assembly, testing, and packaging for MNCs."[46] The high import content of Malaysia's semiconductors is com-mon throughout the country's entire electrical and electronics industry, which, in the early 1990s, imported over 69% of intermediate inputs.[47] Similarly, Thailand became one of the world's largest exporters of hard disk drives in the 1980s and 1990s. But there are no significant Thai suppliers of parts or services to the foreign-owned disk drive producers. This contrasts with the significant development of local precision engineering and other suppliers to foreign firms seen in Singapore and, to an extent, Malaysia's state of Penang.[48]

There are also important ASEAN-4 vs. NIC differences with regard to local firms' ability to shift from original equipment manufacturing (OEM)

---

[43] ASEAN stands for Association of Southeast Asian Nations.
[44] For example, Dhanani (2000); Chen (1999).
[45] Chen (1999, 127).
[46] Ibid. (127, 130).
[47] Ibid. (134).
[48] McKendrick, Haggard, and Doner (2000); Rasiah (2000).

TABLE 1.1 *Structural Changes in East Asia*

	GDP Growth (% Change, 1965–1999)	Manufactured Exports (% of GDP, 1965)	Manufactured Exports (% of GDP, 1999)	Agric. (% of GDP, 1965)	Agric. (% of GDP, 1999)	Labor Force in Agriculture (% of Labor Force, 1980)	Labor Force in Agriculture (% of Labor Force, 1995)	Medium % High-tech Products as % of Total Mfg. Exports, 1985*	Medium % High-tech Products as % of Total Mfg. Exports, 1994*
Taiwan	5.8	35.06	26.59	6.77	2.55			34.0	61.1
Korea	7.96	17.34	31.8	36.45	4.99	34	12.5	32.3	62.3
Japan	4.57	33.73	23.51	9.82	1.72	10.4	5.7	n.a.	n.a.
Singapore	8.79	14.79	25.88	2.85	0.16	1.3	0.2	46.9	79.4
Hong Kong	6.85		6.18		0.13			33.5	42.3
East Asian NICs Avg.	6.79	25.23	22.79	13.97	1.91	15.23	3	36.7	61.3
Thailand	6.94	14.17	32.37	31.92	10.46	70.8	52.1	19.7	49.8
Malaysia	6.86	9.45	31.52	28.75	10.68	37.2	20	36.5	69.1
Indonesia	6.12	8.35	25.44	55.99	19.48	55.9	46.1	8.7	23.2
Philippines	3.76	19.5	21.48	25.85	17.73	51.8	44.1	n.a.	n.a.
ASEAN-4 Avg.	5.92	12.87	27.70	35.63	14.59	53.93	40.57	18.3	47.4

Sources: World Bank Development Indicators, 2001; Asian Development Bank Economic Indicators, various years.
*Lall (1998), cited in Wong and Ng (2000, 15).

to original design manufacturing (ODM) to original brand manufacturing (OBM).[49] Moving along this continuum requires that local firms develop the capacity to innovate, and innovation requires what Cohen and Levinthal label "absorptive capacity": the ability of local producers to recognize the value of new (to the firm) information, to assimilate it, and to apply it to commercial ends.[50] Korean and Taiwanese firms have, to varying degrees, proceeded along this trajectory, but firms in the ASEAN-4, even large business groups with extensive experience, have been much slower to move beyond OEM.[51] This contrast in moving up the value-added ladder also extends to low- and mid-tech industries such as footwear and textiles, where ASEAN-4 firms might be presumed to have comparative advantage. Only in resource-based industries, such as plywood, food, palm oil, and jewelry, have the ASEAN-4 improved, and even in some of these, such as the sugar case discussed later in this book, local firms have had difficulty contending with low-wage competitors on the one hand and higher productivity rivals on the other.[52]

These differences reflect contrasting levels of productivity and technology competencies as reflected in Table 1.2 and noted especially by scholars of East Asian development. Robert Wade, for example, has questioned the robustness of development in the ASEAN-4, noting the heavy export profile of foreign investment in these countries (i.e., the fact that growth does not depend on domestic economic expansion), the heavy reliance of foreign subsidiaries on imported inputs, and what he calls their generally "technologyless industrialization."[53]

III. STRUCTURAL CHANGE VS. UPGRADING: WHY IT MATTERS

But growth is growth. Why should it matter if growth is "technologyless"? Why should we be concerned about upgrading if countries are able to continue shifting into new sectors on the basis of foreign technology and/or

---

[49] See fn. 12.

[50] Cohen and Levinthal (1990).

[51] See Rasiah (2003); Kim (2001); Ernst (2000); Wong and Ng (2001); Amsden (1989; 2001); Amsden and Chu (2003). I discuss technological weaknesses in large Thai groups in later chapters.

[52] On footwear see Cheng (2001), Chiu and Lui (2001). On garments and textiles, see, Chen, Chen and Chu (2001). On shrimp, see Brimble and Doner (2007).

[53] Wade (2005). Others highlighting the NIC vs. ASEAN-4 distinction include Booth (1999); MacIntyre (1994); Wong and Ng (2001); Rasiah (2003); and Doner and Hawes (1995).

TABLE 1.2 *Productivity and Technology Competencies*

Country	Value Added/Worker in Mfg. (US$) 1980*	Value Added /Worker in Mfg. (US$) 1994 (% Growth 1980–1994)*	Gross Exp. on R&D as % of GDP, 1996*	World Competitiveness Rankings of Science and Technology 1999*	Tertiary Science and Engineering Students as % of Population, Early 1990s*
Hong Kong	7,840	26,436 (9.1)	0.1	22	0.47
Korea	9,545	52,760 (13)	2.8	28	1.34
Taiwan	7,470	33,766 (11.4)	1.8	10	1.09
Japan			3.0	17	0.46
Singapore	13,942	56,329 (10.5)	1.4	12	0.56
Asian NICs					
Average	9,699	42,323 (11.1)		16.75	
Thailand	5,675	18,734 (8.9)	0.1	46	0.32
Indonesia	3,499	6,954 (5)	0.2	47	0.13
Malaysia	8,060	15,317 (4.7)	0.2	32	0.15
Philippines	4,552	12,334 (7.4)	0.2	33	n.a.
ASEAN-4					
Average	5,447	13,335 (6.5)		39.5	

Sources: www.taiwan; www.info.gov.hk.; Taiwanese Ministry of Economic Affairs Indicators, 2000; World Bank Development Indicators, 2002; MASTIC, 1998; Thai National Research Council, 1998; UNESCO yearly report, various years.
Note: * = Wong and Ng (2001: Tables 1.5, 1.7).

existing factor endowments?[54] For example, Alwyn Young, who argued that the NICs' growth was based on factor accumulation, not productivity growth, was sanguine about the potential "gains from factor accumulation and the sectoral reallocation of resources ..."[55] But Paul Krugman, who drew on Young's work, came to different conclusions, arguing that development based on rapid growth of inputs rather than productivity would be subject to the law of diminishing returns.[56] And despite challenges to both Young's calculations and Krugman's conclusions,[57] there are other important reasons to question the sustainability of diversification-based growth. One is the finding that sectoral diversification constitutes the key force for national growth up to a certain income level, past which growth occurs through more concentration, involving domestic linkages and agglomeration.[58] Put differently, diversification seems to be the key for low-income countries, while concentration is more important for richer economies. But even this finding does not capture some of the short-term risks of not upgrading.

One has to do with the danger that a combination of low innovation in agriculture and reliance on foreign technology without local linkages promotes capital intensive manufacturing and fails to absorb rural populations. This phenomenon is evident in the ASEAN-4 (Table 1.1). It is likely to constitute a drag on economic growth in light of the finding that "the transition from low productivity farming, absorbing the bulk of the labor force, to high productivity farming absorbing little is the essence of development."[59] Relatedly, the persistence of low productivity in agriculture and weak labor absorption in industry contributes to inequality which in turn discourages growth.[60] Another set of problems has to do with the economic and political consequences of weak linkages. As Wade argues, the lack of a "dense set of input–output linkages between sectors" limits the expansion of domestic demand and thus increases vulnerability to export volatility. Such a weak, internally integrated production structure can also discourage cross-class alliances and thus the potential for a broad constituency for growth promotion.[61]

---

[54] I am grateful to Stephan Haggard for emphasizing this concern.

[55] Young (1994, 973).

[56] Krugman (1994).

[57] Haggard and Kim (1997; Easterly (2002, 65–66).

[58] Imbs and Wacziarg (2003).

[59] Pritchett (2004, 76); there is a "... strong inverse relationship between a nation's level of per capita income and the size of the rural population" (Cypher and Dietz 1997, 331).

[60] For example, Birdsall, Pinckney, and Sabot (2000, 4).

[61] Wade (2006, 13).

Also troubling is the transience of low-wage advantages, especially in a region as competitive as East Asia and as exposed to the demands of global value chains. Since the mid-1990s to late 1990s industrialists in Thailand and elsewhere have spoken of operating in a "nutcracker," squeezed between new, low-wage competitors and those countries with higher wages but stronger technological and innovation capacities. In effect, developing countries have limited time in which to capture wage-based rents in global value chains.[62] Sustained growth (rents) will require meeting value chain requirements for higher skills and more extensive domestic linkages. For example, as discussed in Chapter 6, global garment buyers have begun to move to "full package production" which often involves direct sourcing from a complete supply chain within one country.[63]

Weak linkages reflect the coexistence of technologically advanced foreign firms producing for export on the one hand, and weak local technology and innovation capacities on the other. How do we account for the fact that knowledge, whether basic research or applied technology, is available from foreign subsidiaries and foreign buyers but not always "absorbed" by local producers? This puzzle applies to agriculture as well.[64] How, for example, do we explain that despite the birth of the Green Revolution in the Philippines (at the International Rice Research Institute), the country has been "in the embarrassing position of not being self-sufficient" in rice?[65]

IV. THE ARGUMENT

My answer begins from well-accepted assumptions about the centrality of collective action problems and institutions for development. The central dilemma plaguing economic change is the gap between private and social benefits.[66] As North and Thomas note, growth requires that individuals "be lured by incentives to undertake ... socially desirable activities."[67] Institutions are the mechanisms through which individuals are lured. Economic

---

[62] Kaplinsky (2000).

[63] Bair and Gereffi (2002). Even when developing country firms improve their skill and technology levels, interfirm and international competition may reduce the returns to such upgrading (Schrank 2004) .

[64] This is a puzzle in the sense that it runs against neoclassical growth theory's emphasis on the benefits of technology (Solow 1957) and the World Bank's (1993) expectations, influenced by the "new growth theory," that export production would actively expose developing country to new technology. For a review, see Haggard and Kim (1997).

[65] Billig (2003, 101).

[66] Waldner (1999, 166).

[67] North and Thomas (1970, 2).

development depends critically on institutions through which "political and economic actors organize and manage their interdependencies."[68] Institutional deficiencies plague poor countries

This institutionalist turn has been a cross-disciplinary one with real-world policy implications.[69] World Bank publications such as *Institutions Matter: Beyond the Washington Consensus*[70] have encouraged development practitioners to focus more on urging states to construct pro-market institutions and less on advising them to cease intervening in markets. The consensus among development specialists has become: "to get prices right and to get policies right, it is also necessary to 'get institutions right'."[71] But recommendations that "institutions matter" risk being (1) vacuous or even misleading when it comes to specifying the kinds of institutions needed for growth;[72] and (2) naive when it comes to why such capacities actually exist.[73] My argument addresses each of these problems.

The Demand for Institutional Capacities: Analyses of the NICs' impressive achievements have led to the general recognition that not only is development institutionally demanding, but that different development strategies demand different institutional capacities.[74] Successful development thus requires a "goodness of fit between the chosen strategy ... and the institutional environment in which the strategy is to be implemented."[75] For our purposes, "chosen strategies" refer to development objectives, such as

---

[68] Eden and Hampson (1997, 362). Despite some overlap, I distinguish economic from political institutions. I understand the former to refer to the rules, norms and organization that determine the production, allocation and distribution of goods and services, such as firms, groups and networks of firms, property rights, training institutions, and other arrangements that have a direct influence on firms' operations. Political institutions include those that determine the broad parameters of resource allocation within which firms operate, e.g., courts, police forces, electoral rules, party structures, unitary vs. federalist arrangements, and political regime type (democratic vs. authoritarian). On this distinction, see Frye (2000, 4); Jutting (2003, 15); and Hallerberg (2002). This distinction is especially important for identifying the independent impact of veto players, discussed later.

[69] Emphasis on the developmental role of institutions has drawn on transaction and information costs, and collective action approaches from economics (Williamson 1985; Olson 1965), network approaches from sociology (e.g., Eden and Hampson 1997), and political scientists' analyses of states and the incentives facing state leaders (e.g., Haggard 1990; Bates 1995).

[70] Burki and Perry (1998).

[71] Meier (2001, 23). A forceful statement of this point is found in Frye's analysis of Russian financial markets (2000, 4).

[72] Pritchett and Woolcock (2004, 204).

[73] Knight (1992).

[74] For example, World Bank (1993, 6); and Page (1994).

[75] Biggs and Levy (1991, 366).

diversification and upgrading. Attaining those objectives require implementing sets of tasks or policies, each of which involves collective action
dilemmas. The challenge here is twofold: to distinguish among the collective
action problems inherent in various tasks; and to specify the kinds of
institutional capacities required to address such dilemmas. As Greg Noble
warns, we need to understand how "varying problems call on different
types of capacities."[76] In its simplest form, my response is as follows:

Economic development through upgrading, and thus reliance on local technological
competencies and linkages, involves difficult collective action problems that in turn
require greater institutional capacities than does growth through static comparative
advantage or through economic diversification.

I develop this argument in three steps. The first involves identifying a range
of possible difficulties inherent in development policies. I draw from the NIE
to highlight large numbers-related problems of free riding and high transaction costs; information requirements; and distributional tensions. This
leads to three sets of questions about the collective action problems inherent
in policies related to structural change and upgrading: (1) How many actors
need to be involved for a policy to be successfully formulated and implemented? (2) Does the policy require highly technical knowledge and/or site-
specific information? Is there a template for the policy or are actors operating
blind? (3) Are there big losers? Are they organized? Are their losses immediate? These dimensions provide a metric for assessing a development task's
difficulty. Other things being equal, I predict these difficulties are cumulative,
that the more actors involved in implementing a policy, the newer or more
complex information required, and more severe the distributional consequences, the more difficult the task will be to accomplish.

The second step involves specifying the institutional capacities needed for
accomplishing various tasks. Three sets of capacities are most relevant:
consultation, in which actors learn each others' preferences with regard to
goals and mechanisms for achieving those goals; *credible commitments*, in
which actors develop belief in each others' willingness and ability to follow
through with stated preferences and agreed courses of action; and *monitoring*, in which actors obtain information about each others' actual
behavior. My assumption is that the more difficult the policy task, the more
extensive the required institutional capacities.

I am more agnostic with regard to institutional design, especially since
the NICs' experience suggests that equally strong institutional capacities

---

[76] Noble (1998, 21).

can emerge from different kinds of organizational arrangements.[77] However, I do anticipate that capacities will follow a continuum consistent with specific organizational dimensions: cohesion and independence in the public bureaucracy; collective strength in the private sector; and transparent, function-based linkages between public and private actors. At the top of this continuum are a small number of "developmental" or "capitalist cohesive,"[78] states that exhibit the bureaucratic coherence, organized private actors, and systematic, transparent public–private coordination constituting what Evans[79] labels "embedded autonomy." Somewhat lower along this continuum lie "intermediate states" characterized by uneven bureaucratic coherence, significant clientelism in public–private relations, and factionalism within the private sector.[80]

These steps constitute the basis for anticipating the kinds of capacities and arrangements required for the tasks involved in structural change vs. upgrading. Both involve serious challenges. The former involves mobilizing and investing capital in new, typically risky ventures, whereas the latter involves making these ventures productive and moving up the product cycle based on local resources. But making investments more productive requires innovation and thus learning new technologies and skills. Such learning is far from automatic.[81] Because productivity-enhancing techniques are often new to developing country firms, even if well understood elsewhere, this learning is often tacit and costly. Technology spillovers from even the most supportive foreign partners, buyers, or suppliers require deliberate and systematic efforts. These efforts may themselves have to be stimulated by rewards and threats from public authorities – what Alice Amsden[82] labels "reciprocity." And because upgrading draws on multiple actors as sources of information, intermediate inputs, and selective benefits, it typically involves collective efforts. All of this confirms a core insight of endogenous

---

[77] Wong and Ng (2001).

[78] Kohli (2004).

[79] Evans 1995.

[80] Evans (1995, Ch. 3). In the East Asian developmental states, institutional strength at the national level coexists with clientelism and inefficiency in particular sectors. Such bifurcated situations reflect the more "clientelised" sectors' role as mechanisms to generate political support for the more rigorous governance arrangements in competitive sectors (Kang 2002; Cox and McCubbins 2000). There is thus some degree of differentiation between competitive and clientelistic sectors in most middle-income developers. The key distinction hinges on the degree of clientelism and whether sectors governed by strong institutions are buffered from clientelism elsewhere in the political economy.

[81] Romer (1990; 1994).

[82] Amsden 2001.

growth literature: Because technology is not a costless public good, technological progress depends not simply on physical and human and capital but also on the "institutional structures of the economy."[83]

Development is not, of course, *only* about collective action and institutions. There are problems that can and should be resolved by arms-length, market pressures.[84] There are problems whose distributional nature is so extreme and/or places where institutions are so inefficient that attempts to organize collective action are fruitless or bound to end in inefficiency and even corruption, such as what Cox and McCubbins label the "dark side of corporatism."[85] A major challenge for development scholarship is explaining the variation among collective action efforts.

The Supply of Institutional Capacities: The fact that institutions can promote efficiency by resolving collective action problems has led some new institutionalists to presume that institutions emerge and evolve for pure market reasons, that is, as the result of choices by private parties to enhance mutual welfare in response to shifts in factor prices. As Bates notes, this account is flawed by its neglect of politics:

The new institutionalists have been slower to acknowledge that the creation of economic institutions takes place not on the 'level playing field' of the market but rather within the political arena, in which some are endowed with greater power than others. ...The reality is that non-market institutions are often created in the legislature or the court room or by economic actors who anticipate the appeal of others within the political arenas. Property rights, contract law, the power to regulate the production and exchange of commodities – these and other economic institutions are created by the state.[86]

Developmental state scholars, for their part, have emphasized broad political considerations, especially nationalism, security threats, and state autonomy.[87] But there is little guidance as to why nationalism should stimulate growth-promoting institutions in some places (Northeast Asia) but inefficient populism in others (Latin America). Relatedly, it remains unclear why some states respond to external threats through institutional strengthening and industrial change, whereas others simply build up military forces. And finally, reliance on political autonomy reflects the developmental state writings' "thin politics" by begging the question of why

---

[83] Cypher and Dietz (1997, 247; Romer 1994, 16).
[84] See for example the discussion of overcapacity problems in Chapter 3.
[85] Cox and McCubbins (2000, 55).
[86] Bates (1995, 42).
[87] For example, Woo-Cumings (1998).

political leaders, independent of political pressures, should expend scarce resources to create efficiency-enhancing institutions.[88]

My answer starts from the argument that politicians will attempt to create strong institutions when they perceive their countries confronting pressures similar to those faced by firms in highly competitive markets.[89] Drawing on the concept of "systemic vulnerability"[90] I identify three sets of systemic, background factors leading to such perceptions and behavior: external security threats, popular pressures, and resource constraints. External threats and popular pressures constitute claims on resources. Where such resources are scarce and pressures are high, political elites will attempt to build growth-promoting institutions to generate needed resources. Thus,

The availability of institutional capacities depends on the ways in which resource claims and resource availability influence the calculus of national political elites and the concentration of political authority through which elites operate.

Three aspects of this argument may be less obvious but merit explicit mention and close scrutiny in light of this book's evidence. The first has to do with the explanatory status of the structure of national political competition operationalized through what are more commonly known as the number of effective "veto players."[91] I presume that such competition is an "intervening variable," that is, it is influenced by systemic variables but in turn influences institutional creation. More specifically, and contrary to more path-dependent arguments, I expect that the number of veto players will move from very high to very low toward a moderate number as systemic pressures increases. The second is that, unlike the original version of systemic vulnerability,[92] my argument allows for ordinal variation. That is,

---

[88] Wade (1992); see also Moon and Prasad (1998).

[89] This argument is found in a range of scholarship: Juhana Vartiainen argues that central to an explanation of institutional strength in Taiwan, South Korea, Finland, and Austria were external political challenges and projects of national integration and mobilization under which "these countries could ill afford an economic failure" (1999, 223). Drawing on Mexican examples, Careaga and Weingast argue that "good governance" occurs when greater electoral competition and greater dependence on locally generated revenues increases political leaders' propensities to provide market-fostering public goods (2003). Judith Tendler (1997) traces the unexpected, good government in Northeast Brazil to electoral competition. Finally, even Jack Knight notes that actors' more common distributional impulses in institutional creation will be minimized in rare situations where actors are constrained to search for the most efficient arrangements (Knight 1992). See also Schneider and Maxfield (1997, 25).

[90] Doner, Ritchie and Slater [DRS] (2005).

[91] Cox and McCubbins (2000).

[92] DRS (2005).

I anticipate that variation in degrees of systemic pressures will result in degrees of change in institutional capacities. Rather than dichotomous shifts from "developmental" to "intermediate" state status, such changes may occur as "blips" over time and/or as "pockets of efficiency" (or inefficiency) in particular policy realms. Finally, my argument privileges *national* level variables as determinants of sectoral performance. In this, I follow a large body of scholarship on national production regimes, innovation systems, or varieties of capitalism nicely reflected in David Waldner's contention that "even greater variation in efficiency and innovation distinguish almost all firms in an industrial sector of one national economy from almost all firms in another national economy."[93]

But this argument that "national trumps sectoral" would seem to be inconsistent with my view that ordinal shifts in systemic pressures can lead to sectoral pockets of efficiency. How do I account for important "hints" of significant strength in otherwise weak national institutional systems?[94] I expect that a sector exhibiting institutional strengths at odds with modal, national patterns should reflect political elites' estimation of that sector's significance in light of serious, systematic pressures. Put differently, elites economize on resource-intensive institutional efforts by focusing not on all sectors but on those with obvious potential.

V. THE THAI CASE(S)

What damn good is this country – you can't compare it with anything![95]

I believe that David Wilson's frustration is unwarranted, that the Thai "case" lends itself well to methodologically sound comparative analysis.[96] As designed in this study, the analysis offers significant variation and thus opportunities for evaluating (and refining) my arguments. And because Thailand exhibits features common in the developing world, Thai-based

---

[93] Waldner (1999, 170). On production regimes, see Kitschelt (1991). On national business systems, see Whitley (1992). On "national innovation systems," see Nelson (1993). On "varieties of capitalism," see Hall and Soskice (2000). It bears emphasis that while this national institutionalist approach affirms the centrality of firms, it views firms as "relational" institutions whose success in exploiting core competencies involves not just internal resources but also links with other actors, such as suppliers, competitors, and clients (Ibid., 6).

[94] For example, Kohli (2004, 382).

[95] David Wilson, cited in Phillips (1976, 452).

[96] I understand a "case" to refer to a given study's unit of analysis, an instance of a phenomenon (e.g., national economic growth, a social movement, a party system) that we wish to understand (Brady and Collier 2004).

findings are potentially generalizable to other, especially middle-income, developing countries.

Cases, Observations, and Variation: Studies of development are often weakened by "selection on the dependent variable." Many studies focus on either the developmentally challenged, such as Latin American countries hobbled by protection and rent seeking, or on impressive successes, such as the East Asian NICs.[97] Studies of intermediate cases, such as Thailand and its Southeast Asian neighbors, tend to emphasize either their achievements or their shortcomings.[98] The problem, as Stephan Haggard has observed with regard to the debate on industrial policy, is that "the analysts pick a successful (unsuccessful) industry, demonstrate that policy support existed, and then conclude that the case for industrial policy is made (or rejected)."[99]

By contrast, the present study offers numerous within- and cross-case opportunities both to assess our expectations in the context of *mixed or uneven* performance, and to avoid the small-N problem common in studies of single cases.[100] I begin in Chapter 4 at the country level by assessing change and sequence over time in Thai national institutions. This historical overview generates different observations that allow me to assess the congruence of the Thai case with my arguments about institutional origins. Some of these observations focus on whether the variables actually line up or correlate in the way I predict. Others focus on the sequences of the variables, the mechanisms that link them, the presence of new variables, and the actors' perceptions of and responses to the variables.[101]

The sectoral analyses (sugar, textiles, and automobile) in Chapters 5–7 can be considered cases in and of themselves. That is, I shift the level of analysis to gain analytical leverage for our principal case of Thailand. I have selected these sectors on the basis of their similarities and differences. All three are important to the Thai economy; all face growing external pressures to upgrade; and all have been the target of development attention by Thai policy makers. However, they differ from each other with regard to entry barriers. As global value chain analysis suggests, the opportunities and conditions for upgrading in sugar, while significant, are lower than those in

---

[97] For example, Lall (1998). For a useful effort to address both Northeast and Southeast Asia, see Booth (1999).
[98] For example, Bello and Rosenfeld (1990). For an exception, see Perkins (1994: 661).
[99] Haggard (2003, 21).
[100] For example, Snyder (2001).
[101] Brady and Collier (2004) label these "data-set" and "causal-process" observations respectively.

apparel and textiles, which are in turn lower than those in automobiles.[102] As such, the sectors afford opportunities to assess expectations through both congruence and cross-case analysis.

Longitudinal analysis of each sector provides the opportunity to assess whether the sector's overall correlations of variables and causal process are congruent with the expectations derived from my arguments. And because they exhibit different entry barriers, they constitute a loose hierarchy of "harder" to "easier" cases for our contention that upgrading requires extensive institutional capacities.[103] The three sectors also allow for a "most-different/similar outcome" comparison. Because they differ with regard to entry barriers and particular sectoral arrangements but operate within a common national institutional and political context, they provide opportunities to assess our "supply-side" contention that sectoral arrangements follow national patterns, except where elites consider that sector's performance to be an especially important source of resources in light of politically important pressures.

I seek further evidence by supplementing the analysis of Thai sectoral performance with a comparison of two other countries' outcomes in each sector. I have selected these "shadow cases" on the basis of two criteria: The first is variation in growth outcomes, with one country's sectoral performance stronger than that of Thailand, the other's performance weaker. The second is that my cases, especially the "weaker" performer, must have had the possibility of generating the outcome of interest, that is, sectoral growth.[104] If my arguments are correct, the variation in growth outcomes

---

[102] In this sense, sugar, apparel/textile, and automobiles constitute a hierarchy of rising technology levels and more rapid rates of technological change. In addition, access to technology varies across these sectors: As an "international trader-driven" value chain, sugar offers clear upgrading opportunities (higher quality, product shifts, and more local processing), but the level of technology required is low relative to the other two sectors as is the difficulty of access to such technology (see e.g., Gibbon 2001). As a "consumer-driven" value chain, apparel/textiles offers easier access to production technology (but still-difficult access to marketing and design technology, which is controlled by lead firms, e.g., final retailers). Conversely, automobile production is a "producer-driven" chain in which production technology is more directly controlled by lead firms, (e.g., auto assemblers and foreign component producers). On entry barriers presented by different kinds of global value chains and their relations to upgrading, see e.g., Kaplinsky (2005); McKendrick, Doner, and Haggard 2000, Ch. 11).

[103] That is, sugar constitutes a relatively "hard" case for our argument since, other things being equal, one might assume that upgrading in a low-tech industry would not involve extensive information exchanges and learning and would thus not require significant institutional capacities.

[104] For example, our shadow sugar cases, the Philippines and Brazil, exclude those countries whose weather and soil preclude the possibility of sugar production and export and whose

will reflect variation in our key independent variables: institutional capacities and, in turn, pressures on elites to promote such capacities.

In assessing my arguments, the three national cases examined in each sectoral chapter constitute a "most-similar," cross-case design to the extent that their different performance outcomes correlate with differences in institutional and political variables.[105] But this design is flawed. Although contrasts in national institutional and political variables may correspond with variation in performance outcomes, the restricted population of potentially strong performers does not allow us to control for the possibility that other variables may have played a more important role in accounting for performance. Within-case analysis, especially process tracing of sequence, actors' perceptions, and the presence of other variables, thus bears significant explanatory weight in this analysis.

Generalizability of a non-NIC: This effort to gain multiple sources of analytical leverage for our principal case, Thailand, presumes that lessons from the Thai case are in fact generalizable to other developing countries. One way to appreciate the broader value of Thailand's development experience is to view it relative to lessons drawn from the East Asian NICs. Although the NICs have inspired an extensive body of research, some have questioned their utility for understanding broader development patterns because their upgrading and institutional capacities are well beyond those of other less developed countries (LDCs);[106] and because their background variables – regional context, scarce resources, relative ethnic homogeneity – are uncommon. In my view, this perspective minimizes the value of outliers. It is more helpful to see these cases as a source of purposive sampling through which to examine cases that do not fit into regular patterns in order to improve one's understanding of more commonly occurring dynamics.[107]

The challenge is to find cases that are (1) sufficiently similar to *and* different from the NICs to isolate the factors that matter the most for development outcomes and (2) sufficiently similar to other developing countries, especially middle-income countries, to offer more useful lessons for the developing world than do the NICs. Thailand meets these criteria. It shares with the NICs a distinctive regional context and an emphasis on

leaders have never exhibited any interest in such activities. On this "possibility principle," see Mahoney and Goertz (2004).

[105] A "most-similar" design is based on cases that differ in their dependent variables but are similar in all of their independent variables except those anticipated by the theory. Those differences are predicted to account for different outcomes.

[106] For example, Noland and Pack (2003).

[107] Babbie (2004, 180).

export growth; but it exhibits a different development trajectory (described in Chapter 2) and a much weaker set of institutional capacities, described earlier in this chapter as "intermediate" rather than "developmental."[108]

At the same time, Thailand is closer than are the NICs to most developing countries with regard not only to development outcomes and institutions, but also to structural, background variables that potentially influence development. As reviewed in Chapter 4, this is a country that has benefited from a less threatening security environment, less domestic unrest, and easier access to foreign exchange (due to natural resource exports and military aid), than have the NICs.[109] Furthermore, whereas three of the key NICs, South Korea, Taiwan, and Hong Kong, are ethnically homogeneous, in Thailand, ethnic Chinese (Sino-Thais) constitute some 10% of the population but have historically dominated the economy.

Chapter 2 lays the groundwork for this analysis in two steps. It first establishes our empirical puzzle by reviewing the strengths and weaknesses of Thai economic change since the late 1950s. It then reviews a range of contending but unsatisfactory explanations for this performance in light of Thai and other developing country experiences. This discussion provides background material on Thailand while also demonstrating the need for an approach that addresses the demand for and supply of institutions. Chapter 3 presents such an approach.

[108] As such, Thailand and its (non-Singaporean) Southeast Asian neighbors constitute what Collier and Mahoney (1996) label a "contrast space" with the NICs. For a systematic comparison of institutional features in the NICs vs. the ASEAN-4, see Doner, Ritchie and Slater (2005, Table 1).

[109] On Thailand as "resource rich," see Birdsall, Pinckney, and Sabot. (2000: 14).

Puzzles of Thai Development in Comparative Perspective

Thailand poses two challenges to students of economic growth. One is to determine the degree and nature of the country's development: "Is Thailand a case of successful development or rather a case of maldevelopment?"[1] My answer, presented in Section I, is that neither of these options is accurate. Thailand has experienced impressive but still uneven development, whose weaknesses threaten the sustainability of the economy's growth. The second and central challenge of this book is to understand the reasons for this mixed performance. Section II establishes the background for my answer by assessing several prominent, noninstitutional approaches: investment capital, human resources, entrepreneurship, policy, and political regime type. This empirically based assessment draws on Thai and other East Asian experiences and highlights the insufficiency of these explanations, while also noting their value. In the process, it demonstrates the importance of attention to the demand for and supply of institutional capacities.

I. THAILAND: THE "FIFTH TIGER"?

A. Achievements

Thailand has, by many criteria, been an economic superstar. Its position as one of the World Bank's High Performing Asian Economies reflects the country's consistent growth and structural change.[2] GDP growth has averaged roughly 7.6% during the 1960s and 1970s, dropping to 5.55%

---

[1] Glassman (2004a, 2).
[2] World Bank (1993).

during the debt crisis years of the early 1980s, and then rebounding to 9% during the boom years of 1985–1995 (Table 2.1). The weak (1.54%) growth of the late 1990s reflects the 1997 financial crisis, but Thailand rebounded to annual rates of over 5% in the first five years of the twenty-first century. The initial stages of this growth reflected successful use of existing resource endowments, especially in paddy (rice), as well as rubber, jute, maize, and cassava flour. Paddy production expanded from under six million rai in 1857 to some 25 million rai in the 1940s; rice exports grew from 58 tons to over 1,000 tons over the same period; and the average annual value of rice exports jumped from five million baht in the 1870s to around 100 million baht in the 1940s.[3] And as seen in Table 2.2, rice production continued to grow from 1960 through to the twenty-first century. The economy's growth also reflected significant export expansion, with export growth rates averaging over 12% from 1970 through the mid-1990s and over 16% between 1985 and 1994 (Table 2.3).

Thai growth was also fueled by impressive structural change after World War II. The country "successfully transformed itself from an agrarian economy, heavily dependent on rice and land-intensive production, to an export-led economy that combines agriculture, agro-industry, manufacturing and services."[4] Agriculture's share of GDP fell from 27% in 1970 to 12% in 1993 as manufacturing expanded to account for over a quarter of GDP (Table 2.4). Indeed, manufacturing expanded at over 8% annually from 1977 to 2003, and at a 10% annual rate from 1977 until 1966, just prior to the Asian crisis.[5] Agriculture itself has diversified significantly: in 1961, the top five products – natural rubber, jute, maize, cassava flour, and of course rice – accounted for 88.4% of total agricultural exports (Table 2.5). By the year 2000, the identities of the top five had shifted significantly and their overall position had declined to just over 50% with a shift not only to upland crops, such as maize, sugarcane, and soy beans, but also to products such as canned pineapple. At the beginning of the twenty-first century, Thailand was "Southeast Asia's most successful agricultural exporter."[6] By 2005, roughly half of Thailand's processed food output was exported; Thailand had become one of the world's few new producers of a broad range of fishery and agricultural products and either the top or close to the top exporter of rice, rubber, cassava

[3] Pasuk and Baker (1995, 16).
[4] Bidhya (1995, 367).
[5] World Bank (2005b).
[6] Crispin and Goad (2000, 58).

TABLE 2.1 GDP Growth (Annual %)

	1961–1969	1970–1974	1975–1979	1980–1984	1985–1989	1990–1994	1995–1999	2000–2004
Australia	5.42	3.47	2.89	2.82	3.92	2.39	4.31	3.1
China	3.02	8.08	6.8	9.64	9.86	10.66	8.76	8.52
India	3.99	2.13	3.72	5.58	6.21	4.86	6.53	5.74
Indonesia	3.74	8.21	7.42	6.72	6.04	7.99	1.68	4.63
Japan	10.44	6.13	4.44	2.65	4.78	2.17	1.23	1.66
Korea, Rep.	8.28	8.05	8.52	6.18	9.18	7.82	4.69	5.41
Malaysia	6.55	8.23	7.22	6.87	4.88	9.31	5.19	5.14
Philippines	5.06	5.42	6.16	1.35	2.68	1.86	3.71	4.58
Singapore	9.45	11.27	7.36	8.68	6.33	9.23	6.05	4.24
Thailand	7.82	7.06	7.96	5.55	9.04	9.01	1.54	5.03
Vietnam	–	–	–	–	4.54	7.32	7.51	7.09
Latin America*	5.25	6.51	4.77	1.33	2.19	3.51	2.52	2.26
Africa**	4.65	5.55	2.47	1.72	2.62	0.61	3.49	3.77

Source: World Bank World Development Indicators.
Notes: * Average for Latin America.
** Average for the Caribbean region.

27

TABLE 2.2 *Output of Major Agricultural Production – Thailand (Thousands of Metric Tons)*

Grains and Food:	1960	1970	1975	1981	1985	1990	1995	2000	2004
Rice*	6770	13410	13386	17800	20599	17473	21052	24948	29082
Vegetable and fruit						38	44	55	65
Sugarcane**	5382	6585.9	19910	30260	24000	37641	54323	45892	69808
Maize	543.9	1938.2	2863.2	4000	5030	3813	4147	4492	4300
Cassava	1222	3431	8100	17744	19263	19953	15970	19094	20209
Mungbean	60.3	150.5	120.6	283.7	323.4	317	211	214	165
Onion and shallot						178	211	282	318
Garlic						111	120	125	96
Chilli						21	29	35	41
Sorghum						233	121	81	101
Oils:									
Palm						1192	2255	3256	5182
Coconut	1040	714	677	709.6	980.8	1426	1413	1400	1499
Soybean	25.6	50.4	113.9	131.5	307.8	557	454	313	245
Groundnut	152	124.9	99.9	146.5	171	161	146	135	74
Sesame	18.6	20.2	17.4	28.5	25.4	29	34	39	41

Grains and Food:	1960	1970	1975	1981	1985	1990	1995	2000	2004
Raw Materials and Fibers:									
Rubber†	171.8	287.2	348.7	502	722	1250	1810	2378	3005
Tobacco††	n.a.	20.2	36.9	51.6	35.2	67	49	74	68
Cotton	45.5	26.8	28.7	175.7	101.5	95	83	39	14
Jute and Kenaf	187.5	384.9	307.6	208	266	181	114	28	25
Kapok Fiber	n.a.	103	106.4	39.2	43.5	37	43	45	45
Castor Seed	43	42.7	38.5	36	32.9	23	6	9	13
Beverages:									
Coffee						70	86	128	44

Source: Bank of Thailand.

Notes: *Paddy production in year t includes the first crop in year t / t+1 and the second crop in year t.

**Office of the Cane and Sugar Board.

†Rubber Research Institute, Ministry of Agriculture and Co-operatives.

††Thailand Tobacco Monopoly.

TABLE 2.3 *Exports of Goods and Services (Annual % Growth)*

Country	1970–1974	1975–1979	1980–1984	1985–1989	1990–1994	1995–1999	2000–2004
Australia	4.49	5.55	4.24	5.99	8.39	7.21	1.9
China	–	22.46	7.99	4.18	13.65	10.19	24.39
India	6.69	10.1	4.58	6.27	10.47	13.45	14.48
Indonesia	15.84	5.47	–2.67	5.96	10.38	0.49	7.28
Japan	13.2	6.29	8.94	2.73	3.64	4.19	6.09
Korea, Rep.	–	–	–	–	–	15.27	11.35
Malaysia	7.73	8.74	7.83	10.58	15.93	9.47	6.81
Philippines	8.23	8.63	9.31	6.48	7.39	5.44	4.98
Thailand	10.12	10.68	7.96	19.14	13.92	6.89	8.01
Vietnam	–	–	–	–	25.69	21.78	15.6

Source: World Bank World Development Indicators.

TABLE 2.4 *GDP by Sector, 1970–1993 (Million Baht at 1972 Prices)*

Year	Agriculture	Industry	Manufacturing	Services
1970	42,046 27	39,201 25	24,893 16	74,429 48
1980	61,770 21	92,287 31	64,948 12	145,415 48
1990	90,711 14	226,402 36	156,043 25	314,497 50
1993	97,700 12	300,400 38	208,800 26	391,500 50

Source: Bank of Thailand, cited in Pasuk and Baker (1995, Table 5.4, 153).

TABLE 2.5 *Top Agricultural Exports*

Year	Items (% value share in total Thai agricultural exports)					Total Share
1961	Milled paddy rice (42.7)	Rubber (25.7)	Jute (7.5)	Maize (7.3)	Cassava flour (5.2)	88.4
1970	Milled paddy rice (24.3)	Rubber (21.7)	Maize (18)	Cassava dried (9.8)	Jute (6.9)	80.7
1980	Milled paddy rice (28.1)	Cassava dried (19.8)	Rubber natural dry (18.1)	Maize (10.5)	Sugar centrifugal raw (4.3)	80.8
1990	Milled paddy rice (18.5)	Rubber natural dry (16.2)	Cassava dried (14.7)	Sugar centrifugal raw (9)	Chicken meat (5.5)	63.9
2000	Milled paddy rice (20.3)	Rubber natural dry (17.7)	Chicken meat (5.4)	Meat canned chicken (4.6)	Sugar centrifugal raw (4.6)	52.6
2002	Rubber natural dry (17.3)	Milled paddy rice (17.1)	Chicken meat (6.5)	Meat canned chicken (5.2)	Sugar refined (4.6)	50.7

Source: Calculated from FAOSTAT in Bhanupong (2005, Table 4, 33).

(tapioca), shrimp, canned pineapple, processed tuna, cane sugar, soy, and frozen chicken.[7]

Thai exports also diversified considerably. Manufactured products, including electrical products (computers, parts and integrated circuits),

---

[7] Singh (2005, 219); Bhanupong (2005).

jewelry, footwear, vehicles and parts, textiles, as well as agro-industrial goods, accounted for over 85% of exports by the end of the century, up from only 15% in 1970 (Table 2.6).[8] New exports emerged and grew rapidly. As described later in this book, Thailand became a major garment supplier, one of the world's largest producers of hard disk drives, and, since the mid-1990s, Southeast Asia's largest automotive exporter– labeled by its leaders, the "Detroit of Asia."[9] The growth of Thai electronics exports, highlights the increasingly technological nature of the country's exports (Table 2.7). Finally, the export of services grew significantly. Remittances from Thais working abroad, especially in the Middle East, jumped from 8 billion baht in the early part of the decade to 24 billion baht in 1985. The expansion of tourism was especially impressive: tourist earning grew from 3 billion baht annually in the mid-1970s to 32 billion baht in 1985 and exceeded rice as Thailand's largest foreign exchange earner. Over the 1980s, "Thailand was converted from an exporter of agricultural goods to an exporter of manufactures and tourism."[10]

B. Limitations

By the mid-1990s, weaknesses in this hugely impressive record began to emerge. After annual growth rates of over 20% from 1985 to 1995, the stock market began to fall in 1995 and exports failed to grow at all in 1996, culminating in Thailand's becoming the first victim of the 1997 Asian economic crisis.[11] Several short-term factors contributed to the economy's fall, including cronyism in bank lending, mismanagement of foreign funds, growth in Mexican exports, and a cyclical slowdown in global demand for all Asian exporters. But the manufacturing export decline in Thailand was significantly higher than elsewhere in the region, leading economists to conclude that the most important contributing factor was Thailand's deteriorating international competitiveness.[12]

From this perspective, the central component of the crisis was the 1996 collapse of export growth in labor-intensive manufactured goods. As

---

[8] While agriculture's role in the economy declined from over a third of GDP in the 1960s to around 10% in the 1990s, the farm sector was linked to as much as 25% of manufacturing activities (Asian Development Bank 1996, 1, cited in Abonyi 2005, 16). On the growing importance of jewelry, footwear, and electronics, see Pasuk and Baker (1995, 160-Table 5.9).

[9] For disk drives, see McKendrick, Doner, and Haggard. 2000. For autos, see Doner, Noble, and Ravenhill 2004.

[10] Pasuk and Baker (1995, 153; 148).

[11] Nipon and Somkiat (2001, 121).

[12] Warr (1998); Nipon and Somkiat(2001).

TABLE 2.6 *Export Earnings Percentage Composition – Thailand*

	1970	1975	1980	1985	1990	1995	1999	2001	2002	2004
Manufactured Products	15.40	15.40	26.80	49.50	73.80	82.02	84.49	85.11	85.72	86.77
Agricultural Products				38.00	18.00	11.26	8.19	7.31	7.62	8.36
Fishery Products	77.10	75.10	68.30	5.50	5.30	5.07	3.58	3.14	2.45	1.87
Forestry Products				0.20	0.20	0.04	0.05	0.06	0.07	0.05
Mineral Products	0.10	0.10	2.10	5.20	1.40	0.55	0.63	0.91	1.04	1.29
Other Goods	3.20	2.20	1.50	0.80	1.10	0.90	2.85	3.31	2.89	1.49
Re-Exports	3.60	1.90	1.30	0.90	0.20	0.17	0.22	0.15	0.21	0.17

Source: 1970–1990 (Dixon (1999); 1995–2004 Ministry of Commerce; see also Pasuk and Baker (1995, Table 5.3, 152).

TABLE 2.7 *Distribution of Thai Manufactured Exports by Technological Categories (%)*

Sector	Korea			Singapore			Taiwan			Thailand		
	1980	1990	1999	1980	1990	1999	1980	1990	1999	1980	1990	1999
Resource-based	9.0	6.8	11.6	44.4	26.9	13.2	9.8	8.2	9.2	21.7	13.8	10.7
Labor-intensive	49.2	40.8	23.2	10.6	10.3	7.6	54.3	41.2	31.0	47.0	45.5	35.8
Scale-intensive	23.6	19.3	21.0	9.3	5.9	5.5	9.1	10.3	10.6	7.8	6.3	7.7
Differentiated	11.3	15.6	18.7	20.5	22.3	21.2	12.4	20.6	22.2	14.1	19.5	
Science-based	6.9	17.4	25.5	15.1	34.6	52.5	14.5	19.8	28.9	1.2	20.2	26.4

Source: Patarapong (April 2004, Table 1; Calculated from UN Comtrade data base).

Thailand began to face new, low-wage competitors, such as India, China, Vietnam, and the Philippines, the country experienced sharp rises in wage rates during the early 1990s that were "not matched by an increase in labour productivity."[13] A 1998 study concluded that, despite its intensive growth during the 1980s, Thailand's export structure was closer to that of the Philippines than Taiwan, Singapore, South Korea, or even Malaysia.[14] Thai firms failed to use "their temporary low production cost advantage as a stepping-stone for the creation of more durable competitive advantages based on productivity, quality, and timeliness."[15] Thailand had essentially lost its comparative advantage in labor-intensive manufactured goods after only a decade. The mid-1990s thus marked the "end of the era of 'cheap labor'."[16]

The underlying problem was Thailand's weak engineering base: "the country's ability to absorb new technologies and to raise the capacities of indigenous firms was much more limited than in the NICs at a similar stage in their development."[17] Thailand's more sophisticated manufactured exports came from foreign, not domestic firms; the latter are heavily oriented to the domestic market and have much lower technical capabilities.[18] The weaknesses of Thai-owned and managed companies, were confirmed by a 1999 Thai Ministry of Industry survey's conclusion that most Thai firms competed mainly at the low end of global markets, where value added and product differentiation are minimal.[19] Perhaps most troubling are Thai weaknesses in supporting industries – plastic parts and mold production – whose mid-range technology, relatively low entry barriers, and significant demand from foreign assemblers in autos and electronics make them reasonable, if not ideal niches in which upgrading might occur.[20]

The weak supplier base was reflected in and contributed to productivity problems even in Thailand's higher technology-based exports noted earlier. World Bank studies have concluded that "total factor productivity (TFP) growth has contributed little to Thailand's growth over the last 30 years

---

[13] Nipon and Somkiat (2001, 122). Thai wages grew at a 2% annual rate from 1982 to 1990 and then at 9% a year in the following four years (Warr 1998, 57; see also Nipon and Somkiat 2001, 122).

[14] Lall (1998).

[15] Lauridsen (2002b, 159).

[16] Warr (1998, 57).

[17] Coloco (1998).

[18] Ibid. Overall, by the late 1990s foreign firms were estimated to account for 50–60% of Thailand's manufactured exports (Brooker 2001, 18).

[19] Nipon and Somkiat (2001, 121); see also Montobbio and Rampa (2005, 535).

[20] Laurdisen (2005).

and currently lags those of its competitors."[21] Improvements in labor quality, as measured by gains in educational attainment represent a relatively minor source of growth, 0.3% per year.[22] Much of the growth in manufacturing has been a function of increased factor inputs, including finance. From the mid-1980s through the Asian financial crisis, capital accumulation was critical, leading one Thai scholar to label the country's development strategy one of "FDI-led industrialization."[23] Through its own 1984 devaluation, export-oriented investment incentives, quota opportunities, and cheap labor and land, Thailand succeeded in attracting Foreign Direct Investment (FDI) from Japan, Taiwan, and South Korea pushed by rising labor costs and currency appreciations after the 1985 Plaza Accord. Thailand was, in sum, "in the right place at the right time" to benefit from a regional relocation of production in East and Southeast Asia.[24] Since 1999, Thailand's growth has been driven not by capital accumulation but by "the increasing employment of its large reserves of underemployed labor in the rural sector."[25] Confirming the overall picture of Thai productivity weaknesses is the fact that during the 1990s, "many East Asian economies achieved rates of output growth similar to Thailand's with lower rates of investment."[26] And by late 2006, the World Bank argued that sustained growth would depend on domestic innovation and technological development.[27]

Productivity gaps are also reflected by three related problems: limited local inputs, high trade dependency, and, in some cases, denationalization, including in high-technology areas. The country's high-technology exports reflect not real local competitiveness but "rather simple, labour-intensive assembly of high-tech components imported from advanced industrialized countries (including the Asian NICs)."[28] This emphasis on assembly, especially by foreign firms, is reflected in the fact that the growth in Thai

---

[21] World Bank (2006a, 1).

[22] World Bank (2005, vi).

[23] Intarakumnerd (2005, 2). For an overview of Thai reliance on foreign capital, see Jansen (1997b).

[24] McKean, Toh, and Fisher (1994, 31). Thailand's investment ratio rose from 26% in 1986 to 41% in 1991 and stayed at that level until 1996. These were largely private-sector investments financed in part by domestic savings which rose from 28% of GDP in 1986 to 36% in 1996. But this left a fairly large investment–saving gap that was filled by external finance – direct and portfolio investment (Lauridsen 2002b, 158).

[25] Lauridsen (2002b 158).

[26] Nipon and Somkiat (2001, 118).

[27] World Bank (2006a).

[28] Lauridsen (2002b, 158).

manufactured exports "has been more than compensated by an even more phenomenal increase in imports ..."[29]

This pattern of "weak linkages and value-added leakage"[30] is certainly borne out in Thailand's leading, high-tech electronics sector, hard disk drives, where, in contrast to Singapore and the Malaysian state of Penang, there are no significant local Thai component suppliers.[31] More generally, the World Bank concluded that "high-tech exports ... (was) ... a misleading indicator of technological performance," and that Thailand has remained an assembler, rather than a manufacturer or designer.[32] A similar process seems to have occurred in more mid-technology sectors such as automobiles, especially as the industry shifted to exports after the 1997 crisis. The dwindling role of local auto parts producers over the past decade prompted one foreign expert to re-label the country's auto industry a "maquiladora of Japan" rather than the "Detroit of Asia."[33] Weak local linkages are evident even in the low-tech and Thai-dominated garment industry, where, as discussed in Chapter 6, local garment exporters rely on foreign textile and fabric suppliers for a significant percentage of their inputs.

Productivity and innovation levels are problematic in Thai agriculture as well. The country's impressive agricultural diversification had largely occurred through "extensification," – expansion of output based largely on land abundance: "Abundance meant that agricultural growth could be easily achieved, and it gave agriculture a comparative advantage."[34] This growth was, to be sure, facilitated by large public infrastructural investments, especially in transport and irrigation; by a liberal trade and exchange rate regime; by extensive mechanization; and by highly fluid rural labor markets. But the seed–fertilizer technology (embodied in the Green Revolution) that has been so important for agricultural growth elsewhere in East Asia played a relatively small role in Thailand.[35]

This "land-abundant" model has become less of an option since the early 1980s, when Thai farmers reached the end of the country's land frontier. A 1999 economic survey concluded that "since the 1950s ... (Thai agricultural production) ... has undergone considerable diversification but

---

[29] Jansen (1997a, 198). On the worsening trade deficit, see Dhanani and Scholtes (2002, 6).

[30] Lauridsen (2005, 73).

[31] McKendrick, et al. (2000); interview with Seagate official (June 21, 2006).

[32] World Bank (2005a, 98).

[33] Author interview with manager, Eastern Seaboard Industrial Estate (January 6, 2005).

[34] Siamwalla (1991b, 171).

[35] Abonyi (2005, 12); Siamwalla (1991b, 172).

relatively little technical change."[36] Despite increased commercialization, yields and productivity "continued to be among the lowest in Asia ..."[37] Overall, the country's agricultural productivity growth lagged not only behind Thai manufacturing but also by international standards.[38] And finally, despite agricultural diversification and growth, agriculture and manufacturing have until very recently been "trivially linked" in Thailand. Many of the processing industries in Thai agriculture do not generate much value added per worker; growth in rural incomes tend to be spent more in services (e.g., construction materials) than in manufactured goods (with the exception of vehicles); and Bangkok-based interests have been reluctant to locate factories in rural areas.[39]

C. Sustainability

These weaknesses bear on related questions of equity and sustainability in Thai development. The country's growth has contributed significantly to a reduction in poverty, as per capita GNP has roughly tripled from $625 in 1975 to $1,831 in the late 1990s. From 1962 to 1992, the portion of the Thai population under the poverty line fell from 57% to 23.2%, and then to 11.4% in 1996. But inequality has worsened. As the country's gini coefficient rose from 0.41 in 1965 to 0.50 in 2004,[40] "Thailand has become one of the more inegalitarian countries in the world, in terms of income distribution," with most of the poor found in rural areas.[41]

At first glance this urban–rural gap is surprising: ideally, Thailand's impressive structural change should have involved not just a reduction in agriculture's overall role in the economy but also an improvement of agricultural productivity combined with a reduction in the rural population as farming becomes more mechanized and workers are drawn into well-paying, urban-based industrial and service occupations. But while Thai agriculture has become more mechanized, it has not become more

---

[36] Dixon (1999, 174; see also Porter (2003, 46).
[37] Abonyi (2005, 11).
[38] From the late 1980s to 2002, Thailand's agricultural productivity (value added per worker) rose 12.4% compared to much higher rates for countries with agricultural sectors of roughly equivalent size: 28% for Chile, 19% for Uruguay, and 21% for Malaysia (Bhanupong 2005, 28; 39). In rice, Thai yields have been lower than all its neighbors except Cambodia and Bangladesh (Dixon 1999, 174; Table 5.10, p. 156; Porter 2003, 46). On sugar, see Chapter 5 of the present volume.
[39] Siamwalla (1991b).
[40] Somboon (2008).
[41] Glassman (2004a, 152); see also Motonishi (2003).

productive. Indeed, it has traditionally suffered from government policies that transferred funds to the urban sector, invested less and less in agricultural infrastructure and technology. Because agriculture has been largely "left to fend for itself ... (p)oor and marginal farmers, those with poor quality soils and degraded land, and those who were unable to participate in commercially-oriented contract farming arrangements, were in the most difficult and vulnerable position."[42]

Nor has the manufacturing sector, due to high capital–labor ratios, been able to absorb rural migrants.[43] Low-skill, assembly opportunities have begun to shrink as Thai wage rates have risen: Thai manufacturing has thus become squeezed between high-skill, high-wage Singapore and low-wage (and sometimes high-skill) competitors such as Indonesia and China. Reinforcing this problem has been a mismatch between the more skill- and technology-intensive demands of the increasingly foreign-dominated manufacturing sector and Thailand's ability to supply technical personnel. And as noted with regard to electronics and automotive operations, Thai-owned firms, which tend to be more labor intensive than their foreign-owned counterparts, have not expanded sufficiently to absorb much of this surplus labor. The result has been that farming continues to be a safety net for the poor: agriculture's share of GDP has shrunk but it remains the dominant source of jobs, accounting for between 40% and 50% of Thai employment.[44] In sum, inefficient agriculture and weak indigenous manufacturing has resulted in a farm-heavy employment structure more typical of an agricultural economy than one led by manufactured exports.

These problems threaten the sustainability of Thai growth in ways noted in Chapter 1. First, the kind of increasing inequality and sizeable rural populations seen in Thailand are likely to constitute a drag on economic growth. Second, as the 1997 Asian crisis demonstrated, low wages constitute a weak basis for sustained growth. This is in part because of the emergence of low-wage rivals. A 1998 study concluded that, despite its intensive growth during the 1980s, Thailand remained an assembly base whose cost advantage would prove as temporary as its success in low-technology exports.[45] Finally, the lack of linkages weakens domestic demand and the long-run political constituency for growth-promoting

---

[42] Abonyi (2005, 11).

[43] Bhanupong (2005, 39); Ahmad and Isvilanonda (2003, 1).

[44] Abonyi (2005, 55). This pattern is consistent with economists' views that industrialization, in the presence of a weak rural sector, can reinforce problems of widespread poverty, inequality, and unemployment (Todaro 2000, 364).

[45] Coloco (1998, 12–14).

policies, especially those based on engagement with global production chains.

Our review of Thai weaknesses should not detract from the country's significant accomplishments. Thailand has successfully built on its existing endowments to develop an economic structure whose consistent growth, diversity, and cost advantages far exceed those of the vast majority of developing countries. As noted, dynamic agricultural growth has been based in part on strong infrastructure, trade and exchange rate regimes, and fluid labor markets. Underlying Thailand's impressive diversification has been success in attracting capital into new, often risky activities; promoting labor market shifts; and keeping exit barriers sufficiently low to encourage competitive market structures. None of this occurs "naturally," and a good part of this book is devoted to demonstrating the indigenous institutions and related political calculations underlying these achievements.

But I am also interested in identifying and explaining the limits to Thailand's growth trajectory. Most importantly, I am interested in explaining the gap between the advanced nature of the country's export structure and the much more modest technological levels in its production processes.[46] I seek to explain why, when Thailand's relatively high wages require a shift to "competitive advantages that result from knowledge and spillovers, rather than merely resources and labor costs,"[47] the country's upgrading-related abilities remain so modest, especially in historical and comparative perspective: Thai capacities for exploiting technology and generating innovation lag significantly behind what they were in the NICs at similar stages in their development.[48] Even more troubling is the fact that Thailand's

commitment to building these ... (knowledge) ... resources, both by government and by the private sector, lags far behind the commitments that were being made 10–20 years ago in ... (Korea, Taiwan and Singapore) ... when their economies were at levels and structures of economic development roughly similar to those in Thailand today.[49]

Perhaps the clearest indication of this problem is the worsening gap in research and development (R&D), already a problem in the mid-1990s (see Table 1.2). Since that time, R&D spending in East Asia rose more than in any other region. Yet disparities within the region also grew: the NICs'

---

[46] Lall (1998, 4).
[47] Veloso and Fuchs (2004, 133).
[48] Bell (2003, 4).
[49] Ibid (1).

R&D spending grew to 2% or more of GDP; China's rates have risen toward an official target of 1.5% of GDP; but R&D in Thailand remained at under 0.2%, a level the World Bank labels "miniscule" and "low relative to other economies at similar per capita income levels."[50]

II. ALTERNATIVE EXPLANATIONS

In this section I explore several explanations for this uneven growth. Each sheds some light on aspects of the Thai experience. But none is anywhere near sufficient to account for development trajectories in Thailand or elsewhere in East Asia. Instead, the shortcomings of alternative arguments highlight the value of an account that targets the demand for and supply of institutions.

A. Investment Capital

The growth impact of traditional economic variables, especially investment capital, is murky at best.[51] The fact that capital stock in Hong Kong and Nigeria increased equally, yet Nigeria's output-per-worker rose only 12% compared to 328% in Hong Kong[52] suggests that financing is at best a necessary condition for growth. In addition, endogeneity complicates the relationship between investment and growth. For example, although the growth results of FDI are typically strong, overall FDI flows and the specific composition of those investments themselves must be explained, since foreign investment "will be pulled into countries already doing well, or expected to do well in the future."[53] Finally, the impact of investments on different kinds of economic performance remains underspecified, a fact that reflects economists' general failure to explore the sources of different levels of economic growth.[54] The experience of the East Asian NICs, as well as specific Latin American cases, such as Chile, suggests that success in promoting technological and managerial spillovers from foreign investment depends in large part on deliberate policies and cohesive institutions, both public and private.[55]

---

[50] Gill and Kharas (2006, 99–100).
[51] For example, Temple (1999).
[52] Easterly (2002, 67).
[53] Temple (1999, 138); see also Haggard and Kim (1997, 33).
[54] Structural transformation "has not been sufficiently addressed in the macroeconomic literature" (Temple 1999, 150).
[55] On FDI screening, see Mardon (1990); Schein (1996); and Felker and Jomo (2003).

Thailand's experience illustrates both the importance of capital and the limited explanatory value of what amounts to an "accumulationist" account of economic performance. As noted earlier, capital inflows, especially foreign portfolio and FDI, did lead to increases in private investment, exports, and economic growth in Thailand.[56] In fact, Jansen, the foremost analyst of finance and Thai development, argues that "exceptional growth is only possible in Thailand when external conditions are favourable and, in particular, when external finance is available to help finance high levels of investment."[57] But this leaves unexplained Thailand's great success in attracting and translating these inflows into new, dynamic export-related activities in the 1980s and early 1990s in contrast, for example, with the Philippines and even Indonesia. As I describe in Chapter 4, astute macroeconomic policies and export incentives played a positive role, but those policies themselves were implemented by capable macroeconomic institutions, such as the Finance Ministry and central bank, often in conjunction with private sector organizations, such as the country's commercial banks.

There is also the absence of a capital-based explanation as to why Thailand has not succeeded in using capital inflows to promote local technological strengthening. Again, I shall argue that the explanation lies in policies and institutions. Here I note simply that Thai policies on promoting spin-offs from higher technology investments to technology promotion have ranged from vague to nonexistent. The country's key investment promotion agency, the Board of Investment (BOI), traditionally focused on generic incentives designed to generate employment and foreign exchange from large investors. Owing to its lack of sectoral expertise and the influence of private interests, technology promotion played little if any role throughout the 1980s. Until the mid-1990s, the Board has applied investment incentives "liberally to a wide range of industries – ranging from high-tech electronics to mature sectors like agriculture and hotel and tourist projects – rather than as an instrument for implementing focused strategic industrial policies."[58] This relatively indiscriminate approach has been sufficient for diversification, but it has also led to excess capacity and upstream protection, not local technology growth.[59]

---

[56] Jansen (1997a, 204).
[57] Jansen (1997b, 2).
[58] Felker and Jomo (2003, 11).
[59] Felker (1998).

B. Entrepreneurship

If capital inflows do not correlate with growth variations, perhaps the answer lies in the levels or quality of entrepreneurship, that is, the capacity and drive required to "make markets."[60] But the animal spirits of entrepreneurship have never been in short supply, even in the poorest countries. The question is why entrepreneurship varies so much across time and place in both form and consequence. In some places, such as 1950s Java, entrepreneurs got stuck as what Clifford Geertz[61] called "enterpreneurs without enterprises," independent peddlers barely able to promote static efficiency. Later in Southeast Asia, entrepreneurs organized as diversified but largely finance- and trade-based business groups were critical to the economic dynamism and structural changes seen in Malaysia, Indonesia, the Philippines, and Thailand.[62] On the other hand, Kunio Yoshihara[63] argues that Southeast Asian entrepreneurs are "ersatz," and that these business groups generally have not developed the manufacturing and innovative strengths of industrial conglomerates in South Korea and Taiwan.[64]

How do we explain variations in entrepreneurial impact? One approach draws on sociological factors, such as religion, ethnicity, or social capital.[65] But these do a poor job of explaining variation in entrepreneurial performance. Confucianism, for example, was less of a problem for postwar Taiwan than for prewar China, despite leadership by virtually the same political party and ruling elite espousing similar cultural commitments. Muslims, who had established one of the world's preeminent mercantile traditions in precolonial Indonesia, ended up economically marginalized.[66]

But where ascriptive linkages overlap with the trust, reputation, and network communications of social capital, such accounts are more satisfying explanations of growth, up to a point. Economists have argued that indigenous, "traditional" arrangements – especially networks and business groups – fulfilled the functions of more "modern" institutions. Scholars such as Avner Grief[67] and Janet Landa[68] showed how horizontal ethnic

---

[60] Liebenstein (1968).
[61] Geertz (1963).
[62] For example, Leff (1978); Suehiro (1989).
[63] Yoshihara (1988).
[64] For example, Fields (1995); Amsden and Chu (2003).
[65] For example, Unger (1998).
[66] Hefner (1998); Robison (1986).
[67] Grief (1993).
[68] Landa (1991).

trading networks functioned as mechanisms for the provision of market information, of matching and referral services, and for "collectivist" contract enforcement to deter opportunistic behavior. Others stressed the benefits of business groups based on patriarchal family structures but also dependent on horizontal networks among families.[69] More than simple interorganizational alliances, these groups were multicompany arrangements. Linked by interpersonal trust based on similar family, ethnic, or communal background, these groups could mobilize financial, technical, and managerial resources beyond the resources of a single family or firm. Common to all of these approaches is the argument that nonmarket institutions, by combining group cohesion (i.e., solidarity) with scale and cosmopolitanism (i.e., links to outsiders), are able to fill "institutional voids."[70]

This literature helps answer the puzzle of development without modern institutions. But it also raises two other questions central to the present study. The first involves "goodness of fit": to what degree are "premarket" institutions second-best alternatives, destined to become obsolete or even counterproductive as the market imperfections they initially resolved get "modernized" away? Are the family business groups that helped to overcome capital market imperfections and to socialize risks less useful when it comes to promoting technological competence?[71] The second question involves origins. How do we explain variation in degree of cohesion and cosmopolitanism across groups? Why did some groups become self-dealing enterprises that "turn into relief organizations rather than businesses," while still others, exhibiting both "cohesion and cosmopolitanism," help to mobilize capital for new economic activities?[72] Why in only some places does locally based social capital scale up "to generate solidarity ties and social action on a scale that is politically and economically efficacious"?[73] How do we explain that family-based groups in South Korea and Taiwan seem to have met the upgrading challenge much more successfully than their counterparts elsewhere in the developing world, even as groups in these two countries differ significantly with regard to their relative weight and economic roles?[74] How do we explain what Michael Billig[75] describes as the "death and rebirth of entrepreneurism" in southern Philippines?

---

[69] Leff (1978).
[70] Bratton (1989, 415); Geddes (1994, 31).
[71] For example, Hoff and Stiglitz (2001, 405).
[72] For example, Geertz (1963).
[73] Evans (1997, 191).
[74] For example, Fields (1995).
[75] Billig (1994).

Analyzing the ethnic Chinese (Sino-Thai) experience in Thailand illustrates the developmental contributions of ethnic networks and the limits to those contributions, while also helping to explain those limits. Chinese have been central to the Thai economy's growth and diversification. Waves of Chinese immigrants, arriving in the late nineteenth and early twentieth centuries, helped to organize and expand the rice industry, to introduce sugar cultivation and tin mining into Thailand, to spread upland crops, while promoting the adoption of new chemical inputs and varieties.[76] Middlemen frequently played a multiplicity of roles, acting as technical, commercial, and financial advisers to farming communities."[77] Further, as discussed in Chapter 4, Sino-Thai commercial banks mobilized funds from agriculture to promote growth in new, industrial activities, including textiles/garments and agro-business. On the basis of capital accumulation from agro-exports, ethnic Chinese established (1) large commercial banks in the 1950s that went on to become conglomerates in the 1970s; (2) industrial groups based on import substitution in conjunction with foreign capital beginning in the 1960s; and (3) agro-business groups emerging in the 1970s through the integration of agricultural exports and industrial activities.[78]

But if social capital-based ethnic groups have successfully diversified the Thai economy, they have not, by and large, promoted economic upgrading, especially in manufacturing.[79] What accounts for this limitation? The answer does not lie in some innate, merchant-based aversion to technology on the part of ethnic Chinese, whether in Thailand or elsewhere. By the turn of the twentieth century, for example, Chinese engineers in Thailand had not only pioneered novel rice milling processes but also replaced Western milling equipment with their own designs.[80] More contemporary illustrations of technology potential by ethnic Chinese are the high rates of innovation among Chinese firms in Taiwan, Singapore, and even Hong Kong. Nor can the technology-related weaknesses of Thai entrepreneurs be attributed to a lack of access to foreign technology. Sino-Thai firms, for example, have had similar exposure to foreign disk drive firms as their Singaporean counterparts but have proven much less adept at seeking out and absorbing this knowledge.[81] One potential answer to this puzzle,

---

[76] Unger (1998, 55); Dixon (1999, 51–52).

[77] Ibid. (177).

[78] Suehiro (1989).

[79] Personal communication from Danny Unger (November 2002). The point is implicit in Unger (1998).

[80] Skinner (1957, 104).

[81] McKendrick, Doner and Haggard (2000).

prominent in the economic growth literature, involves access to qualified human capital.

C. Human Capital – Education and Training

Expansion of education and training has two potential benefits for economic growth. Indirectly, a large pool of technically capable workers can reduce inequality which, as noted earlier, typically improves growth.[82] Directly, human capital investment enhances worker productivity and firms' "absorptive capacity," that is, their ability to recognize the value of new information, to assimilate it, and to apply it to commercial ends and new technologies.[83] This direct impact is important in part because technological change may well drive capital accumulation, not the other way around.[84] But more critically, as "endogenous growth" theories have argued, technology is not a costless public good, but rather a body of knowledge whose tacitness makes it difficult to appropriate without existing technical capacity.[85]

Despite these potential benefits, educational expansion does not necessarily lead to better economic performance. An "explosion" in all levels of schooling at all levels throughout the world over the past 40 years has not been associated with convergence in output and productivity. Instead, "the basic fact is that the raw cross national dispersion of output per capita has gone up substantially and of schooling down substantially."[86] Indeed, in places such as Venezuela, the Philippines, and Brazil schooling per worker has risen consistently but output per worker has fallen.[87]

The potentially virtuous cycle between education and growth can be short-circuited in a number of ways.[88] Simply expanding the number of classrooms and teachers rarely translates into improved educational quality; indeed, such an expansion is often less of an "investment" good that improves output and more of a "consumer" good demanded by the rich or awarded to political constituencies. Relatedly, an expansion of existing educational services may not serve emerging developmental goals, such as the needs for greater technological capacities required for upgrading. Even

---

[82] Birdsall, Pinckney, and Sabot (2000).
[83] Cohen and Levinthal (1990).
[84] Easterly (2002, 66).
[85] Romer (1990).
[86] Pritchett (2004, 10; 12); see also Easterly (2002, 73).
[87] Pritchett (2004, 14).
[88] Birdsall, Pinckney, and Sabot (2000), from which the rest of this discussion is drawn. See also Nelson (1999); Grindle (2004).

if educational quality is improved with regard to technical competencies, there may be problems on the demand side: firms may lack the capacity and/ or willingness to take advantage of such a supply.[89] And finally, more education does not necessarily promote income equality. As reflected in the case of Brazil, wage inequality results from an expansion of educational opportunities targeted at a small number of workers, compared to the equity-producing outcomes of educational expansion focused on broader sections of the working population, as in South Korea.[90]

The key question then is not whether education can promote growth; it clearly can. The question involves rather the quality of educational opportunities, their match for specific development tasks, and the factors influencing educational opportunities. First, the quality and appropriateness of education and training are functions of incentives and, by extension, development strategies and political coalitions. Birdsall, Pinckney, and Sabot conclude that where educational expansion is associated with a capital-intensive growth path, as in Brazil, the focus will be on a small number of workers, resulting in a deterioration of most of the educational sector.[91] By contrast, the more equitable and productivity-enhancing education expansion in South Korea was associated with a more labor- and skill-intensive growth path. The structure of political coalitions may also encourage the expansion of (low-quality) education as pork or "consumer" goods as noted earlier. Second, existing institutional arrangements may inhibit the formulation and implementation of broad-based, productivity-enhancing educational strategies even when political leaders support such strategies. Jonathan Temple, after an extensive and inconclusive review of the empirical evidence regarding educational expansion and growth, concludes that a "perhaps more interesting task for future research is to explore the fine detail of the institutional and incentive structure that best allocates a fixed amount of educational expenditures."[92]

This issue of institutional capacity lies at the heart of the present study, but raises still a third level of questions – namely, the origins of development strategies and related capacities. A prominent argument on this question has to do with resource abundance: economists argue that natural resource-rich countries, especially those with "point-source" (e.g., minerals) or inequitably distributed resources (e.g., land), will tend *not* to pursue

---

[89] Radosevic (1999).
[90] Birdsall, Pinckney, and Sabot (2000, 5).
[91] Ibid.
[92] Temple (2001, 917).

labor-demanding growth paths that demand/require institutions supporting quality and appropriate education.[93] This can occur due to one or a combination of several mechanisms: Agriculture can constitute a labor "sink" through which there is little pressure to improve worker productivity. Natural resource rents can allow governments to pursue inward-looking development strategies that do not impose competitive pressures on local firms and thus weaken demand for skilled workers. Finally, because resource abundance tends to concentrate income, political leaders may find themselves under populist pressures to provide education as a consumption good to assuage frustrated poor and/or to shore up particular constituencies.

The Thai experience confirms the argument that a human capital explanation of economic growth is seriously incomplete without a focus not just on the match between education and specific development stage but also the strategies, institutions, and background factors accounting for a country's educational assets. Thailand's overall educational investment has been impressive in quantity but poorly suited to move the country out of a reliance on agro-exports and labor-intensive manufacturing. The country's education expenditures as a percentage of government budgets were the highest in Southeast Asia from 1970 to 1990.[94] Primary education was expanded significantly beginning in the 1960s, and by the 1970s achieved high enrolment and literacy rates relative to regional and general developing country standards.[95] By 2003, primary education was, in the words of the World Bank, a "remarkable success" with over 100% enrollment rates, 92% transition to lower secondary levels, retention rates of 90%, and literacy rates of 96%.[96] A subsequent wave of investment focused on tertiary education, resulting in a level of university enrolment of 25% in 1982, over twice the rate of Singapore.[97]

However, Thai universities have emphasized the social science and humanities rather than science and engineering.[98] The situation in vocational and secondary education is especially bad. In the mid-1990s, only 40% of Thai workers had finished secondary or postsecondary education.[99]

---

[93] Unless noted, this discussion draws on Birdsall, Pinckney, and Sabot (2000); and Birdsall, Ross, and Sabot (1997).
[94] Dixon (1999, 91). Unless otherwise noted, this discussion draws on Ibid. (91–92).
[95] Ibid.
[96] World Bank (2005b, 68).
[97] Dixon (1999, 92).
[98] Schiller (2006a). The exception is civil engineering, reflecting Thai security-related concerns with the development of rural infrastructure (Christensen 1993a, 132–133).
[99] Brooker (2001, 26).

By 2000, Thailand's secondary education completion rate was "by far lower than the norm" for the country's income level: 4.1% in 2000 compared to 23.6% in Malaysia and 17.5% in the Philippines.[100]

All of this translates into both skills shortages and persistent mismatches, especially in Thai manufacturing. Skilled production workers are in especially short supply. A 2005 World Bank survey found that 50% of garment firms, 25% of textile firms, and roughly 35% of auto parts firms identified skills and education of available workers as a "severe" or "very severe" obstacle to improved operations.[101] Under conditions of skill shortages, firm managers must operate with a ratio of skilled to unskilled workers that is lower than the optimal level for their industry and significantly less than is the case for regional competitors such as Malaysia. This skill mismatch results in average losses, based on potential sales, of almost 15% of output.[102] Weaknesses in human resources are also associated with weaknesses in other areas reviewed earlier, for example, R&D capabilities, IT infrastructure, and general competitiveness rankings, as well as rates of ISO certification.[103]

Thailand is, in sum, a regional laggard in the kinds of technological competences generally understood as necessary for upgrading. This is problematic on two fronts. First, the country's particular type of educational expansion seems to be contributing to the kind of unequal wage structure noted earlier. Second and more critically, given Thailand's relatively higher wages, the skills shortage impedes the country's ability to "move from low-tech assembler to high-tech manufacturer and escape the strong competition from Bangladesh, China and Vietnam on the low-end of manufacturing."[104]

A part of the explanation for this very uneven human capital record lies in the depressing effect of Thailand's development strategy on the demand for technical personnel. Yet Thailand's export success seems to run counter to Birdsall, Ross, and Sabot's argument that weak educational systems reflect inward-looking strategies. In fact, the anomaly is only apparent. Thailand's export promotion has been tempered with protection – a sort of "insulated export promotion."[105] In response to balance of payments

---

[100] World Bank (2005b, 67).
[101] World Bank (2005a, 60).
[102] World Bank (2005b, 39; 66).
[103] Nipon and Somkiat (2001, 122); Arnold et al. (2000a).
[104] World Bank (2005b, xii; 65).
[105] Nipon and Fuller (1997, 480) use the term "export-oriented protectionism." Unless otherwise noted, the following discussion draws largely on Felker (1998: Chs. 5 and 6), and to a lesser extent, on Nipon and Pawadee (1998), and Nipon and Fuller (1997, 479–482).

problems resulting from import substitution policies, Thailand initiated an extensive program of export promotion in the early to mid-1980s.[106] However, until the early 1990s, these export-oriented reforms were grafted on to protection for local suppliers of raw materials and intermediates and for local downstream firms producing for the domestic market. In addition, the country's overall tariff levels actually increased during the 1970s and 1980s, even as the government proclaimed its export orientation. And while tariff rates declined in the 1990s, they remained high relative to those of other large developing countries.[107] The result was a combination of rising effective rates of protection for upstream firms, most of which were locally owned, and countervailing export subsidies for downstream firms, most of which were foreign owned.[108] Added to this protection were local content requirements in the automotive and agricultural machinery industries and a set of specific business tax and tariffs that discouraged linkages between final exporters and domestic suppliers.[109]

The gaps in this export policy were clearly critical in reducing competitive pressures on local Thai firms to meet global market requirements. This should not obscure the fact that effective free trade did occur in certain areas. High rates of protection in the domestic market were offset by smuggling – "water in the tariffs" – and large numbers of illegal firms. The result was intense competition in otherwise protected markets where declining profits forced firms, especially in textiles/garments, to seek foreign outlets for their products.[110] Yet as demonstrated in the textile/garment case analyzed later in this book, exposure to competition stimulated exports

---

[106] These incentives included tariff and tax exemptions, customs reforms, EPZ development, relaxed ownership requirements, and, perhaps most critically, "protection offsets" that involved partial refunds of duties and business taxes. By 1987, such offsets amounted to 10% of total merchandise exports, up from 4% in 1984 (Herderschee 1993, 356).

[107] Nipon and Fuller (1997, 479–480). See also Christensen et al. (1993, 10).

[108] Rock (1995, 754).

[109] The business tax was levied not on the value added but on the complete value of inter-firm sales. Any product manufactured through inter-firm subcontracting suffered a higher tax burden than one produced in-house. A value-added tax (VAT) replaced the business tax in 1992. One problematic feature of the tariff regime was its cascading nature, in which the highest rates were levied on final goods. This encouraged firms to concentrate in final assembly since local suppliers had to pay duties on their own imported inputs. A related problem was that in most industries, including electronics, knocked-down assembly kits paid lower tariffs than individual components, further discouraging local assembly firms from unpackaging their kits and obtaining parts locally. Finally, in order to obtain tariff exemptions, firms initially had to export at least 80% of their product. Although this was subsequently relaxed to allow domestic distribution, it still required the costly separation of production lines devoted to the domestic and export markets. For example, Felker and Jomo (2003).

[110] Herderschee (1993, 353).

and some product *diversification*, but not pressure for product and process upgrading and a resulting demand for technical personnel.

Equally serious have been supply-side weaknesses in the country's education-related institutions. First, ministries responsible for human resource development, especially the Ministry of Education, have been technically incompetent and frequently corrupt.[111] This is reflected in an institutional weakness to which I return in the rest of this book – namely, the inability to monitor policy implementation. For example, as part of its project to establish seven university "centers of excellence" financed with $70 million from the Asian Development Bank (ADB), the Commission of Higher Education never put in place a performance monitoring system during the first five years of the project's existence, despite the fact that such a monitoring system was a requirement of the ADB loan.[112]

A related weakness lies in the university and technical training systems. Thai universities have been underfunded; their financing is based not on performance with regard to the quality of graduating students or services to industry but on relative bargaining power and the ability to develop new programs.[113] Indeed, linkages between universities and industry are generally weak in Thailand due to a combination of factors: protection afforded upstream by firms noted earlier; the incentives facing university faculty; the fact that foreign firms possess their own, in-house innovation capacities; and Thailand's very low R&D expenditures.[114]

In the wake of alarms raised by science and technology (S&T) manpower studies conducted in the late 1980s and early 1990s, Thai policy makers initiated an effort, focused largely on the universities, to expand the supply of trained personnel as a way of both stimulating and satisfying growing demand. The efforts met little success, in part due to attractive alternatives in foreign firms and in the country's burgeoning financial services sector, but largely due to the universities' inability to address the range of technology absorption and diffusion needs of both Thai and more technologically advanced foreign firms.[115] A final institutional factor seriously

---

[111] Pasuk and Sungsidh (1994, 38).

[112] Interview, consultant on the Centers of Excellence project, Bangkok, June 16, 2006.

[113] Schiller (2006a).

[114] Brimble and Doner (2007). In 2002, Thailand spent 0.26% of GDP for R&D, in contrast to 0.5% by Malaysia, and roughly 2% by the NICs. (Schiller 2006a).

[115] I have not found data on the movement of engineers to the financial sector, but the problem was frequently cited in author interviews with Thai autoparts firms during the 1990s. See, for example, Deyo and Doner (2000a).

exacerbates problems in education and training: the provision of vocational training is strikingly fragmented, with responsibility shared and contested among at least seven ministries.[116]

Accounting for these institutional weaknesses brings us back to some of the resource-related issues noted earlier. Thailand is characterized by neither point-source resources nor highly inequitable land distribution. But the country is considered "resource rich."[117] And its agriculture has constituted not only a relatively easy source of foreign exchange but also as noted, a consistent labor sink. The resource abundance argument thus helps to explain otherwise puzzling educational outcomes, including the question of why some countries, such as the Philippines, squander impressive educational resources developed by colonial power whereas others, such as South Korea, improve on existing educational legacies.[118] But as I argue later in this book, the resource approach is itself insufficient without a consideration of competing claims on resources from popular coalitional pressures and external security threats. Where such competing claims are strong and resources scarce, political leaders, *ceteris paribus,* are compelled to promote education-related policies and relevant institutions to improve productivity. This emphasis on political constraints suggests a broader critique of the resource-based argument: whereas education obviously does influence equality, the reverse causal arrows are equally if not more important. That is, pressures to build broader, more equal coalitions, can help to explain productivity-enhancing education.[119]

The impact of these structural factors is also indirectly transmitted through politics: the incentives and structures of coalitional governments ruling Thailand essentially since the early 1970s. Central to the formation of coalitional governments is the allocation of ministerial portfolios among prospective coalitional partners.[120] Parties seek those ministries that provide politicians with resources useful both for personal enrichment and for funding local electoral machines: discretionary power in key policy areas; control over large budgets and personnel; access to project biddings by private firms owned or controlled by the minister; and control of state enterprises. On the basis of these kinds of criteria, politicians commonly rate ministries into grades A, B, and C in declining order of desirability. Education is an A minus or B plus ministry: although it does not have the

---

[116] Ritchie (2005).
[117] Birdsall et al. (2000, 14).
[118] Booth (1999, 311); Jeong and Armer (1994).
[119] I am grateful to Bryan Ritchie for emphasizing this point.
[120] Unless noted, this analysis is based on Bidhya (2001, 289–293).

clout of defense and finance or control over profitable infrastructure of Transport and Communications, Education controls a resource critical for election campaigns: half a million teachers dispersed throughout the country. In addition, Education is responsible for procurement of school equipment involving large funds. All of this contributes to a combination of policy instability, lack of knowledge, and corruption.

The Thai–Singapore comparison in the hard disk drive industry illustrates the impact of these weaknesses on upgrading.[121] Both countries are global giants in disk drive production; both have operated roughly since the early 1980s; and as noted earlier, disk drive production in both countries is dominated by the same group of multinationals. Yet unlike Thailand, Singapore has institutionalized technical education and training programs that have in turn prompted the multinationals to develop new products and to promote indigenous (precision engineering) suppliers not seen in Thailand.

D. Policy

A fourth set of explanations for growth variations hinges on various policy packages seen by development economists and practitioners as necessary, and in some cases sufficient, for economic growth. A neoclassical "accumulationist" approach associated with the Washington Consensus focuses largely on the importance of attracting and mobilizing capital through macroeconomic stabilization, liberalization, and deregulation. This approach is useful but seriously incomplete, if not misleading. It highlights the importance of macroeconomic stability for growth, and the fact that price distortions, often the result of government interventions, impede investment and efficiency throughout the developing world. But the accumulationist approach fails to account for the fact that policies that "got prices wrong," that promoted growth through selective protection and state ownership, have sometimes contributed to successes not simply in the East Asian NICs (including Hong Kong), but also, for example, in high-growth Botswana, where the government "intervened massively in the economy, and the public sector accounts for a much larger share of the economy than is true on average in Africa."[122] As Przeworski and his colleagues note, the relatively "mindless" statistical research on the topic of state spending fails

---

[121] McKendrick et al. (2000).

[122] Rodrik (2003, 11). The classic statement on "getting prices wrong" in South Korea is Amsden (1989). See also Wade (1990) on Taiwan; on Singapore, see Lim (1983).

to recognize the possibility that private and public capital are complementary to each other.[123]

Further, as reflected in the difficulties encountered not only in Latin America and Russian market liberalization, but also the 1997 Asian economic crisis, the "sound money free markets" framework often founders on an "orthodox paradox" in which the very process of sustained economic reform requires significant state capacities.[124] Such capacities, including the ability to learn from and coordinate with private actors, are especially important in such neoclassical areas of trade liberalization, especially when it comes to reconciling trade reform in downstream *and* upstream sectors. Finally, the accumulationist approach is largely silent on whether and how its prescriptions relate to "2nd generation" reforms in areas such as health and education, and improvements in firms' technology capacities.

The Thai case illustrates these gaps. First, although a good part of Thai success can be attributed to maintaining sound, free market fundamentals, decidedly heterodox and even interventionist measures also played important roles in promoting growth and diversification. These include varying levels of protection noted earlier, promotional privileges favoring large firms, and highly selective, often successful, interventions in particular sectors, such as cassava, autos, textiles, gems and jewelry, rubber, and tourism.[125] Second, as discussed in Chapter 4, Thailand's traditionally sound macroeconomic policies were possible only due to the presence of a set of coherent, capable, and relatively insulated technocratic agencies; indeed, the more recent politicization of these agencies was an important factor in the country's 1997 financial meltdown.[126] Finally, these macroeconomic agencies had little understanding of challenges, especially upgrading issues, facing the real sectors. Indeed, until the 1990s the Thai state was a highly bifurcated one in which finance technocrats were ignorant and, at times, disdainful, of ministries' grappling with challenges of the "real" sector.[127] As discussed later in this book, these problems were especially striking in the failure of Thai institutions to coordinate tariff

[123] Przeworski et al. (2000, 164).
[124] Kahler (1990).
[125] On tourism, see Muscat (1994, 197–198). On cassava, see Somboon (1998). On gems and jewelry, see Laothamatas (1991). On rubber, see Petchanet (2006). Textiles and autos are covered later in this book. For an overview and sympathetic treatment of Thai interventions, see Rock (2000).
[126] Thitinan (2001).
[127] Doner and Ramsay (1997).

liberalization among diverse niches of the same sector.[128] The failure of such coordination has constituted an important obstacle to the local linkages so central to upgrading.

An especially important policy approach to upgrading builds on endogenous growth theory to explain firms' willingness and capacity to assimilate technology.[129] While acknowledging that technological strengths are in part a function of firm-level organizational routines and other aspects of firm-specific history,[130] the assimilationists split into two schools in explaining the fact that firm performance tends to vary cross-nationally. The more neoclassically oriented answer limits policy prescriptions to "functional" measures "aimed at remedying generic market failures, without favoring particular activities or sets of activities over others."[131] Such policies include worker training, openness to foreign technology, export promotion, and nontargeted incentives for R&D to *complement* competitive market processes. With these kinds of policies, dynamic firm practices and performances are presumed to occur through competitive emulation.[132] An alternative, more interventionist answer is skeptical about the process of competitive imitation; in this view, productivity gains are "too time-consuming for most private firms to underwrite without government support, the amount and duration of support depending on the industry."[133] Here, the policy prescription involves selective interventions that directly influence resource allocation to particular sectors to raise their productivity and relative importance within the manufacturing sector.[134] Such interventions involve various combinations of trade restrictions, credit allocations/subsidies, and targeting of foreign investment and technology flows.[135]

A key empirical point of contention between the two assimilationist perspectives is whether (sector-specific) interventions actually promoted growth in the NICs – the interventionist view, or whether they simply did not hurt – the functionalist view. My view is that sectoral policies had significant growth benefits in the NICs that would not have occurred otherwise.[136] Positive results of intervention are also clear outside the NICs,

---

[128] Lauridsen (2005).
[129] Romer (1990); Kim and Nelson (2000).
[130] Nelson and Winter (1982).
[131] Lall (2000, 23).
[132] Pack (2000b, 87).
[133] Amsden (1994, 632).
[134] Amsden (2001); Wade (1990); Pack (2000a, 48).
[135] Lall (2000).
[136] The functionalist view is that the policies are simply a "marginal gloss on the governments' nonselective macroeconomic policies." The "aggregate impact of such ... (industrial

including in the cases of agro-exports in Chile and Argentina,[137] electronic exports in Penang – Malaysia,[138] as well as Thailand's own industrial policies in sectors such as tourism, sugar, rubber, autos, and textiles. Conversely, there is evidence from the Thai auto case that best practices do *not* get diffused through competitive imitation in the absence of broader sets of incentives to weaker firms.[139] Many of these cases also challenge the functionalist perspective by highlighting the presence and potential benefits of a sort of a mid-range type of industrial policy: this "new" or "open economy" industrial policy is designed to focus on the development of worker and firm competencies necessary to accelerate new activities at broad sectoral or cross-sectoral levels. Examples include extension of services to support and encourage the growth of aquaculture in Chile, venture capital networks with special expertise in precision engineering, and supplier and skills development programs for existing electronics (Singapore) or auto producers (South Africa).[140]

For my purposes, the question is not whether industrial policies, whether narrowly or more broadly targeted, can promote growth, especially upgrading. They clearly can, but often do not. The question emerging from this whole literature on policy and growth is then: under what conditions can targeted policies succeed? And here the more functionalist skeptics of sectoral interventions raise a point central to this book: more targeted policies require significant institutional strengths. Indeed, this is one of the primary justifications for neoclassical economists' warning that developing countries should not emulate the NICs.[141] But "new" industrial policies are institutionally demanding as well. It is no coincidence that a highly sophisticated,

---

policy) ... efforts was limited (Pack 2000a, 51; 63). The interventionist position is that these industrial policies actually transform the industrial structure and increased productivity growth. Lall, for example, argues that "there is a clear positive relationship within the group of HPAEs between the extent of industrial deepening and the degree of price distortions: the most successful industrializers in Asia ... distorted their prices significantly" (1994, 650). See also Amsden (1994), as well as Wade (1990, 20–21).

[137] For example, Kuznetsov (2004); McDermott (2005).

[138] Rasiah (2000).

[139] See the case study of Aapico, a highly successful, but little emulated Thai-based parts producer in Deyo and Doner (2000b).

[140] For an overview of "new" industrial policy, see the World Bank's "Knowledge 4 Development" at www.worldbank.k4d.

[141] "Countries attempting to extract the benefits from industrial policy that Japan and Korea obtained have to possess not only an exceptionally capable bureaucracy but also the political ability to withdraw benefits from nonperforming firms. Experience in dozens of other countries suggests that these conditions rarely obtain" (Pack 2000a, 64). See also World Bank (1993, 6); and Page (1994).

technically proficient organization, Fundacion Chile, has acted as the hub for the organizational experimentation, the process of public–private discovery and problem solving, and the identification and diffusion of emerging best practices so important for Chile's agro-industry success.

Two cases from Thailand illustrate the importance of institutional capacities for effective policy implementation, especially when it comes to upgrading. The first involves one of Thailand's largest textile entrepreneurs, Sukree Photiratanangkun. A series of targeted incentives, involving protection and promotional privileges (as well as important political ties), helped Sukree to build Thai Blanket Industries, the largest integrated textile operation in Thailand in the 1980s and one of the largest in Southeast Asia.[142] As discussed in Chapter 6, these policies were implemented through a set of institutions that were technologically weak and highly clientelistic. They proved incapable of encouraging and supporting the kinds of technological improvements required for increasingly competitive markets. By the late 1990s, Sukree's group had dissolved. Also illustrative is a comparison between Thai and Singaporean supplier development initiatives. Singapore's Local Industry Upgrading Program (LIUP) has played a central role, through the provision of finance and the coordination of technology support from foreign multinationals, in the promotion of indigenous precision engineering firms capable of supplying foreign electronics producers.[143] A subsequent Thai effort, inspired in part by Singapore's program, achieved much less. In response to weak local participation in the country's burgeoning auto and electronics industries, the Thai government established two programs designed to upgrade local suppliers through linkages to foreign producers: the Board of Investment Unit for Industrial Linkage Development and the National Supplier Development Program. As described in Chapter 4, neither was successful.

The point here is not to deny that selective industrial policies require a stable macroeconomic environment and various types of competitive pressures on firms. Some level of complementarity among selective and functional policies is clearly required. But equally important is the institutional environment. Specifically, for a policy to be successfully implemented, its "degree of complexity has to reflect ... (local) ... administrative capabilities."[144] I also find this issue of institutional environment emerging in research on the developmental impact of democracies vs. authoritarian political regimes.

---

[142] Rock (2000, 188).
[143] McKendrick et al. (2000, 176).
[144] Barnes, Kaplinsky, and Morris (2004, 170).

E. Regime Type

Recent scholarship has cast considerable doubt on a clear relationship between regime type and economic growth. Some scholars argued that democracy encouraged economic growth because it excelled at guaranteeing property rights while avoiding the predatory tendencies of authoritarian rulers. Others suggested that because authoritarian regimes were more insulated from particular interests and exhibited longer time horizons, such regimes were better at mobilizing savings that could be devoted to growth. After a review of the statistical evidence, Przeworski and Limongi concluded that "we do not know whether democracy fosters or hinders economic growth."[145] Democracies are not always or uniquely committed to private property rights; and authoritarian regimes are neither always insulated from particularistic interests nor superior at mobilizing savings for investments.[146] Politics clearly do matter, as we shall see, but not through regime type.[147]

The more immediate influences on growth are institutions "that enable the state to do what it should but disable it from doing what it should not."[148] Recent empirical work has found that a key feature of the institutional context is the degree of uncertainty perceived by economic actors. Such uncertainty is a function of institutional credibility, for example, rule predictability, security of property, fears of policy surprises, and reversals.[149]

These two conclusions – that the impact of regime type is indeterminate for growth but that institutional context does count – find confirmation in the Thai case. As illustrated in Table 2.8, there is no clear association between regime type and growth rate. Military dictatorships had roughly the same annual GDP growth rates (7.9%) as did semidemocratic regimes (7.8%), and whereas military dictatorships in the early 1970s averaged lower (4.6%) growth rates, the democratic regimes of the 1990s (except for 1991) had average annual rates of just over 3% (although the average was roughly 7%) without the two years of East Asian economic crisis. Note also that the crisis occurred as well in much more authoritarian regimes elsewhere in the region. Further, the principal regime types all experienced both

---

[145] Przeworski and Limongi (1993, 64); see also Chang (2002); and Keefer (2003).
[146] Przeworski et al. (2000, 158).
[147] Nor is development correlated with specific electoral rules (e.g., majoritarian – first-past-the-post electoral systems with small electoral districts or presidential vs. parliamentary forms of government) (Keefer 2003, 316).
[148] Przeworski and Limongi (1993, 65).
[149] Brunetti and Weder (1994).

TABLE 2.8 Growth Rates and Regime Type in Thailand

Year	GDP Growth	POLITY	POLITY Regime Type	POLITY Democracy Score	Timeline Description
1961	5.4	−7	Military Dictatorship	0	**1957–1962:** Army chief Sarit Thanarat suspends the constitution, dissolves parliament, and bans parties, using the motto "Nation-Religion-King." Sarit calls for a new constitution but sits as a powerful interim prime minister for years, laying the basis for development through economic policies that expand education, investment, and infrastructure. U.S. troops arrive in 1962 as war in Vietnam builds.
1962	7.6	−7	Military Dictatorship	0	
1963	8.0	−7	Military Dictatorship	0	**1963–1967:** After Sarit's death, his defense minister, Thanom Kittikachorn, becomes prime minister and continues his policy of political stability, economic development, and anticommunism while allowing some democratization. Insurgencies by Communists and ethnic groups provide a genuine threat, as well as a convenient label for opposition of any kind.
1964	6.8	−7	Military Dictatorship	0	
1965	8.2	−7	Military Dictatorship	0	
1966	11.1	−7	Military Dictatorship	0	
1967	8.6	−7	Military Dictatorship	0	
1968	8.1	XXX	Semi-Democratic	XXX	**1968–1970:** The constitution is at last completed in 1968, and the first elections return Thanom to power, beginning a short experiment in parliamentary democracy.
1969	6.6	2	Semi-Democratic	4	
1970	11.4	2	Semi-Democratic	4	

(continued)

59

TABLE 2.8 (*continued*)

Year	GDP Growth	POLITY	POLITY Regime Type	POLITY Democracy Score	Timeline Description
1971	4.9	-7	Military Dictatorship	o	**1971–1973:** Thanom repeals the constitution, ending parliamentary democracy and wielding power through a National Executive Council and a largely appointed assembly. After bloody protests, the king negotiates the coup leaders' exile as new pressures from a more educated and prosperous population begin a period of alternating democratization and authoritarianism.
1972	4.3	-7	Military Dictatorship	o	
1973	10.2	XXX	Semi-Democratic	XXX	
1974	4.5	3	Semi-Democratic	4	**1974–1975:** The king appoints legal scholar Sanya Thammasak prime minister. A 1974 constitution provides for an elected House of Representatives. With many new parties, elections do not produce a clear majority, though center and right parties dominate. A series of coalitions fail to achieve stability or reform. Right-wing power increases, and anticommunist laws are used against labor and student organizers.
1975	5.0	3	Semi-Democratic	4	
1976	9.3	-7	Military Dictatorship	o	**1976–1979:** Paramilitaries attack student protesters, the army again seizes power, and many students flee to the forests to join communist rebels. An army-backed, anticommunist ex-judge is soon replaced as prime minister by Gen. Kriangsak Chamanand. Kriangsak promises elections, while a new constitution creates an elected House and an appointed Senate.
1977	9.8	XXX	Semi-Democratic	XXX	
1978	10.3	2	Semi-Democratic	3	
1979	5.4	2	Semi-Democratic	3	

Year	GDP Growth	POLITY	POLITY Regime Type	POLITY Democracy Score	Timeline Description
1980	5.2	2	Semi-Democratic	3	1980–1987: The effects of the oil shocks increase opposition to the ruling moderate right, and Kriangsak resigns. The National Assembly elects the economically savvy Gen. Prem Tinsulanon, who encourages democratization and with the king's help survives two coups. Continuity in policies and stability allows faster growth, while improved ties with China stanch Chinese resource flow to communist insurgents.
1981	5.9	2	Semi-Democratic	3	
1982	5.4	2	Semi-Democratic	3	
1983	5.6	2	Semi-Democratic	3	
1984	5.8	2	Semi-Democratic	3	
1985	4.6	2	Semi-Democratic	3	
1986	5.5	2	Semi-Democratic	3	
1987	9.5	2	Semi-Democratic	3	
1988	13.3	3	Semi-Democratic	4	1988–1990: National elections bring to power Gen. Chatichai Choonhavan, a retired major general, businessman, and head of the Thai Nation Party.
1989	12.2	3	Semi-Democratic	4	
1990	11.2	3	Semi-Democratic	4	

(continued)

TABLE 2.8 (continued)

Year	GDP Growth	POLITY	POLITY Regime Type	POLITY Democracy Score	Timeline Description
1991	8.6	−1	Semi-Authoritarian	1	**1991–1994:** Generals overthrow the elected government and name a new prime minister, ending a dozen years of relative freedom. After another round of mass protests, with many students killed, the military government and its undemocratic constitution are revoked. Democratic progress under an interim government is followed by a coalition under Chuan Leekpai running on a pro-democracy platform.
1992	8.1	9	Democratic	9	
1993	8.4	9	Democratic	9.0	
1994	9	9	Democratic	9	
1995	9.3	9	Democratic	9	**1995–1996:** The government falls in a scandal tied to manipulation of forest lands, and a no-confidence vote in 1996 ousts another prime minister, Banharn Silpa-archa, requiring selection of the sixth prime minister in as many years. While this instability raises concerns, no-confidence votes and a free press are among the few checks on power in the absence of an independent judiciary.
1996	5.9	9	Democratic	9	
1997	−1.4	9	Democratic	9	**1997–2000:** As a crisis sets in, the prime minister resigns, and Chuan Leekpai returns to guide recovery. The most democratic constitution yet mandates more public participation, decentralization, and fairer elections. The first-ever Senate elections take place in 2000, and 78 candidates are disqualified for fraud, another first. But reform comes slowly, and parties still rely on money politics to win votes.
1998	−10.8	9	Democratic	9	
1999	4.7	9	Democratic	9	
2000	4.7	9	Democratic	9	

high and low growth rates. On the other hand, the Thai case illustrates the benefits of credibility. Despite the fact that Thailand had 13 constitutions, 17 military coups and several mass riots between the establishment of the constitutional monarchy in 1932 and 1994, entrepreneurs operating in Thailand perceived property rights as being "predictably enforced" and economic policies remaining "foreseeable."[150] As numerous authors have stressed, relatively insulated technocrats in the country's macroeconomic agencies were key to maintaining such certainty, at least through the mid-1990s.[151]

But if Thailand's experience confirms that institutional context is more important for growth than is degree of democracy, it also highlights the need to address two other challenges emerging from our review of other noninstitutional approaches.

We need greater specification of the fit between specific institutional features and levels of growth. Clear, well-enforced property rights and stable macroeconomic policies effectively facilitated the capital mobilization underlying the country's impressive growth and diversification. But, as I argue in subsequent chapters, Thai state institutions rarely exhibited consistency or inspired confidence in policy areas where (1) effective formulation and implementation required extensive information exchanges, (2) numerous actors' participation was critical, (3) significant distributional tensions were likely to occur, and (4) opportunities for free riding were abundant. These are precisely the features of technology promotion and linkage development key to upgrading.

We also need a "supply-side" account of institutional capacity. How do we account for the impressive credibility of Thailand's property rights and macroeconomic policies, especially in light of the country's numerous coups (as well as its rampant clientelism)?[152] How do we explain the insulation and capacity of Thai macroeconomic officials in contract, for example, to their Philippine and Indonesian counterparts? Conversely, how do we explain the much more circumscribed scope of influence and expertise of Thai officials relative to their Singaporean counterparts? These questions bring us squarely back to politics: the structural pressures on state leaders and the more proximate political institutions within which they operate.

These two challenges – understanding institutional fit and explaining institutional supply – are the focus of the following chapter.

---

[150] Brunetti and Weder (1995, 130).

[151] Muscat (1994); Thitinan (2001).

[152] On the inverse correlation between clientelism and strength of property rights, see Keefer (2004, 29).

3

Development Tasks, Institutions, and Politics

"Uneven development" in this book refers to the fact that many middle-income, developing countries, such as Thailand, succeed at structural change but not, or much less, at upgrading. Why is upgrading rare? I contend that the tasks required for economic diversification, although difficult, are less challenging than those of upgrading. This is so in part because of potential tradeoffs among the three aspects of the latter. Increasing value added with local inputs *and* doing so at export levels of price, quality, and delivery require that private and public actors overcome a particularly tough set of collective action challenges. Doing so in turn requires significant institutional capacities. But politics makes such capacities rare in the developing world. The creation of institutional capacities is itself a difficult collective action problem that leaders will attempt to resolve only when facing a particularly tough set of domestic and external pressures.

I develop this framework as follows: Section I briefly reviews two approaches – developmental state analyses and new institutional economics (NIE) – whose treatments of collective action are central to my arguments. Section II presents the core of the demand-side component of my argument by identifying (1) types of difficulty along which to differentiate among policy tasks and (2) the institutional capacities appropriate for addressing those tasks. Section III applies the framework to differentiate between the tasks of structural change and upgrading and to anticipate the challenges of more specific policy tasks. Section IV addresses the question of institutional design. Although there is no strict correspondence between capacities and design, cross-national analysis does suggest the benefits of certain organizational structures and practices. But prescriptions of institutional design are typically vague if not silent on the sources of institutional capacities.

64

I address this origin question in Section V. I contend that institutions for upgrading will emerge to the degree that internal and external pressures, "systemic vulnerability," compel political elites to encourage economic productivity and innovation. Of course, leaders do not automatically translate structural pressures into institutions and policy. They must operate within more proximate structures of authority and preferences that influence opportunities for policy change and the very nature of policies.[1] In Section VI, I acknowledge the impact of "veto players" but suggest that they are themselves largely a result of the broader pressures on political elites.

I. COLLECTIVE ACTION, INSTITUTIONS, AND DEVELOPMENT

Market failures pervade the developing world's economies.[2] At the core of market failures are collective action problems: situations in which individual rationality does not allocate resources that maximize social welfare.[3] In most of these situations, maximizing social welfare requires institutions, that is, mechanisms that help individuals to enhance social welfare by rising above their own interests. Our growing awareness of these issues is due in large part to work by scholars of the NIE and of developmental states. Both have emphasized that good policies are of limited utility for resolving collective action problems without effective governance mechanisms. In so doing, both developed institutionalist responses to flaws in the earlier Washington Consensus view that "getting prices right" through free markets and sound money was largely sufficient for economic growth. Both signaled the need for a more *comparative* institutional approach to economic growth, one that specifies differences across institutions and

---

[1] Tsebelis (2002); Cox and McCubbins (2000).

[2] Market failures connote situations – externalities and public goods (bads) – in which "the necessary and sufficient conditions for market equilibrium fail to hold" (Bates 1995, 28). Externalities involve spillovers – the unintended consequences of an individual's activities on others. In negative externalities, an individual's activities impose a cost on others without the individual having to bear that cost; as a result, such goods are oversupplied. In positive externalities, the individual generates benefits for others without being able to capture them him/herself; as a result, such goods are undersupplied. Public goods are those whose consumption by one does not reduce the goods' supply to others (non-rivalrous) or their opportunity to consume the good (non-excludable). In such situations, rational individuals will free ride on the production of public goods or on opposition to public bads. Indeed, both market failure problems are plagued by free riding: individuals will tend not to contribute "to the costs of providing them or remedying their negative effects" (Waldner 1999, 166).

[3] For a useful overview, see Sandler (1992). For applications, see Waldner (1999) and an especially astute analysis of collective action in East Asian industrial policy by Noble (1998).

recognizes the importance of context-specific factors in accounting for such differences. And both have in turn stimulated more applied analyses of development tasks on which I draw later in this chapter.

I do not wish to minimize the differences between the two schools. Developmental state scholars have, for example, exhibited much greater interest in major economic transformations and openness to the potential benefits of government sectoral interventions than have their NIE counterparts.[4] Nor do I wish to deny the weaknesses of these schools. But if the explanatory power of each is limited, they provide important conceptual tools to understand what kinds of capacities are required for what kinds of development and the origins of those capacities. I first note the limitations of the two approaches and then highlight their key contributions.

Although early developmental state writings highlighted dynamic efficiency and structural transformation in the East Asian NICs, they (1) said little explicit about upgrading and provided only vague guidelines for distinguishing among tasks and identifying the institutional capacities required; (2) paid little attention to the contribution of *private* actors, especially organized business;[5] and (3) failed to provide a coherent explanation of institutional origins.[6]

New institutionalists, for their part, have emphasized broad definitions of development (e.g., GDP growth) as well as important but relatively

---

[4] These differences reflect divergent origins. The Developmental state literature has its origins in an appreciation of nationalism, of country- and time-specific concepts of development, and of the institutional requirements of growth, especially by late developing countries (Gerschenkron 1962; Johnson 1982, 1999). Chalmers Johnson's pioneering work distinguished among capitalist economies with regard to developmental ideologies and institutions, a line of analysis that has been extended by "varieties of capitalism" scholars (Hall and Soskice 2000). Finally, the developmental state's primary disciplinary affinities are with history, political sociology, and political science rather than economics. The NIE, in contrast, is best understood as an "expanded neoclassical economics" (Clague 1997, 16). It is neoclassical by virtue of its focus on choice, by its embrace of neoclassical price theory, and by its view of institutions as largely derivative of interests (Evans 1995, 33). It is "expanded" by virtue of its willingness to relax core neoclassical assumptions about perfect information and to move from simple assumptions of utility maximization to incorporate strategic calculations represented by game theory. Overall, these features translate into three core foci of the NIE: exchange (through transaction costs); control and hierarchy (through principal–agent relationships); and cooperation (through collective action dilemmas). For a review, see Doner and Schneider (2000).

[5] See, e.g., criticisms by Kuo (1995) and Moon and Prasad (1998). Alice Amsden's attention to the role of business groups constituted an important exception to the lack of attention to private actors (1989). On organized business, see Schneider (2004) and Doner and Schneider (2000).

[6] For example, Wade (1992).

macro institutions (e.g., property rights, antitrust regulation, judicial systems, and quality of bureaucracy/degree of corruption). But the NIE has failed to offer much "concrete analysis of how variations in state structure can have consequences for industrial change."[7] This failure reflects three related problems. First, transaction costs, one key component of the NIE, have not been systematically applied to the specific and diverse challenges of development, in part because of the difficulties of measuring such costs.[8] Second, the application of another NIE component, principal–agent relations, is problematic since in the economic development process it is often difficult to know "who is whose agent."[9] Finally, the assumption that institutions emerge and change as the result of choices by private parties responding to shifts in factor prices in order to enhance mutual welfare is flawed by its silence on the distributional fights and existing institutional arrangements that constitute politics.[10] All of this has contributed to an overly functionalist account of how institutions emerge to address such dilemmas.

The two schools nevertheless provide important concepts that structure the rest of this chapter:

Distinguishing Development Tasks as Collective Action Problems: As institutionalist scholars have argued, collective action problems inherent in development policies can be differentiated with regard to numbers of participants;[11] the nature and extent of information required to implement a task-related policy;[12] and the costs and benefits accruing to participating parties from the policy's implementation.[13] Taken together, these three sets of factors allow me to assess degrees of difficulty among development tasks and their related policies. These dimensions are also, to varying degrees, reflected in later developmentalist scholarship, such as Noble's "varieties of collective dilemmas" and Evans' typology of state "roles."[14]

---

[7] Evans (1995, 33–34).
[8] Harris, Hunter, and Lewis (1995, 12).
[9] Dixit (1998, 52).
[10] Bates (1995); Knight (1992).
[11] Olson (1965).
[12] For example, Stiglitz (2000).
[13] Key works include Olson (1965) and Stiglitz (2000). Transaction costs are of course central to my approach. Oliver Williamson (1985) identifies uncertainty, asset specificity, and frequency of transactions as the sources of transaction costs. My emphasis here is on uncertainty, as influenced by number of actors, information challenges, and distributional tensions.
[14] Noble distinguishes among the challenges of capacity cartels, R&D consortia, and standards setting (1998: Ch. 1). Evans' roles include regulation by the state as "custodians," direct state production by the state as "demiurge," promote new activities by private actors

Institutional Capacities: Success in policy implementation requires an alignment between the difficulties or complexities of the transactions and governance mechanisms.[15] The NIE identifies at least three sets of capacities potentially necessary for successful governance (depending on the difficulties or complexities of the transactions). Through *consultation,* parties can gain information about each other's preference, interests, and capacities with regard to a particular issue.[16] But because actors are tempted to free ride and/or to renege on agreements, implementing policies also requires *credible commitments*, including commitments to compensate losers through selective benefits and/or to sanction defectors.[17] Finally, the enforcement of credible commitments presumes the parties' access to information about each other's behavior, typically through *monitoring*. Ostrom is emphatic on this point: "Without monitoring, there can be no credible commitment. ..."[18] These three sets of capacities are more or less necessary depending on the difficulties inherent in specific policies or, following Clague's formulation, the "institution-intensiveness" of the policy.[19]

Institutional Design: The availability of these capacities does not map evenly onto any particular organizational structure. But the developmental state literature, in both its empirical analyses and its theoretical formulations, has drawn attention to the importance of characteristics such as the public sector's cohesion, expertise, independence, and linkages with key societal actors.[20] This literature has in turn prompted greater attention to the ways in which such attributes in private actors themselves, as well as in the linkages between public and private actors, can produce the kind of credibility required for solutions to complex market failures.[21] Such attention to the role of private actors is especially important in light of the fact that solutions to market failures can come from decentralized bargaining or from specialized, nonstate institutions.[22]

Origins of Institutional Capacities: Even if such solutions do emerge out of private governance mechanisms, the availability and capacities of such

---

with the state as "midwife," and nurturing and further prodding private firms by the state as "husband" (1995: Ch. 4).

[15] Williamson (1985; 1995).

[16] Williamson (1985).

[17] Ibid.; Olson (1965); Clague (1997, 21).

[18] Ostrom (1990, 45).

[19] Clague (1997, 3).

[20] Useful reviews include Woo-Cumings (1998); and Shafer (1994).

[21] Schneider and Maxfield (1997: Ch. 1).

[22] Waldner (1999, 166).

mechanisms depend on the preferences and resources of the political leaders holding state power.[23] Herein lies what is perhaps the most significant set of contributions by developmental state scholars: They have not only recognized and demonstrated that state actions *could* encourage major economic transformations but have also demonstrated that in doing so, state actors could be motivated by more than just the immediate accumulation of wealth and power. As Peter Evans has argued, if states are simply aggregations of individual maximizers, it is difficult to explain why all officeholders are not corrupt "free-lancers."[24]

But developmental state theorists have not provided a clear account of why some officeholders build strong institutions. Early writings emphasized autonomy without providing any sense of why autonomous leaders should promote growth.[25] Some have saved the question for others to address.[26] But several scholars have identified pressures, both internal and external, under which political leaders feel compelled to promote growth-promoting institutions. I draw from these and other writings a set of three factors – external security threats, domestic discontent, and resource constraints – that help to account for institutional capacities. I argue that these factors operate both directly and through intervening structures of political competition – namely, the number of effective veto players within which political leaders operate. This allows me to assess path-dependent arguments emphasizing the impact of preexisting political arrangements in the face of new pressures.[27]

II. GOODNESS OF FIT

My objective in this section is to understand how "varying problems call on different types of ... capacities."[28] Development problems can be distinguished by their degree of difficulty or number of challenges: the number of actors involved, the kinds of information required, and the distributional differences resulting from the policy. Institutions can help actors resolve these challenges through consultation, monitoring, and credible commitments. My core contention is that more difficult problems require greater degrees of institutional capacity.[29] Figure 3.1 portrays the argument in its

---

[23] Schneider and Maxfield (1997); Schneider (2004).
[24] Evans (1995, 24–25).
[25] For example, Amsden (1989); Wade (1990).
[26] Evans (1995, 42).
[27] For example, Thelen (2003); Pierson (2000).
[28] Noble (1998, 21).
[29] The argument is an ordinal one that presumes the dimensions of both task difficulties and institutional capacities as additive. Thus, tasks are more difficult if they involve not only

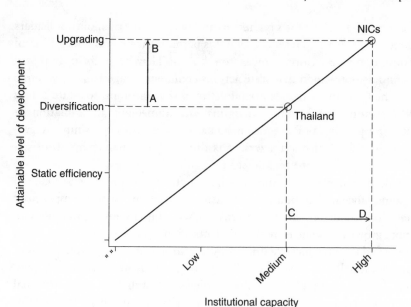

FIGURE 3.1. Development Potential and Institutional Capacities

simplest form: Thailand's success in diversification is a function of its "medium" level of institutional capacities. Its potential to upgrade (to move from A to B) and move closer to the East Asian NICs requires further expansion of its capacities (from C to D).

A. Dimensions of Development Difficulties

Breadth of Participation: How many actors need to be involved for a policy to be formulated and implemented successfully? Does the solution require contributions by all parties concerned or can it "withstand a certain amount of abstention or free riding"?[30] To what degree does the delivery of a service require a large number of transactions, many of which involve some face-to-face contact? The importance of this dimension lies in the implications of large numbers in collective action situations: greater risks of free riding and what Pritchett and Woolcock label "transaction intensiveness."[31]

---

many actors but also require extensive information and result in immediate, widespread losses. Similarly, institutions that facilitate "only" consultation are weaker than those also facilitating monitoring and credible commitments. Further research would explore the potentially multiplicative nature of these variables, e.g., that larger numbers of actors would intensify a task's information challenges.

[30] Noble (1998, 21).
[31] Pritchett and Woolcock (2004, 194).

Information: Policy tasks differ with regard to their information requirements. Collective action problems become more difficult where the issue area is more technical, place-specific, and/or lacks a clear template. Since technical information is both costly and has a tendency to leak out, there are greater dangers of free riding in these kinds of situations. Problems whose solutions depend on different local contexts compel national reformers to accumulate and synthesize large amounts of complex information. And, as Merilee Grindle has argued, where there is no clear agreement as to an appropriate solution, policy makers are often "walking blind as to what needs to be done."[32] Indeed, to the degree that the formulation and implementation of a policy requires decisions made "on the basis of information that is important but inherently imperfectly specified and incomplete," decisions about such policies are "discretionary."[33]

Distributional Consequences: Who wins and who loses when a particular policy is implemented? How quickly do the winners get their benefits and the losers suffer losses? How powerful are the losers? Other things being equal, development problems are more challenging when losses are greater than benefits, when losses are felt quickly while benefits are experienced over a longer period of time, and when the losers are more powerful or better able to get organized than the winners.[34]

Together, these dimensions provide a rough but useful basis for evaluating the obstacles to resolving the policy tasks inherent in different stages of development. Ceteris paribus, problems whose solutions are characterized by the need for participation by numerous actors, the need for unfamiliar, site-specific, or more technical information, and immediate losses for powerful interests will be especially difficult to resolve. Grindle's comparison of macroeconomic vs. education reform challenges illustrates the value of such distinctions.

Education reforms involve many more moving parts in terms of how they are planned and put into practice. They also require extensive consultation, negotiation, and consensus building if they are to be successfully adopted. They call for

---

[32] Grindle (2001, 373).

[33] Pritchett and Woolcock (2004, 194).

[34] The problem of rapid, concentrated losses vs. slow, diffuse benefits has been a core component of scholarship on the political economy of trade reform (e.g., Haggard and Webb 1994). Gains and losses can of course be measured in different ways, e.g., money, market access, access to information, social status, influence over future policies, etc. Distributional impacts may also be affected by "rivalrous consumption," i.e., the degree to which one actor can consume or use the good without reducing its supply to others in the group. Other things being equal, the more "rivalrous" the consumption, the sharper the distributional differences.

decentralized forms of decision making and need continual and time consuming monitoring and capacity building if they are to be implemented. In contrast to the general consensus that exists about macroeconomic policy, many of the newer reforms do not have well recognized templates that explain the central problem and the appropriate solution to it. Policymakers are thus dealing in much more political environments and often walking blind as to what needs to be done to resolve issues of public importance.[35]

B. Institutional Capacities

Grindle's analysis goes beyond the admonition that "institutions matter." It suggests that overcoming such collective action problems requires particular sets of institutional capacities. I identify three interdependent sets of capacities: consultation, monitoring, and credible commitments.[36]

Consultation: Overcoming collective action problems requires that actors know each other's interests or preferences with regard to goals and mechanisms for achieving those goals. This kind of information can be transmitted through consultation, which can involve exchanges of information about (1) the capabilities and organization of others; (2) the preferences of others: each side learns what the other wants and assesses possibilities for bargaining; and (3) intentions: each side learns what the other is likely to do. Further, consultation can be analyzed on several dimensions.[37] In terms of direction, consultation can be a top-down process in which government officials inform private actors of decisions. A more complex form would involve a more bidirectional flow involving private input into policy formulation. Consultation may also involve participation in policy implementation as well as formulation. Finally, we might measure consultation by the degree of formality and repetition. Other things being equal, the more difficult the task, the more consultation should be bidirectional and involve numerous, often informal, discussions/negotiations on carrying out as well as formulating policies.

Credible Commitments: Actors need to believe in each other's willingness and ability to comply with their stated preferences and agreed courses of action. The ability to make commitments credible is thus central, with one study arguing that "problems of credibility constitute the major obstacle to a better growth performance in many LDCs [less-developed

---

[35] Grindle (2001, 373).

[36] In addition to the sources cited below, the following discussion draws on Lin (1999); and Eggertsson (1996).

[37] Ritchie (2005).

countries]."[38] Credibility is especially important with regard to rewards and sanctions. Private interests must believe in government's willingness and ability to implement its commitments to reward firms for compliance with agreed performance goals and to withdraw benefits and even punish those whose performance has been poor. Reform efforts often run into difficulties because of "time inconsistency," that is, surprising policy shifts or even reversals due to factors such as changes in government or payoffs to government officials. Such shifts undermine the willingness of private actors to invest resources in line with prior agreements. On the other hand, government policies often need to change and government officials require discretion. When conditions change, stability can translate into rigidity. Indeed, sometimes policies are credible precisely because they are flexible. Private agents must thus believe that agreed-on policies will not change or, if they do, that the change will reflect new conditions and will be based on consultation among relevant actors.[39]

Monitoring: Actors, whether public or private, cannot credibly commit to reward or punish each other without information about each other's actual performance. Further, monitoring (as well as consultation) can help actors to develop a sense of what constitutes "responsible behavior" and reputations for such behavior. This point underlies Alice Amsden's analysis of reciprocity in South Korea: The Korean state's credibility in exacting performance standards from firms in exchange for subsidies was based in part on officials' abilities to track firms' export performance.[40]

But effective monitoring for development is often much more complex and challenging than implied by this Korean example. If a government is providing businesses with subsidies to encourage exports, it can monitor business performance simply by checking trade data. But it may be more difficult to assess whether firms are fulfilling their commitments to improve the quality of training and/or whether the incentives to do so are well designed. Indeed, the information requirements of upgrading reviewed earlier in this chapter mean that monitoring is not only a way to ensure that partners do not shirk on their commitments, it must also be a multidirectional process "designed to evaluate outcomes as they appear" and to revise policies and responsibilities as necessary.[41] This is, in essence, what Charles Sabel has called "learning by monitoring."[42]

---

[38] Brunetti and Weder (1994, 27).
[39] Ahrens (2002, 107–110).
[40] Amsden (1989).
[41] Rodrik (2004, 18).
[42] Sabel (1994).

III. DEVELOPMENT CHALLENGES AND POLICY TASKS

This section provides an initial application of the demand-side framework. After contrasting the general challenges inherent in upgrading vs. structural change, I analyze the difficulties of specific policy tasks and suggest institutional capacities required to address these challenges.

A. Upgrading as Learning and Linkages

David Waldner[43] distinguishes between structural change, or "Gerschenkronian collective dilemmas," and upgrading, or "Kaldorian collective dilemmas." The former involves mobilizing resources that are "hidden, scattered, or badly utilized" for investment in new productive activities that raise national incomes.[44] As such, structural change requires accumulating and investing capital in new activities characterized by uncertainty and risks. Upgrading, on the other hand, involves increasing efficiency of existing facilities and/or moving up the product cycle with both efficiency and local inputs. Both stages present serious challenges. But Waldner argues that difficulties increase as countries and sectors attempt to move to higher development levels: "It is a great deal easier to find the capital for the construction of a modern industry than to run it."[45] Why is this the case?

Upgrading, more than structural change, requires innovation, understood as the diffusion of a product, process, or practice that is "new," not to the world, but to a particular firm or group of firms.[46] Rather than a passive process in which developing country firms wait for new technologies to appear, diffusion instead requires an absorptive capacity – an endogenous, cumulative learning process in which local producers recognize the value of new information, assimilate it, and apply it to commercial ends.[47]

The *information requirements* of such upgrading efforts are significant in part because the very magnitude of the market failures involved in them is uncertain.[48] Technology new to developing country firms is usually complex, costly to obtain, and uncertain in its mode of employment and benefits. This uncertainty stems in part from its tacit nature: Even if codified,

---

[43] Waldner (1999).
[44] Hirschman (1958, 5); Waldner (1999, 163).
[45] Hobsbawm (1968, 61); cited in Waldner (1999, 160).
[46] For example, Kuznetsov (2004).
[47] Cohen and Levinthal (1990).
[48] Rodrik (2007, 100).

that is, written down or embedded in technology, a firm's ability to internalize new knowledge requires trial and error. This is in part because the technology is new to the firm, and in part because the knowledge is being applied and must be adapted to a context different from that in which it was originally developed. Absorbing technology is thus typically a site-specific, technical process with which most developing country firms have little experience or clear templates. Further, designing incentives for firms to engage in new behaviors is fraught with challenges. Cooperation required to formulate and implement new programs can be weakened by uncertainty as to "whether the causal mechanisms that supposedly generate the high payoff to cooperation actually do deliver that outcome" and "what exactly constitutes 'defection' and what constitutes 'cooperation.' "[49]

In part because it is characterized by so much uncertainty and complexity, this process also requires the involvement of *multiple actors* in a process of collective problem solving through ongoing deliberation. This involves iterative discovery processes in which firms (and farms) draw on the resources of multiple partners, including competitors, buyers, suppliers of intermediates and capital equipment, company-oriented service providers, public research institutions, universities, and relevant state agencies.[50] These institutions must be linked as "networks of innovation" so that, for example, agricultural research institutes have access to "outlets to put their research into use, conduits to receive problems, and consultation mechanisms to deal with both of these issues in collaboration with stakeholders."[51] To illustrate, a comparative analysis of Southeast Asian firms found a strong association between innovation activities and extra-firm cooperation, with Bangkok-based firms ranking lowest on both dimensions, Singaporean firms highest, and Penang in the middle.[52]

Two particular considerations – the role of the state and the need for upstream and downstream complementarities – contribute to the expanding constellation of actors required for upgrading. Even if (1) we assume that private-sector actors will be the primary sources of new technology and (2) we focus not on narrowly targeted industrial policies but on "mid-range" measures devoted to promoting broad sets of worker and firm competencies, local firms engaged in learning and productivity improvement face significant risks and information uncertainties. Overcoming these challenges typically

---

[49] Culpepper (2001, 283).
[50] Nelson (1993); McDermott (2005).
[51] Etzkowitz (2002, 18).
[52] Berger and Revilla Diez (n.d.).

requires the intervention of a third party, often a state agency.[53] But successful upgrading does not involve officials telling firms what to do or doing it themselves. It is rather a process of supporting, prodding, and nurturing in which the state elicits information from business and other private actors on key externalities and their management as part of an ongoing process of information exchange, goal setting and adjustment, and mutual monitoring.[54] The importance of linkages between upstream (suppliers) and downstream (buyers) intensifies these challenges of upgrading. Structural change, especially with regard to manufacturing, often occurs through investments in protected and/or foreign-dominated upstream industries, typically resulting in upstream inefficiency and "a transfer of rents from the finished-goods producer to the intermediate-input producer."[55] Upgrading, by contrast, requires dynamic *complementarities* between upstream and downstream firms in which the former provide higher quality and cheaper inputs that promote the competitiveness of the latter.[56] It "involves import replacement, especially at the upstream level, with attention to international prices so as not to impose on domestic users price-quality combinations that would hinder their international competitiveness."[57]

For example, the establishment of a steel mill constitutes structural change in a country whose economy has traditionally relied on agriculture and light manufacturing. But in upgrading, the mill's products must not only be attractive to downstream producers of goods sold in competitive markets; ideally, the two sets of firms will also stimulate each other's technology development. This process requires extensive interaction and information exchanges between steel producers and downstream users, such as shipbuilders. Indeed, it is precisely such "downstream leadership" and linkages with upstream producers that distinguishes the NICs from other developing countries.[58] As I demonstrate later in this book, weaknesses of such linkages in auto, textiles, and even sugar have impeded Thai upgrading in these sectors.

The importance of efficient backward linkages is one of at least two factors that intensify the *distributional challenges* of upgrading. Precisely

---

[53] Rodrik (2007).
[54] Ibid.; Evans (1995); see also Sabel (1994).
[55] Waldner (1999, 169).
[56] For example, Gore (2000, 797).
[57] Wade (2006, 20).
[58] The outstanding works here are Amsden (1989) and Wade (1990). For a useful comparison of Brazilian, Indian, and South Korean steel industries along these lines, see D'Costa (1999).

because upgrading requires a combination of efficiency and local inputs, it is inconsistent with the process of rent transfer from finished-goods producers to the intermediate-input producers more typical of structural change. As David Waldner notes, solving this upstream–downstream tension "requires resolution of a distributive conflict, which is a type of collective dilemma."[59] This particular distributive conflict is most obvious in the case of trade liberalization (discussed later). But the efficiency pressures of upgrading translate into other potential losses, such as the potential for underperforming firms or sectors to lose investment incentives.

B. Policy Tasks

In the face of these difficulties, I argue that upgrading, other things being equal, will require greater capacities for consultation, credible commitment, and monitoring than will diversification. I now illustrate this general argument by examining a range of more specific policy tasks inherent in efforts at structural change and upgrading (Table 3.1).[60]

Property Rights: Investors must believe that they can appropriate the rewards of their investments and other productive activities. Such assurance is based on rules – property rights – "that assign rights of control over or access to something to an individual or a community."[61] Establishing such mechanisms may require resolving distributional tensions based on sunk investments in prior, often multilayered arrangements (e.g., land ownership), as well as the relevant parties' costs in moving to new sets of rules. Although the information requirements for basic property rights in physical assets are not technical, local knowledge can be required, as is the case with regard to the governance of particular community resources.[62] Local knowledge is also required in light of fact that efficiency-generating arrangements in one country rarely "work" in another.[63] New knowledge will also be required for intellectual property rights, whether in the development of new agricultural varieties or low-tech areas such as modification

---

[59] Waldner (1999, 169).
[60] The following discussion does not cover most of the tasks analyzed in succeeding chapters. Nor does this chapter's analysis explore differences *within* particular tasks. For example, within irrigation, the challenges of locating main canals differ from those of allocating water flows and of providing standpipes in multiple villages (Pritchett and Woolcock 2004, 195). For an earlier predictive typology of tasks and capacities, see Noble (1998, 22).
[61] Siamwalla (2001, 28).
[62] Ostrom (1990).
[63] For example, Lin (1999, 12).

TABLE 3.1. *Selected Development Tasks and Requisite Institutional Capacities**

Tasks (Listed in Increasing Relevance for Upgrading)	Task Difficulties			Requisite Capacities		
	# Actors Required	Information Required	Distribution Consequences	Consultation	Credible Commitment	Monitoring
Property rights	Low–high	Medium	Medium–high	Low–medium	High (initially)	Low–medium
Macroeconomic stability	low	Medium	High	Low–medium	High	Low
Risk socialization	Low	Medium–high	Low	Medium (initially)	High (initially)	Medium (initially)
Trade liberalization	High	Medium	High	Medium–High	High	Medium
Capacity reduction	High	High	High	High	High	High
FDI – for technology promotion	High	High	Medium–high	High	High	High
Supplier development	High	High	Low	High	High	High
Training and education	High	High	Medium–high	High	High	High

*Coding based on author's judgment and intended to be illustrative.

of equipment designs. Finally, the number of actors whose participation is required varies with factors such as the number of agencies with jurisdiction over these rights and the fragmentation of assets affected.[64]

In light of such variation in property rights challenges, requisite institutional capacities vary as well. Credible commitment is, of course, always critical, but especially where distributional consequences are severe. Such consequences, when compounded by high information requirements and the need for broad participation, can require extensive consultation and, depending on the enforcement needs, ongoing monitoring. However, because most property rights regimes are self-reinforcing, institutional capacities are typically more important at the initial stages of institutional creation than after the regime has been in operation.[65]

Macroeconomic Stability: If investors are to put their money in new ventures, they need some assurance as to the stability of their input costs and markets. A key source of such confidence is the ability to ensure macroeconomic stability through interest rate, exchange rate, and fiscal measures. The information requirements of such policies are not especially high: Although effective macroeconomic management requires significant professional training and judgment, there are clear templates and guidelines for this policy area.[66] In addition, the breadth of participation is, ceteris paribus, relatively narrow in the sense " '10 smart people' can handle the actual decisions and mechanics" of macroeconomic policy reform.[67] In the sense that macroeconomic reforms can be achieved with "the stroke of a pen," consultation is only moderately important, especially at initial stages, although more consultation may be required to consolidate a reform. Indeed, the real challenge comes from distributional impacts, especially at initial stages. These require credibility in the capacity to provide side payments and/or to punish defectors. Credibility is also important in light of the fact that macroeconomic policy can suffer from time inconsistency. Political pressures "can lead the politician to discount the future gains ... (of stabilization measures) ... deeply ... because of impending elections or the fear of sparking demonstrations or riots."[68]

---

[64] Reflecting the large number of small farms, Taiwan's land reform involved government-sponsored organizations – tenancy committees – to resolve over 62,000 landlord–tenant disputes between 1952 and 1956 (Nordhaug 1997, 174).

[65] Property rights constitute a "battle of the sexes" situation in which, once equilibrium is reached, there are few incentives to defect. The challenge is overcoming the distributional differences blocking an agreement in the first place (Scharpf 1997).

[66] Grindle (2001).

[67] Pritchett and Woolcock (2004, 194).

[68] Haggard (1997, 124).

Risk Socialization: Structural change involves getting economic agents to engage in risky economic behavior where there is uncertainty as to whether new activities will generate profits and to whom such benefits will accrue.[69] Also challenging is the scale or accumulation problem: new investments involve the need for volumes of capital exceeding the capacities of any one particular firm. Investors must thus deploy significant sums of capital in the face of uncertainty about customers, new kinds of equipment, and the availability of workers to overcome technical problems. This problem of uncertainty is especially severe for upstream investors since downstream producers of finished goods might well be averse to purchasing domestically produced inputs of higher price and lower quality than imported alternatives. The challenge in this area is thus to socialize the risks of new investors and ensure that such investments are made.[70]

The number of actors in these situations is often relatively small, usually involving large public or private financial institutions. Despite risks, distributional tensions are fairly low since the key transaction involves financial support for new activities. But information requirements are typically high given the need to identify potential financial sources and investors on the one hand, and potentially lucrative opportunities on the other. In this context, some consultation and performance monitoring are required at initial investment stages, but the need for credibility of offers to provide subsidies and protection is especially high.[71]

Trade Liberalization: Success at socializing risk for new investments typically leads to protection for inefficient producers and, as a result, the need for trade liberalization. Such reform is notoriously difficult in large part because the costs of liberalization are typically felt quickly by a relatively discrete group of firms, whereas benefits are more diffuse and take longer to appear.[72] Since liberalization typically implies a significant reduction in the transfer of rents from the downstream to upstream producers, distributional problems are especially serious in upstream–downstream relations central to upgrading.[73] The capacity to make credible commitments with regard to side payments and the ability to resist pressure from losers is thus critical, especially at the initial stages of trade reform.

---

[69] Waldner (1999, 165).

[70] Rodrik (2007, Ch. 4).

[71] Huang (2002, 547).

[72] The literature on the political economy of trade reform is vast. For useful reviews, see Haggard (1997); Haggard and Webb (1994).

[73] Waldner (1999).

On the other hand, the informational and participatory difficulties of trade liberalization might seem relatively moderate. After all, these are often macro reforms whose technical requirements are the stuff of basic graduate courses. But the optimal degree and complexity of trade reform are contested and, when it comes to efforts at ensuring competition while also promoting local linkages, quite complex. Effective imposition of competitive pressures on upstream firms requires information sufficient to calibrate and gradually reduce tariff rates. For example, liberalization efforts that promote upstream–downstream linkages can be confounded by products that can be counted as either intermediate inputs or finished products. Finally, trade reform that promotes upgrading requires the participation of numerous parties to encourage producer–user interactions among multiple firms in complex value chains. In sum, when trade reform is designed both to ensure competitive pressures *and* to promote local linkages, consultation and monitoring, along with credible commitments, grow in importance.

Capacity Reduction: Risk socialization often leads to excessive entry. For example, the number of auto assemblers operating in Thailand rose from 8 to 22 between 1960 and 1978, precisely the period in which tariffs on auto imports rose from 60% to 150%.[74] Excessive entry in turn often leads firms to incur an "economy of scale penalty cost" in which each is unable to reduce unit costs due to the large number of competitors in a limited market. Under these kinds of conditions, each entrant typically lacks the opportunity to advance "on the learning curve far enough from the rest of the domestic firms sufficient to deter new entry on its own."[75]

Overcapacity is thus a "public bad" which, in most developing countries, proves resistant to resolution through market mechanisms. In principle, inefficient, high-cost producers should either go bankrupt and diversify into other products, or move overseas. But firms often decide to stay in the market, even at very low capacity utilization rates, for one or several of the following considerations: (1) firms' expectation of future demand growth; (2) minimal interfirm differences in marginal costs and financial structures; (3) firms' desire to cover large fixed costs and to recoup large investments; (4) firms with pockets deep enough to withstand low margins; and/or (5) the availability of continued protection or subsidies, which become increasingly necessary as firms fail to improve efficiency.[76]

[74] Kesavatana (1989), cited in Huang (2002, 549).
[75] Huang (2002, 567); see also Waldner (1999, 174).
[76] Huang (2002).

Responses to this kind of market failure typically involve variants of entry restrictions or exclusions, such as the formation of capacity consortia or the threat to withdraw support in the face of weak performance.[77] Such efforts frequently fail. Industry consortia for capacity reduction usually involve numerous firms and are notoriously prone to cheating. And as Huang argues, attempts to promote consortia or conglomerations, whether by state officials or other third parties, run up against both distributive and information challenges. Because it implies a reduction in benefits to particular firms, consolidation is often politically costly, while policies that *reward* good performers "tax government's analytical ability."[78]

The potential losses from overcapacity reduction thus require credibility in either the provision of side payments to losers or resistance to the protests of such firms. The need for clarity about weak performers and/or free riders also requires a significant analytical capability within the state itself, a capability which is unlikely without extensive information-intensive consultation and subsequent monitoring by both public and private actors.[79]

Foreign Direct Investment (FDI) Promotion: FDI can contribute to upgrading as a source of technology and managerial expertise, as well as a stimulus to make use of such knowledge. Yet success in capturing technology and managerial spillovers varies significantly across countries. Success seems to reflect "a much broader and more energetic" approach to investment promotion than is common among LDCs.[80] Specifically, promotion strategies will have to shift (1) from an emphasis on negative restrictions and tax holidays, to more positive financial incentives and to active strategies of matchmaking between investors and suppliers; (2) from a focus on foreign exchange and employment to dynamic effects on industrial structure through market access, technology transfer, and human resource development; (3) from a focus on discrete industries to the growth of "clusters" of complementary activities; (4) from a one-size-fits-all approach to strategies targeted to specific product areas and even firms; and (5) toward greater post-investment services such as support for new skills and troubleshooting obstacles posed by government agencies.

In this kind of effort, distributional tensions may grow, as host countries forego simple job- and foreign-exchange-generating investments in exchange for the long-term benefits of more technologically sophisticated investments. Information requirements will also expand significantly:

---

[77] Noble (1998: Ch. 1).
[78] Huang (2002, 550).
[79] Ibid.; Noble (1998: Ch. 1).
[80] Moran (1998, 153). The rest of this paragraph draws on Felker and Jomo (2003).

Tailoring the local investment environment to the needs of globally linked production requires an understanding of the widely varying technological properties of specific industries, the logistical and strategic concerns of multinational businesses, and the rapidly evolving international investment environment.[81] And the provision of such expertise will require involvement by new actors, such as consultants, universities, and research institutes.

The preceding considerations suggest that FDI policies designed to promote technology spillovers have tougher institutional requirements than is the case for FDI policies designed only to generate jobs and foreign exchange. Governments must possess significant expertise and flexibility as well as credibility in providing and withholding benefits to private actors. For their part, local firms, individually and collectively, must learn to search, screen, and bargain more effectively. The East Asian NICs' experience suggests that developing such public and private capacities requires extensive, overlapping consultation and monitoring capacities.[82]

Local Supplier Development: But upgrading also requires the expansion of local capacities to absorb FDI resources, especially by suppliers. The simultaneous development of indigenous capacities to complement FDI "might be the *sine qua non* of continued technology access ..."[83] Such development requires improving local enterprises' capabilities and strengthening education and training provision. Early approaches include the strengthening of local firms, especially small and medium enterprises (SMEs), centered on state provision of various supports by stand-alone Business Development Services (BDS).[84] Subsequent research suggested that BDS would achieve better results if they focused more on creating markets for private providers of technological services. But local firms, especially smaller ones, can often not afford the costs of relevant services. Further questions have been raised as to the actual benefits of even privately provided stand-alone services, at least in the absence of support from buyers of local products. Indeed, there is a growing consensus that the buyers (e.g., final assemblers), by providing specifications, technical guidance, and ongoing performance monitoring, are most effective in diffusing the capacities needed to compete in global markets.

---

[81] Felker and Jomo (2003).
[82] For example, Mardon (1990).
[83] Felker and Jomo (2003, 17).
[84] Unless noted, this discussion is based on Schmitz (2005: Ch. 5).

However, buyers may lack the organizational capacities to nurture suppliers and/or the belief that such support is worth the time and effort. Cross-national variation in supplier–buyer linkages within the same industry indicates that host country incentives, often in the form of supplier development programs, are a key influence on buyers' linkage activities.[85] Although such programs are widespread in the developing world, they typically involve "simple matchmaking" exercises that "rarely lead to sustainable linkages."[86] Successful support programs require that public agencies possess knowledge about the kinds of competencies required by buyers; they must develop a sense of the specific incentives attractive to buyers; and they must encourage the design of programs to large numbers of local producers. Experiences in Singapore and Penang (Malaysia) indicate that such capacities emerge only through extensive consultation with both final suppliers and producers; and that investment by private actors in such programs demands credibility and flexibility on the part of public agencies, as well as ongoing monitoring by both business and government.[87]

Training and Education: The supply of technical training is necessary for upgrading but notoriously prone to a range of imperfections and failures.[88] Imperfect information is a common problem. Investment in training may be low because workers who want jobs may not be certain of getting offers, and firms needing workers are uncertain about getting applicants. Information problems often become more serious with upgrading efforts. Questions emerge, for example, in the *design* of training as providers, whether public or private, find it difficult to judge precisely how broad training curricula ought to be. The design of high-skill training systems thus requires information about both market needs and the "cooperative proclivities of firms, and this is information that governments will not be able to acquire on their own."[89] "Poaching externalities" are also frequent, especially when skills are under great demand. Workers receiving "transferable" training, that is, training useful to at least one other firm in addition to the firm doing the training, may be hired by competitors, thus reducing all firms' incentive to invest in training. This free riding problem inherent in the positive externalities of training is intensified in the presence of large numbers of participants.

---

[85] For example, McKendrick et al (2000).

[86] Schmitz (2005, 30–31).

[87] Mckendrick et al (2000: Ch. 7); Rasiah (2000).

[88] "[T]he free-market system cannot usually be expected to lead people to acquire sufficient skills, and this is true in general, quite independently of the cyclical conditions and historical experience of individual countries" (Booth and Snower 1996, 7–8).

[89] Culpepper (2001, 278).

In light of these difficulties, effective training programs require what Culpepper calls "a politics of decentralized cooperation in which governments try to convince private actors to cooperate with each other."[90] Central to this process are consultation and monitoring that allow state policy makers to incorporate private information accessible to business associations.

Although lower in technology content, the effective provision of basic but high-quality education is no less of a challenge. Empirical evidence suggests that the social sector reforms emerging in the 1990s, including education, "pose even more formidable political obstacles" than the "1st generation" economic stabilization efforts emphasized by multilateral institutions in the 1980s.[91] The informational requirements of education reform are significant. Such changes lack accepted templates and must often be adapted to particular locales. Successful reforms also require broad participation by teachers, administrators, and community members.[92] Distributional tensions often emerge as basic education reforms threaten the use of educational goods, such as construction contracts or book sales, as pork and/or the interests of groups such as unions and favored locales.[93] Also, developing the strong secondary (and public vocational training) so critical to the capacity for basic technology absorption often means devoting fewer resources for universities and thus requires overcoming the preferences of wealthier interests.[94] Grindle's conclusion as to the institutional capacities needed to address such difficulties merits emphasis: "extensive consultation, negotiation and consensus building ... decentralized forms of decision making ... and time consuming monitoring."[95]

IV. INSTITUTIONAL DESIGN

Running through the previous sections is the idea that the institutional capacities appropriate for overcoming upgrading-related challenges are more likely with cooperation, "strategic collaboration", or "collaborative

---

[90] Ibid. (276).

[91] Nelson (1999, 2); Clague (1997).

[92] My emphasis here is on educational quality through, e.g., effective classroom teaching and teacher preparation, rather than the less information-intensive components of education such as the provision of school lunches or construction of school buildings. For an example of the different difficulties of various educational components, see Pritchett and Woolcock (2004, 195).

[93] Grindle (2004).

[94] Jeong and Armer (1994).

[95] Grindle (2001, 373).

problem solving." Two assumptions underlie this notion. One is that the complexities of upgrading tasks render their solutions highly idiosyncratic. As a result, resolving these tasks presents "the biggest headache for even the most astute and well-intentioned practitioner, because they are intrinsically incompatible with the logic and imperatives of large-scale routinized administrative control."[96] The second is that solutions to such challenges require engagement by both public and private actors, each making particular contributions. Organized business, for example, is often relatively weak in monitoring but is quite well situated to access and circulate relevant, but private, information. States, on the other hand, are relatively weak with regard to information circulation but stronger with regard to policy initiation, sanctioning, and the provision of transition aid, such as subsidies.[97]

All of this is consistent with, indeed in many cases inspired by, Peter Evans' emphasis on the value of "embedded autonomy," that is, a state that exhibits both independence in policy formulation and systematic linkages "to particular social groups with whom the state shares a joint project of transformation."[98] The challenge is finding the balance between autonomy and embeddedness.[99] The specific kind of institutional design that facilitates such a relationship and its associated capacities is unclear: "Formally, there is no single mapping between the market and the set of non-market institutions required to sustain it."[100] Instead, optimal institutional arrangements seem to be context specific, reflecting geography, historical trajectories, sociological characteristics, and so on.[101] The importance of context-based variation emerges even in the East Asian NICs, which differ in degrees of state centralization, business organization, and modalities of public–private relations.[102] Yet acknowledging that efficiency-generating institutions are home-grown does not preclude identifying three broad organizational features that appear empirically and causally associated with the institutional capacities reviewed above.

The first includes what might be termed a Weberian state bureaucracy "on steroids": In addition to the features highlighted by developmental state scholars, for example, competitive recruitment, merit-based promotion,

---

[96] Pritchett and Woolcock (2004, 195).
[97] For example, Culppper (2001).
[98] Evans (1995, 59).
[99] Rodrik (2007, 110–111).
[100] Ibid. (162).
[101] For example, Jutting (2003, 22).
[102] Wong and Ng (2001).

competitive remuneration, and relative autonomy in preference and policy formulation, such a bureaucracy rewards officials "who seek out close ties to business rather than hide behind a desk in a ministry."[103] Secure tenure can permit extended links with business even as the promotion and transparency rules under which they operate discourages more collusive clientelist or particularistic relationships.

The ability to maintain such relationships is also encouraged by the presence of well-organized private actors. Despite a long tradition of (often justified) suspicion that business associations are largely price fixing arenas, comparative research has demonstrated that collusive, inefficient behavior is far from universal. Associations have, often in collaboration with public officials, made important developmental contributions in areas ranging from infrastructure, to quota allocation, standard setting, market development, R&D, quality control, and technical training.[104]

These contributions are typically associated with specific organizational features: density, as measured by proportion of the sector (or potential group) output produced by members; effective interest mediation facilitated by voting rules weighted by firm size and transparency in allocation decisions; and the provision of selective incentives (e.g., privileged access to public officials, revenues from export taxes) that discourage exit. But these strengths themselves are in large part a function of state policies and behavior. Schneider argues in his study of Latin American business associations that "*states organized or disorganized business*" through a combination of threats and side payments (including privileged access as well as financial incentives).[105]

Finally, systematic and transparent linkages between public officials and business representatives to facilitate the kinds of signaling, reputation development, and buy-in assumed in the preceding sections on consultation and monitoring. The growing interest in "public–private consultative mechanisms" over the past decade reflects awareness of the benefits of such arrangements.[106]

Together, these broad organizational guidelines constitute a hierarchical taxonomy of "developmental," "intermediate," and "predatory" states. Given the strong presence of all three components in the East Asian NICs, these are "coded" as developmental, a category consistent with

---

[103] Schneider and Maxfield (1997, 17).
[104] Doner and Schneider (2000).
[105] Schneider (2004, 5); Ibid. (238).
[106] Yet the actual workings of these linkages remain underexplored. See Campos and Root (1996); World Bank (1993); Weiss (1998); Doner (1991). Evans provides little specifics on how "embeddedness" actually operates. On this point see Moon and Prasad (1998, 15–19); Kuo (1995); Schneider and Maxfield (1997).

corporatism.[107] As will be seen in Chapter 4, Thailand falls more in the intermediate category characterized by uneven bureaucratic coherence, significant clientelism in public–private relations, and factionalism within the private sector.[108] Yet Thailand's intermediate status itself constitutes a puzzle, especially in light of nineteenth-century predictions that the newly centralized Thai state would promote greater economic growth than would the newly established Meiji state in Japan.[109]

One way of responding to puzzles such as this is simply to include "political leadership at the top" as a component of institutional architecture.[110] This is useful insofar as it highlights political leaders' role as "principals" in raising the profile of industrial transformation, as well as in pushing public agencies and monitoring their behavior. But this response simply begs the question of political leaders' motivations: Why do a small number of political leaders indeed play these "virtuous" roles whereas most others do not? Why, for example, did postwar Philippine leaders squander colonial legacies of a well-educated population and a bureaucracy that exhibited impressive pockets of bureaucratic expertise, whereas Korea actively built on its legacy and even strove to learn from the Philippines' experience by sending its officials to Manila for training?[111] How do we explain the fact that Thai institutional capacities, while rarely approaching those required for upgrading, have in fact varied over time and even across sectors?

V. SYSTEMIC VULNERABILITY AND THE ORIGINS OF INSTITUTIONAL CAPACITIES

My response to these questions begins from three assumptions: First, as Robert Bates[112] has stressed, institutional capacities are themselves difficult collective action problems whose resolution requires resources and long-time horizons.

---

[107] Wade (1990, 375). This hierarchy itself requires some qualifications. One already noted is that the NICs institutional commonalities cover significant cross-national differences, especially in the degree of multilateralism characterizing public–private linkages. In addition, coherent, expert bureaucracies interacting with organized private sectors in transparent arenas often coexist in the NICs with clientelist and even corrupt arrangements in highly "bifurcated" state structures. The NICs' particular strength seems to lie in their ability to have hived off such corruption from leading economic sectors (e.g., Kang 2002). Finally, the optimal degree and combination of bureaucratic strength, private sector organization, and consultative mechanisms differ across developmental tasks.

[108] Evans (1995: Ch. 3).

[109] Feeny (1998, 6).

[110] Rodrik (2004, 19–20).

[111] Chang (2002, 224).

[112] Bates (1988).

Second, given these requirements, political leaders or "ruling elites" are crucial to the creation of institutional capacities, whether in the bureaucracy, the private sector, or public–private networks.[113] Third, political leaders' goals of securing power typically results in clientelist institutions to channel largesse to key constituencies interested in quick profits through rents or speculation, not in arrangements to promote public goods such as productivity improvement.[114]

Neither the benign motivations found in some NIE writings nor the autonomy emphasized in early developmental state accounts can thus account for institutional strength. The challenge is to specify the constraints that make it difficult for politicians to maintain power simply through clientelist connections, *and* the incentives pushing them to undertake the difficult task of building institutions for economic change. As noted in Chapter 1, a useful starting point in answering this challenge comes from a disparate set of writings all suggesting that politicians will attempt to create strong institutions when they perceive their countries confronting pressures similar to those faced by firms in highly competitive markets. This book locates the origins of institutional capacities in three pressures that, when occurring simultaneously, result in what Doner, Ritchie, and Slater[115] label "systemic vulnerability": (1) popular protests, or "contentious politics," ranging from demands for land reform, to labor protests, to communal demands;[116] (2) external security threats; and (3) hard budget constraints, due to a lack of exportable natural resources, foreign loans, and/or military aid.

The causal logic of this argument is as follows: other things being equal, political leaders try to keep coalitions as narrow as possible.[117] But elites are often pressed to enlarge coalitions by the credible threat of disruptive popular protests and by growing security threats. Addressing domestic and external threats simultaneously is especially difficult in the face of hard budget constraints: leaders must satisfy claims on revenues to satisfy popular pressures and national defense in the face of revenue scarcity. The experiences of the East Asian NICs suggest that doing so requires sustained growth to expand the national pie. Diversified, low-wage exports can support growth up to a point; but the emergence of lower wage rivals imposes limits on such a strategy. The challenge is then to develop a growth

---

[113] Schneider and Maxfield (1997).
[114] Geddes (1994).
[115] Doner, Ritchie, and Slater (2005).
[116] On contentious politics, see Slater (2006).
[117] Riker (1962).

strategy without following a "race to the bottom" approach that can alienate popular sectors who feel the brunt of such squeezing. The East Asian NICs' response has been an export trajectory based on higher skills and higher product quality. Put differently, political survival has required local producers to produce and export high value-added goods, which is upgrading. Doing so has in turn required institutions capable of consultation, monitoring, and credibility to address the specific challenges of upgrading discussed earlier.[118]

Using the East Asian NICs as "extreme cases," the systemic vulnerability approach addresses weaknesses in studies of institutional origins based on security threats, coalitional pressures, and resource endowments *viewed in isolation*.[119] It echoes the work of scholars such as Chalmers Johnson[120] on nationalism and Meredith Woo-Cumings[121] on security threats; but it argues that when the effect of external threats has been compounded by coalitional pressures and resource constraints, nationalist impulses go well beyond simple patriotism to prompt the creation of developmental institutions. It acknowledges the impact of coalitional pressures on institutional formation[122] and the potential for *broad* coalitions (or pressures to build such coalitions) to stimulate public goods.[123] But it highlights the ways in which external threats and resource constraints encourage payments to popular sectors that promote growth rather than inefficient populism.

Finally, the framework goes beyond existing scholarship on the "resource curse."[124] It explains the ways in which geography "is not destiny"[125] by emphasizing the importance of resource endowments as mediated by claims on those resources. It thus follows Rajah Rasiah's[126] argument that natural-resource exports reduced fiscal pressure on Southeast

---

[118] On the specific pressures facing the NICs and their institutional responses, see Doner, Ritchie, and Slater (2005).

[119] An extreme case has two dimensions. It is selected due to its unusual nature, i.e., "extreme value on an independent of dependent variable of interest." And, unlike an "outlier" whose values challenge an established argument, extreme cases are less useful for disconfirming than for generating hypotheses (Gerring 2007, 101). In other words, Doner, Ritchie, and Slater (2005) presume that there is no widely accepted hypothesis regarding the origins of institutional capacities, and that we have much to learn about the absence of upgrading in Southeast Asia from its presence in the NICs.

[120] Johnson (1982).

[121] Woo-Cumings (1998).

[122] Waldner (1999); Campos and Root (1996).

[123] Bueno de Mesquita et al. (2003).

[124] For example, Ross (1999); Birdsall, Pickney, and Sabot (2000).

[125] Rodrik (2003, 12).

[126] Rasiah (2003, 66).

Asian states to promote the kinds of "complementary institutional and linkage development" seen in the NICs.[127] But it disputes the implication that simple resource scarcity would have led to institutional strength in the NICs. And as illustrated in Chapters 4–7, it accounts not just for institutional weaknesses in Thailand (compared to the NICs), but also for institutional strengths that helped to promote Thai structural change and for variations in Thai capacities over time.

This last point highlights an important goal of this book – namely, to provide a more nuanced understanding of how vulnerability affects institutional capacities than currently available. The book's longitudinal and cross-sectoral analysis of the Thai case, as well as its single sector, cross-national comparisons, allow us to assess the impact of degrees of change in the three sets of pressures, rather than their simple presence or absence as emphasized in previous assessments of this argument.[128] This kind of ordinal analysis can help us to understand how much vulnerability is necessary to trigger and to sustain efforts at institutional strengthening. It provides the opportunity to assess the impact of variation in specific vulnerability pressures. In the following chapter, for example, I assess the impact of a sudden constriction in available resources owing to exogenous shocks – the 1980s debt crisis and the 1997 financial crisis – in the absence of security threats or internal contentious politics. It allows us to assess the impact of vulnerability on the *evolution*, as well as the creation, of development-related institutions, and allows me to identify intervening variables, especially political institutions.

VI. VETO PLAYERS AS INTERVENING VARIABLES

The preferences of political leaders may be influenced by security threats or hard budget constraints, but the ability to translate those preferences into institutions and policies depends in part on more proximate political arrangements through which leaders act. More specifically, it depends on (1) the political system's institutional separation of power (i.e., subunits of the polity), and (2) the diversity of preferences among those holding such institutional positions; and (3) the distance among the preferences of diverse players. Together, these constitute what Cox and McCubbins label "the

---

[127] See also Anne Booth's emphasis on the negative growth impact of "easy to tax" sectors in Southeast Asia (1999, 311).

[128] Doner, Ritchie, and Slater (2005) considered ordinal variation in the analysis of the ASEAN-4, but nominal variation between the NICs and ASEAN-4 was the article's primary focus.

effective number of vetoes."[129] And although the veto player literature largely focuses on democracies, the framework also applies to authoritarian regimes, including Thailand's numerous nondemocratic governments.[130] My interest in veto players is with their developmental impact and their origins.

Developmental Consequences of Veto Players: The number of effective vetoes can affect development policy by influencing the balance between "decisiveness" – the ability to shift or modify policy, and "resoluteness" – the ability to commit credibly to a policy.[131] Large numbers of veto players reduce policy makers' decisiveness while increasing their resoluteness. Transaction costs are central to this argument: With more, diverse interests provided with vetoes, "it becomes increasingly difficult to ensure that every party to the negotiation receives sufficient value to accept" a deal to change policy.[132] The corollary of this logic leads to significant dangers at both extremes: With a single veto player there are risks of policy volatility and thus weak commitment to a particular policy. With a very large number of veto players, the risk is one of stalemate or gridlock.

One might assume that gridlock translates into high credible commitment. But large numbers of veto players can also result in policy *balkanization*,[133] a situation in which each actor has the ability to initiate policies in his/her particular area of authority. More specifically, the result may be gridlock with regard to public goods but a free-for-all for less public goods, that is, fiscal pork (geographically divisible public expenditures based on political rather than economic logic), and/or rents (special favors extracted from state officials).[134] Thus, numerous veto players can undermine the capacity for credible commitments, at least with regard to upgrading-related policies.

---

[129] Cox and McCubbins (2000, 26); see also Tsebelis (2002).

[130] Andrew MacIntyre notes that there are few pure autocracies, and in most authoritarian regimes, politics are shaped in important ways by a range of formal and informal rules (2003, 5; 42). Factors potentially influencing institutional separation of power in a democracy include the structure of the national executive (presidentialism vs. parliamentarianism) and of the national legislature (bicameralism vs. unicameralism); national–subnational relations (federal vs. unitary state); the independence of the national judiciary; independence of the military; and the electoral system (structure of electoral districts, entry, voting and the conversion of votes into seats). Separation of purpose is reflected in the number and strength of parties (including the number of party factions), as well as ideological distance and sectoral differences among relevant actors (Cox and McCubbins 2000, 26).

[131] Cox and McCubbins (2000).

[132] Ibid. (27).

[133] Ibid. (46).

[134] "[E]ach veto player will be able to demand, and receive, side payments in the form of narrowly targeted policies" (Ibid., 28). We should, however, view with caution the implied correlation between more veto players and clientelism. As will be seen later in this book,

But what is the optimal number of effective veto players for upgrading? Assuming that upgrading requires the capacity (1) to adapt decisively to new challenges *and* (2) to do so credibly enough that private actors will undertake new investments, the answer is to avoid both extremes.[135] This can occur in several ways. First, political elites in multiple veto player contexts can provide assurance of decisiveness as well as resoluteness by delegating authority to an agency, such as an independent central bank[136] or a specialized R&D agency as Israel's Office of Chief Scientist,[137] with the autonomy to shift policies when needed. Second, single veto players can provide assurance that they will avoid radical policy changes, or at least shift only with justification, by consulting with key private actors to decentralize policy design and implementation, a strategy practiced by Singapore's People's Action Party (PAP).[138] Third, a coup can produce an authoritarian regime and thus reduce at least the number of official veto players. And fourth, fewer veto players can result from a reduction in the number and strength of parties (or factions).

Origins of Veto Players: How would such political arrangements emerge? Despite the potential impact of veto players, there is very little written on their origins.[139] This may reflect the fact that most of the veto player literature has analyzed developed countries whose political arrangements are more stable than in the developing world. Under these conditions, it makes sense to emphasize the path dependent nature of political arrangements and to view them as independent variables.[140] But in less-institutionalized developing countries, veto players are best understood as potentially malleable, intervening variables. *The hypothesis explored in this book is that increasing systemic vulnerability pushes both extremes – single and many veto players – toward the middle.* In this interpretation, the need to generate new resources led Singapore's PAP to consult with multiple parties and thus to act more like a multiple veto player system.[141] Conversely, vulnerability can reduce an otherwise large number of effective veto players by (1) limiting the material basis

---

the Philippines under martial law exhibited extensive clientelism, i.e., cronyism. Nor does a highly competitive form of clientelism, as seen in Thailand from the late 1950s to the early 1970s, necessarily preclude the provision of certain public goods.

[135] MacIntyre (2003) applies this logic to exchange rate management.
[136] Hallerberg (2002).
[137] Breznitz (2007).
[138] Hicken and Ritchie (2002).
[139] A partial exception is Streeck (2001).
[140] For example, Thelen (2003).
[141] Hicken and Ritchie (2002).

on which clientelist-type factions operate; (2) prompting actors to launch a coup; and/or (3) by prompting an alignment of preferences among veto players, as seems to have occurred in Israel's creation of an insulated body devoted to upgrading-related functions.[142] In this book, I ask whether such dynamics operates in the more intermediate case of Thailand as well.

The framework developed in this chapter predicts that economic upgrading will occur only to the extent that public and private actors succeed at consultation, credible commitments, and monitoring. It predicts that such capacities are more likely to emerge in the presence of more cohesive and transparent organizational structures but that the most important influence on these capacities is the degree to which political leaders feel compelled by external and domestic pressures to promote them. Finally, the framework predicts that while institution-building efforts must operate through existing structures of political competition, that is, veto players, such structures will themselves shift in the face of external and domestic pressures. In the following chapter I assess these arguments through an analytical chronology of Thai development from 1958 to 2006. This country-level analysis sets the stage for the sectoral and cross-national analyses in Chapters 5–7.

[142] Breznitz (2007).

4

Origins and Consequences of Thailand's Intermediate State

The creation of the modern Thai state in the mid-to-late nineteenth century prompted predictions that Thailand's economic growth would rival that of Japan's newly established Meiji state.[1] Instead, Thailand emerged from World War II and moved into the late 1950s as a preindustrial economy with a healthy but relatively undifferentiated agricultural sector.[2] Beginning in the early 1960s, however, the economy took off. Agriculture began to diversify, and new industrial activities attracted investment. By the 1990s, dynamic growth and diversification had made Thailand an "East Asian Miracle."[3] Yet apprehension about the shallowness of the country's industrialization grew as diversified export dynamism was matched by rising import dependence and competition from other low-wage producers. The 1997 Asian economic crisis made it clear that these concerns were justified. Upgrading became a central focus of the country's recovery efforts. But almost a decade after the crisis, the World Bank warned that Thai growth could not be sustained unless the country's technological base was improved.[4]

The present chapter traces the institutions and politics of this evolution in order to provide both background for the subsequent sectoral analyses and an initial assessment of the book's framework. The chapter is organized into six time periods, each of which is distinguished by shifts in reform pressures and political competition. The analysis of each period begins with

---

[1] Feeny (1998, 6).
[2] Ingram (1955); Baker and Pasuk (2005).
[3] World Bank (1983).
[4] World Bank (2006a).

a demand-side focus on key policy tasks and institutional responses. This allows me to evaluate the degree to which policy outcomes were, as anticipated by the framework, the result of existing institutional capacities. These tasks exhibit different degrees of difficulty and therefore offer opportunities to assess the importance of variation in institutional capacities. Also, each of the tasks was perceived by Thai officials and business leaders as being important for development. Each section's analysis then shifts to the supply side, with a focus on political competition/veto players and on the vulnerability pressures facing state leaders.

I. IGNITING GROWTH UNDER AUTHORITARIAN RULE, 1958–1973

The Thai economy experienced impressive growth in the period 1958–1973. Manufacturing value added rose almost threefold, and its contribution to GNP increased gradually.[5] Thai agriculture entered a "first wave" of diversification from rice, rubber, and teak into upland field crops that were both exports and inputs into other agro-related products; but yields remained low, as did manufacturing productivity and backward linkages.[6] The country's impressive but uneven performance was a function of available institutional capacities, which were strongly influenced by political shifts and broad pressures facing the country's leaders. In 1958, Field Marshal Sarit Thanarat unified the armed forces and consolidated a military regime that endured for a decade beyond his death in 1963. Externally, Sarit and his successors faced a regional context of Cold War-related instability, albeit with significant U.S. support. Internally, rural unrest was simmering, especially in the northeast, though the extensive land frontier helped to moderate this pressure.

A. Macroeconomic Performance

Thailand's growth under Sarit owes much to effective, market-conforming macroeconomic policies.[7] The government's main goal was fostering continuous economic growth while maintaining monetary stability. The regime unified the exchange rate, limited the size of the fiscal deficit and external borrowing, prohibited state guarantees of private debt, and refrained from establishing new government enterprises. Centralized and rationalized

---

[5] Muscat (1994, 107).
[6] Christensen (1993b, 6); Muscat (1994, 75; 101; 107).
[7] Ibid. (100).

macroeconomic agencies established under Sarit formulated and implemented these policies. These included the Bureau of the Budget within the Prime Minister's Office, the Office of Fiscal Policy in the Finance Ministry, the Board of Investments (BOI), and the National Economic Board, which initiated the country's first Five Year Plan in 1961.[8] The first two agencies, linking technocrats in the central bank, Finance Ministry, and prime minister's office, reformed the budgetary process. The ban on government guarantees of private sector debt strengthened the autonomy of these agencies from other parts of the bureaucracy and from elected officials, who were forced to operate under hard budget constraints.[9]

B. Risk Socialization

During the 1960s, Thai commercial banks coordinated a shift of resources from agriculture to manufacturing and within agriculture itself.[10] Corporatist-like linkages between public agencies and the commercial banks were important to these investments: the central bank (Bank of Thailand – BOT) cooperated with the Thai Bankers' Association (TBA) in formulating and enforcing key banking regulations; extending domestic credit to exporters, industrialists, and farmers; and funneling commercial deposits into government bonds, thus helping the government avoid costly foreign development loans.[11] These activities produced Thailand's first wave of agricultural diversification and encouraged the growth of large business groups, including agro-business conglomerates[12] and industrial conglomerates in textiles, electronics, and capital goods.[13]

C. Productivity

Sarit undertook some productivity-related measures, encouraging highway expansion, launching water projects, and establishing a graduate program in agriculture that laid the base for the first wave of agricultural

---

[8] The planning agency was named the National Economic Board from 1950 to 1959. It then became the National Economic Development board until 1972. From 1972 to the present, it has been the National Economic and Social Development Board (NESDB), the name henceforth used in this volume.

[9] Ibid. (79).

[10] Christensen (1993, 135).

[11] Thitinan (2001, 71).

[12] Christensen (1993, 136–137); Suehiro (1992, 58–59).

[13] Rock (2000, 187–88).

diversification.[14] Perhaps the most serious effort at ensuring product quality pre-dated the Sarit regime, however. In the mid-1950s, when intense competition resulted in product adulteration that threatened the country's export reputation and thus a key revenue source, the government established a corporatist arrangement centered on the Board of Trade, a peak association empowered, in conjunction with the Commerce Ministry, to allocate rice export quotas in exchange for maintaining quality standards and a minimal export price.[15] Overall, however, public and private actors focused on investment promotion, not productivity.

D. Explaining Outcomes

Policy Difficulties and Institutional Responses: As noted in Chapter 3, macroeconomic stabilization requires technical expertise and the ability to resist opposition from those disadvantaged by the introduction of stabilization policies. Yet the Sarit regime could follow accepted blueprints in this area, and the number of actors required for implementation was small. Facilitating investments in new, often risky activities, on the other hand, involves gathering information about unfamiliar markets and, in the case of Thailand, required the accumulation of savings from large numbers of small farmers. Finally, productivity improvements required the development of expertise in new, unfamiliar areas and the capacity to translate and deliver such knowledge to large numbers of geographically dispersed producers. Thailand's impressive success in the first two areas and general neglect of the third reflects the uneven capacities of Thai institutions during this period.

Specifically, this mixed record reflected a Thai version of Evans's "intermediate state" discussed in Chapter 3: a bifurcated structure pairing efficiency in macroeconomic agencies and commercial banks with a distinctly politicized and clientelistic set of arrangements governing manufacturing and productivity-related tasks. While this "macrosectoral split"[16] did little for upgrading, its ability to impose hard budget constraints and the competitive nature of its clientelism limited the costs of inefficiency in sectoral arrangements.

The "strong" side of this bifurcated structure consisted of the macroeconomic agencies, especially the Ministry of Finance and BOT, which

---

[14] Christensen (1993, 132–33).
[15] Laothamatas (1991); Christensen (1993, 220).
[16] Christensen (1993, 126).

"shared a technocratic corridor" until the mid-1970s.[17] Often operating under off-budget rules, they were staffed by foreign-educated economists sent abroad on central bank scholarship programs. Dr. Puey Ungpakorn, the first director of the Bureau of the Budget, the first director of the Fiscal Policy Office, and governor of the BOT from 1959 to 1971, embodied the expertise, autonomy, and credibility, of the macro-agencies. Puey succeeded in blocking crony practices in government contracting and commodity trading. By unifying distortionary multiple exchange rates, Puey and his colleagues in the National Economic and Social Development Board and Budget Bureau helped reduce postwar inflation and eliminate the state's monopolistic rents based on control of the rice trade. They limited state spending while directing funds into infrastructure projects such as roads and basic utilities. As noted, they pushed commercial banks to invest deposits in government bonds, thus avoiding expensive foreign loans. They contracted World Bank loans less to bolster foreign reserves and more to impose high standards of feasibility analysis, planning, and implementation on domestic project spending. Finally, through corporatist links to the TBA noted earlier, they increased credit available to the private sector by developing legislation to increase domestic savings.[18]

Government macroeconomic policies were consistent with the expanding agro-export interests of Thailand's large commercial banks. The banks coordinated a rice export-tax regime that was key to state revenues. Working with rice millers and exporters, as well as with state officials, the banks helped to organize a syndicate-like structure through which prices were set, risks were shared, and product quality was monitored.[19] By extracting revenues from a multitude of geographically dispersed and marginally profitable small cultivators, the banks effectively substituted for the "flexible, deeply penetrating" state tax regime otherwise expected in small-farm, rice producing countries.[20] In addition, the banks were *the* key institution for diversification. Through consultation with and monitoring of diverse producer groups, they organized export cartels in products such as maize and sugar[21] and coordinated the establishment of agro-business

---

[17] Thitinan (2001, 66). The rest of this paragraph draws on Ibid., Ch. 3.
[18] Commercial bank deposits grew from B5.3 billion in 1960 to B26 billion in 1969 (Ibid., 71).
[19] Christensen (1993); Silcock (1967).
[20] Shafer (1994).
[21] Silcock (1967, 184).

groups.[22] In effect, the banks, rather than the state, coordinated investment.[23] Corporatist-like linkages between key public agencies and the
commercial banks, discussed earlier, constituted the third pillar of the
strong side of Thailand's bifurcated arrangement.

Line ministries, along with the BOI, formed the weaker side of Thailand's bifurcated structure. The Ministries of Industry, Agriculture, and
Commerce, among others, exhibited little of the sector-specific expertise,
coordination, or autonomy of their macroeconomic counterparts. Competition and duplication were common: five departments in three ministries
had authority over permits and licenses, and at least four agencies controlled trade policy, with Finance torn between its preference for export
promotion and its reliance on tariffs as a source of government revenues.[24]
Such fragmentation undermined credibility, especially with regard to policies on protection and entry.[25] Industries discouraged from expanding by
the Industry Ministry due to concern about excess capacity often expanded
to take advantage of high tariffs imposed by the Finance Ministry[26] or as a
result of aggressive promotion by the BOI.[27]

This lack of coordination was largely a function of the line ministries'
participation in clientelistic networks linking firms or groups of firms to
individual members of the political–military elite. The latter typically sat on
the firms' boards of directors and leveraged these positions to reward their
own supporters. The ministries' role in such arrangements was to help firms
obtain rents through the provision of licenses, protection, and other goods.
Fragmentation among and within line ministries promoted particularistic
lobbying to the detriment of systematic public–private consultation or long-
term planning.[28] The resulting lack of consultation, monitoring capacity, and
credibility undermined upgrading by fostering the "higgledy-piggledy growth
of Thailand's industrial sector" and its "spotty performance in terms of
efficiency."[29] The Finance Ministry's desire for revenue, in combination with
line ministries' interest in particularistic rents, resulted in tariff and taxation
systems that discouraged efficiency-based linkages within sectors.[30]

---

[22] Suehiro (1992).
[23] Christensen and Siamwalla (1993, 14).
[24] Rock (2000); Corden (1967, 165–167).
[25] For example, Somboon (1998, 86).
[26] Rock (2000, 185).
[27] Siamwalla (1975, 38).
[28] Muscat (1994, 96).
[29] Siamwalla (1975, 38).
[30] Muscat (1994, 105).

But the competitive nature of Thai clientelism also reduced entry barriers in most sectors and thereby facilitated new investments and promoted more competitive market structures than would otherwise have obtained.[31] Intra-elite rivalries helped to ensure that aspiring businessmen could find patrons concerned about their own economic security and willing to provide licenses or protection or both. Multiple patrons were available to bribe, keeping the level of bribes fairly low.[32] As a result, market structures in many areas, such as control over remittances to China, rice exporting, cassava, sugar, and textiles, were competitive, albeit sometimes oligopolistic.[33] Other factors complemented the low entry barriers to business. Linkages with prominent politicians and the growth of joint ventures with BOI-promoted foreign investors constituted de facto property rights for risky investments.[34] *Exit* barriers were also low: technocratic control over the budgetary process meant hard budget constraints on line ministries, limiting their ability to bail out failing firms.

Political Competition and Veto Players: This set of institutional capacities emerged under an authoritarian regime whose political–military elite was factionalized when it came to the pursuit of economic rents but unified behind the country's economic and political strategies. In 1958, Sarit exiled competing factions, unified the armed forces, and consolidated his military regime. Yet cooperation within his coup group quickly turned into factional rivalry that only intensified after his death.[35] This intra-elite rivalry had both costs and benefits. With regard to sector-specific and productivity-related policies, the regime effectively had a large number of veto players, with the predicted result of policy balkanization anticipated by Cox and McCubbins.[36] With regard to macroeconomic policy and risk socialization, the regime had a very small number of veto players.

Vulnerability Pressures: That sectoral policy balkanization did not break the bank and macro policy did not swing wildly reflected the broader set of pressures within which Sarit and his successors operated. By the late 1950s, Thai leaders faced significant challenges and had access to equally significant resources. The country found itself in the midst of Cold War tensions reflected in instability in Indo-China and a more assertive China. But

---

[31] Doner and Ramsay (2000, 152–155).
[32] Schleifer and Vishny (1993, 607).
[33] Skinner (1958, 304); Christensen (1993a, 192; 220); Somboon (1998).
[34] Hewison (1985).
[35] Morell (1974, 846).
[36] Cox and McCubbins (2000).

external threats to Thai stability were not as serious as those faced by Korea, Taiwan, and Singapore.[37] They were also offset by an alliance with the U.S. that not only provided important security guarantees but also reduced hard budget constraints resulting from the post-Korean War depression and drought-induced declines in crop production. U.S. military expenditures, especially in the 1960s, *"provided sufficient exogenous foreign exchange earnings to free Thailand from the reserves constraint that might otherwise have materialized as economic conditions turned less favorable."*[38] Domestically, there was significant concern that regional instability might stimulate unrest in Thailand's historically poor northeast region, where the Communist Party of Thailand (CPT) launched an insurgency in 1965. Yet rural discontent was moderated by a large land frontier, which made it "possible to extract resources from agriculture without impoverishing the peasantry and to build an indigenously owned commercial banking system and an import-substitution base in Bangkok behind protective barriers"[39]

This moderate set of pressures encouraged the creation of institutions devoted to a gradual expansion of economic activities, even as it allowed for arrangements with little capacity for the monitoring, consultation, and credibility required for technology and linkage development. The significant exceptions in corporatist, nonclientelist arrangements in macroeconomic policy and rice exports reflected the importance of those areas for state revenues.

II. ECONOMIC DIVERSIFICATION AND THE RISE OF POLITICAL COMPETITION, 1973–1979

The first six years following the end of military rule were a period of significant diversification and growth in the Thai economy, particularly in manufactured goods and exports, which expanded at an annual rate of almost 40%.[40] Although agriculture's role in the economy declined, the sector began a second wave of diversification. Such increases in agricultural and manufacturing value added clearly involved some degree of upgrading, but the growth was largely based on "agricultural inputs and in labor-intensive production."[41] Demand for foreign intermediates and capital goods climbed in part due to weak export linkages: as exports grew, so did

---

[37] Doner, Ritchie, and Slater (2005).
[38] Muscat (1994, 101; italics added).
[39] Rock (1995, 13).
[40] Mingsarn (1992a, 2–12).
[41] Muscat (1994, 152).

the need for imported raw materials and intermediates. And technological changes in agriculture were uneven at best.

Innovative commercial banks and increased state capacity in rural areas were key to the achievements and persistent problems of this period. Important political changes – the overthrow of military rule in 1973 and subsequent intensified party competition – encouraged limited institutional strengthening in a context of growing domestic unrest in the northeast and a more volatile external environment. These pressures were offset by U.S.– China rapprochement and growing access to external finance.

A. Reform in Agriculture

Thai governments during this period undertook three sets of efforts in agriculture. One focused on farmers' *productivity*. The Ministry of Agriculture (MOA) was reorganized and strengthened, assuming direct control of irrigation and cooperatives. Formerly fragmented extension functions and crop research activities were consolidated and expanded, and extension officials began making routine visits to villages throughout the country.[42] These efforts achieved little, however, as reflected in stagnant rice yields. The government also initiated a system of *rice price supports* in which proceeds from the rice premium would be shifted from the Commerce to the Agriculture Ministry for market interventions. But the effort failed; it was "at best an ad hoc method for rewarding supporters of select political parties, and at worst an utter financial scam ..."[43]

Results were much more positive in *agricultural finance*. Until the mid-1970s, commercial credit to rural producers was scarce, forcing most farmers to rely on informal lenders for working capital. Long-term risk capital was almost unknown. In response, the Finance Minister requested that the commercial banks devote at least 5% of their loans and advances to rural households; ordered the ministry's Bank for Agriculture and Cooperatives (BAAC) to expand its loans to rural households; and allowed any commercial bank unable to lend the required amount directly to deposit the balance of its requirements in the BAAC. These measures expanded formal credit to farmers and significantly reduced the role of informal lenders. By 1990, some 60% of agricultural families had access to formal institutional credit, compared to 15–20% before 1975. Growth in lending also

---

[42] Christensen (1993a, 162).
[43] Christensen (1995, 1–2).

stimulated diversification via an increase in commercial bank lending to agribusinesses in new product areas.[44]

B. Explaining Outcomes: Agriculture

These contrasting results reflect different fits between available capacities and task difficulties. Improving irrigation and extension services, both key to productivity, required the engagement of multiple actors, as well as site-specific technical information. Yet the MOA remained fragmented into uncoordinated departments and lacked expertise.[45] Equally important, farmers' groups of the sort capable of absorbing new technologies did not expand in this period. Raising price supports posed significant distributional and information challenges. Higher prices for producers meant higher food costs for urban consumers, and price supports lent themselves to particularistic schemes yielding rents not for farmers but for almost everyone in the rice industry, including cabinet ministers and their provincial supporters, such as rice millers and traders.[46] Effective implementation also required information about different grades of rice, region-specific needs, and the impact of price supports on overall market prices.[47] The two agencies within the Agriculture and Commerce Ministries responsible for implementing the program had neither the staff nor the expertise to monitor basic price information and compliance with program goals. Finally, neither had the political will or capacity to bypass the politicians who had discretion over site-specific subsidy distribution.[48]

The challenges of lending to small farmers were more easily addressed by existing institutional capacities. Because loans were designed to benefit the agricultural sector as a whole, lending had fewer information and coordination requirements than did productivity and price supports, while distributional differences were limited by the broad focus of the effort. Institutional reforms also helped. Because the BAAC operated under the Finance Ministry and the central bank, it was supervised by the technocrats who ran these institutions. Further, in 1975, the Finance Ministry initiated an extensive reform of the BAAC, developing new credit monitoring techniques and an innovative group lending strategy known as the "peer monitoring system"[49]

---

[44] Muscat (1994, 168).
[45] Christensen (1993, 162).
[46] Christensen (1995, 10).
[47] Ibid. (10).
[48] Siamwalla and MacIntyre (2001, 252–254).
[49] Christensen (1993; 1995).

While state agencies and associated farmers groups managed loans to small producers, the commercial banks were important in mobilizing funds for agribusiness. Although the BOT mandated increased commercial bank lending to farmers, it had neither the capacity nor the desire to regulate such loans. It therefore permitted the commercial banks to count loans to large agribusiness firms as "agricultural."[50] The commercial banks reacted quickly to the 1975 lending requirements by searching out investment opportunities in farming, encouraged by the launching of what was in effect an industrial policy for large-scale agriculture. In the late 1970s, the BOI began to issue promotional certificates for large chicken exporters and require promoted firms to have large minimum working capital.[51]

The key organizer in this effort was the Bangkok Bank, which developed an agricultural credit center focused on integrated livestock investments. Its partner was Charoen Pokphand, an animal feed producer established in 1970, which was anxious to move into integrated livestock production and export. Commercial bank investments into this and other such agricultural groups, facilitated by finance companies and the Stock Exchange of Thailand (SET) established in the mid-1970s, constituted a "dominant channel which facilitated Sino-Thai agribusiness investments into the countryside in the 1970s"[52]

This growth also required mechanisms to overcome rural market imperfections in extending credit, information, and technology to large numbers of farmers. After encountering problems raising poultry and swine based on arms-length relations with small farmers, Charoen Pokphand shifted to contract farming. The Bangkok Bank's agricultural credit center was instrumental in this innovation, requesting that the company develop contract arrangements in exchange for financing.[53] Using this system, it became one of the world's largest integrated livestock producers.[54]

The achievements of contract farming were less impressive in non-livestock products.[55] The contract system failed to increase rural technological capacities, even as it increased farmers' indebtedness.[56] These outcomes reflect persistent institutional weaknesses on the part of both the state and rural producers, which contract farming reinforced. Agribusiness

---

[50] Ibid. (1993; 151).
[51] Muscat (1994, 156); Goss and Burch (2001, 979).
[52] Christensen (1993a, 270); Muscat (1994, 161).
[53] Christensen (1993a, 269–270).
[54] Singh (2005, 219).
[55] Siamwalla (1992a, 22; 1996).
[56] Singh (2005, 222–223).

arrangements seem to have alleviated any pressure for improvements in state capacity, especially with regard to local extension services. The system also did little to promote farmer organizations with the capacity to influence policy through consultation or to monitor compliance with contracts.[57]

C. Trade Policy

Thailand became more protectionist during the 1970s, with a doubling of the average effective rate.[58] Yet protection in Thailand was not designed to encourage linkages and technology absorption. The Thai system of tariffs and business taxes favored vertical integration, not local supplier development. Nor, because it favored domestic-oriented producers, did the Thai trade regime encourage learning. Unlike in the NICs, where levels of protection and dispersion were also high, the Thais did not combine temporary protection with exposure to competition.[59] In the face of pressures such as oil price increases, the government's principal goal was revenue generation: import tariffs accounted for one-quarter of tax revenues in the second half of the 1970s.[60] Of course, exports were also a potential revenue source, and Thai technocrats did initiate export-promoting tax concessions and duty rebates. But these were neither extensive nor designed to push protected firms toward greater competitiveness.[61] They were instead the seeds of what would later become a system of "export-oriented protectionism."[62]

But the trade regime did encourage investments, relatively competitive markets, and even exports. The regime was in fact "fairly liberal or laissez faire partly by design and partly by default."[63] The design component refers in part to a series of tax concessions and duty rebates for exporters[64] and in part to the minor role of Thai state enterprises in manufacturing and thus the relatively minimal political pressure on commercial banks to direct funds into specific sectors requiring protection.[65] The default component refers to the beneficial consequences of institutional weaknesses, to which I now turn.

---

[57] Ibid. (224).
[58] Lauridsen (2000, 18–20).
[59] Ibid. (35); Wade (1990).
[60] Muscat (1994, 148).
[61] Herderschee (1993, 356).
[62] Paopongsakorn and Fuller (1997, 480).
[63] Lauridsen (2000, 35).
[64] Herderschee (1993).
[65] Muscat (1994, 149).

D. Explaining Outcomes: Trade Policy

Developing a trade policy conducive to upgrading posed significant challenges that Thai institutions were ill-equipped to address. First, severe fragmentation in the bureaucracy and among trade associations impeded consultation and coordination of the numerous parties whose interests would have to be reconciled by such a policy. Instead, public officials in rival agencies, often linked to political parties, brokered between competing private interests.[66] In addition, Thai agencies typically adopted a top-down approach to policy decisions rather than involving "sector agents in identification of problems, in monitoring and in feedback of result(s)."[67] Third, the key agencies administering trade policy lacked the capacity to assess potential effects and to monitor outcomes.[68] This weakness was in part due to the state's poor statistical base, itself a result of "the modest collection of data by trade associations and a prevailing unwillingness among Sino-Thai enterprises to provide information."[69] The BOI, driven by conflicts among ministers and business associations, lacked the capacity to use performance requirements as criteria for investment promotion.[70] All of these problems contributed to ad hoc policy changes that undermined the state's credibility.

But these very weaknesses had their benefits. Bureaucratic balkanization discouraged capture by one set of particular interests. Further, the state's inability to monitor allowed smuggling and illegal firms, both of which stimulated competition in otherwise protected markets. Where such competition led to overcapacity, firms were forced to seek out export markets. Such exports, however, were based largely on varying combinations of low wages, existing natural resources, and foreign know-how.

E. Explaining Outcomes: An Overall View

Political Competition and Veto Players: Thai politics became more democratic and more crowded in the 1970s. The process began with the contested 1969 parliamentary elections and culminated in a popular, student-led uprising that led to a democratic regime in 1973. Some 42 parties contested the 1975 election, with success increasingly based on funds from business and

---

[66] Lauridsen (2000, 35).
[67] Ibid. (39).
[68] Muscat (1994, 151).
[69] Lauridsen (2000, 35).
[70] Unger (1998, 75).

local influence.[71] The military remained influential, overthrowing the democratic government in a bloody 1976 coup, ruling directly for two years, and then remaining as a key player through the quasi-democratic governments of most of the 1980s. Multiple contending parties operating in shifting coalitional governments "became the norm for Thai politics."[72]

Sectoral ministries became cash cows for parties operating in multiparty coalitions.[73] With cabinet portfolios used for particularistic purposes, the sectoral ministries became a "representative kleptocracy."[74] Three top parties competed for Agriculture, while the Ministries of Industry and Commerce became the fiefdoms of particular parties. This process culminated in the 1978 Constitution, which increased rent-seeking opportunities by expanding the cabinet from 30 to 44 posts. This increase in veto players resulted in policy balkanization and pork, as seen in the trade and agricultural policies reviewed earlier.

Vulnerability Pressures: A more threatening set of external and domestic factors pushed Thai leaders to focus on rural issues and revenue generation in this period. With industrial growth limited to Bangkok, rural–urban income gaps had widened.[75] Rural problems fueled an expansion of the CPT as well as the creation of the Peasants Federation of Thailand, a group whose organization was "unprecedented in rural Thailand."[76] Adding to domestic political concerns was an upsurge in urban activism stimulated by growth-inspired urban migration, expanded secondary and university enrollment, and growing factory and white-collar workforces.[77] These urban forces, especially students, were key to the overthrow of authoritarian rule in 1973.

External factors intensified the impact of domestic political upheavals. The 1975 U.S. defeat in Vietnam, the fall of Cambodia to the Khmer Rouge in 1975, and China's explicit support for Thailand's domestic insurgency coincided with the withdrawal of U.S. forces and consequently the rapid reduction of U.S. military aid.[78] Finally, in the fall of 1973, Thailand was hit by OPEC's fourfold rise in oil prices. As predicted by the arguments presented in Chapter 3, these pressures led to a reduction in veto players in the form of the military's overthrow of democracy in 1976.

---

[71] Hewison (1989, 143).
[72] Ockey (2004a, 25).
[73] Christensen (1993a, 156–157).
[74] Siamwalla (1991).
[75] Christensen (1993a, 145–146).
[76] Pasuk and Baker (1995, 298).
[77] Anderson (1977).
[78] Christensen (1993a, 146–147).

But this increased vulnerability was offset by a number of factors. Thailand's democratic transition did not create broad-based popular coalitions.[79] Also, with the land frontier still not exhausted, land-hungry farmers could move into upland crop areas. Externally, security threats eased with Thai- and U.S.–China rapprochement. In terms of revenue, the costs of the first oil shock in the early 1970s and the losses of U.S. military spending in 1975 were moderated by significant global rises in food and commodity prices, by remittances from increasing numbers of Thais working in the Middle East, and by Japanese investment. There was also significant growth in public sector borrowing of petrodollars from global commercial institutions. By reducing foreign exchange constraints, these financial inflows financed an increase in veto players, facilitated "debt-financed growth" in the latter half of the decade, funded increases in defense spending, and weakened the need for upgrading.[80]

III. HARD-BUDGET CLIENTELISM, PARTIAL INSTITUTIONAL REFORM, AND EXPORT BOOM, 1979–1988

Thailand's impressive growth-cum-diversification of the 1970s masked important weaknesses, especially low savings, capital-intensive manufacturing, and heavy reliance on oil imports. With falling agricultural exports and oil price hikes at the end of the decade, the country was forced to borrow $542 million from the World Bank, thus becoming the world's fifth largest recipient of Bank funds.[81] Adding to pressures of external indebtedness were rural discontent and growing protectionism in foreign markets. But the threats facing Thailand were offset by favorable regional conditions: security problems had abated, and currency realignments resulted in lower prices for Thai exports and rising investment inflows. These conditions prompted limited political consolidation and institutional strengthening. Under a "quasi-democracy" led by General Prem Tinsulanonda from 1980 to 1988, Thailand adopted aspects of "societal corporatism" in macroeconomic policy and general export promotion,[82] while party-based clientelism continued to dominate the line ministries.

The result was impressive economic growth and diversification with little upgrading. In the last half of the 1980s, Thai exports increased threefold,

[79] Ibid. (154).
[80] Jansen (1997b,Ch. 4).
[81] Muscat (1994, 155).
[82] Laothamatas (1991).

with manufactured exports rising fivefold. This growth was broad-based, including textiles (which became the largest export sector by the end of the decade), jewelry, toys, furniture, plastic products, processed foods, tourism, and, by the later 1980s, higher-technology products such as electronics and auto parts. Thailand also continued its "second wave" of agricultural diversification into new products, such as oilseeds, horticulture, dairy, and advanced aquaculture.[83] This growth was, however, based largely on institutional mechanisms that promoted export flexibility, not productivity and linkages.

A. Stabilization, Export Promotion, and Tourism

Thailand succeeded in three policy areas that laid the basis for its impressive recovery and subsequent boom. In *macroeconomic stabilization,* the government cut public sector deficits, devalued the exchange rate in 1984, raised interest rates, and maintained oil prices at reasonable levels.[84] Even with a lower exchange rate, however, export growth was hindered by a lack of market information, weak product quality standards, and bureaucratic inefficiency and corruption, especially in customs. Processing exports was a "management nightmare."[85] To *promote exports,* the National Economic and Social Development Board worked with businesses to improve services in areas such as quality standards, packaging, and trade fair participation. Also, liberalized BOI incentives freed foreign firms proposing to export from local ownership requirements.[86] In addition to this general export push, the government succeeded in a large-scale effort to increase foreign exchange through *tourism promotion.* Tourist revenues jumped from around $1 billion in 1985 to over $3 billion (and roughly 15% of goods and services revenues) in 1988.[87]

Enhanced institutional capacities to address specific policy difficulties were key to these accomplishments. Success in macroeconomic stabilization reflected the fit between the technical expertise, cohesion, and political leverage of the Prem-backed technocrats and the fact that most of these issues posed few informational challenges and could be implemented by a relatively small number of actors. There were significant distributional challenges, especially from military leaders and import-substituting business interests who opposed devaluation because it would reduce the ability to

---

[83] Christensen (1993b, 6; 1993a, 17).
[84] Doner and Laothamatas (1994).
[85] Muscat (1994, 196).
[86] Ibid.
[87] Ibid. (197).

purchase new weapons systems and raise the cost of needed imports. But this opposition was weakened by distrust between business and the military leaders and by support for devaluation from commercial banks with extensive export activities. Equally important was the credibility of the government's commitment to stabilization and its ability, through consultation with peak associations, to provide compensatory measures, such as temporary import surcharges and price controls.

Improving services to exporters in areas such as quality, marketing, and logistics posed greater informational problems and demanded the cooperation of numerous actors. Enhanced public–private consultation and monitoring, centered on a Joint Public and Private Sector Consultative Committee (JPPCC), were key to success in this area. The JPPCC, established in 1981, was composed of top state economic officials and representatives of the major business associations.[88] Through the JPPCC, the government identified administrative obstacles to exports and designed appropriate remedies.[89]

Success in tourism promotion involved the active participation of multiple actors, including hotels, restaurants, and tour operators. The government's Tourism Authority of Thailand (TAT) created an integrated program of global promotion and domestic investments in accommodations and services targeted at the "Visit Thailand Year" of 1987. The TAT was one of the few agencies with "a clear sectoral strategy," and it made a major effort "to coordinate its limited resources both with other government agencies and the private sector to achieve its goals."[90]

But success in tourism also demonstrates the limits of Thai institutional capacities. Tourism development was relatively "easy" in terms of information and distributional tensions. Tourism had already proved itself successful in the 1970s, and further development benefited existing actors. Yet by the early 1990s, observers were expressing deep concerns about the sustainability of the industry's growth due to the public sector's "appalling" management of Thailand's environment and infrastructure.[91]

B. Trade Liberalization without Upgrading

Although Thai policy makers recognized that trade protection impeded export promotion, success in trade liberalization was uneven at best. Duties and premiums on several agricultural products were removed, the most

---

[88] Laothamatas (1991).
[89] Muscat (1994, 196).
[90] Mingsarn (1992b, III-13); see also Muscat (1994).
[91] Mingsarn (1992b, III-13).

important being rice, but overall tariff liberalization did not succeed, as the average level of effective protection actually rose over the decade.[92] Thai technocrats responded by initiating a more encompassing effort to improve the competitiveness and domestic linkages by eliminating local content requirements and other promotional but protective regulations in industries ranging from autos to textiles to electrical products.[93] This was, in effect, an upgrading effort, led by a newly established, high-level Restructuring Committee (RESCOM) operating under the National Economic and Social Development Board. Background studies were conducted, but the actual programs "foundered in every case"[94]

Finally, to increase rural incomes and exports without raising energy imports, the government extended its second wave of agricultural diversification.[95] BOI incentives were expanded to include larger-scale, more technical products, and tariffs on agribusiness-related equipment were reduced. By the mid-1980s, agro-based processing operations represented 40% of total manufacturing value added, leading Thai policy makers to talk of Thailand as a newly agro-industrializing country, or NAIC, rather than a NIC.[96] But efforts to improve agricultural productivity through improved irrigation, credit provision, and research and development were generally not successful.[97]

Problems in these areas reflected institutional weaknesses. The one area of trade liberalization in which the government was successful – reducing the rice premium – involved low distributional tensions, a small number of implementing actors, and low information requirements. In contrast, other areas of protection posed severe distributional and informational challenges. Because cutting tariffs threatened government revenues, the Finance Ministry *raised* duties in 1985 following partial rate reductions in the first part of the decade. The Ministry of Industry was hamstrung by conflicts between protected upstream interests and downstream producers demanding cheaper inputs. The overall result was a "jungle of rates lacking any rational economic structure."[98] As RESCOM, the institutional mechanism created to address these challenges, lacked links to and knowledge of particular industries, there was little consultation or monitoring. Indeed, the

---

[92] Doner and Laothamatas (1994, 424–426).
[93] Industrial Management Co. (1984; 1985).
[94] Muscat (1994, 199).
[95] Hewison (1986, 6–7).
[96] Christensen (1993a, 164–167).
[97] Ibid. (167).
[98] Muscat (1994, 198).

committee rarely met and was, according to one observer, simply "set up for the [World] Bank."[99]

In the case of agricultural upgrading, distributional challenges proved especially onerous in the face of bureaucratic fragmentation. Attempts to improve the productivity of small and medium Thai farmers were undermined by the NESDB's focus on industrial infrastructure, by agribusiness interests, and, most critically, by the military's desire to defeat insurgents and to counter the political influence of elected politicians. Rural development became welfare projects as the military built reservoirs, distributed water jugs, established buffalo banks, and set up village "self-defense" squads. Such divisible goods fueled fragmentation among competing public agencies.[100]

Uncertain property rights also impeded agricultural upgrading. Rooted in late-nineteenth-century reactions to colonial threats, Thai agriculture operated under a "segmented and inconsistent … framework" governing land.[101] This became especially problematic in the mid-1980s when the looming end to the land frontier and a de facto state policy to encourage expansion of cash crop expansion pushed farmers into illegally clearing and settling in public forest reserve lands. By 1988, squatters totaled 8 million, roughly 15% of the country's total population, and formed 22% of its villages.[102] The result was environmental destruction and "great insecurity and confusion" in the matter of land titles for the residents of nearly half of Thailand's total land area.[103]

The government's inability to establish clear property rights reflected its impotence in the face of informational, coordination, and distributional challenges. In 1985, at least 14 government agencies or para-statals were providing different types of land use documents. With little administrative, record-keeping, or surveying skills to implement comprehensive land surveys, the government could simply not keep land registration up-to-date with population growth and cultivation expansion. Nor could these diverse agencies provide any uniform way of resolving disputes among the many parties to land use conflicts. Finally, with a large land frontier but no regional nobility, there was no politically powerful group interested in promoting the enclosure of community lands or the establishment of comprehensive rural property rights.[104]

[99] Doner and Laothamatas (1994, 441).
[100] Christensen (1993a, 164–167).
[101] Christensen (1993b, 10).
[102] Christensen and Akin (1993, 8); Muscat (1994, 193).
[103] Christensen and Akin (1993, 7).
[104] Ibid. (5).

Nor did the closing of the land frontier encourage investments in farming productivity. Under pressure to improve forest cover and from urban industrial interests hungry for inputs, the government encouraged an expansion of commercial livestock, of commercial tree planting, and of related user-industries, such as pulp and paper factories. This strategy opened opportunities for land seizures by influential politicians linked to the MOA. It prompted fights between individual farmers, between small-scale farmers and commercial interests, and between agricultural interests and the state itself. Finally, because large livestock and lumber-related interests needed only access to land at a nominal rate, not necessarily land owner-ship, the strategy promoted diversification but did not generate much demand for the secure property rights of the sort that would justify productivity-related investments.

C. Industrial Infrastructure

A central policy focus of this period was the promotion of industrial inputs and infrastructure designed to support exports, to deepen import substitu-tion, and to reduce production and traffic bottlenecks caused by industrial concentration in Bangkok. The effort had two principal components: Bangkok mass transit, and the Eastern Seaboard (ESB) project, which included port development, transportation links, petrochemicals, and fer-tilizer production. These were massive undertakings. All involved the need to obtain and diffuse new kinds of information about technical specifica-tions and uncertain returns; all challenged authorities to coordinate multi-ple actors attracted by divisible benefits; and all involved investments of a scope that required government commitments to be credible.

Given Thailand's lack of forums within which groups could coordinate and share information, the implementation process was rocky and results were uneven. Unger summarized the overall effort as one of "incredible commitments and policy chaos," one in which "officials' announcement of decisions ... served as the starter's gun signaling a political scramble."[105] But under debt crisis-induced pressure to increase exports and with full backing from Prime Minister Prem, National Economic and Social Devel-opment Board technocrats developed a coherent vision, expanded links with key actors, and succeeded in convincing Japanese funders of the pro-jects' potential.[106] The greatest success came in port and petrochemical

---

[105] Unger (1998, 142).
[106] Interview # 125.

development. Relative to other projects, these could be implemented through a top-down process without extensive evaluation or coordination among multiple parties. As Unger notes, these conditions "suited local administrative strengths."[107]

D. Explaining Outcomes

Political Competition and Veto Players: This period is one in which the effective number of veto players declined. General Prem served as prime minister throughout most of the 1980s, surviving two coups, three elections, and five cabinets. Political competition thus persisted, but it was effectively circumscribed in a quasi- or semi-democratic system that balanced business-backed parties against the military in a bicameral system. Although governments came to power through competitive elections, party leaders could not agree about who should lead the government; at the same time, they knew that it was precisely the coalitional instability and related excesses of the 1973–1976 period that helped justify the return to military rule in 1976–1978. Prem, a retired general with significant royal backing and un-beholden to party constituencies, was both acceptable to key military factions and sufficiently independent of the military to satisfy party leaders. Prem capitalized on each side's belief in the need for stability and each side's fear of the other.[108]

In his position as a balancer, Prem managed what Hicken[109] termed a "pork-policy" compromise under which real institutional strengthening in areas such as macroeconomics and general export promotion coexisted with persistent clientelism in most sectors of the economy. On the "pork" side, one party, Chart Thai, dominated the Ministry of Industry by virtue of its interests in textiles, glass, sugar milling, and banking; the Social Action Party, involved more in agribusiness, dominated the Commerce Ministry, which allocated quotas for exports of these products. The two parties shared control of the Agriculture Ministry.[110] The "policy" side of the compromise involved several layers of institutional strengthening. At the top was the Council of Economic Ministers, a committee of the cabinet composed of party-based heads of sectoral ministries, technocrats, and mid-career officials from macroeconomic agencies. This group, especially its technocratic component, constituted a distinctly centralized authority with

---

[107] Unger (1998, 140).
[108] Hicken (2004).
[109] Ibid.
[110] Wingfield (2002, 260).

explicit backing from the prime minister.[111] Decisions were made by consensus; technocrats usually prevailed because they had better information
and a more coherent intellectual perspective than the parties.

The technocrats went to great lengths to persuade and, when necessary, to
compromise with party-based cabinet ministers. As Muscat notes, this apex
group "took the dual functions of brokering and defining policy and of
monitoring and encouraging the implementation activities of the relevant line
organizations."[112] Officials were aided in these efforts by a more organized
private sector. By the late 1980s, the number of associations had risen to 233
from under 50 in the late 1960s, in part due to business's concern with
looming economic threats in the late 1970s.[113] Equally important was
encouragement by state officials who viewed organized business as a key
source of information and legitimacy for addressing the country's economic
ills.[114] It was the technocrats who helped to incorporate organized business
into effective public–private consultation that eventually became the JPPCC.
Systemic Pressures: The reduction in veto players reflected serious threats
facing Thailand. The capital account was of special concern. Foreign
investment was falling drastically in response to a deteriorating situation on
the Cambodian border, while higher offshore rates were attracting an
outflow of short-term capital. Thailand's external indebtedness had jumped
sharply to exceed even that of the Philippines – a particular problem, since
many of the loans for defense and state enterprises had commercial terms.
All of this undermined Thailand's ability to secure foreign commercial loans
in 1979–1980.

These problems were especially serious in light of the economy's long-
term weaknesses. The capital-intensive nature of Thai manufacturing
increased foreign exchange needs as the country became the fifth largest
petroleum importer in the developing world. And problems in the agricultural sector raised serious doubts about the country's ability to continue its
tradition of financing growing imports through agricultural exports.[115] As
Muscat noted, "no previous Thai government had been under the kind of
severe and sustained economic pressure that now brought the technocrats to
the conclusion that a thoroughgoing shift to an export orientation could no
longer be delayed."[116]

[111] Doner and Laothamatas (1994, 436–38).
[112] Muscat (1994, 177).
[113] Christensen et al. (1993, 11); Doner (1991).
[114] Laothamatas (1991).
[115] Siamwalla (1996).
[116] Muscat (1994, 195; italics added).

Finally, coalitional dynamics intensified concerns about economic stagnation and resource access. Fear that agricultural stagnation would fuel rural discontent was reflected in Prime Minister Prem's statement that "the weakness that threatens the whole future of the nation is rural poverty."[117] Although not as mobilized as in the 1970s, popular sectors, especially in the rural areas, were politically salient as potential allies for the military and because increasing numbers of elected representatives were businessmen from outside Bangkok.[118]

On the other hand, external threats had declined. China and Vietnam were preoccupied with each other and with internal consolidation. And by the mid-1980s, the regional context provided new resources. Realignments of the world's major currencies, combined with a Thai devaluation in 1984, cut the costs of Thai goods almost in half. In addition, rising labor costs in Japan and the East Asian NICs encouraged a jump in FDI to Thailand from an annual average of $150 million between 1970 and 1985 to $1.4 billion a year for the 1986–1994 period.[119] With abundant resources generated in part by institutional strengthening, Thailand had little need to undertake more difficult institutional changes required for upgrading.

IV. BOOM YEARS AND BUFFET CABINETS, 1988–1997

With GDP growth of 9.5%, 13.3%, and 12.2% in 1987, 1988, and 1989, fiscal deficits were replaced by boom-induced surpluses.[120] This boom, along with a reduction in external threats, encouraged a political opening and an expansion of veto players. Prem was replaced by Chartichai Choonavan, the first elected civilian prime minister since 1976, whose party-based government became known as the "buffet cabinet" for its ministers' practice of feeding at the trough of government contracts. The pervasive corruption of the regime and, as discussed later, concern with the challenges of impending trade liberalization, prompted a brief return to military-backed reform under two governments led by Anand Panyarachun in 1991–1992. Anand was followed by unstable coalition governments, all of which experienced frequent cabinet reshuffles and fell due to scandals. The damage to Thailand's institutional capacities resulting from intensified

---

[117] Hewison (1986, 6).
[118] Pasuk and Baker (1995, 344).
[119] Dixon (1999, 157).
[120] Thitinan (2001, 197).

political competition was reflected in areas ranging from financial liberalization to supplier development.

A. Financial and Trade Liberalization

Pressures for financial sector liberalization had built up by the end of the decade. Macroeconomic officials were concerned that the country's persistent savings–investment gap left it unable to finance the trade deficit running through the economic boom.[121] Financial opening became a way to bridge the gap by mobilizing foreign and local funds. There was also hope that financial liberalization would increase competitive pressure on Thai firms and help Thailand to become a regional financial hub.[122] The result was a series of measures, including interest rate deregulation, liberalization of foreign exchange controls, and financial institutional deregulation.

The Bangkok International Banking Facility (BIBF) was a critical part of these efforts. Established in 1993, the BIBF opened up the capital market and stimulated massive foreign investment into the Thai economy. This inflow of foreign funds loosened trust-based links between lenders and borrowers that had been so successful in mobilizing and investing Thai savings.[123] It also posed regulatory challenges for which Thailand was unprepared, due in part to the volume of debt but more importantly to the fact that many of the loans were short-term and unhedged against currency fluctuations. These funds went to capital-intensive sectors with long-term returns and into nonproductive activities, especially real estate and property sectors, where politically connected firms were the most active. The result was a combination of speculative booms in the real estate and stock markets, declining Thai competitiveness due to rising inflation and currency values, and rising current account deficits due to a fall in export growth from 15% to 0% by 1996.[124]

These problems highlighted the need for more effective monitoring and supervision. The Anand governments responded by creating a Stock Exchange Commission, improving fiscal policy, liberalizing tariffs, and reforming bureaucratic procedures such as bidding on public works. The greatest successes involved the VAT, which did not require new technical information or the participation of large numbers of actors.[125] But Anand's

---

[121] Ibid. (202).
[122] Hicken (2004, 19).
[123] Siamwalla (2000, 13).
[124] Siamwalla (1997b, 1).
[125] Siamwalla (2000); Hicken (2004).

short tenure in office limited his ability to improve financial supervision. Margin financing, chain-listing, and insider trading became common on the SET.[126] A World Bank report concluded that this financial system, lacking supervision, favored private gains at public expense.[127]

Regulating the expanding financial system posed challenges that overwhelmed Thailand's politicized and weak institutions. Supervision required understanding new kinds of transactions and keeping tabs on many new actors ranging from political parties to business interests in telecommunications, real estate, and services who could tap new financial sources.[128] These players benefited from a hyper laissez-faire environment and took advantage of the country's decentralized policy-making process to prevent more rigorous financial sector regulation.[129] Traditional regulatory institutions lacked the competence, cohesion, and leverage to address these challenges. Boom-inspired salaries in the private sectors discouraged qualified personnel from work in the traditionally strong macroeconomic agencies, especially the BOT and Finance Ministry. These in turn suffered from leadership instability and politicization that undermined credibility.[130] Multiple politician-ministers and their inexperienced but compliant subordinates replaced experienced career officials.

The Anand government was much more successful in trade-related areas, such as reducing tariffs, ending bans on imports and new factories, and proposing the creation of an ASEAN Free Trade Area (AFTA). As was the case with the VAT, such measures involved little new technical information. They presented distributional challenges, but without electoral, partisan, or coalitional constraints and through consultation with peak associations, Anand overcame opposition, which was, at any rate, weakened by differences within affected industries.

B. Agricultural Planning and Productivity

In the late 1980s and early 1990s, government officials and agribusiness executives became increasingly concerned with declining commodity prices. In response, they proposed a consultative policy-making forum for the whole agricultural sector known as the National Agricultural Council (NAC) to help plan agricultural production, especially with regard to the

---

[126] Wingfield (2002, 268).
[127] Dollar and Hallward-Driemeir (1999, 2).
[128] Handley (1997, 98).
[129] Hicken (2004, 20).
[130] Satyanath (2006,.Ch. 4).

location of staple food crop cultivation. This ambitious and comprehensive initiative never succeeded, despite being reintroduced in several administrations. One obstacle was distributional: Farmers, as well as academics, argued that the NAC would become a mechanism through which agribusiness and the state would control farmers. Another problem involved the challenge of coordinating multiple interests. The vast number of agricultural producers and their diversity in size, wealth, and political power made true collective action problematic. Politicians preferred to respond to rural issues on an ad hoc basis than to make policy for agriculture as a whole.[131]

C. Research and Development

To promote R&D, Thai governments of the 1990s exempted tariffs on new equipment, increased public R&D expenditures via a new Thai Research Fund, and established a series of new industry "institutes" and technology institutions to function as "centers of excellence" to foster technology and innovations useful for Thai firms.[132] But the agencies designing soft loan programs had little sense of how to spread the risks of technology initiatives; nor were they successful in designing incentives for large firms, whose main constraint was qualified R&D personnel, not financing. Implementing agencies lacked both experience in evaluating technology proposals and a willingness to shoulder all the risk, especially for small firms lacking collateral. Technology promotion policies were also poorly integrated with export promotion schemes, whose "general and unconditional" nature did little to encourage firms to invest in technological improvements.[133] More broadly, these efforts also reflected a lack of support from the Finance Ministry as well as from the BOI, whose major interests were revenue accumulation and the promotion of physical assets. Bureaucratic rivalries among state technology institutions remained intense.[134] The linkages with the private sector in various industries, themselves highly fragmented, were anything but dense.

Finally, the industry institutes required understanding sector-specific needs, reconciling multiple interests, and assuring firms that such institutes would draw consistent state backing. But their only real support came from Anand's government, and given his relatively short tenure and the difficulty

---

[131] Christensen (1993b, 29).
[132] Lauridsen (2002a, 110).
[133] Ibid. (109).
[134] Doner and Ritchie (2003, 212).

of reforming the sectoral ministries, it is not surprising that he gained cabinet approval for only one of the numerous proposed institutes.

D. Supplier Development

Thailand's export boom weakened linkages to local producers, as reflected in the rising import levels for industries ranging from electronics to garments to autos.[135] Underlying this problem was the fact that local suppliers lacked technical personnel, up-to-date equipment, and modern financial and managerial systems.[136] One set of responses involved the trade and tax reforms implemented under the Anand governments that could provide access to lower-cost raw materials, while the VAT increased incentives for final assemblers to shift from in-house parts production to purchasing from outside suppliers. But these measures were insufficient without complementary measures to support the development of technology, skills, and management expertise.[137] Developing such measures meant shifting away from Thailand's "passive and liberal approach to investment promotion" that focused largely on targeted financial inflows, foreign exchange earnings, and jobs.[138] BOI officials attempted just such a shift. Along with the Industry Ministry, the BOI launched a series of initiatives to upgrade local suppliers, including the BOI Unit for Industrial Linkage Development in 1991, a National Supplier Development Programme in 1994, a multiagency effort to develop small- and medium-enterprise suppliers, and a 1995 Master Plan for the Development of Supporting Industries in conjunction with the Japan International Cooperation Agency.[139]

These efforts were largely ineffective. Thai firms experienced high mortality rates not just in the aftermath of the 1997 crisis but also in the subsequent shift to full-fledged export competition in its aftermath. The BOI lacked the sector-specific expertise, as well as the political support, needed to formulate, much less monitor, the supplier development efforts.[140] As a result, the Board subcontracted many of its matchmaking functions to consultants. The efforts were also stymied by conflicting policies: Even as it talked of promoting local suppliers, the Board allowed foreign-owned firms to sell all of their output in the domestic market (up

---

[135] Mingsarn (1992a, 2–20); OECD (1999, 7).
[136] Lauridsen (2005, 34–35).
[137] Ibid. (49).
[138] Lauridsen (2004, 573).
[139] Ibid. (576).
[140] For example, McKendrick, Doner, and Haggard (2000); Felker (2001).

from 20% in 1991) and intensified a campaign to attract investments from Japanese SMEs. Public policy on supplier development thus lacked credibility.[141] The BOI's weaknesses themselves reflected the Thai state's failure to integrate export-promotion, traditionally under the Commerce Ministry, with industrial development, under the Industry Ministry. To address this problem, technocrats proposed the merging of these functions into a Ministry of International Trade and Industry. But turf battles between the two key ministries, backed by political–business interests, blocked the effort.[142]

Weak private sector motivations and organization further undermined these efforts. Many firms were more concerned with solving day-to-day production issues than with upgrading. In some cases, influxes of cheap labor from neighboring countries reduced pressures to improve technological competences. And public policies designed to promote industrial upgrading were of little interest to the large, especially foreign firms that exerted significant influence in the peak Federation of Thai Industries. Collectively, sector-specific trade associations, especially supplier groups, focused more on trade issues than on productivity.[143] The FTI had difficulty reconciling the interests of diverse enterprises.[144] These conditions did not encourage open, systematic public–private linkages, consultation, or monitoring. The BOI's relations with organized producers were especially weak. Overall, Thailand's technology- and productivity-related institutions "functioned in isolation from each other and worked in isolation from the local industry."[145]

E. Explaining Outcomes

Political Competition and Veto Players: The boom fueled the expansion of veto players in the form of factionalized political parties. The political influence of business, especially rural interests, grew by virtue of their roles as middlemen in the expanding cash crop economy; their investments in service and trading activities encouraged by local demand; the expansion of public contracts; and profits from semilegal or illegal businesses.[146] Further, provincial constituencies accounted for 90% of parliamentary seats, and

---

[141] Lauridsen (2004).
[142] Interview # 69.
[143] Lauridsen (2005, 39).
[144] Ibid. (11).
[145] Lauridsen (2002a, 111).
[146] Pasuk and Baker (1997, 30–31).

many politicians preferred to avoid highly competitive Bangkok elections by running in rural constituencies.[147] The growing influence of rural business intensified the parties' tradition of personalism and programmatic weakness. The country lacked a tradition of local mobilization and organization, and Thailand's multimember constituency system encouraged parties to factionalize. Factional power derived from the amount of money spent on election campaigns and "MP-buying." Under a quota system, the more Members of Parliament (MPs), the more cabinet seats allocated to the faction. Faction leaders in turn used their cabinet positions to accumulate funds for frequent elections.[148] And given the industrial boom, funds were available. The Chartichai government raised the 1989 fiscal budget by 10% and lifted the limit on public sector foreign borrowing from $1 billion (under Prem) to $2.5 billion in 1990.[149]

Parties used ministerial positions to enhance factional power in a continuing process of logrolls.[150] The cabinet consequently became the focus of factional conflict. Governing coalitions were unstable, with scandals bringing down all four of the coalition governments between 1988 and 1997. From 1979 to 2001, Thailand underwent 25 governing coalitions and 43 cabinet reshuffles.[151] Andrew MacIntyre counts no less than six veto players in the government of Chavalit Yongchaiyudh in power at the time of the financial crisis.[152] The result was the weakening of Thai institutions: The Council of Economic Ministers was left to wither. The National Economic and Social Development Board was told to stop interfering with government work, its governing board sacked, and its pivotal role in overseeing public projects ended, with oversight shifted to ministries headed by cabinet cronies. Three parties shared the leadership and resources of the lucrative Interior Ministry.[153] Politicians even took over technology agencies, including the Institute of Scientific and Technological Research.[154] With business-financed politicians in direct control of key agencies, there was less need for collective business organization and consultation between public and private actors. As a result, the JPPCC was dissolved. In sum, "The further evolution of institutionalized relationships between government and business organizations

---

[147] Ockey (1992); McVey (2000).
[148] Ockey (2004a, 26); Wingfield (2002, 265).
[149] Thitinan (2001, 86, 197).
[150] For example, Pasuk and Baker (2000, 138).
[151] Chambers (2006, 13).
[152] MacIntyre (2003, 60).
[153] Ibid.
[154] Thitinan (2001, 83–85).

was put on hold as the individual businessmen/politicians and government leadership became one and the same."[155]

This combination of coalitional instability and institutional weakening led to rampant pork. Chartichai's "buffet cabinet" was no worse than its post-Anand successors. The House Speaker during the (1995–1996) government of Banharn Silpa-archa declared that corruption took half of all budget project funds.[156] Legislation was narrowly focused, with little if any developmental vision.[157] As reflected in policy initiatives, many were aware of the economy's underlying weaknesses, which culminated in the 1997 crisis, but "(p)olitics got in the way" of addressing these problems.[158]

Systemic Pressures: Politics could "get in the way" in part due to reduced systemic pressures. In addition to impressive GDP growth and budget surpluses, Thailand benefited from a decidedly less threatening external context in this period. Vietnam's decision to withdraw from Cambodia and to focus on its own development transformed Indo-China from a threat to a market of almost 100 million potential consumers. This permissive context encouraged political opening, contributing to Prem's removal from office in 1988.[159] It also drowned out research highlighting a broad range of weaknesses in the Thai supplier base.[160]

How then to account for the reduction in veto players represented by the 1991 military coup? The precipitating factors included broad opposition to rampant corruption and the military's reaction against Chartichai's sharp cuts in defense budgets. These were compounded by an economic downturn and growing uncertainty triggered by rising oil prices following the 1990–1991 Gulf Conflict.[161] Systemic pressures were even more directly influential in the military's decision to name a respected businessman, Anand, as prime minister, and in Anand's reform efforts.[162] Anand was actively concerned with the need to prepare Thai firms for the potential loss of FDI to NAFTA participants and the liberalization required by looming WTO membership: his proposed AFTA aimed to raise competitive pressures on Thai firms; the VAT would encourage backward linkages; a better bureaucracy would support private sector adjustment; and the institutes

---

[155] Muscat (1994, 184).
[156] Pasuk and Baker (1998, 260).
[157] Siamwalla (1997b, 8).
[158] Hicken (2004, 8).
[159] Handley (1997, 96).
[160] Lauridsen (2005).
[161] Thitinan (2001, 202).
[162] This interpretation is based on Siamwalla 1992b; and interviews # 60, 63, 69.

would encourage overall productivity growth. As described earlier, however, Anand's achievements were limited, reflecting shallow support for reform under what remained, despite a short downturn, a boom economy. The costs of these limits became evident in the 1997 crisis.

V. CRISIS AND COALITION GOVERNMENT, 1997–2000

The World Bank had touted Thailand as a dynamic success,[163] Thai officials anticipated 8% growth into the new millennium.[164] But by mid-1997, the stock market had lost two-thirds of its value, the baht was pushed by speculators into a major devaluation, two-thirds of all finance companies were suspended, and unemployment was close to 6%. Over three million people were pushed back into poverty, as households poor before the crisis became even poorer. Thailand was in a state of insolvency, and it accepted the IMF's second-largest-ever support package – $17 billion – in exchange for a commitment to significant reform.[165]

This shock highlighted problems in financial supervision and weaknesses in the economy's overall competitiveness. Thailand's response was initially impressive, including reform initiatives in finance, agriculture, education, and especially industrial restructuring. But success was uneven at best, encompassing some achievements in financial restructuring but little else. Reform efforts were stymied by persistent coalitional rivalries and corresponding bureaucratic fragmentation. And as aid funds flowed in and the crisis ebbed, so did enthusiasm for reform.[166]

A. Financial Sector Reform

The crisis demonstrated the toxicity of "financial market liberalization without adequate preparation."[167] Following the November 1997 resignation of Prime Minister Chavalit, a new coalition led by the Democrat Party's Chuan Leekpai focused largely on financial sector reform, particularly regulatory oversight, managing insolvent financial institutions and the large number of nonperforming loans (NPLs), and restoring bank liquidity and lending. The government made significant progress in supervision and regulation through new loan classifications, provisioning requirements, and improvements in the

---

[163] World Bank (1993).
[164] Pasuk and Baker (1998, 5).
[165] Ibid. (124).
[166] Hicken (2004).
[167] Siamwalla (2000, 33).

central bank's organizational structure.[168] It also succeeded at restructuring nonbank financial institutions: through two new public agencies, it closed 56 of 58 failed finance companies by the end of 1997.[169]

But the government made only limited progress in commercial bank restructuring, as evidenced by the fact that NPLs constituted almost half of total loans in early 2000, roughly 30% by the end of that year.[170] These disappointing results reflected two kinds of difficulties. One was the need to coordinate many actors. Because small- and medium-sized firms accounted for over two-thirds of corporate debt, restructuring involved small, costly, diffuse transactions with firms scattered throughout the country. In the face of such transaction costs, banks opted simply to cut their lending.[171] There were also distributional issues: Whereas the finance companies were essentially defunct at the time of the crisis, the still-viable commercial banks faced significant short-term losses from restructuring, as did firms in the real sector that had already suffered from the government's initial adherence to IMF austerity measures. Faced with these challenges, the government lacked credible instruments with which to force debt restructuring, despite its new bankruptcy and foreclosure rules.[172] This was due in part to policy differences within the Chuan government as to the value of focusing on financial restructuring while neglecting the needs of the real sector.[173] It also reflected opposition to restructuring from senate supporters of firms in the real sector.[174]

B. Agricultural Sector Reform

Agriculture took on added political significance following the crisis, in part because of the countryside's electoral dominance and the popular perception that the crisis originated in the machinations of Bangkok financiers. Agriculture was also central to the economy. Though its contribution to GDP had declined over the years, it functioned as a "shock absorber" for the almost three million unemployed, and it continued to account for roughly 50% of the country's employment.[175] Yet agricultural yields and

---

[168] Asian Development Bank (2000, 30).
[169] World Bank (2005b, 39
[170] Asian Development Bank (2000, 30).
[171] Asian Development Bank (2001, 30).
[172] Wingfield (2002, 279).
[173] Pasuk and Baker (2000, 142).
[174] Wingfield (2002, 277).
[175] Abonyi (2005, 17).

quality had been slow to improve. Thai policy makers knew that the state needed "to move up the value-added ladder" by making farming "more knowledge-based."[176]

An Agricultural Sector Program Loan (ASPL) from the ADB provided the opportunity to address these challenges. The ASPL was a comprehensive program of agricultural reform that included measures ranging from water resource management to credit to land tenure to R&D.[177] But the actual implementation of these reforms proved elusive. Most of the reforms required not only coordinating multiple existing actors (some 20 government agencies, NGOs, banks and farmers' groups) but also creating new committees, advisory councils, agencies, and task forces. Getting "ownership" of the reform projects by such a large number of participants required "close coordination," while implementation required monitoring mechanisms.[178] Many of the reforms also required an understanding of local conditions, anticipating interactions among policy areas, and a clear understanding of their actual meaning.[179] Such complex coordination and information requirements demanded extensive consultation and monitoring. Finally, reform required overcoming distributional tensions. Special interests who traditionally used their ties to the Ministry of Commerce to benefit from government involvement in input markets opposed removing the government from fertilizer provision. And many of the reforms imposed short-term costs in return for uncertain gains. Farmers viewed "cost recovery in irrigation" as imposing new fees during a dire economic crisis and protested the program.[180]

Thai institutions were unprepared for these challenges. Monies for agricultural investments "often disappeared into the black void of old-fashioned rural politics," unobstructed by a "hidebound" MOA.[181] Bureaucratic fragmentation was extensive. Ministers were largely autonomous within their portfolio area, and, illustrating the pork-generating potential of mutual veto players, practiced "mutual non-interference."[182] Within ministries, key resources lay within departments, which in turn became targets of party or faction competition. Control of the MOA's Royal Irrigation and Agricultural Extension Departments – precisely the departments most relevant to productivity – was especially lucrative by virtue of those departments'

---

[176] Crispin and Goad (2000, 59).
[177] Abonyi (2005, 23).
[178] Ibid. (25; 36).
[179] Ibid. (30).
[180] Ibid. (30).
[181] Crispin and Goad (2000, 58).
[182] Painter (2005, 5).

responsibility for contracts.[183] Neither the ADB nor the government knew much about the preferences of Thai farmers, and both were surprised by their resistance.[184] Nor did the program designers have the mechanisms for the kinds of stakeholder consultations necessary to build constituencies for various reforms.[185] All of these problems affected the government's credibility, culminating in the decision by the new Thaksin government, elected in January 2001, to cancel the whole program with half of the total loan undisbursed.

C. Training

In the wake of the crisis, the Chuan government initiated a series of skills development initiatives.[186] A Skills Development Fund, adopted in 1997, had little bearing on higher-order manufacturing skills. The government subsequently proposed a broad Education Reform Act and a more targeted Skills Development Act (SDA) modeled on Singaporean and Malaysian strategies of levying payroll taxes to finance skills training. The draft SDA legislation, however, remained pending at the end of the Chuan administration. The failure to implement such badly needed measures reflected a combination of private sector shortsightedness and public sector weakness. Following a long-standing emphasis on wage repression and labor discipline, Thai firms were reluctant to pay for technical training. Government consultation with business in the design of the plan was minimal, and the responsible agency had little capacity to monitor or enforce compliance. Firms managed to evade "the disciplining aspects of the levy scheme."[187]

D. Industrial Competitiveness[188]

The most ambitious effort to improve manufacturing performance was the Industrial Restructuring Program (IRP). Launched in late 1997, the IRP aimed to upgrade 13 sectors through 8 sets of measures ranging from equipment

---

[183] Bidhya 2001).

[184] Abonyi (2005, 39).

[185] Ibid. (21).

[186] For a review, see Ritchie (2005).

[187] Lauridsen (2002a, 117).

[188] The following description is based on author interviews (# 48, 85, 92), as well as information provided by Greg Felker (personal communication). See also Lauridsen (2005); Paopongsakorn and Somkiat (2001, 131–132); and National Industrial Development Committee (1998).

modernization to labor skills to product design. The entire effort was led by a respected technocrat, Sompop Amatayakul, who saw the crisis as an opportunity to address long-standing competitiveness problems and who was given a free hand by the Chuan government's first Minister of Industry.

Consultation was extensive. A multiagency team drew up a first draft of an Industrial Master Plan. The Ministry of Industry (MOI) then invited individuals and groups from both industry and government to a series of sector consultations lasting from December 1997 to March 1998 at which "vision exercises" and break-out sessions maximized information sharing and opinion exchanges. The result was a strategic plan subsequently submitted to all public and private sector participants, who were invited to make project proposals. Sectoral participants were then asked to assess and prioritize the 400 proposals received, producing an "action plan" from which a planning subcommittee selected 24 projects in September.

In the year 2000, a senior MOI official labeled the IRP "a failure in terms of boosting efficiency and cooperation."[189] The capacity for the kinds of coordination and information gathering required to monitor and evaluate was undermined by weak business association involvement in the IRP process.[190] This problem was reinforced by ministries' reluctance to give up resources to the quasi-autonomous institutes designated to help implement the project.[191] Bureaucratic turf defense and leadership instability remained problems. Sompop worked under three different Industry Ministers, each of whom had a somewhat different set of reform preferences. As a result, many of the projects were selected to match the preexisting wish list of various agencies, especially the MOI. This undermined the coherence of the sectoral reform packages, discouraged "ownership" by other agencies, created confusion in financial disbursements, and further undermined evaluation and monitoring. In fact, pressure from officials monitoring the IRP led to more favorable project evaluations than actual project outcomes warranted.[192]

E. Explaining Outcomes

Political Competition and Veto Players: Chuan's government was a minority-led coalition of eight factionalized parties that presided over a fractious legislature and reshuffled the cabinet four times.[193] Ministerial

---

[189] *Bangkok Post/Mid-Year Economic Review* (July 2000).
[190] Lauridsen (2005, 69).
[191] See Nexus (2000, 80–81).
[192] Interview # 122.
[193] Chambers (2003, 254).

turnover was frequent, as parties and factions strove to gain control of those agencies with the greatest potential for resource control.[194] The level of political competition for ministerial resources was especially intense due to the looming implementation of a new Constitution. With the number of cabinet seats slated to fall from 49 to 35, the parties engaged in a "feeding frenzy" for control of ministries.[195]

Systemic Pressures: The reform efforts of this period were prompted not only by the 1997 crisis-induced stock market crash but also by the poverty increases and import price rises due to devaluation. The crisis also intensified rural protests that had been building during the 1990s. In 1998, farmers demanded agrarian debt relief. Rice farmers, cattle raisers, cassava farmers, and sugar growers held large protests in Bangkok. Unemployed workers and displaced villagers occupied empty land. For most of 1998, the economy seeming "locked in a downward spiral."[196]

But pressures for reform lessened in 1999. The Chuan government abandoned the more draconian fiscal and monetary components of the IMF program.[197] The balance of payments improved, foreign exchange reserves grew, and the baht stabilized as a result of devaluation-induced export growth.[198] Foreign funds also provided some breathing room. The IMF program permitted a slight fiscal expansion, the Japanese government's "Miyazawa Fund" contributed around $1.5 billion for development, and the ADB contributed $300 million for agriculture.[199] These conditions fueled the persistence of veto players and associated inefficiencies. Pressure to improve productivity through greater consultation and monitoring declined, as reflected in the IRP's demise. The availability of funds both reinforced the role of government agencies as patronage sources for parties and factions and encouraged fragmentation within public and private institutions.

VI. THAKSIN AND THE ERSATZ DEVELOPMENTAL STATE, 2001–2006

In early 2001, a new government under Thaksin Shinawatra promised to address competitiveness problems in the real economy with an eye to solving the dual challenges of rural poverty and inequality on the one hand

---

[194] Bidhya (2001, 291).
[195] Overholt (1999, 1023); cf also Chambers (2003, 256).
[196] Abonyi (2005, 14).
[197] Hicken (2006a).
[198] Pasuk and Baker (2004b, 127).
[199] Abonyi (2005, 6).

and industrial competitiveness on the other. He couched this whole effort in explicitly nationalist terms.[200] Thaksin's focus on upgrading was striking for its departure from past governments' lukewarm attention to real sector problems. He and his advisors spoke of the "nutcracker effect" created by the combination of cost pressure from low-cost rivals and technology pressure from more advanced rivals.[201] They were explicit in their desire to move the country "further up the value chain" and away from excessive dependence on exports that used cheap labor to produce goods relying on foreign technology and investment.[202] Further, they took a systematic and market-based approach, classifying industries and focusing on adding value in sectors – autos, tourism, food, and textiles – where Thailand had a positive track record.[203] This strategy involved linkages through support for basic and support industries, related infrastructure, and technical personnel, and it involved combining "local know-how, knowledge and dedication ... with world-class modern design, cutting-edge technology, appropriate cost-effective engineering, modern packaging, advanced marketing and Internet capabilities."[204] Finally, Thaksin proposed to pursue a cluster strategy in emulation of Italy's "industrial districts."[205]

This emphasis on productivity growth was coupled with extensive bureaucratic reform.[206] Thaksin declared his intention to end turnover, fragmentation, and overall inefficiency through a "massive overhaul" of the Thai state.[207] Committed to infusing the bureaucracy with performance norms of the "New Public Management," Thaksin aimed to improve cross-agency coordination, to break down the gap between macroeconomic and sectoral agencies, to create an elite group of high-performing senior executives, and to encourage private sector input.[208] In a sort of "top-down decentralization," Thaksin appointed "CEO Governors" to be responsible for implementing government policies by coordinating local representative and bureaucratic agencies.[209]

---

[200] Glassman (2004b)
[201] Pansak (2004, 30).
[202] Pasuk and Baker (2004b, 104); interview # 127.
[203] Pasuk and Baker (2004b, 114).
[204] Thaksin (cited in Ibid., 113).
[205] Interviews # 61, 113.
[206] Ockey (2004b, 143).
[207] Connors (2004, 2).
[208] Unless otherwise noted, this discussion of bureaucratic reform draws on author interviews # 58, 59, 63, 69, 78, 82, 90, 91, 111, 115. Written sources include Ockey (2004b); Painter (2005); and the *Nation* (2005 various issues).
[209] Painter (2005, 12).

Thaksin also pledged to help Thai producers upgrade. He designated the Industry Ministry's Office of Industrial Economics as a key source for information regarding productivity and linkages.[210] He ordered the National Economic and Social Development Board to oversee the development of sector-specific "master plans" and the BOI to focus on technology development and cluster promotion rather than employment.[211] He elevated the status of the industry-specific institutes established in the 1990s. He established a National Committee on Competitiveness and a National IT Committee. And he proposed integrating industrial and export promotion by merging the Ministries of Commerce and Industry.

This ambitious set of objectives was backed up by impressive electoral strength. Thaksin's Thai Rak Thai (TRT) party co-opted or allied with other parties to create a 70% parliamentary majority that allowed it to do what no other elected government had done – survive a full four-year term. After winning roughly two-thirds of the popular vote in the next (2005) elections, Thaksin could govern without a coalition partner or any fear of a parliamentary censure vote. This success reflected Thaksin's attention to the concerns of both local business and the rural poor. He flirted with economic nationalism in defending large, local firms threatened by globalization in the form of the 1997 crisis and the subsequent increase in foreign economic influence. For these firms, the TRT provided investment privileges, debt relief, new credit, delayed privatization, access to state contracts, and a seat at the policy-making table.[212]

But Thaksin's regime was also the first in decades to devote explicit attention to popular sectors. For labor, there were commitments to workers' rights;[213] for small businesses, there were promises of targeted credit; and for farmers, there were promises of an inexpensive health care plan, a debt moratorium, and soft loans to encourage sub-district-level products. Though Thaksin abandoned his pledges to labor and small business,[214] he fulfilled his commitment to farmers.[215]

Given this combination of political strength and capacity to deliver rural welfare policies, one might have expected decisive, effective action toward the stated goals of institutional reform and industrial competitiveness. Yet,

---

[210] Dhanani and Scholtes (2002).
[211] Ritchie (2005).
[212] Pasuk (2004); Pasuk and Baker (2002); Hicken (2006); Glassman (2004b).
[213] Brown and Hewison (2005, 363).
[214] Ibid.; Glassman (2004b, 53).
[215] Pasuk and Baker (2002, 9).

in September 2006, when Thaksin was overthrown in a military coup, his record was disappointing.

A. Rural Development and Entrepreneurship

The results of Thaksin's rural development initiatives were mixed. The highly popular health care program provided important insurance and the loan program stimulated growth in consumer spending.[216] But design flaws and inadequate financing in health care led to demoralized staff and serious doubts as to the program's financial sustainability.[217] The loan program seems to have stimulated a rise of household indebtedness, not of rural enterprises.[218] Finally, the CEO Governors appear mainly to have weakened rather than promoted the consultative capacities of local representative organizations and marginalized the bureaucracy rather than strengthening its capacity for credible policy development.[219]

B. Education Reform

Thaksin pledged to "overhaul the educational structure."[220] He pushed through a National Education Act (1999), consolidated operations of the Ministry of Education, and established a series of new agencies ranging from an Office of Education to supervisory commissions for basic, vocational, and higher education.[221] The results were disappointing: McCargo identified education as the area in which "the blunting of reform ... [was] most clearly evident."[222]

These efforts did yield important benefits. They raised public awareness of the need for curriculum reform in basic education. They also extended compulsory education to nine years and expanded state support. But after several years of reform efforts, the system remained "a shambles," in the

---

[216] Tejapira (2006); Pasuk and Baker (2004b, 109–109).

[217] Worawan (2005).

[218] During a July 2007 visit to one village in Srisaket province, the author observed wreath production based on household flower cultivation and weaving by multifamily groups of women. According to villagers, this activity was initiated by villagers themselves but facilitated by rural loans and a newly energized agricultural extension service under Thaksin. But overall, there is little if any evaluation data on the rural debt relief and credit programs (Personal communication, Chris Baker, March 20, 2008).

[219] Weerayut (2006).

[220] Thaksin (2001, 11).

[221] Bangkok Post Mid-year Economic Review (2004).

[222] McCargo (2002a, 123).

view of the Office's director.[223] Persistent fragmentation in the Education Ministry undermined the capacity to consult with teachers on training needs and to coordinate and monitor in-service training providers.[224] Distributional obstacles were significant, as reform efforts ran up against a "maze of organizations and stakeholders," including both bureaucratic and partisan political interests.[225] These conditions fed patronage pressures to favor suppliers of educational goods while not imposing tough requirements on rural teachers. The result was an emphasis on lumpy, rent-generating investments in buildings and offices.[226]

In the area of vocational education and technical training, Thaksin confronted a dysfunctional system in which responsibilities and budgets were divided among seven different agencies.[227] This arrangement blocked systematic consultations with either business or labor. Recognizing that the quality of technical training influenced the vitality of local firms, Thaksin ordered the merger of the Department of Vocational Education into the Ministry of Education and created the Thailand Vocational Qualification Institute in 2003. But the mismatch between the economy's demand for technical personnel and the supply of vocational graduates persisted in the face of ministerial turnover and bureaucratic competition.[228] An extensive BOI effort to improve the quality of Thai electronics personnel ended up gathering dust after leadership changes.[229] The Vocational Qualification Institute was undermined by Ministry of Labor control of certification standards.[230] There were also conflicts between public and private training providers, as the latter mobilized to block standards legislation which they feared would be too expensive to meet. Without central coordination, there was little pressure to establish benchmarks through consultation with local businesses, and without them there is little capacity for monitoring performance.

The 1997 crisis also solidified a consensus that Thai universities performed poorly in training personnel and exposing companies to new ideas. Despite some strengths in agro-industry, medicine, and life sciences, engineering training was weak, overall research output was low, research topics were inconsistent with industrial needs, and faculty ties with business were

---

[223] *The Nation* (November 6, 2006).
[224] Fry (2002, 27).
[225] Ibid. (13).
[226] Ibid. (8); interview # 103.
[227] Ritchie (2005).
[228] Chularat (2006).
[229] Brimble and Doner (2007).
[230] Interview # 107.

individual and temporary.[231] These weaknesses were in part the result of low demand: in most sectors, local firms' technological and absorptive capacities were insufficient to stimulate much demand for university inputs. More technologically advanced foreign firms were either uninterested or skeptical as to the institutions' capacities to provide needed services. But the incentives and structures of the universities themselves were also a key part of the problem.[232] The most prestigious Thai universities are public; their funding has been largely unrelated to research productivity, teaching effectiveness, or market-related services.[233]

To address these supply-side problems, the Thaksin government committed itself to a series of reforms, the most important of which was a continuation of efforts to make public universities "autonomous" by 2002. Autonomy involved not privatization but rather a comprehensive reduction in levels of state funding combined with more self-governance designed to push faculty toward greater research, teaching, and service productivity in conjunction with closer links to business. As of 2007, only one university became autonomous and with some partial exceptions, university–industry linkages remain very weak.

The autonomy effort required crafting a new set of rules and management systems and coordinating and overcoming the opposition of numerous actors – both the universities themselves and particular interests within them – for whom reform meant considerable short-term uncertainty, if not costs. But reformers never succeeded in clarifying what autonomy would mean or devising adequate incentives and management structures to convince universities to make the transition. These problems reflected broader institutional failings, one of which was a lack of credibility. Owing to instability in the Education Ministry and Commission for Higher Education, some backtracking on the part of Thaksin, and stagnant funding for education in the first two years of his government, key actors could not be sure about the government's actual plans or the level of its commitment to change.[234] Finally, due to preexisting budgetary arrangements, reformers found monitoring universities' financial conduct virtually impossible.[235]

More positive outcomes in two sectors – shrimp and disk drives – merit brief analysis.[236] Following the collapse of its shrimp industry in the late

---

[231] Schiller (2006a).
[232] Brimble and Doner (2007).
[233] Schiller (2006b, 6).
[234] Schiller (2006b, 7).
[235] Ibid. (7).
[236] Information on shrimp and disk drives is drawn from Brimble and Doner (2007).

1980s, Thailand became the world's largest producer of cultivated (farmed) shrimp in the mid-1990s. Support from Japanese trading companies and Taiwanese technicians, as well as public support for financing, property rights adjustments, and infrastructure, help explain this success. But a strong set of university–industry linkages was especially important. Thailand's major bio-medical institution, Mahidol University, worked with the giant Charoen Phopkand (CP) group to address disease problems that had killed Taiwan's shrimp industry. This effort was undertaken in conjunction with an industry consortium, the Shrimp Culture Research and Development Company, established in 1996, and then institutionalized in a quasi-governmental Center of Excellence for Shrimp Molecular Biology and Biotechnology.

In disk drives, Seagate Technology, Thailand's largest employer, initiated significant training and research efforts, which the firm itself judges to have been successful.[237] Initiatives include the organization of a loose consor-tium of universities to offer customized courses focused on the management and automation of Seagate's high-technology production facilities, the development of a "cooperative training program" with two universities in northeast Thailand, and the establishment of R&D centers, again with northeastern universities. In addition, Seagate has worked with other pro-ducers and the Bangkok-based Asian Institute of Technology to create a Certificate of Competence in Storage Technology, as well as a "road map" for industry-wide efforts to improve training and to address industry-wide needs for process improvement.

Two aspects of these cases merit note. First, each occurred at the initiative of a large, dominant firm that viewed broad-based training and research as beneficial to itself. Second, public sector participation in each has been inconsistent at best. Government officials have not drawn lessons from either set of experience to inform initiatives in related industries. In electronics, at least, Thailand has lost investment to other countries as a result.[238]

C. Explaining Outcomes

Political Competition and Veto Players: Thaksin came to power under a new (1997) Constitution designed to reduce coalitional instability, as well as to improve checks and balances and to expand citizens' rights.[239] The Constitution's shift from multimember to single-member constituencies was

[237] Brimble and Doner (2007).
[238] Dong (2006).
[239] McCargo (2002c).

intended to encourage a smaller number of larger, more policy-based parties. In addition, the Constitution created a number of special "anti-graft" agencies designed to increase accountability and transparency in the political system.[240] The electoral reforms were partially successful in their goal of party consolidation, either weakening or actually wiping out smaller and medium-sized parties.[241]

But the actual reduction in veto players was more limited than it appeared. The TRT's success reflected Thaksin's success in appealing to both rural and business interests and using patronage to translate that base into a coalition of multiple parties and factions. Both of these factors actually discouraged institutional strengthening. Consider first Thaksin's rural programs: health care, debt relief, and development loans involved little if any systematic attention to productivity through, say, education and training. Further, these initiatives were financed not by productivity-related growth but by expanding state credit: government banks' share of total credit rose from 27% at the end of 2000 to 35% in 2003.[242] As such, this strategy was more akin to financially unsustainable Latin American populism than to South Korean or Taiwan-style rural reforms.[243]

Nor was upgrading a major a concern for Thaksin's business supporters, the most influential of whom came from the service sectors, especially telecoms, the media, tourism, construction, and real estate. These were sectors that either benefited from natural protection or, as in the case of Thaksin's own telecommunication empire, grew on the basis of government contracts.[244] Where local manufacturing interests were influential, they were largely subservient to foreign firms capable of providing their own technology and not highly interested in promoting local suppliers. Thaksin seemed to have ceded manufacturing to Thai-based multinationals.[245] Further discouraging institutional innovation was business's increasingly direct influence over policy. Well-placed business interests within the TRT coalition occupied ministerial positions and exerted direct influence over the policy process to an even greater extent than in the past, prompting Hewison to label Thaksin's regime "Thailand's first government of tycoons."[246] And challenges to this influence were undermined by

---

[240] Ockey (2004a, 167–170).
[241] Hicken (2006b).
[242] Pasuk and Baker (2004b, 111).
[243] Laothamatas (2007).
[244] Sakkarin (2000).
[245] Glassman (2004b).
[246] Hewison (2003, 10); see also Pasuk and Baker (2002, 4).

Thaksin's antidemocratic turn. Thaksin exerted increasing control over the media, harassed the opposition and, most critically, manipulated watchdog agencies established by the 1997 Constitution to increase accountability.[247]

He further subverted his otherwise impressive institutional initiatives by centralizing bureaucracy-based patronage to co-opt other parties and satisfy TRT factions. Thaksin continued the practice of "benefit-sharing" and "remained captive to a quota system of ministerial allocations."[248] Thaksin increased the number of ministries and departments from 14 and 126, respectively, to 20 and 143, thus expanding patronage opportunities while undermining any sense of stability in organizational operation.[249] He also orchestrated eight cabinet reshuffles involving 55 individual new appointments from 2001 to 2004.[250] In education, for example, five different Education Ministers from 2001 through 2004 undermined the credibility of education reform.[251] Science and technology institutions suffered from conflicting pressures and internal disputes.[252]

Existing pockets of efficiency in budgeting, planning, and performance monitoring also suffered. Thaksin inserted a political ally as head of the central bank and, in expanding the use of discretionary funds for rural projects, marginalized the Bureau of the Budget. The National Economic and Social Development Board also saw its responsibilities and capacities reduced as the TRT's platform and reelection strategy, not the National Economic and Social Development Board, became the country's planning framework.[253] The practice of outsourcing National Economic and Social Development Board evaluation activities to private consultants further effectively weakened the Board's internal monitoring capacity and undermined its role as the lead agency in the country's Five Year Plans, as monitor of the sectoral master plans, and as overseer of large infrastructural projects.[254] The government's overall data collection system suffered, especially on productivity-related issues. A 2002 study rated the system "poor for a country at Thailand's stage of development" because data on issues such as value added and labor costs were dispersed over numerous nonstatistical agencies.[255]

[247] Mutebi (2006).
[248] McCargo (2002d, 247)
[249] Painter (2005, 14); Ockey (2004b, 148).
[250] *The Nation* (March 12, 2005, cited in Painter 2005, 5); Glassman (2004b, 55).
[251] Fry (2002, 13).
[252] Interviews # 92, 115; Bell (2003, 29–30); Ritchie (2005, 33).
[253] Painter (2005, 11).
[254] Ibid.; interviews # 67, 122; Pasuk and Baker (2004, 114).
[255] Dhanani and Scholtes (2002, 71).

Finally, even Thaksin's productivity-oriented institutional reforms suffered. The consolidation of the Industry and Commerce Ministries and the strengthening of the institutes were either blocked or delayed by bureaucratic and factional interests. Improvements in the Office of Industrial Economics (OIE) and BOI and the creation of the Senior Executive Service were undermined by what emerged as the central function of the bureaucratic reforms: to reduce traditional bureaucratic power centers and to centralize power in the executive's hands.[256] The role of organized business was also minimal, despite Thaksin's pledge to expand private sector policy input. Efforts by FTI leaders to promote upgrading were met largely by government indifference and undermined by differences within the FTI itself.[257] Public–private consultation thus became more erratic and fragmented, with meetings of the JPPCs being rare. Reflecting all of these problems, the quality of most "master plans" was weak, as was follow-up by relevant agencies, which lacked monitoring and evaluation capacity.

Systemic Pressures: The disappointing results of ambitious upgrading policies reflected growing, albeit centralized clientelism facilitated in turn by economic growth. On taking office in early 2001, Thaksin confronted a weak but improving economy. Although income (per capita GDP) had not reached pre-crisis levels in 2001 and would not do so until 2004, the baht had stabilized; with the devaluation promoting exports, growth rates averaged over 4% from 2000 to 2005; and gross domestic investment began to rebound.[258] Under these conditions, the budget shifted from deficit (57.6% of GDP in 2001) to a slight surplus in 2003. These improved conditions facilitated the use of state credit as demand stimulus. This included direct lending by state financial institutions for rural welfare and small and medium enterprises; state-supported credit to lower expenses for goods such as computers, taxis, health care and insurance; and state encouragement of commercial credit, including for consumer durables and housing.[259] In addition to stimulating overall economic expansion, the strategy helped to finance the pro-poor, pro-rural welfare programs so critical to the TRT's electoral success.

In Chapter 2, I argued that explanations based on capital investment, education, culture, policy type, or political regime could not account for Thailand's impressive but limited economic growth. In the present chapter,

---

[256] Painter (2005, 9; 16).
[257] Interviews # 54, 59, 63, 66, 69, 117, 121, 126, 127, 128.
[258] Hicken (2006, 6).
[259] Pasuk and Baker (2004b, 104–107).

I have presented evidence that the framework elaborated in Chapter 3 accords well with Thailand's mixed performance. By distinguishing among development tasks and available institutional capacities, the framework helps to explain *both* impressive strengths in areas key to diversification (e.g., macroeconomic stabilization, risk socialization, export promotion, and infrastructure), *and* weaknesses in areas necessary for upgrading (e.g., trade liberalization, research and development, technical training, supplier development, and agricultural extension).

The framework also helps to account for institutional capacities themselves. The overall intermediate levels of vulnerability facing Thai political elites during most of the postwar period provide an explanation for the bifurcated state structure characterizing much of Thailand's postwar history, a structure consistent with Peter Evans' "intermediate state" category.[260] Tracing shifts in vulnerability pressures has also shed light on variations in capacities. As seen in agricultural initiatives during the 1973–1976 democratic period, corporatist arrangements during the 1980s debt crisis, and the post-crisis IRP, short-term increases in pressures have led to corresponding institutional strengthening. The fact that such strengthening has been limited reflects the limited nature of threats facing Thai political elites, not obstacles posed by veto players. Indeed, such political institutions were themselves malleable in the face of shifting vulnerability pressures.

How robust are these conclusions? Does sectoral performance reflect capacities and background pressures? Do national institutional capacities also help to explain sectoral performance? Or do sector-specific characteristics trump national conditions? Chapters 5–7 address these questions in sugar, textiles, and autos. The core of each chapter is an analysis of Thai performance through the lens of sector-specific developmental challenges, available capacities, and political pressures. For further evidence, I conclude each chapter with brief comparative analyses of stronger and weaker national performers. If the arguments presented in Chapter 3 are correct, cross-national performance differences reflect variation in institutional capacities and, in turn, pressures on national elites to promote such capacities.

---

[260] Evans (1995).

5

Sugar

Co-authored with Ansil Ramsay

The sugar industry exemplifies both the impressive diversification and the modest upgrading characteristic of the broader Thai economy. In the mid-nineteenth century, the Thai sugar industry was robust and promising: taxes on the industry constituted the largest source of cash revenue for the government, and British colonial officials predicted that Thailand would become a major sugar exporter.[1] However, competition from colonial plantations elsewhere in Southeast Asia largely destroyed the Thai sugar industry, and by 1950 it was unable to produce enough sugar to meet domestic demand. The classic postwar study of the Thai economy concluded "there was no prospect of exporting sugar from Thailand."[2]

Yet the industry revived and thrived. Sugar production rose from 35,000 tons in 1953–1954 to an annual average of 5.3 million tons from 1995 to 2000. Sugar exports rose as well, from under 2,000 tons in 1961 to over 5 million in 2002 making Thailand one of the world's three largest exporters along with Australia and Brazil. Between 1993 and 1999, sugar brought in more net foreign exchange for the Thai economy than any agricultural product except rice.[3] With 46 sugar mills and over 100,000 farms, the industry employs over 1 million people.[4]

Comparative advantage only partially explains this turnaround. While Thailand has soil and weather conditions well suited to growing sugarcane, so do the Philippines and Brazil. Yet in the Philippines we see an industry that

---

[1] Prasertkul (1989, 112); Ingram (1955, 10).

[2] Ingram (1955, 127).

[3] "Thailand" (1997, p. 4).

[4] On numbers employed, see Office of the Cane and Sugar Board (2006); and *Far Eastern Economic Review* (November 23, 2000, p. 76).

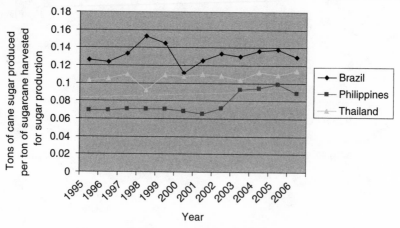

FIGURE 5.1 Measure of Sugarcane Processing Efficiency

devolved from "one of the world's most efficient and technologically advanced producers of cane sugar" in the 1930s to a technologically challenged laggard in the postwar period.[5] Brazil, on the other hand, has become one of the most efficient sugar producers in the world (Figure 5.1), has far surpassed both the Filipino and Thai industries in export earnings (Table 5.1),[6] and in 2005 became the world's largest producer of sugarcane and sugar.[7]

Thai institutions, both public and private, as well as the country's underlying political arrangements, were key to sugar millers and growers taking advantage of good weather, good soil, and an extensive land frontier. Nevertheless, these same institutional and political factors contributed to weaknesses that became evident in the 1990s. Relative to Brazil, Thai sugar producers suffer from low farm productivity and inefficiency as expressed in yields of sugarcane per acre and sugar from sugarcane (Figure 5.1). Thailand's weaknesses in cane varieties, farm mechanization, and irrigation have made the industry especially vulnerable to global market shifts and, even more centrally, to limits on land suitable for mechanized harvesting and variable rainfall. As a result, while Thai sugar export growth has been impressive, it has also been highly volatile, with drought-induced declines especially sharp in 2005 (Figure 5.2).

In the past Thailand could offset these weaknesses with low labor and land costs, low environmental and social standards, and hopes for good

[5] Billig (1993, 122).
[6] Martines-Filho et al. (2006, 92).
[7] The figures include both centrifugal raw sugar exports and refined sugar exports.

TABLE 5.1 *Brazil, Philippines, and Thailand Sugar Exports (1000 US $)*

	Brazil	Philippines	Thailand
1961	65,511	141,240	127
1965	56,730	136,723	4823
1970	126,631*	187,876	4547
1975	1,099,946	583,453**	281,642
1980	1,290,579	624,051	145,555
1985	390,557	168,775	231,310
1990	493,183	111,737	692.713
1995	1,925,510	67,177	1,157,890
2000	1,202,874	52,021	650,898
2005	3,924,506	77,679	714,536

Source: http://faostat.org/site/535/DeskTopDefault.aspx?PageID = 535. (accessed April 9, 2008).
Notes: *Raw sugar exports only. Refined sugar exports not available
**Refined sugar data are from 1976. 1975 data unavailable.

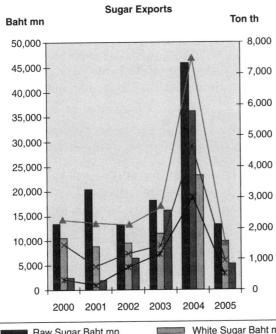

FIGURE 5.2 Thai Sugar Exports, 2000–2005

weather,[8] but with rising domestic factor costs relative to new competitors such as Vietnam and lower cane and sugar yields relative to leaders Brazil and Australia, weak productivity became a significant liability. Improving productivity required solving informational, coordination, and distributional challenges for which the Thais were institutionally ill-prepared. By 2002, Thai government officials were warning that the industry faced "collapse unless the government either increases domestic prices or bails it out."[9] Despite such warnings, in 2006 observers viewed the government as "losing control" over the industry.[10]

To explain Thailand's mixed performance, Section I reviews key drivers of the global sugar industry. Sections II–V analyze Thailand's responses to industry pressures from the early 1950s through 2006, focusing on tasks ranging from capital mobilization for new investments, to mill modernization and capacity limits, to upstream–downstream revenue conflicts, to productivity challenges. We account for varying performance on these tasks as a function of the country's institutional capacities, pressures on its political leaders, and political institutions. These have been brought to bear on an industry that is highly organized and, owing to its foreign exchange earnings and employment levels, politically influential.[11] As a result, Thai sugar has been the focus of ongoing controversy and extensive consultation. The results have been decidedly mixed, as producers succeeded more at expanding than upgrading production, especially by growers. Section VI assesses these findings in comparison with the Philippines and Brazilian sugar industries.

I. THE SUGAR VALUE CHAIN

The sugar value chain consists primarily of the cultivation of sugarcane or sugar beets, their processing into (raw or refined) sugar, and distribution of the finished product to domestic or export markets. Since Thai sugar comes from sugarcane our focus in this chapter is on cane production and sugar milling. Entry barriers in each of these stages are low relative to the other industries in our study. Small farms are viable production units, as evidenced by the operation of over 100,000, mostly family-owned cane farms in Thailand.[12] The technological problems are modest with regard to

---

[8] Prayong (1988, 16); Zimmerman and Zeddies (n.d.).
[9] *The Nation* (September 14, 2002).
[10] *Thai News Service* (March 9, 2006); *Bangkok Post.* (January 15, 2006).
[11] Somboon (1998, 83).
[12] "Thailand" (1997, 2); House (2000, 2).

farming and farm-related equipment; challenges lie more in design innovation than invention. Capital requirements are significantly higher for mills and refineries, but the technology of sugar milling is relatively mature and accessible to developing country producers.

Despite these relatively low capital and technology barriers, several factors complicate the production and export of sugar, even for countries endowed with appropriate soil and weather conditions. One is the high level of interdependence between growers and millers who are forced into close contact due to sugarcane's rapid spoilage rate.[13] Sugarcane growing and sugar milling are "separate economic activities that can achieve economic efficiency only through cooperative behavior."[14] Sugar industry development thus creates collective action problems more than is the case in most sectors.

The need for grower–miller coordination emerges within a particularly demanding set of global market conditions, the most important of which are severe price fluctuations.[15] This market volatility leads farmers and millers to seek government assistance and protection. Because sugar millers are usually much better organized for political action than consumers, protectionism tends to be high and sticky. Subsidies have led to oversupplies of sugar being dumped into world markets, lowering global sugar prices. The result has been a long slide in the average world price of sugar. Only a few countries, including Australia, Brazil, and Thailand no longer provide significant levels of protection. Australia and Brazil export sugar without subsidies, while Thai subsidies are relatively small.

Agricultural trade liberalization is beginning to undermine this pattern of subsidies–gluts–price declines–more subsidies. WTO rules restrict the kinds of subsidies allowed, and tariff reductions on sugar are already underway in the AFTA.[16] As subsidies are cut, sugar exporters will be pressed to upgrade. This trend represents both an opportunity and a threat for Thailand. Because the Thais have relatively low costs and some of the lower subsidies among sugar exporters, they would benefit if countries with much higher subsidies were forced to reduce them.[17] On the other hand, Thailand is a "low-to-medium" cost producer in which domestic prices have been set at levels high enough to support competitive exports. As such,

[13] Paitoon, Auansakul, and Supawan (2001, 33).
[14] Larson and Borrell (2001, 14).
[15] Information in this paragraph is drawn from Borrell and Duncan (1992, 171–172; 182–183); Larson and Borrell (2001, 3); Billig (2003, 100); and Zimmerman and Zeddies (n.d., 3–4).
[16] Paopongsakorn and Viroj (2000, 8); Viroj (2000, 2).
[17] Zimmerman and Zeddies (n.d., 8).

the Thais have been increasingly squeezed by two groups of low-cost producers: those, such as Vietnam, who benefit from lower labor and land costs
than Thailand, and those such as Australia and Brazil who have already
upgraded sugar production and largely eliminated subsidies.[18]

II. (RE-) IGNITING GROWTH: MID-1950S–MID-1960S

The end of World War II brought a flood of imported sugar to Thailand
that made new domestic investments a risky proposition.[19] The fact that
investment did indeed occur reflected Thailand's success in meeting such
policy tasks as ensuring property rights and socializing the risks of investment (Table 5.2), all in a context of relatively limited information
requirements, coordination challenges, and distributional difficulties.

A. Policy Tasks and Responses

Property Rights: Sugar cultivation was encouraged by a relatively informal
set of rules that combined customary practices with usufruct land tenure.
Despite their weaknesses (discussed later), Thailand's rights regime provided sufficient security for basic investments in land by sugarcane growers,
who more than doubled acreage planted under sugar from the early 1950s
to the mid-1960s.[20] Sugar milling was dominated by four Sino-Thai firms
that had begun in rice trading, engineering, and sugar-planting.[21] In principle, these family-owned firms were vulnerable to predation by political
elites. However, consistent with the clientelist arrangements described in
Chapter 4, these millers enjoyed de facto property rights based on protection by powerful patrons – a veritable "who's who" of the Thai political–
military power elite.[22]

Another feature of Thailand's property rights regime – ownership of
sugar once it is milled – merits note: in Thailand, farm and mill are separate,
as is ownership, with cane belonging to the grower and milled sugar
belonging to the mill owner. In this system, the benefits of investments in

---

[18] Paopongsakorn and Viroj (2000, 8). Data on "low-cost," low-to-medium cost," and
"medium-to-high cost" producers (such as the Philippines) from Billig (2003, 64). On Brazil
and Australia as the only countries with "a rather liberal, unprotected sugar market," see
Zimmerman and Zeddies (n.d. 8).

[19] Ingram (1955, 126).

[20] Pasuk and Baker (1995, 54, 135).

[21] Ibid., (135).

[22] Warin (1986).

TABLE 5.2 *Sugar Industry Challenges*

Policy Tasks	1950–mid-1960s	Mid-1960s–late 1980s	1990s–2005
Property rights	Land tenure for farmers and mills for millers	NA*	Incentives for innovations in harvest equipment and new strains of sugarcane
Risk socialization	Building mills and switching from rice to sugar	Investing in modern integrated sugar mills	NA
Reducing overcapacity	NA	Sugar production exceeds demands of domestic market	Sugar mills' capacity exceeds cane supply
Up–downstream: revenue sharing	NA	Serious conflicts between growers and millers over cane prices	Matching supplies of cane with mill capacity
Quality standards	NA	Attempted but failed	CCS – adopted but little impact on cane quality
Research and development	NA	Some technocrats recognize the problem, but it is not seen as a major problem by many in industry	Improved cane varieties; harvest equipment – little success
Infrastructure	roads	NA	Irrigation; transport facilities

Note: *NA = not a major challenge in this period.

mill equipment accrue directly to the mill owners, with the result that Thai mills are some of the most modern in the world.

Risk Socialization: In 1961, the otherwise liberal Sarit regime adopted two measures that provided millers with assurance that a market for sugar would exist: Sarit prohibited the import of refined sugar in what was "perhaps the single most important change in state policy in this area;"[23] and the state-managed Thai Sugar Corporation handled exports and established a guaranteed domestic retail price higher than world market

---

[23] Hewison (1986, 11).

prices.[24] The country's commercial banks were equally important for their role in overcoming market imperfections in the mobilization and allocation of capital. Led by the Bangkok Bank, the commercial banks coordinated the shift of resources from rice to sugar, extended credit to farmers each season, financed crop expansion into new regions, became the largest sources of credit to sugar exporters, supported the establishment of agribusiness groups, organized sugar export cartels, and helped individual firms during periodic downturns.[25] Risks were also reduced by a highly concentrated and organized market. Sarit's 1961 import ban on refined sugar resulted in four entrants into sugar milling. Consistent with Thailand's competitive clientelism, each of these entered via a political patron.[26] These producers subsequently organized an export cartel in the face of domestic market saturation.

The four firms competed intensely with each other for shares of the lucrative domestic market and, eventually, in exports. With greater market opportunities following the democratic opening of 1973, production capacity and market shares became even more dispersed.[27] Sugar millers had to face hard budget constraints as well as competition. Thai governments were "generally reluctant to expend budgetary resources in support of the sugar industry, particularly in the period after 1958."[28] This was demonstrated in the 1964–1965 sugarcane growing season when sugar producers were faced with a disastrous shortfall in revenues because of declines in the wholesale sugar prices. Ten sugar mills closed down because of losses. The Finance Ministry technocrats refused industry requests for loans in 1965 for fear of having to bailout other troubled industries and/or not being repaid if and when another sugar slump occurred.[29] This episode reflected the ways in which the technocrats' fiscal caution, a preference shared by the commercial banks, could trump the clientelist side of Thailand's bifurcated state. Technocrats were willing to help, however, if funds could be generated without endangering state revenues. Funds from domestic profits were subsequently used to reopen mills closed during the crisis in the mid-1960s.[30] Commercial banks also provided help for individual firms, but, in return expected firms to turn a profit by improving performance and paying off loans.

[24] See Silcock (1967, 184); Ramsay (1987).
[25] For example, Christensen (1993); Silcock (1967, 184); Hewison (1989).
[26] Warin (1986, 5); Krirrkiat and Yoshihara (1983, 4).
[27] Pasuk and Baker (1995, 135); Hewison (1989).
[28] Siamwalla and Setboonsarng (1987, 92–93).
[29] Phitsanes (1977, 72).
[30] Ibid. (71–73).

B. Explaining Outcomes

Policy Difficulties and Institutional Capacities: Successful (re)creation of the industry reflected the fit between local institutional capacities and the challenges of property rights creation and risk socialization. Information requirements for the industry were relatively limited. The specifics of farmers' property rights had been worked out earlier, while those for millers remained largely informal. Technical demands of growing sugarcane and managing the mills of the 1950s were relatively simple. The imported machinery could be maintained by local mechanics or technicians from Taiwan. Commercial banks that invested in the industry were able to help with information on financial and managerial complexities as the industry grew. It made few informational or technical demands on government ministries.

The number of actors whose participation was required to promote the industry was also small. Farmers were numerous and dispersed, but socializing financial risks and promoting competition in milling involved less than half a dozen firms, a similar number of commercial banks, a small number of high-ranking political-military officials, and the Ministry of Finance. Finally, achieving early success did not require resolving significant distributional differences. The key challenge was allocating rents among millers and high-ranking Thai officials. Farmers had not yet become organized into effective associations and, at any rate, were largely benefiting from the expansion of cane cultivation.[31] Nor did Thai political leaders have to pay much attention to downstream interests. In the 1950s and 1960s, demand from bakeries and soft drink producers meant high sugar prices could be passed along to domestic consumers.

Politics and Veto Players: Despite authoritarian rule in this period, a factionalized military and fragmented line ministries translated into pervasive clientelism. But the competitive nature of Thai clientelism served to reinforce property rights; and a small-veto players corporatist financial facilitated risk socialization, and thus industry financing.

III. SUSTAINING GROWTH: MID-1960S THROUGH 1970S

The industry's growth quickly resulted in domestic market saturation. By the early 1960s, Thai sugar millers were producing 120,000–180,000 tons/year in excess of domestic demand.[32] The government, with varying levels

---

[31] Prayong (1988).
[32] Phitsanes (1977, 56).

of private sector support, attempted a number of solutions involving production limits or capacity reductions combined with an improvement in farm efficiency designed to encourage exports. These proved well beyond the capacities of public or private institutions. Finally, severe market pressure, combined with state incentives, stimulated a private sector response that combined collective export controls with individual investments to improve mill efficiency. The result was export expansion via *mill* upgrading.

A. Policy Task and Responses: Overproduction

Confronted with a saturated domestic market, Thai public officials could have let market forces consolidate productive capacities, leaving only the most efficient mills. But millers benefited from patrons' backing, while commercial banks were willing to help them survive, assuming a reasonable chance of repayment. Exports offered that possibility, but millers could not produce sugar cheaply enough for competitive export. In one of the worst years, 1961–1962, world market prices were only half of millers' production costs.[33] The government might alternatively have opted to subsidize exported sugar, but the Ministry of Finance was unwilling to throw state funds at uncompetitive firms. The industry had to find a way to either limit production or export excess.

Private sector efforts to reduce capacity failed. Millers could not even agree to hold sugar in warehouses and limit sales to amounts that would not drive prices down. They believed "it is better to break an agreement and make 100 million baht than keep an agreement and wind up with only one million baht." Once one miller began selling sugar to take advantage of others' restraint, other mills followed quickly."[34]

A prominent public–private alternative, reflected in the Sugar Act of 1961, was for the mills to sell all of their produce to a jointly owned entity, the Thai Sugar Corporation (TSC). The TSC would use its monopoly profits from domestic sales to subsidize sugar exports and to improve farm productivity without using government funds.[35] A tax on domestic sugar sales was to create a fund devoted to promoting expansion (by subsidizing exports and encouraging cane cultivation) and the improvement of sugarcane quality through R&D. For a few years, roughly 85% of the fund went

[33] Ibid. (51).
[34] Interview # 9.
[35] This review draws on Phitsanes (1977, 52–63).

to export subsidies. When the world price of sugar plummeted in the 1965–1966 season, however, the fund was insufficient to make up the difference between production costs and world market prices, and it was discontinued.

In the Sugar Act of 1968, technocrats at the National Economic and Social Development Board proposed still another efficiency-based approach to exporting surplus sugar, this one focused on lowering costs through mill, not farm, improvement. Many mills had obsolete, imported second-hand machinery and inefficient management; and they suffered from high transaction costs due to small deliveries from large numbers of farmers.[36] To address these problems, the Act stipulated that Thai millers limit their production to the needs of the domestic market while working to improve their mills' efficiency. Once mills became more efficient, Thailand could begin exporting sugar to world markets. The strategy foundered again on the industry's inability, even with the state acting as a third-party enforcer, to control sugar production. Millers continued to produce more than was needed for the domestic market and by 1971 had created a huge surplus of sugar.

The solution to the overproduction crisis – a combination of export coordination and mill modernization – was finally initiated by the private sector, albeit with considerable state support and incentives. Until the mid-1970s, exports were managed by the government-backed TSC. In 1973, after several years of government opposition, two of the mill operators finally obtained approval to establish a second exporting firm, the Thai Sugar Trading Corporation (TSTC). The millers complemented the cartels' export coordination by becoming more efficient: Beginning in the late 1960s, they began building new, technologically sophisticated mills. The new mills not only produced higher quality sugar; they also cut transaction costs by purchasing larger volumes of cane directly from producers.[37]

At first glance, this would seem to have been a "pure" market solution. Exports grew rapidly in the early 1970s, reaching 1 million tons in 1976.[38] But state-supported risk socialization was also necessary. In May 1971 the government officially adopted an export promotion policy, publicly subsidizing sugar exports by fixing the domestic retail price of sugar, usually at a higher level than the international price.[39] In addition, the government allocated domestic sugar quotas based on mill capacity. This combination

[36] Pakorn and Khubbol (1976, 266).
[37] Sayon (1987, 123); and Suthat (1987, 88).
[38] Pasuk and Baker (1995, 135).
[39] "Thailand Sugar ..." (2006, 2).

of high domestic prices and production-based quotas helped to finance new mill construction; and it encouraged a race by mill owners to expand production capacity.[40]

B. Explaining Outcomes

Policy Difficulties and Institutional Capacities: In this period, the millers expanded exports through improved export management and upgraded mills, but they failed to limit production or to improve farm productivity. Reducing sugar production exceeded the capacities of Thai institutions. Preventing growers and millers from defecting from agreements by limiting production or sales required accurate information about how much sugarcane was being grown, how much sugar was being produced, who was producing it, and how much was in warehouses, but the millers and growers had strong incentives to hide this sort of information. The less the government knew about mills' production and profits, the lower their taxes. The less sugarcane growers knew about mills' profits, the less the millers had to pay growers for cane. Given these incentives, all knew there would be massive defections; anyone who restrained production received a sucker's payoff.

Preventing free riding would have required strong monitoring capacities, the capacity to facilitate consultation and information sharing, and credible commitments to providing benefits to growers and millers who cooperated, while punishing defectors. Such capacities were absent. The Ministry of Industry could refuse to issue licenses for new mill construction, but mill owners could "close a mill and use the existing license to build a new plant in a different location with greater capacity."[41] In the private sector, sugar associations were fragmented and focused on immediate gains.[42] In contrast, the private-sector-led strategy of mill modernization avoided the complexities of information sharing and monitoring. With information needed to modernize mills the responsibility of millers and their bankers, there was no need to obtain sugar growers' cooperation. Nor did this strategy require any credible state sanctions against capacity expansion by millers. The state's main role was side payments for risk socialization. These were paid for by Thai domestic consumers who lacked the capacity to oppose higher sugar prices.

---

[40] Viroj (2000, 4); and Suthat (1987, 99).
[41] "Thailand" (1997, 2).
[42] Ramsay (1987, 256).

Politics and Veto Players: Politics in this period were important in two key ways. The overthrow of authoritarian rule and the advent of party competition in 1973 ended the military-backed export monopoly and encouraged more export competition among millers. Competitive politics also had more negative consequences: Because it offered sugar interests diverse opportunities for influence through parties with little if any developmental policies, competitive politics translated into multiple veto players and discouraged collective action. Only with the onset of economic crisis, concern with popular frustration, and the quasi-democratic arrangements of the 1980s did greater collective action occur.

IV. UPSTREAM–DOWNSTREAM CHALLENGES: REVENUE SHARING IN THE 1980S

Thailand's entry into world sugar markets resulted in revenue disputes between growers and millers. Sugar growers had gradually become more organized and assertive in their demands for a share of sugar profits. The resulting dispute and its potential for impeding revenue-generating sugar exports was especially troubling, as the country confronted severe fiscal imbalances in the 1980s, and Prime Minister Prem viewed agricultural exports as critical to address both popular pressures from rural areas and the country's debt-induced resource constraints. Sustaining export growth now involved a significant new actor, the growers, in an issue whose distributional consequences were more prominent than was the case for capacity reduction and mill modernization in the 1970s. Despite these obstacles, by the mid-1980s Thai officials and sugar interests reached a revenue-sharing agreement via a new set of institutional arrangements.

A. Policy Task and Responses: Sharing Revenues

Conflicts between growers and millers over the price of sugarcane had begun with the establishment of growers' organizations. These associations emerged first in the mid-1960s and expanded later in the decade, as the efficiency of the new integrated mills depended in part on coordinating the rapid delivery of tons of sugarcane to the mills from large numbers of farmers.[43] The solution was to contract with suppliers, or "quotamen," who could guarantee large deliveries of cane. The coordinating functions of these quotamen were especially important given both the logistical

---

[43] Ramsay (1987), from which the rest of this discussion is drawn, unless otherwise noted.

complexity of sugar delivery and the weakness of the transport infrastructure available to sugar growers. The quotamen, who had a strong incentive
to raise the price of cane and could easily organize smaller cultivators, took
the lead in creating growers' associations.

Stronger organization helped the growers to bargain more effectively
with what was essentially an oligopsony of millers. With better access to
market information, they countered millers' export declarations and claims
of fair prices for sugarcane. The result was escalating confrontation as both
sides sought to win larger shares of the growing profits in the sugar
industry. In the 1975–1976 season the two sides deadlocked and the government was drawn into the bargaining as a mediator for the first time. This
annual mediating role became standard practice, and government officials
found themselves in the middle of intense pressures from both sides. Millers
relied on contacts with high-level officials and military officers to pressure
the state, while growers took advantage of more open politics in the late
1970s and early 1980s to elect members of parliament and to stage mass
demonstrations in Bangkok.

This approach to revenue sharing was clumsy at best, but achieving a
solution involved new difficulties. The industry had more and better organized participants, information requirements were greater, and distributional conflicts were more intense. Participants in negotiations included
representatives from the two major millers' associations, the two major
sugarcane growers' associations, and relevant government officials in the
Ministries of Agriculture, Commerce, and Industry. Considerable distrust
between farmers and millers made the task even more difficult, and the
industry lacked encompassing associations that could speak for each side.[44]

Extensive negotiations among the parties led by Chiryu Issarangkul na
Ayuthaya, a Deputy Minister of Industry selected by Prime Minister Prem,
resulted in a form of revenue sharing that would give growers 70% and
millers 30% of all revenues. Adopted on an experimental basis during the
1982–1983 season, the 70:30 system subsequently became institutionalized
in the Cane and Sugar Act of 1984 and remains the main law governing the
industry.[45] The Act established a Cane and Sugar Board with representatives from the Ministries of Agriculture, Commerce, and Industry, along
with representatives from growers' and millers' associations. At the beginning of each growing season, this Board sets the preliminary price of cane to
be paid to sugarcane farmers based on projections of world market

[44] Interview # 9.
[45] As of 2006.

conditions and domestic supply. Millers receive specific quotas for domestic and export sales. The Board calculates the final price of cane once the season's industry income is known. The Act also created a set of other implementing mechanisms: the Thai Cane and Sugar Trading Corporation, to set a benchmark price for exported sugar; a Central Sugar Distribution Agency to provide farmers with information about millers' profits by monitoring domestic sales; and a Sugar Fund to reduce sugarcane farmers' vulnerability to falling prices.

Establishing this set formula and associated mechanisms increased transparency and trust, and thus helped mitigate conflicts that had turned violent in the past. It raised and stabilized growers' and millers' incomes.[46] In doing so, it encouraged further growth in exports and cultivation: the planted area of sugarcane rose from 3 million to 6 million hectares in the 1985–1997 period.[47] However, the arrangement also sustained and even encouraged intra-industry distributional tensions that would impede the industry's willingness and ability to resolve such issues.[48] First, the quota system weakened the millers' incentive to support measures that might increase farm productivity by giving them an incentive to expand milling capacity rather than to improve yields. Second, the system did not address all of the reasons for growers' mistrust of millers. Recall that domestic prices were set at levels presumed to exceed export prices. Where these levels were reversed, millers were tempted to engage in illegal sales of sugar to the export market, thus reducing domestic supplies. Conversely, when the domestic price was higher, the millers would sell sugar destined for export in the domestic market. In addition, because cane prices were determined by a weighted average of the domestic and export prices, export growth in a context of low export prices reduced cane prices and thus growers' revenue.

B. Explaining Outcomes

Policy Difficulties and Institutional Capacities: The 70:30 agreement was a function of extensive consultations between government officials and industry groups. This consultation conveyed credibility in part through the establishment of monitoring mechanisms, the engagement of technocratic leaders with significant political backing, and the engagement of the

---

[46] Viroj (2000, 5).
[47] Thippawal, Molle, and Chompadist (1999, 1); Pichai (1999, 4).
[48] Viroj (2000, 5).

financial sector. The leader of the effort, Chirayu, was a prototypical technocrat, an economist with a reputation for impeccable integrity. He assembled a team of knowledgeable advisers who gathered information about other countries' experience with revenue sharing in sugar and proposed the 70:30 plan on the basis of that investigation.[49] The group then met extensively with the various actors in the industry to adjust the proposed solution. It sponsored studies providing accurate, credible information about the income and profit consequences for different actors from the 70:30 arrangement. It worked with all parties to design arrangements, particularly the Cane and Sugar Board, which would facilitate continuing consultation, information sharing, and monitoring.

This group also acted to overcome distributional obstacles and to build credibility. It organized side payments, critical to easing financial difficulties facing specific mills and many growers, by leading government pressure on commercial banks to provide some $78 million dollars in low-interest loans. The group designed a provision under which the mills collected membership fees for growers' associations from each grower when cane was delivered to the mill. This made it difficult for individual growers to free ride on associational efforts to bargain for better cane prices.[50] Finally, the group sequenced the plan's implementation by adopting it on a trial basis and then, to ensure its credibility, holding extensive hearings and adopting it into law as the Cane and Sugar Bill in 1984.

Politics and Veto Players: Success in this effort reflected the small number of effective veto players during this period's quasi-democracy.[51] Chirayu's ability to construct a quasi-corporatist arrangement was highly dependent on backing from the prime minister. But even Prem and Chirayu were limited in their ability to reform an industry so political that a grower's association leader heavily involved in the drafting of the 70:30 scheme was assassinated in 1984, reportedly by associational rivals. Connected to the multiple veto players of the Thai party system, the sugar industry remained part of the "pork" side of the "pork-policy" compromise of the period. Its rural base made the industry especially important to pork-based political parties. Even after the adoption of the 70:30 scheme, one of the major parties traditionally leading the Industry Ministry used advocacy of higher cane prices to attack Prem. By 1985, Chirayu, although still a deputy minister, had lost influence over sugar policy to a party-based minister, Ob Vasuratana.

[49] Ramsay (1987); interview # 1.
[50] Interview # 2.
[51] The following two paragraphs are based on Ramsay (1987).

This renewed political influence helped to limit the industry's reforms, as illustrated in Ob's decision to abolish the Central Sugar Distribution Agency, reportedly at the behest of a large miller, over Chirayu's objection. This Agency was the mechanism established by the Cane and Sugar Bill to provide farmers with information about millers' profits by recording domestic and export sales. As such, it was especially important for monitoring millers' responses to domestic–global price shifts. Its abolition reduced information available to growers and fueled conflicts within the sugar value chain.

By institutionalizing negotiations, the revenue-sharing scheme was key to continued growth and successful diversification. Yet the technocrats' expertise about the industry was relatively superficial and their ties to it were fragile, certainly weaker than the clientelist ties of the parties. These weaknesses impeded their undertaking the even more difficult reforms required to improve the sugar industry's productivity in a pattern consistent with the broader failure of Prem's Restructuring Committee. They established a set of institutions devoted almost totally to prices and revenues, and even these would prove vulnerable to external price shocks. These new arrangements did "not create an environment that would support research, development, or productivity improvement – elements crucial to the preservation of Thailand's competitiveness in the future."[52]

V. THE CHALLENGES OF UPGRADING: 1990S TO THE PRESENT

By the 1990s, Thailand began to face growing competition not only from high-yield producers, such as Brazil and Australia, but also from producers such as China, India, and Vietnam with lower land and labor costs and the ability to import modern mill technology.[53] The new competitive pressure highlighted the need to increase productivity. As noted, the Thai sugar industry suffered from low yields of sugarcane *and* low sugar content of cane relative to its competitors. Ironically, these problems were in part a function of technological improvements in Thai mills which, by the early 1990s, were among the most advanced in the world. The wave of mill expansion and modernization continued in the late 1980s and 1990s due to rising world sugar prices and the particular incentives of Thailand's quota

---

[52] Viroj (2000, 3).

[53] On the fear of low-cost competition, see (Pichai 1999, 8). By 2001, Vietnam had displaced Thailand as the largest sugar exporter to Indonesia and Singapore (*Bangkok Post* January 10, 2001). In the mid-1990s, Thai cane *yields* were below those of 59 other countries (Paopongsakorn and Viroj 2000: 30).

system, in which millers' sales quotas are based on past volumes of cane crushed. To satisfy their expanded capacity, millers subsidized the expansion of cane planting. When millers needed cane, farmers were able to sell it without improving quality.[54] Even with the latest equipment, then, the mills' efficiency was low because of poor cane quality and the difficulties of obtaining cane. Faced with overcapacity, millers scrambled against each other to obtain cane, especially due to Thailand's short growing season.[55] Further, because roughly 90% of Thai sugarcane is grown in rain-fed areas, Thailand suffers from weather-induced fluctuations in annual cane output.[56]

Industry and government officials responded to these problems by (1) establishing a new rating standard designed to encourage all parties to work toward higher sugar content and (2) attempting to provide cane growers with infrastructure, cane varieties, and equipment necessary to improve yields.

A. Policy Task and Responses on the Demand-side: Standards

Thai sugar mills traditionally purchased cane by weight. As a result, sugarcane growers had no incentive to increase the cane's sugar *content,* even though low sugar content kept production costs high for millers. To address this problem, technocrats in the Ministry of Industry's Cane and Sugar Board proposed adopting a Commercial Cane System (CCS) used in other sugar growing countries in which cane would be purchased on the basis of sugar content rather than weight. The industry adopted a partial version of the CCS system, beginning in the 1992–1993 growing season: Cane price is based 60% on content and 40% on weight.[57] Because the system increased cane prices, it led to an expansion in acreage,[58] but it had little impact on sugar content. As late as October 2006, Thailand's production of sugar per ton of cane was much lower than major competitors.[59]

B. Explaining Demand-side Outcomes

Policy Difficulties and Institutional Capacities: Getting farmers and millers to switch to the CCS involved overcoming a number of obstacles significant enough to require deliberate efforts by many of the same set of actors that

---

[54] Viroj (2000).
[55] Interview # 80.
[56] Viroj (2000).
[57] Ibid. (8).
[58] Pichai (1999, 5).
[59] "Thailand: Agriculture and Cooperatives ..." (2006).

had pushed through the 70:30 revenue arrangements. Gaining the support of the mills was particularly important, but it was also necessary to convince farmers that the new system would benefit them. While the industry's 46 mills and over 100,000 farmers were organized into three millers' groups and three growers' federations, conflict among these groups persisted. There were sure to be losers as well as winners from the switch, but the short-term distributional consequences were not extreme. Millers in different parts of the country would gain more from the switch because different soil conditions resulted in higher sugar yield per ton,[60] but these differences were offset by the fact that the milling groups owned mills in different parts of the country. In addition, growers' associations in those regions that stood to gain from the change had become increasingly influential in the decision-making committees set up by the 1984 Act.[61] On the other hand, raising sugar yields from cane would require investments with a relatively long time-to-payoff. The more significant issue involved simple uncertainty: What would in fact be the costs and benefits of the new system, both across regions and between growers and millers? Although answering this question was not technologically complex, it did require credible information and forecasts.

Success in getting the industry to adopt the CCS was a function of initiatives built on arrangements established to implement the 70:30 system. The moving force for the change came from the Office of the Cane and Sugar Board, especially the director.[62] He hired experts to generate credible data about the distributional consequences of the switch and organized industry-wide seminars to disseminate this information, to work out a 60:40 compromise, and to assure growers that that the sugar content of their cane would be measured accurately and that millers would not take advantage of them. The Office of the Cane and Sugar Board would take responsibility for sampling deliveries of cane and testing for sugar content, installing and maintaining the necessary equipment and training the personnel necessary to operate it.

But these same arrangements lacked the capacity for credible commitment to reward sugar growers for better cane or to punish them for poor quality cane. Such consequences had to come from the millers who purchased cane. With continuing expansion of mill capacity (twofold growth between 1980 and 2000), millers were operating at only 65–89% of

[60] Interview # 18.
[61] Prayong (1988, 13); interview # 16.
[62] Interviews # 17, 18.

installed capacity in the late 1990s.[63] As a result, they competed among each other for cane supplies, seeking "to maximize sugarcane volume, not sugar yield."[64] It was necessary to reduce mill capacity in order to improve cane quality, but doing so required overcoming tough distributional and informational challenges. The most direct strategy would have been to liberalize domestic sugar prices and drop the quota allocation system based on production capacity, but this would have resulted in immediate losses with uncertain gains. Closing mills or limiting their production was equally if not more difficult. To avoid defection and free riding, such a strategy required accurate information, available to all, as to each party's production and investment activities. In addition, this strategy would have incurred losses not just to millers but also to the growers relying on specific mills.

Addressing the Thai sugar industry's overcapacity problem thus required arrangements capable of monitoring the activities of numerous parties, as well as of coercion, the provision of substantial side payments, or both. Neither was available: A 1999 industry analysis concluded that mill expansion and relocation had occurred "with lax regulations and vague guidelines in site and size ... (and) ... without proper monitoring and evaluation."[65]

Politics and Veto Players: This combination of institutional strengths and weaknesses reflected political shifts in the number of veto players during the 1990s. Political competition was decidedly muted under the military-backed government of Anand Panyarachun (1991–1992). As during the Prem period, a broader reformist agenda drove Anand's initiatives, including those in sugar; and centralized political support for these initiatives made it difficult for doubters in the industry to resist change by finding sympathetic ministers to support their resistance. But as under Prem, a more centralized economic elite's concern with economic reform was insufficient to promote the capacities needed to address core productivity issues.

Nor did the Anand government have the time to develop such capacities. With the return of elected governments in 1992 came fragmentation and the overlapping of agency functions, with responsibility for the sugar industry divided among the Agriculture, Commerce, and Industry ministries. Under these conditions, sectoral policy in sugar became primarily a "distributive game."[66] State incoherence was mirrored by and probably reinforced fragmented sugar organizations. Thailand's three millers' associations

---

[63] Viroj (2000, 4).
[64] "Thailand" (1997, 6).
[65] Pichai (1999).
[66] Christensen, Dollar, Siamwalla, and Vichyanond (1993, 1).

narrowly represented the interests of the three largest milling groups who cooperated only on issues that clearly benefited all: lower sugarcane prices, higher domestic sugar prices, and lower taxes. On more divisive issues, they agreed to work as individual associations.[67]

One might have expected the 1997 currency crisis to provoke a break with such dynamics, especially since cheap foreign loans had resulted in a mill expansion that was clearly unsustainable, but several factors blocked the shakeout. The Thai baht's depreciation fueled hopes that the lower cost of Thai sugar would spur new growth. Domestic banks were willing to support overextended mills.[68] And interparty competition provided political support for mills hoping to survive, leading to a government-backed restructuring package of over $2 billion to aid 28 (out of 46) mills.[69]

C. Policy Tasks and Responses on the Supply-side

By the late 1990s, it was clear that demand-side standards alone would not provoke improvements in cane yields and sugar content. According to an industry analysis, cane yields not only lagged behind those of Australia and Brazil; they also fluctuated significantly due to "inadequate water supply, lack of proper cane varieties, insufficient control of diseases and insects, erosion of soil conditions and shortages of farm laborers."[70] In response, the Cane and Sugar Board along with the major associations developed a five-year plan designed to increase cane and sugar yields by improving inputs.

One important goal of the plan involved securing adequate and consistent *access to water*, especially through irrigation, for higher and more stable yields. Expansion of irrigation was especially important since the government's efforts to limit capacity in the 1970s and 1980s had resulted in an expansion of mills, and thus sugarcane farms, in the rain-reliant north and (drought-prone) northeast of Thailand.[71] Because cane rapidly loses its sugar content, the plan also sought to extend appropriate *farm mechanization,* since efficient harvesters, handling and transport equipment can increase the speed in which cane is harvested and delivered to mills.[72]

---

[67] Interview # 49.
[68] *Far Eastern Economic Review.* (November 23, 2006, 75–76).
[69] Pichai (1999); Bangkok Post (March 11, 2003).
[70] Pichai (1999, 4).
[71] "Thailand" (1997, 3).
[72] Viroj (2000); "Thailand" (1997, 6).

Finally, given the low sugar content of Thai cane, the plan emphasized the importance of improving *cane varieties*.

Some 10 years later, the industry had made little progress in these areas. The sugar content of Thai cane had not risen, and its average cane yield in 2006 was 7–10 tons per hectares compared to 13–15 tons for its more efficient competitors.[73] The industry's continuing vulnerability to weather shifts was starkly illustrated in the 2004–2005 season when a drought resulted in a 26% decline in sugarcane production and contributed to a sharp decline in sugar exports over the previous season.[74] Progress on farm mechanization was also minimal: harvesting equipment in use was usually too large for most Thai farms, which also continued to suffer from inefficient transport systems that reduced sugarcane weight and quality and, eventually, mill productivity and revenue.[75] Finally, lack of progress on new cane varieties was reflected in the fact that, as of October 2006, the sugar associations and the Minister of Agriculture and Cooperatives were still discussing the need for research and development on new cane varieties and related technologies, such as fertilizer quality.[76]

D. Explaining Outcomes on the Supply-side

Water: Increasing farmers' access to water required overcoming distributional conflicts. Allocating funds for irrigation meant resolving competing claims from other sectors; increasing irrigation in the rainfall-reliant northeast would give the millers and farmers in this region an advantage over farmers in older sugarcane growing regions in the areas west and south of Bangkok; and there were questions as to how the costs of the water delivery system would be divided between millers and farmers.[77] Improving water access also required coordinating large numbers of actors both in the public and private sectors. Finally, it required extensive information regarding appropriate site-specific facilities for accessing and controlling water.[78]

These difficulties exceeded the capacities of relevant Thai institutions which were themselves limited by large numbers of veto players. Agricultural policy prior to the 1997 crisis was heavily politicized by interparty and interfaction competition that promoted institutional weakness, especially in

[73] *Thai News Service* (July 13, 2006).
[74] CEIC Data; Figure 5.1.
[75] Paitoon, Auansakul, and Supawan (2001).
[76] "Thailand: Agriculture and Cooperatives (2006).
[77] Viroj (2000, 3).
[78] Thippawal, Molle, and Chompadist (1999).

the public sector. The Ministry of Agriculture continued to exhibit "fractious competition among agencies"; and conflict between the Irrigation Department and agencies responsible for property rights impeded the development and management of tertiary canal projects.[79] Such clientelist control was not conducive to broad consultation, policy consistency, or effective monitoring in areas such as irrigation.[80]

Farm Mechanization: Potential returns to investments in equipment to harvest and handle cane seemed to be large in light of the sugar industry's size and the proven willingness of Thai farmers to use new equipment.[81] The challenge was not so much to invent new machinery but to modify existing, often foreign, designs. Given the technical weaknesses of public agricultural agencies and the potential gains, the likely source of such innovations was the private sector, but private sector R&D on farm machinery remained quite low. Key design improvements originated "mainly from imported machines and the public sector."[82] Two sets of institutional problems have impeded a private sector response. In terms of equipment improvement, Thailand lacks patent protection for innovations by local machinery producers.[83] In terms of transportation, relevant ministries and associations are unable to coordinate large numbers of independent actors. The industry's over 100,000 small-sized, often family-owned farms decide independently when to harvest, a decision that depends on the availability of workers and transport, each of which is subcontracted to independent providers. Despite coordination by quotamen, the result is "an uneven sugar cane supply at the mill ... and ... excess time spent at the mills waiting to unload the sugar cane."[84]

Improved Cane Varieties: Market failures impede the development of new, higher yielding sugarcane varieties. When crops are grown from seeds "the profitability of seed production acts as a spur to the development of new varieties"; but since sugarcane is not grown from seeds, and since new varieties can be quickly appropriated by competitors, potential gains are diffuse, thus weakening an incentive to invest.[85] Furthermore, there is a long time to payoff from developing new strains of cane: often 10 years or more from beginning research to making the new variety commercially

---

[79] Christensen (1992, 27, 30).
[80] Bidhya (2001).
[81] Fuglie (2001, 87).
[82] Ibid. (91).
[83] Viroj (2000, 4).
[84] Karndee, Prichanont, and Buansri (2005, 1586).
[85] Fry (1999, 4).

viable. Given these problems of internalizing benefits in crops such as sugar, there was a prima facie role for the public sector in the development of a collective research effort.[86] To address this challenge, the 1999–2004 five-year development plan established a quasi-public National Cane and Sugar Research Institute funded by sugar export revenues, but the effort was dropped amidst differences between the government and industry regarding control and financing.[87]

Nor did the government's overall research-related record inspire confidence. Public funding for sugarcane R&D as a percentage of industry output between 1994 and 2000 fell steadily. Most of the Cane and Sugar Board's funds were earmarked for price support and administrative costs. The government's three existing cane-breeding programs maintained poor databases and were run by different, uncoordinated agencies, which suffered from a shortage of researchers.[88] Finally, Thailand's public universities had a poor track record on sugar-related research, a reflection of the overall weak university–industry linkages in Thailand. In principle, research could have been supported from a levy on sugar sales. But these funds were used to finance the monitoring of cane and sugar quality, an issue of frequent contention between growers and millers.[89]

The private sector responded to the absence of credible public initiatives in at least two ways. Mitr Phol, the country's largest milling group, established its own R&D center and pilot projects in northeast Thailand.[90] The Mitr Phol initiative covers not only new cane varieties but also innovations in fertilizers and water management. Despite Mitr Phol's size, this initiative is quite localized and its benefits to the firm and the industry itself are far from clear. A second initiative involves the development of an ethanol industry that would use sugar and thus increase grower incomes. As of 2006, however, neither of these initiatives had much effect. The industry continued to be preoccupied by conflict over profits and prices to the exclusion of any focus on productivity.[91] Threatening mass demonstrations, growers demanded that the government set higher preliminary prices to compensate for increased costs of cultivation. Growers also claimed to be

---

[86] Christensen (1992, 24).

[87] Viroj (2000, 8–9); Brimble and Doner (2007); interview # 50.

[88] Viroj (2000, 4); *Far Eastern Economic Review.* (November 23, 2000).

[89] Brimble and Doner (2007).

[90] This account draws on Brimble and Doner (2006); *Thai News Service* (July 13 2006); interview # 95.

[91] See "Thai Sugar and Sugarcane ..." (2006); "Thailand Sugar Semi-Annual 2005" (2005); *Bangkok Post* (December. 31, 2005; January 15, 2006; March 8, 2006).

losing revenues relative to millers who, many suspected, were illegally diverting sugar designated for domestic use to more profitable global markets. Unable to resist growers' pressure, the Cane and Sugar Board continued to borrow from the BAAC to compensate growers, but in so doing, the Board raised its cumulative interest payments to 16–17 billion baht, a level that placed into doubt the BAAC's willingness to extend more loans. Efforts to develop ethanol production were only beginning in 2005; and government efforts to ban molasses exports to secure domestic molasses for ethanol production were opposed by millers.

Several sets of economic factors contributed to these problems. Owing to diversions of sugar to ethanol and WTO restrictions on EU production, global supplies dwindled and prices increased, thus encouraging millers to sell sugar abroad. Growers also experienced rising input costs. Lastly, in the presence of uncertain gains, some producers began adopting "exit" options. Several large millers began establishing cane plantations and mills in China, Laos, Cambodia, and Vietnam.[92] Also, some growers started to shift out of cane production, further discouraging millers from supporting investments in productivity-enhancing measures such as irrigation.[93]

These problems were themselves in part a result of the very arrangements – the 60:40 CCS standards, the 70:30 arrangement, and government price supports and subsidies – that provided income stability and encouraged the industry's tremendous export growth. These arrangements both reflected and reinforced broader institutional weaknesses. For example, the same weaknesses in monitoring and credibility seen in compromise efforts such as 70:30 were reflected in the fact that Thai authorities were "practically incapable" of tracking and limiting illegal diversions of sugar to export markets.[94]

Political competition helps to explain these institutional weaknesses. The persistence of multiple veto players, even under the more centralizing Thaksin, discouraged a more sustained approach to industry reform and upgrading.[95] In fact, the short-term distributional consequences of industry reform, combined with institutional weaknesses, led even the military regime that overthrew Thaksin to avoid any tough decisions.[96]

[92] *Bangkok Post* (March 16, 2006); *Far Eastern Economic Review* (November 23, 2000, 76); interview # 120.
[93] Interview # 80.
[94] "Thailand Sugar" (2006); *Bangkok Post.* (January 15, 2006).
[95] *Bangkok Post* (January 6, 2006).
[96] *Thailand News Service* (November 1, 2005).

VI. THE PHILIPPINES AND BRAZIL

The Brazilian and Filipino sugar industries offer contrasts with the Thai case, which allow further assessment of our arguments. Stagnation in the Philippines and upgrading in Brazil reflect contrasting institutional capacities, themselves a function of variation in elite competition and systemic pressures.

A. The Philippines

Policy Tasks: The most proximate explanation for the Philippines' disappointing performance in sugar lies in the country's failure to address at least three of the policy challenges reviewed in the Thai case: property rights, risk socialization, and R&D.

Ownership relations between Philippine sugarcane growers and millers dating back to the early twentieth century have discouraged efforts to improve productivity in both cane production and mills. Unlike the "cane-purchase" system operating in Thailand, Philippine planters typically retain ownership of as much as 70% of the sugar even after the cane is milled and stored in mill warehouses, reflected in an official coupon or *quedan*.[97] Under the *quedan* system millers have little incentive to invest in mill modernization, since upgrading would benefit growers as much if not more than millers. By 2003, the average age of sugar mills in the Philippines was 50 years compared to an average of less than 20 for Thai mills. This has translated into rates of sugar extracted from cane that are not only lower than those of the Thais but also lower than the average Philippine rates of 50 years prior. For their part, planters have focused on trading ownership shares rather than agricultural productivity. Despite widespread industry support for a shift to the cane-purchase system, distributional differences and institutional fragmentation blocked the change.[98]

The Philippines sugar industry has suffered from a more fundamental challenge to property rights: following the 1972 declaration of martial law, Marcos began seizing property from uncooperative oligarchs.[99] Another blow to existing rights was Marcos' decision to replace existing export arrangements with the Philippine Sugar Commission (Philsucom), under the control of a crony, Roberto Benedicto. This firm had control of the export

[97] The rest of this discussion is drawn from Billig (2003).
[98] Billig (2003, 125–126).
[99] Hawes (1987, 97).

trade and, more importantly for Filipino producers, exclusive rights to purchase all sugar (i.e., all *quedans*). In essence, Benedicto determined the prices at which he bought raw sugar and paid for milled sugar. His monopoly and monopsony profits allowed Benedicto to purchase refineries and related infrastructure while undermining planters' confidence in the marketing system. The result was an environment of economic and political insecurity in which existing sugar interests "could not risk new investments or even maximize production," leading to a steep decline in the production of sugar in the late 1970s.[100]

The process of *risk socialization* was also problematic. Unlike in Thailand, where powerful commercial banks financed sugar operations in a context of relatively hard budget constraints, Philippine sugar producers enjoyed excessive socialization but faced little risk prior to the 1970s. Philippine planters became the largest customer of the National Bank of the Philippines which financed the construction of mills and provided other forms of finance to the industry on easy terms.[101] Indeed, prior to martial law, sugar interests dominated the banking industry. The planters "had easy access to credit, low labor costs, cheap and abundant land, large profits," and thus little incentive to make improvements.[102] Further inhibiting the industry's modernization were guaranteed sugar quotas from the U.S. that ensured profits and reassured bankers they would be repaid. According to a U.S. government estimate, in 1967 alone, U.S. quotas provided some $97 million in "hidden assistance" to the Philippine sugar industry.[103]

The industry's risks rose sharply during the martial law period due in part to the end of preferential access to the protected U.S. market in 1974 and low market prices beginning in 1975. The effects of these shifts were compounded by Benedicto's monopoly and monopsony power. In 1974, operating through a state-backed bank, Benedicto held much of the sugar crop rather than exporting it in the mistaken belief that world sugar prices would rise in 1975. Instead, sugar prices fell from 67 cents per pound in 1974 to only 30 cents in 1975. The consequences were dire for planters and millers, and devastating for impoverished workers in the industry. Then in the 1980s, Benedicto bought sugar at an artificially low domestic price and sold it in world markets at a much higher price with most of the profits going to Ferdinand Marcos and selected cronies.[104] These moves severely weakened existing growers and

---

[100] Ibid. (97–98).
[101] McCoy (1983, 137).
[102] Billig (2003, 49); cf. also Hawes (1987, 97).
[103] Hawes (1987, 94).
[104] Billig (2003, 54–57).

millers. As a result, "(n)either domestic nor foreign investors invested new money in sugar during the martial law years."[105]

Given these conditions, a lack of *research and development* is not surprising. Government-sponsored research facilities did produce new cane varieties in the 1920s;[106] and industry leaders explored new mechanization techniques when faced with market volatility in the mid-1970s.[107] However, none of these efforts were sustained, and by the 1990s government research and extension functions under the Sugar Regulatory Administration (SRA), were disorganized and underfunded. Efforts to have planters' associations take over R&D from ineffective state agencies foundered because the associations could not agree on which group would manage the research. In consequence, the average cost of sugar production in the Philippines priced it out of world markets.[108]

Institutional Capacities: Michael Billig has summarized the Philippine sugar industry as a case of "technical inefficiency and institutional stasis."[109] Until the 1970s, there was little consultation. Disputes tended to involve distributive issues, especially fights over *quedan* allocations, not cane yield or sugar quality. Where public–private exchanges did occur, they involved particular millers or planters and individual legislators, some of whom were sugar producers themselves. This shifted briefly in the mid-1970s when, confronted with market volatility and the loss of preferential access to the U.S. market, Marcos proposed a state-sponsored export organization, Philsucom, as a means to improve market and pricing coordination. Growers and millers welcomed the proposal, in part out of mistrust of the private traders traditionally managing exports.

But as Philsucom became a rent-generating machine for Marcos and Benedicto, consultation was replaced by top-down decisions. In contrast with Thailand's "competitive clientelism" Marcos practiced "monopoly clientelism" which discouraged competition, terminated consultation, made a mockery of credible commitments, and made monitoring impossible. In addition to the direct costs to producers of such practices, the arbitrariness and uncertainty they created deterred new investments.

Since the end of martial law in 1986, consultation both among sugar interests and between them and state officials improved but remained

---

[105] Hawes (1987, 96).
[106] Larkin (1993, 160).
[107] Billig (2003, 68).
[108] Ibid. (64–67).
[109] Ibid. (69). The rest of this review draws on personal communication with Michael Billig, December 20, 2006.

sporadic.[110] The key government sugar agency, the SRA, is responsible for coordinating R&D and extension services, issuing licenses to traders, managing the *quedan* system, and monitoring the industry's operations. However, its capacity for monitoring the large number of actors in areas such as wage-law compliance, quota management, illegal sugar sales, imports and, most critically in *quedan* distribution, was minimal at best.

This state of affairs reflects weakness and fragmentation within both the public and private sectors. Despite having a staff with doctorate degrees in agricultural sciences, the SRA exhibits both "institutional bloat" and internal conflict reminiscent of problems in Thailand Cane and Sugar Board. In terms of the private sector, the idea of a "sugar bloc" is misleading. Conflict within and among sugar associations was rampant. This fragmentation reflected not only a tradition of personalistic organizations, but also real distributional differences pitting planters against millers and both, increasingly, against traders. With sugar industry meetings "frequently end(ing) in greater disharmony than when they started," the industry's emphasis was on short-term advantages obtained through lobbying or the direct exercise of political power.[111]

Two other factors further impeded the industry's organizational cohesion and commitment to upgrading. One is the tendency among large planters to diversify out of sugar into areas such as media and real estate, thus weakening their commitment to the industry overall. The other is the political weakness of perhaps the principal Philippine-based source of pressure for higher cane and sugar quality, namely, the large food processors, including multinationals such as Del Monte, Kraft, Pepsi, and Coke, for whom sugar is a key input. In part because they are multinationals in a country sensitive to behavior viewed as neocolonialist, these firms must work behind the scenes, often through domestic food producers, to press for easier sugar imports or improvements in local productivity. The result of all these factors is a persistent inability to address collective action problems, including improving cane yields and milling efficiency and reforming the *quedan* system, which has endured despite support for a change by powerful sugar interests and extensive research by the World Bank and others demonstrating the superiority of the cane-purchase alternative.

Elite Political Competition: The Philippine sugar industry illustrates the consequences of both many and few veto players. In the premartial law

---

[110] The following three paragraphs are based on Billig (2003).
[111] Ibid. (231).

period, a fragmented sugar bloc with divergent preferences imposed particularistic demands on the bureaucracy via two major parties in a bicameral legislature and presidential system. The result was policy gridlock in the face of significant industry weaknesses.[112] This reflected a broader and persistent pattern of elite relations in which extra-bureaucratic power dominated what Paul Hutchcroft has described as a weakly institutionalized state.[113] Historically, this state generated rent for oligarchic forces operating outside the state but reliant on particularistic access to state-related political machinery via legislative parties.[114] The result was a hamstrung bureaucracy.[115] With martial law, a reduction in veto players did permit a decisive policy shift, as Marcos consolidated the management of sugar exports in the face of external market pressures. But with the new arrangement under crony control, the policy shift undermined overall credibility and discouraged investment in the industry. These developments in sugar reflected the broader consolidation of power by a particular group of Marcos-led interests that involved "a greater degree of purposive rent allocation" but little if any "enforcement of larger performance criteria."[116] The Philippine state remained swamped by oligarchic demands and incapable of playing a coherent role in economic development.

At first glance, this description might seem to fit Thailand as well, but as Hutchcroft notes, public and private spheres in Thailand, while often overlapping, are much more distinguishable than in the Philippines.[117] While oligarchic interests in the Philippines have used their power to ignore technocrats and to dominate large parts of the bureaucracy, in Thailand, macroeconomic agencies have been able to impose hard budget constraints, and technocrats have at times succeeded in fostering collective action.

Systemic Pressures: The "technical inefficiency and institutional stasis" of the Philippine sugar industry, as well as of the Philippine state, was the result of the strikingly permissive environment in which elites have operated. Filipino elites have had virtually no real threats to their power and privileges from external forces. The overall pattern has been one in which the state, *"while plundered internally ... is repeatedly rescued externally."*[118] Ties to the U.S. have provided resources that weakened the incentives of political leaders to

---

[112] Billig (2003, 145; 161).
[113] Hutchcroft (1994; 1998).
[114] Hutchcroft (2000, 218).
[115] Anderson (1988).
[116] Hutchcroft (2000, 227).
[117] Ibid. (218).
[118] Hutchcroft (1994, 226); emphasis added.

build broad coalitions of support and strengthen institutions. Agriculture provided an important basis for economic growth during much of the twentieth century, with sugar accounting for roughly one quarter of the country's total exports from the late 1940s until 1974, when preferential access to the U.S. market ended.[119] The lure of the U.S. market has been particularly pernicious in discouraging institutional strength and upgrading.[120] Popular discontent, a second dimension of systemic pressures, has not been absent in the Philippines, but it has not threatened the established political order.[121] The relative weakness of popular pressures discouraged productivity improvements, allowing cheap labor to remain the key competitive advantage for Philippine sugar producers and an obstacle to upgrading.

B. Brazil

Policy Tasks: In contrast to the Philippines, Brazil has been able both to expand production and to become one of the world's most efficient producers.[122] This performance reflects successes in at least four policy areas, the first of which involves *property rights*. Over 80% of Brazil's sugar comes from the central-south region, especially the state of São Paulo, which benefits from a particular ownership pattern. Unlike both the Philippines and Thailand, large, capital-intensive mills in Brazil own much of the land on which sugarcane is grown, with the rest owned mostly by large-scale sugarcane farmers who displaced small holders. The millers (*usinieros*) also control much of the entire upstream–downstream production process including "supply and manufacture of agricultural and industrial inputs, cane cultivation, and sugar and alcohol refining and marketing."[123] This has given millers strong incentives to expand and improve sugar production, since they do not have to share profits from these changes with planters.

Risk socialization has been more state-led than in Thailand but distinctly more performance-oriented than in the Philippines. Brazil's military government that took power in 1964 gave high priority to improving

---

[119] Larkin (1993, 243).

[120] Ibid. (164).

[121] The Huks never had a strong impact outside their central Luzon heartland, "especially not in the sugarlands of the western Visayas" (Larkin 1993, 241). While the New People's Army was active in Negros, the main sugar island of the Visayas, elites responded through small side payments, localized electoral mobilization, and localized repression (Slater 2006).

[122] "Brazilian Sugar," (2003, 2).

[123] Nunberg (1986, 63).

agricultural and industrial productivity and, eventually, energy independence. Sugar was key to these goals. Government funding was central to the rapid growth of the modern São Paulo sugar complex. Acting through the semiautonomous Instituto do Acucar e do Alcoool (IAA), the regime facilitated relocation of mills to the central-south region,, helped build bulk loading facilities at ports, and offered mill modernization loans with negative interest rates and flexible repayment schedules.[124]

These incentives eventually led to *overcapacity,* especially when world sugar prices collapsed in 1975 and export markets disappeared. Unlike Thailand's purely export-oriented response, the Brazilian strategy was to relieve the problem initially through state-based repression of small farmers and unemployed workers in the northeast, and subsequently by converting surplus cane to alcohol.[125] This took the form of the 1975 National Alcohol Program (*Proalcool*), designed to save foreign exchange by using sugar-based alcohol to supplement gasoline supply. With the growth of alcohol-powered automobiles (demand for which was encouraged by state funds), *Proalcool* became irreversible.[126] This solution to the overproduction crisis created a major alternative to exporting sugar and has continued to give Brazil flexibility in world sugar markets that no other major sugar exporting nation enjoys.

Brazil also went much further than Thailand or the Philippines in promoting R&D to improve sugarcane yields and conversion to sugar, as well as ethanol production and related products. Initial programs to improve cane yields and milling efficiency came from the state, especially the IAA and the São Paulo state government.[127] By the end of the 1970s these efforts were dwarfed by the highly successful programs of the Canavieira Technology Center (CTC), a component of the central-south region's largest private sugar cooperative, Copersucar (Cooperativa Central dos Produtores de Acucar do Estado São Paulo).[128] The Center developed new cane varieties, technologies for ethanol production, products, and mechanical innovations. It benefited from state investments in basic research, molecular genetics, and cane breeding.[129] Together, these efforts significantly raised productivity in both cane and ethanol yield (Figure 5.3).[130]

---

[124] Barzelay (1986, 81); Nunberg (1986, 60–72).
[125] Nunberg (1986, 69).
[126] Barzelay (1986, 81; 139; 198).
[127] Martines-Filho, Burnquist, and Vian (2006, 94); Nunberg (1986, 69).
[128] Nunberg(1986); Martines-Filho, Burnquist, and Vian (2006); and the webpage (http://www.copersucar.com.br/institucional/ing/empresa/tecnologia).
[129] Martines-Filho, Burnquist, and Vian (2006, 94).
[130] See also Brazil Semi-Annual Sugar (2005, 6).

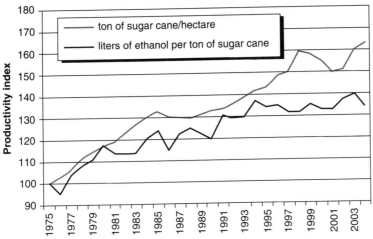

FIGURE 5.3 Sugarcane and Ethanol Productivity in Brazil, 1975–2003

Institutional Capacities: Brazil's success in upgrading its sugar industry reflected explicit efforts to expand institutional capacities both within and between public and private sectors after 1964. It was also part of a longer, uneven process of change in the industry's governance. In the 1930s, the government assigned the IAA to coordinate sugar production and marketing and to channel excess sugar into alcohol production for industrial uses. The IAA functioned as a "corporatist" organization through the 1950s, but its commitment to protecting the incomes of northeast sugar producers transformed it into a case of extreme clientelism.[131]

As exports grew, and as sugar production migrated to the more fertile central-south region, the IAA's functions declined, replaced by a corporatist-type system based on highly organized producers' cooperatives based in São Paulo and on a more centralized state. These cooperatives, especially Copersucar, emerged as "the model for Brazilian agricultural development under the post-1964 military regime."[132] Copersucar's initial focus was on marketing and finance, but it gradually expanded to include packaging and distribution of its own brands, processing and distribution of other commodities, and extensive R&D. By the late 1970s it represented 86% of the millers in São Paulo, and these millers produced over 40% of the country's sugar. In stark contrast to both the Thai and Philippine cases, the cooperative had close ties with local manufacturers of industrial inputs for sugar

[131] Nunberg (1986, 44, 77, 56).
[132] Ibid. (63).

cultivation, refining, and harvesting,[133] and by the 1970s, Copersucar had become one of the largest corporations in Latin America.[134]

The cooperative had a strong voice in sugar policies, including price controls and, most critically, alcohol production. Indeed, the cooperatives became the "new channels of interest intermediation" and, together with the state, constituted "a new centralization of policy-making in sugar."[135] Copersurcar "proposed an enormous expansion of state-controlled alcohol production to help alleviate the balance of payments deficit incurred largely by soaring oil prices."[136] The result, after extensive consultation, was the establishment of Proalcool in 1975. All of Proalcool's production processes were left in private sector hands, but the expansion of private sector distilleries was "the direct result of an extremely attractive credit programme" based on government financing estimated to constitute a subsidy of up to 75% of construction costs.[137]

Institutional strengthening was an ongoing process. Although its basic parameters were established by the late 1970s, Proalcool suffered from "weak programme vision, vague institutional definition and organizational restrictions."[138] Brazil's president responded to these problems in 1979 by committing the government to "strengthening the institutional basis" of the program by improving coordination, setting priorities, refining credit policies, and monitoring and refining as needed.[139] Reinforcing these efforts was a state-led reform of the sugar industry's governance in which the government first reduced the autonomy of the IAA, infusing it with technocratic norms, recruiting technocrats into key positions, and placing military personnel in top leadership. In subsequent centralization, many IAA functions were shifted into policy-making bodies of the state itself, while others were taken over by private sector cooperatives such as Copersucar.[140]

The combination of state centralization and ongoing consultation with an organized private sector approximated what Barzelay[141] labeled a "cooperative game." The arrangement provided credibility, especially in the eyes of private investors. Confidence in the "longevity of favorable policies"

---

[133] Ibid. (86, fn 30).
[134] Barzelay (1986, 138).
[135] Nunberg (1986, 78).
[136] Ibid. (65).
[137] Saint (1982, 227).
[138] Ibid.
[139] Ibid. (228).
[140] Nunberg (1986, 76).
[141] Barzelay (1986, 79).

was especially important to address concerns with time inconsistency that could impede the expensive investments and long time horizons inherent in the kinds of agro-industrial transformation desired by the country's military rulers. By incorporating potential winners, such as *usineiros*, equipment producers, automakers, and small cultivators, governance arrangements also helped to overcome opposition to the development of a sugar-based alcohol program from state financial planners opposed to subsidized credit and from Petrobras, the state oil company, fearful of losing control over fuel production.[142]

Elite Political Competition: Part of the explanation for these strengths is found in the low levels of political competition under military rule. Although divisions clearly existed within the Brazilian officer corps, these were muted by a broader commitment to developmentalism in service of what the military viewed as national security.[143] The relatively small number of veto players contributed to significantly greater cohesion in the Brazilian bureaucracy than in the Thai case. Although many parts of Brazil's state apparatus were fragmented, corrupt, and staffed with patronage appointments, the state had important strengths. Key agencies, especially the Brazilian National Bank for Economic and Social Development, were politically protected and staffed by skilled technocrats with a developmentalist mentality and key roles in spending decisions for the agricultural sector.[144] In addition, the military regime used appointments to "structure access and representation for societal groups," disrupting those the military wanted weakened and facilitating representation for those whose goals meshed with the regime's.[145] The large sugar producers were clearly beneficiaries of this system, while smaller, independent cane suppliers and workers were the major losers.[146]

The Brazilian military used its public power for private ends less than in the Philippines under Marcos in part because the Brazilian regime had more autonomy from producer groups than did the oligarchic-dominated Philippine state. It is true that, for all its statism, the Brazilian military relied on private actors in the sugar industry, whereas Marcos's crony ruled the industry through a state marketing organization. But the Brazilian military used its autonomy to *strengthen* the collective capacity of private sugar interests, especially large producers in the central-south region and

---

[142] Ibid. (12); Saint (1982, 227).
[143] Kohli (2004, 193).
[144] Schneider (1991, 36); Helfand (1999).
[145] Schneider (1999, 297).
[146] Nunberg (1986, 61, 69, 77); Saint (1982, 229–231).

Copersucar. This organization constituted both the embodiment and the mechanism for the military regime's vision of an agro-industrial transformation of Brazilian agriculture.[147]

This arrangement differed from those in Thailand in several ways. In Brazil, agro-industrial elites with a vested interest in upgrading all parts of the value chain were part of the new state coalition, not just the mills, as in Thailand. Also, Brazilian state elites could focus on their relationship with the millers, not with balancing the interests of millers and quotamen, as in Thailand. Thus, to a much greater degree than in Thailand, Brazilian sugar was governed by a corporatist arrangement in which a very small number of veto players represented by the military used consultation with key private actors to complement its flexibility with credibility. Underlying this small number of veto players and the cooperative game it in which it played was the military's perception of threat. As Barzelay notes, "(t)he single unanimous feature" of the policy to convert sugarcane into alcohol was that the effort could not be opposed "by any state official so long as the industry was being 'threatened' by external events."[148] However, the question remains as to why the Brazilian military, unlike its Thai counterparts or Ferdinand Marcos, was so intent on upgrading of sugar in the first place.

Systemic Pressures: At first glance, vulnerability pressures seem an unlikely motivation for the upgrading efforts of Brazilian leaders. Unlike Thailand, Brazil faced no threats on its borders while, like the Philippines, enjoying quota access to the U.S. market.[149] But this comparison masks the ways in which *externally induced resource constraints combined with concerns about domestic political stability* to threaten Brazil's political rulers to a much greater extent than anything faced by their Thai counterparts. These threats stimulated explicitly developmentalist Brazilian states dating back to the 1930s,[150] and by the 1960s, developmentalism took on a national security function.[151] This combination of developmentalism and national security was largely absent in the Thai and Philippine cases but clearly evident in Brazilian sugar.

---

[147] Barzelay (1986, 81–82); Nunberg (1986, 63).

[148] Barzelay (1986, 79).

[149] After the U.S. cancelled the quota for Cuban sugar on the U.S. preferential market, Brazil got a significant share of this quota and in 1962 received a permanent quota on the U.S. market. Brazil's sugar exports to the U.S. rose from 12,000 tons in 1959 to 621,000 tons in 1972 (Nunberg 1986, 57–59).

[150] Schneider (1999).

[151] Further encouraging a preoccupation with national security was a traditional belief in Brazil's regional leadership role. I am grateful to Eric Hershberg for pointing this out.

State intervention in sugar began in the 1930s when President Vargas created the IAA as "an explicit response to the excessively vulnerable position" of the Brazilian sugar industry after the fall of commodity prices in 1929.[152] The IAA was to stabilize prices by reducing production, to safeguard an adequate supply of sugar for domestic consumption, to moderate potentially destabilizing class conflict by protecting small- and medium-sized growers, and to channel any excess production into the production of alcohol as a motor fuel.[153] The developmentalist impulse in sugar (and in general) intensified with the military regime that took power from 1964 to 1985:

> In claiming authority to rule, the military ... propounded an elaborate doctrine of national security that had evolved in response to several perceived threats, including economic crisis and the Cuban revolution. The military's apparent mission in coming to power was to restructure Brazil's political and economic systems in a way that would eliminate these perceived threats.[154]

As part of this national security strategy, sectoral interventions were designed to cultivate the support of specific social groups and, more broadly, to promote the growth central to the military's "legitimacy formula."[155] This emphasis on legitimacy reflected the military's ongoing concern with popular opposition. On seizing power, the Brazilian military "inherited a functioning populist system ...".[156] The military succeeded in dismantling this system through repression, but opposition persisted, including an increasingly militant trade union movement and, as discussed later, electoral opposition.

> Whatever minimal legitimacy and support the military enjoyed thus rested on its performance. Any reduction in growth ... was thus deemed politically undesirable and even dangerous by the military rulers; business profit and the incomes of the middle and working classes depended on sustained growth.[157]

Sugar was an important but challenging component of these efforts. Exports of sugar grew in importance as (1) a source of foreign exchange to finance inputs for the military's domestic industrialization efforts (in 1972 sugar was the second most important foreign exchange earner after coffee,

---

[152] Nunberg (1986, 56).
[153] Ibid. (55–57). Alcohol provided almost half of Brazil's fuel during the oil-scarce years of WWII (Ibid., 130).
[154] Barzelay (1986, 8).
[155] Ibid.
[156] Hagopian (1994, 41).
[157] Kohli (2004, 193).

and by 1974 the most profitable commodity export) and (2) a solution to the industry's chronic overproduction crises, which occurred in 1964–1965 and 1967.[158] Benefiting from access to the U.S. market, the state thus initiated a major export thrust in sugar. But this policy itself posed risks of the same kind of dependence and vulnerability that prompted state intervention in the 1930s. As such, it required more than just a shift to exports, as in the Thai case. Rather, it meant that "the entire system of production and administration of the sugar sector would have to be transformed to meet competitive world-market standards."[159]

Pressures to upgrade sugar intensified in the 1970s. OPEC's quadrupling of oil prices resulted in the country's petroleum imports rising from 16% of imports in 1973 to 40% in 1974, and "appeared to wreak havoc on Brazil's economic miracle."[160] The potential political damage was serious: "the sharp rise in oil prices threatened the military dictatorship's ability to rule."[161] To shore up its declining legitimacy, the generals had decided to hold relatively free congressional elections in 1974. The ruling party suffered a stunning defeat, which the military interpreted "as evidence of its own political isolation."[162] Part of the military's response was the Proalcool program, designed not only to save foreign exchange but also to reduce regional inequality and generate demand for capital goods.[163] The promotion of sugar, as part of an alcohol program, was further intensified in the early 1980s after world sugar prices had declined and, owing to the 1979 oil shocks and U.S. interest rate hikes, Brazil experienced a (1981–1983) depression labeled "the worst ever recorded in Brazilian national accounts, not excluding that of the early 1930s."[164]

By the late 1980s, the level of state intervention in the sugar industry had declined significantly. Ethanol prices were deregulated; the state "Cane, Sugar and Ethanol Harvest Plan" was discontinued; and a 40% tax on sugar exports exceeding a set quota was eliminated.[165] This liberalization occurred because the debt crisis had undermined the state's ability to sustain financial support; agriculture had declined as a source of foreign exchange; and the democratization process which began in the late 1970s undermined

---

[158] Nunberg (1986, 57–59).
[159] Ibid. (59).
[160] Barzelay (1986, 139).
[161] Martines-Filho, Burnquist, and Vian (2006, 93).
[162] Hagopian (1994, 50).
[163] Ibid. (140); Martines-Filho, Burnquist, and Vian (2006, 93).
[164] Diaz-Alejandro (1983, 539); Saint (1982).
[165] Martines-Filho, Burnquist, and Vian (2006); Sheales, Gordon, and Toyne (1999, 56).

the corporatist and sometimes clientelist policy institutions operating under the military.[166] But this liberalization was itself made possible by earlier policies and institutions established in the face of serious challenges.

CONCLUSION

The three sugar industries reviewed in this chapter constitute a hierarchy of performance: deterioration in the Philippines; structural change and moderate upgrading in Thailand; and comprehensive upgrading in Brazil. This cross-national variation, as well as longitudinal variation within each country, reflects institutional capacities and underlying systemic pressures. With minor exceptions, sugar production in the Philippines has been governed by fragmented producers dominating poorly staffed and highly politicized state agencies. Under these conditions, particularistic clientelism aimed at securing quota rents has been the norm. The Thai industry presents a greater level of private sector organization, as well as somewhat more cohesion and autonomy in the state Office of the Cane and Sugar Board. This governance arrangement has facilitated episodes of public–private sector consultation focused largely on income sharing and sectoral stability. In Brazil, a centralized state engaged with organized sugar interests in a deliberate project of agro-industrial transformation.

This cross-national variation reflects important variation in the pressures facing political elites. In the Philippines, localized popular resistance, Cold War security guarantees and aid, and preferential market access allowed elites to plunder the state, as epitomized by the use of a state monopoly to weaken an already-stagnant sugar industry. In Thailand, the industry's importance to large number of farmers and for foreign exchange prompted greater collective organization and more systematic public–private engagement. However, with a large land frontier and favorable climate, and with labor-intensive exports also generating foreign exchange, government and industry focused on export expansion through sectoral stabilization and revenue sharing, and not improvements in cane varieties and farm mechanization. Thailand's "pure export" option was less feasible in Brazil. That country's military rulers viewed sugar as a critical source of foreign exchange not only for import substitution policy-based capital accumulation but also for more general economic growth to address a much more powerful popular opposition than in Thailand. Given the competitive pressures in global sugar markets, reliable exports required upgrading in

[166] Helfand (1999, 27, 37).

precisely the areas neglected by the Thais. The potential of sugar-based ethanol as an alternative to expensive petroleum exports further intensified the pressures for true agro-industrial transformation in sugar.

The importance of systemic pressures can also be seen in within-country "blips and pockets" of institutional strength. In the Philippines, a brief episode of collective consultation and monitoring occurred only in the mid-1970s when the country lost preferential access to U.S. sugar markets. In Thailand, the debt crisis of the 1980s prompted an extended bout of institutional strengthening and public–private engagement. More sustained pressures in Brazil translated into consistent institutional strengthening in sugar, but the Brazil sugar case is interesting as a distinct pocket of efficiency in an otherwise fragmented set of agricultural institutions.[167]

Finally, these cases suggest that systemic pressures constitute a more powerful explanation of institutional and sectoral performance than arguments based on path dependence. One might argue that the Philippines' problems stem largely from the norms, interests, and arrangements associated with the *quedan* system that block its demise even in the face of clear evidence that cane-purchase arrangements could save the industry from catastrophe.[168] But in the absence of significantly different pressures on political elites, it is difficult to know how sticky an institution is; and Billig's own (1994) historical account of the "Death and Rebirth of Entrepreneurism" in the Philippine sugar industry shows how shifting incentives can modify even long-standing cultural practices. Similarly, the lack of systemic pressures in the Philippines facilitated a crony-based monopoly operating not through traditional private arrangements but rather a set of state-backed institutions. Conversely, the Brazilian military's willingness and capacity essentially to do away with the IAA, an organization rooted in powerful agricultural interests, even as it opted to support *private* producer cooperatives as the mechanism of agro-industrial upgrading, provides further evidence of the likelihood of institutional change when political elites face significant threats.

Systemic factors also trump proximate political arrangements, including regime type and electoral competition, as explanations for institutional change and sectoral performance. Authoritarian regimes in both the Philippines and Brazil resulted in distinctly different institutional capacities and sectoral performances. A key source of this difference lies in pressures on military elites for politically legitimizing efficiency. This is not to minimize the potential developmental benefits of greater authority concentration, as

---

[167] Ibid. (8).
[168] Billig (2003, 144).

seen in Thailand in the 1980s and the early 1990s. It is rather to argue that the concentration of authority in the absence of systemic pressures yields few developmental benefits. Further, the fact that Prem and Anand were followed by much more competitive politics reminds us that political arrangements, especially the number of veto players , are often the result of systemic pressures.

6

Textiles

Co-authored with Ansil Ramsay

The Thai textile industry's future seemed bleak in the 1950s when local investments in mechanized spinning collapsed in the face of subsidized cotton imports from Pakistan.[1] But over the next decades, the industry grew (Tables 6.1, 6.2),[2] and by the mid-1980s, a fairly complete textile "complex" had developed (Figure 6.1). The industry's export value also grew from roughly $636,000 in 1981 to over $4 billion in 1991, with garments gradually dominating the industry's exports (Figure 6.2). By the year 2000, Thailand was ranked as the world's ninth largest apparel exporter.[3] The industry also became a key part of the Thai economy: it was the largest export earner by the mid-1980s and the second largest exporter in 2000 (Figure 6.3);[4] it was also the source of 4.5% of total Thai GDP in 2003 employing over 20% of the manufacturing workforce.[5]

[1] Archanun (1995, 33–35). Textile production starts with fiber transformed into yarn, which is then woven or knit into fabric. Fabrics, or in some cases yarn or fiber, are typically dyed or finished to improve aesthetic, cleaning or wearing qualities. Fabric is then transformed into apparel, home furnishings (such as sheets), or industrial products. Our focus is on the process as it results in apparel production. We use the term "textile industry" to refer to this entire process.

[2] Thai textile data is inconsistent, hence the need for separate tables on production data (6.1 and 6.2). For example, the Textile Industry Division shifted its units for fabrics and clothing from square yards to tons in 1994 without, as far as we know, providing any complete, reconciled data. Also, figures provided by the Executive Director of the Thai Textile Institute (Virat 2007) are inconsistent with those on the Institute's website.

[3] Gereffi and Memedovic (2003), 29.

[4] Suphat (1994), 6; IFCT (2543), 1; see also Figure 6.3.

[5] Chalumporn (2004, 1).

TABLE 6.1 *Thai Textile Production, 1966–1986*

Year	Cotton Yarn (1,000 ft)	Synthetic* Yarn (1,000 ft)	Cotton Fabrics (1 million sq. yards)	Synthetic Fabrics (1 million sq. yards)	Synthetic Fiber (1,000 tons)	Clothing (million pieces)
1966	24	1	251	43		
1970	57	8	426	81	1.2	249
1975	71	65	558	338	39	488
1976	73	80	624	430	n.a.	n.a.
1977	94	96	684	446	n.a.	n.a.
1978	83	110	711	527	n.a.	n.a.
1979	90	115	732	596	n.a.	n.a.
1980	96	125	759	672	113	722
1981	97	135	786	723	113	786
1982	101	130	851	794	98	822
1983	110	142	886	847	114	883
1984	119	153	936	904	115	889
1985	131	161	984	971	127	946
1986	169	184	1,060	1,080	131	1,035

Sources: Thai Textile Manufacturing Association, cited in JICA 1989: I-3, Table I-I-I; Thai Textile Manufacturing Association, cited in Suphat 1994: 24, table 3.3.

Note: *We use "manmade" and "synthetic" interchangeably. Strictly speaking, manmade fibers are cellulosic fibers, such as rayon, and synthetic fibers are polyesters and nylons.

But textile's share of Thai manufactured exports fell from around one-third in the mid-1980s to 14% in 1997 and 11% in 2000–2002.[6] Thailand's share of world garment exports fell from 3.2% in 1995 to 2% in 1998.[7] The industry's export growth rates fell from 26% in 1989 to 7.2% in 1995, actually declining by 14% in 1996.[8] These declines reflected an overall fall in competitiveness.[9] Textile exports subsequently rebounded (Figure 6.2), but the country's share of global textile trade continued declining to 1.8% in 2004,[10] and the recovery was largely a function of exchange rate shifts and market diversification, not upgrading.

Upgrading-related weaknesses were evident even during the boom years of the late 1980s and early 1990s. A Japanese aid agency highlighted the

[6] James and Ramstetter (2005, table 1).
[7] Cited in Brooker (2001, 3–7); see also Chalumporn (2004, 5).
[8] Paopongsakorn and Pawadee (1998, figure 2, 343); Warr (1998, 57–58); http://thaitextile.org/statistic/statistico.asp?staat.cate = 1).
[9] James and Ramstetter (2005, table 1).
[10] "Textile Put on Alert," *The Nation*. (May 22, 2004).

TABLE 6.2 *Thai Textile Production, 1987–2006*

Year	Synthetic Fiber (metric tons)	Spinning (metric tons)	Weaving (million square yards)	Knitting (million square yards)	Garments (million pieces)
1987	142,439	400,405	2,498	703	1,218
1988	155,630	419,144	3.023	818	1,348
1989	202,347	451,051	3,356	963	1,630
1990	239,643	476,212	3,490	1,107	1,893
1991	306,100	534,375	3,764	1,314	2,237
1992	359,905	632,974	4,041	1,345	2,283
1993	415,970	557,035	4,163	1,380	2,392
1994	468,283	559,429	4,278	1,403	2,526
1995	540,756	518.171	4,935	1,291	2,587
1996	521,560	546,674	4,756	1,340	2,631
1997	564,575	576,223	5,030	1,401	2,761
1998	733,555	580,137	5,393	1,518	2,964
1999	756,149	601,677	5,234	1,494	2,923
2000	807,406	608,014	5,762	1,707	3,346
2001	806,411	677,899	6,138	1,900	3,620
2002	868,707	735,330	6,592	2,009	3,881
2003	830,701	783,164	6,689	2,032	4,144
2004	893,859	845,893	7,106	2,166	4,399
2005	809,033	775,200	7,108	2,301	4,697
2006	725,356	780,117	7,200	2,373	4,877

Source: Bank of Thailand. Production of Manufactured Goods, Table 66, Historical Data. http://www.bot.or.th/BOTHOMEPAGE/databank/EconData/EconFinance/tab66e.asp

industry's failure to move from assembly of imported inputs to production using local inputs. The supply chain was unbalanced: upstream (fibers) and midstream (spinners, weavers, and dyers/printers/finishers) segments were less efficient than the downstream (apparel) producers. Unable to obtain good-quality, low-priced yarn and finished fabrics from local suppliers, garment producers turned to imports, which more than doubled between 1982 and 1987.[11] These problems persisted into the late 1990s.[12] Underlying the imbalance were problems of outdated equipment, shortages of technical personnel, and tariff and tax structures that discouraged linkages among industry segments.[13]

[11] JICA (1989, I-112, table I-4–5).
[12] Sombat (1998, 1).
[13] Chalumporn (2004).

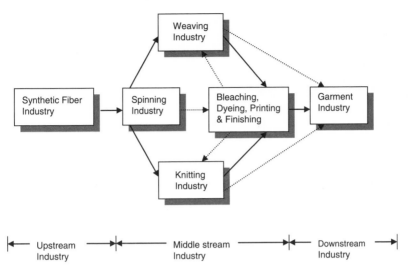

FIGURE 6.1 Structure of the Thai Textile Industry
Source: Brooker Group 2001, 3–4

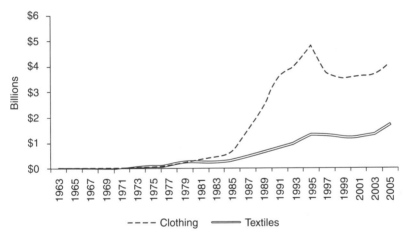

FIGURE 6.2 Thai Textile Exports
Source: UN Comtrade Database

These problems were in part the result of the Thai industry's particular evolution. Protected upstream and midstream producers emerged *prior to and largely unrelated to the growth of export-oriented apparel production.* Because these producers could survive without supplying inputs to garment exporters, and because the latter were able to draw on imported inputs and guaranteed quota markets, there was little pressure to upgrade by establishing linkages among segments or engaging in process and product

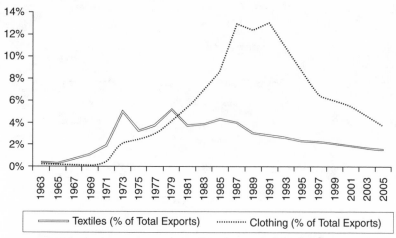

FIGURE 6.3 Textiles as Percentage of Thai Exports
Source: UN Comtrade Database

innovation.[14] As Section I demonstrates, external investment and demand conditions did not impose this pressure. Thailand's responses to external contexts were a function of the fit between its institutional capacities and the particular sets of challenges facing Thai textile firms. Sections II–IV trace these responses in light of our arguments about institutional fit and supply. Section V compares Thailand's textile industry to those of the Philippines and Taiwan, countries whose textile industries emerged at roughly the same time and in the same region as Thailand but performed substantially differently.

I. THE TEXTILE VALUE CHAIN

The Thai textile industry has evolved within a more complex and shifting set of entry barriers than those in sugar. Apart from the more demanding technology requirements, textile firms have operated within dynamic investment and demand conditions that provided opportunities for both expansion and complacency, even as they now punish the latter.

A. 1960s–early 1980s: Japanese Migration to Northeast and Southeast Asia

The initial growth of Thai textiles occurred largely in the upstream and midstream segments. Under extensive protection, Thailand became almost self-sufficient in cotton and synthetic yarn, cotton cloth, and synthetic

---

[14] See Palpacuer, Gibbon, and Thomsen (2004, 412).

fabrics by 1972.[15] This expansion was largely driven by Japanese textile investments, especially from large firms such as Toray and Teijin.[16] As elsewhere in East Asia, Japanese investments in Thailand responded to host country government policies and shifts in comparative costs. In the first half of the 1960s, Japanese investments were designed in part to protect export markets in response to Thai import substitution policies promoting local fabric and yarn production, and in part to create consumers of synthetic fibers, thus increasing Japanese fiber exports.

Further Japanese investments, especially in midstream segments, resulted from Japanese labor shortages and wage increases, as well as from the need for continued access to developed country markets in response to Voluntary Export Restrictions (VERs) on cotton textiles imposed by the Long Term Agreement (LTA) on textiles.[17] From the late 1960s into the early 1970s, some 17 Japanese and Thai-Japanese joint ventures began operations, largely in fiber, spinning, and weaving.[18] Even as local capital became more important in the 1970s, Japanese firms remained critical. As late as 1978, roughly half of Thai textile exports came from Japanese joint ventures.[19]

B. Mid-1980s–Mid-1990s: Triangle Manufacturing

Significant expansion of apparel production and exports characterized the Thai industry's second stage, beginning in the mid-1980s and running through the mid-1990s (Table 6.3). This expansion was in part the result of a shift in East Asia's textile trade and production arrangements to "triangle manufacturing," a system in which Western buyers placed orders with suppliers in Korea, Hong Kong, and Taiwan, who in turn shifted production offshore to affiliated factories in low-wage countries, including Thailand.[20] Outward investments by the "Big 3" reflected rising wage rates, currency adjustments and, perhaps most important, limits on exports to the developed country markets imposed by Multi-Fiber Arrangement (MFA) quotas. This was, then, a regional division of labor between high- and low-cost countries, with the latter possessing plenty of unfilled MFA quotas.[21]

---

[15] JICA (1989, II-1).
[16] Unger (1998, 117).
[17] Suphat (1994, 20, Ch. 4).
[18] Book Club Finance (1976, 2–12); JICA (1989, 2:172–173).
[19] Unger (1998, 15–16).
[20] Bair and Gereffi (2002).
[21] Most Northeast Asian textile investment in Thailand came from Hong Kong and Taiwan in the mid-1980s (Kaewjai 1989: 155).

TABLE 6.3 *Volume and Value of Thai Clothing Exports*

	MFA				Non-MFA				Total	
	Million Pieces	Share%	$million	Share%	Million Pieces	Share%	%Million	Share%	Million Pieces	$Million
1977	37	82	68	82	8	18	15	18	45	83
1980	60	58	175	63	44	42	63	37	104	179
1983	89	54	276	72	77	46	106	28	166	382
1987	183	40	800	55	279	60	654	45	462	1454

Source: Thai Ministry of Commerce, cited in Suphat (1990, table 7, p. 63).

The arrangement provided Thai-based firms stable access to the U.S. and western European markets covered by the MFA. But Thai producers exceeded their quotas to the point of triggering U.S. protectionist pressures.

Exporting countries have followed "three escape paths" from protection.[22] One is *upgrading,* the path followed by the Big 3, in which clothing moves toward high-fashion products, fabrics move toward capital-intensive finishing, and fibers shift to capital-intensive synthetic products.[23] The second is *product diversification,* in which countries expand their product scope to include fabrics such as linen, ramie, or synthetic fibers. Thai producers, as we shall see in Section III, mainly followed a third path: *market diversification.*[24]

C. Mid-1990s–2007: Liberalization and the Challenge of Full-package Production

Persistent weaknesses rendered the industry vulnerable to a more challenging set of external conditions in the early-to-mid-1990s. Thailand faced a liberalized textile trade with the end of the MFA in 2005 and the proliferation of at least 10 free trade agreements.[25] The country also began to lose low-wage advantages; by 2005, Thai costs were reportedly higher than those of the Philippines, Sri Lanka, Vietnam, India, Indonesia, Pakistan, Bangladesh, and Malaysia.[26] Finally, global buyers began to change their procurement methods.[27] In the past, global buyers had ordered from intermediaries, who in turn organized inputs and deliveries from different countries. Now, buyers started to source directly from as complete a supply chain as possible within one country, cutting garment makers' lead time by more than half.

The push is for "deeper" localization, for Thailand to become the site of full-package production where garment producers could source fabric locally.[28] Further, global buyers now require the capacity for both large-scale and small-batch production. This shift has led buyers to reduce the number of their principal apparel suppliers. Survivors will be those firms

---

[22] Suphat (1994, 46–47).
[23] Palcaquier et al. (2004).
[24] Suphat (1994, 47).
[25] Chalumporn (2004).
[26] Tait (2005, 17).
[27] This discussion draws on interviews # 84, 93, 96, 100, 101, 104. See also Brooker (2001, 3–11).
[28] Interviews # 100, 101.

belonging to efficient, relatively proximate supply chains involving textile–
garment industry partnerships and capable of "own-design" and "own-
brand" manufacture.[29] Thus, even as opportunities in low-value segments
were reduced by low-wage competitors, new opportunities in high-value
segments have emerged for the Thai garment industry. Taking advantage of
such opportunities required upgrading, however. But unlike market creation
and diversification, upgrading tasks such as equipment modernization and
expansion of technical personnel have proven more difficult (Table 6.4).

II. CREATING AND MANAGING MARKETS: 1960S–EARLY 1980S

Private investment fueled impressive Thai textile growth in the 1960s and
1970s, but its expansion led to a series of production gluts that nearly
bankrupted the industry in the mid-1970s.[30] Though it emerged from this
crisis intact and expanded exports significantly, overcapacity continued to
plague producers, as did weaknesses in products, processes, and linkages
among segments. This section explores variation in Thai achievements
across three sets of tasks: creating, attracting, and retaining significant
private investment; managing overcapacity problems; and upgrading.

A. Investment Promotion and Risk Socialization

Property Rights and Entry Barriers: In the late 1950s, numerous local
traders and importers entered the industry. By 1960, there were 20 textile
firms in Thailand established by 16 different groups of investors,[31] most
with links to Japanese firms.[32] Stable macroeconomic conditions and government import substitution (ISI) policies help to explain this wave of
investment.[33] Quantitative restrictions on imports in the 1950s (replaced by
tariffs in 1968) were supplemented by the 1960 Investment Promotion Act,
which provided tariff and tax exemptions on new textile equipment and
raw materials, as well as tax holidays for new investments.[34] But without
secure property rights and low entry barriers, ISI policies probably would

---

[29] Tait (2005, 19).
[30] Book Club Finance (1976, 13).
[31] Suehiro (1983); Muscat (1994, 117–118).
[32] Hewison (1985); Pasuk and Baker (2000, 136).
[33] Suphat (1989, 19).
[34] Archanun (1995, 34–36).

TABLE 6.4 *Textile Industry Challenges*

Policy Tasks	1960s–Early 1980s	1985–1997	1997–2007
Property rights	Ban expropriation and abandon discrimination against Sino-Thais	NA	NA
Risk socialization	Provide information and financing; avoid bailouts	NA	Responding to 1997 financial crisis
Overcapacity	Reduce production/encourage exports	NA	NA
Linkages	Adjust tariffs and business tax to encourage use of local fiber and fabric	End ban on new spinning and weaving capacity; adjust tariffs (1) to raise pressure on local producers, (2) encourage dyestuff production; expand cotton cultivation; improve wastewater treatment	Adjust domestic taxes and tariffs, improve wastewater treatment, and promote alliances to improve supply chain capacity for quick response
Equipment	Adjust tariffs and stabilize policy to encourage new equipment purchase	Adjust tariffs and condition new licenses on use of new equipment	Improve incentives to update outdated equipment, especially in spinning, weaving, and dyeing
Trade and markets	NA	Coordinate quota allocation and improve data collection to lower entry barriers and encourage upgrading	Prepare for end of MFA in 2005
Technical personnel	NA	Reduce reliance on foreign personnel; expand pool of skilled labor in response to wage growth	Improve supply of operators, engineers, and specialists in design and marketing to move into ODM and OBM

not have had such an impact. The 1960 Investment Promotion Act, as well as World Bank loans banning expropriation of foreign investment, signaled Thailand's move away from its flirtation with anti-(ethnic) Chinese policies and state-led economic nationalism of the early postwar period.[35] The very presence of foreign investors helped protect local firms' investments.[36] Meanwhile, the government's aggressive and nonselective investment strategy lowered entry barriers: the textile industry accounted for the largest category of BOI-promoted firms from 1962 to 1981.[37]

These policy changes complemented the competitive structures of Thai clientelism. Entry to the industry was facilitated by relationships with powerful officials and by a porous bureaucracy.[38] Rivalry among political leaders encouraged bureaucratic fragmentation, resulting in what Danny Unger[39] labeled "laissez-faire by accident" – a system in which "many centers of state regulatory control and their links to different political factions ensured that no single firm or group of firms could block competition from new entrants." This porous set of arrangements also encouraged competition under an otherwise protectionist trade regime by allowing extensive smuggling.

Risk Socialization (without bailouts): Through ongoing consultation and monitoring, Thailand's commercial banks, particularly the Bangkok Bank, provided key information and financing for the industry.[40] In the early 1960s, the Bangkok Bank helped to attract investors through its overseas contacts, especially in Hong Kong. A decade later, it established a textile center that identified and recruited Thai engineering graduates for the industry. It also became a critical source of textile finance: During a slump of the early 1970s, the bank supported local efforts to contend with the withdrawal of Japanese capital, and by the mid-1970s, it was reportedly financing 70–80% of textile manufacturing. It promoted localization by mobilizing capital from rice exporters to save Thai Durable, one of the country's largest spinning and weaving firms, also managing its subsequent sale. A few years later, in response to its concerns about inefficient family management, the bank set up a Textile Credit Center to facilitate

---

[35] Suehiro (1982, 80).
[36] Hewison (1985).
[37] Paopongsakorn and Fuller (1997, 478).
[38] Doner and Ramsay (2000, 157–160).
[39] Unger (1998, 125).
[40] This paragraph draws on Unger (1998, 132–134); Doner and Ramsay (1997, 261); *Business in Thailand* (April 1976, 21); *Bangkok Post* (February 14, 1977); interview # 12; *The Investor* (Bangkok) (July 1978, 47).

information flows between textile producers and the bank and between public and private sectors.

But this socialization of risk did not extend to guaranteed bailouts for inefficient firms. Exit barriers remained relatively low, as illustrated by government's decision to allow the collapse of a large industrial firm, G. S. Cotton Mills, along with the loss of 1,200 jobs, despite numerous appeals from the company.[41] Key to the government's ability to resist such appeals was the cohesion, expertise, and insulation of the Finance Ministry and Central Bank.

B. Overcapacity

With growth came overcapacity and market instability. In 1975, the industry suffered a massive slump due to a global recession, oil price increases, the dumping of cotton fabric by other countries, a month-long strike, and the closing of Thailand's border trade with Indo-China, which had absorbed 30% of production.[42] Massive investments attracted by the industry's initial growth combined with a tendency to stockpile product to lengthen and deepen the downturn resulted in the withdrawal of several large Japanese producers. Yet the industry recovered in the late 1970s, prompting new investments by large Thai firms, as well as by Hong Kong and Taiwan interests.[43] Institutional arrangements of this period account for both the problem of overcapacity and the relative success of its management.

Thai officials had at their disposal control over the whole package of policy tools commonly used to promote industrial growth: tariffs, taxes, subsidized capital, factory licenses, utility rate adjustments, export subsidies, and capacity controls. But officials never developed a consistent vision of how to use these tools on questions of production capacity. In response to market gluts, the MOI imposed a number of bans on new factories in the 1970s and 1980s. When these proved impossible to implement, the MOI granted amnesties to illegal entrants.[44] Problems of implementation reflected the lack of coordination between the MOI and the two other agencies influencing capacity: the BOI, through its investment incentives, and the Ministry of Commerce, through its control of textile equipment

---

[41] Hewison (1989, 169).
[42] JICA (1989, I-126).
[43] Suphat (1994, 20).
[44] Unger (1998, 126–128); Suphat (1994, 32).

imports. The MOI itself was weakened by splits between its Industrial Works Department and its more politically vulnerable Textile Policy Committee. In part to address such problems, the government created an interministerial public–private group in 1977, the Textile Industry Development Committee (TIDC). But political considerations undermined the TIDC. Capacity policy thus seemed "rather jerky ... first too tight and then too loose."[45] Time inconsistency triggered more instability: new firms simply set up shop illegally, while existing firms, fearing reimposition of capacity limits, rushed in with new capacity that exceeded demand expectations.[46] And although the BOI required exports in exchange for investment incentives, many firms simply dumped their goods on the domestic market.

Yet the industry recovered, and Thai textile exports, especially yarn and woven fabrics, grew significantly in the late 1970s.[47] This growth was in part the result of producers' seeking new markets.[48] Exports were also encouraged by state promotion, involving tax rebates on inputs used for exports and direct export subsidies estimated at 20% of total costs.[49] Firm-specific export initiatives and supportive state policies were themselves encouraged by (1) the fact that insulated macroeconomic agencies precluded bailouts and (2) collective action on the part of the private sector, especially the Thai Textiles Manufacturers Association (TTMA) and the Bangkok Bank.

This second institutional effort helped Thai producers to avoid "a real catastrophe."[50] Recall that reducing overcapacity requires broad participation by and information about an industry's firms, even as it holds the potential for firm-specific losses. The TTMA responded to these challenges by organizing a series of production cartels. Based on extensive consultation and monitoring, these typically consisted of agreements on limits on firms' production capacity monitored by an association committee; agreements on floor prices; associational pressure for export-promoting policies, such as tariff rebates on imported inputs; association-wide agreement on quality of exports, monitored by an association committee; permission to increase production capacity in line with export performance; sharing of large

---

[45] *Business in Thailand* (June 1978, 34).
[46] *Thailand Business* (March 1981, 66–67); Archanun (1995, 48).
[47] Archanun (1995, 44–45).
[48] Interview # 12.
[49] Archanun (1995, 44–45).
[50] *Business Review* (June 1978, 410–414); The rest of this account is based on Doner and Ramsay (2000, 162–167).

export orders among TTMA members; and provision of the association's stamp of approval for commercial bank lending, especially from the Bangkok Bank to textile producers.

Still, these achievements were limited. The cartels had limited capacity to sanction defectors.[51] Overcapacity continued to be a serious problem into the 1980s, until firms became more accustomed to the cyclical nature of demand, more cautious about reinvesting, and more engaged in sub-contracting to address surges in demand. And as temporary arrangements working with fragmented, politicized state agencies, the cartels lacked the means to upgrading challenges.

C. Linkages and Technology

In contrast to its overall growth, the Thai textile industry exhibited little innovation and deepening of intersegment linkages in this first period. This is not to minimize the presence of modern upstream and midstream operations or improved yarn quality as reflected in yarn export growth. But most modern operations were under Japanese ownership or control.[52] As late as 1987, key production and managerial functions were the responsibility of either Japanese or overseas Chinese personnel.[53] Outdated equipment was becoming a major problem, especially in spinning and dyeing/finishing.[54] Finally, linkages within the textile value chain were weak.[55]

Public policy was partly responsible for these weaknesses. According to one analysis, state strategy influenced textile production largely "by restraining the best use of ... new technology."[56] The BOI focused on jobs and foreign exchange; its strategy was to solicit and obtain as much FDI as possible, not to screen investments for technology transfer potential.[57] High tariffs and periodic surcharges also encouraged low-quality dye producers and a general focus on low-quality, low-price domestic markets. They also discouraged quality improvement in yarns and fibers and the use of modern textile equipment.[58] Because tariffs on semi-finished products were equal to or less than those on raw materials, many weavers opted to import finished

[51] Kanitha (1985, 28).
[52] Apinya (1984, 79);"Textiles." (*Business Review*, April 1982, 64)
[53] Tambunlertchai and Yamazawa (1983, 61).
[54] *Prachachat Thurakit* (September 2, 1982, 9).
[55] *Business in Thailand* (June 1983, 24).
[56] Archanun (1995, 52).
[57] Unger (1998, 126–127).
[58] Archanun (1995, 44, table 3.4); *The Investor* (September 1976, 45).

yarn rather than to demand better quality from local fiber suppliers.[59] Because business taxes were imposed on domestic inputs at each stage of processing, moreover, entirely domestic products suffered a higher tax burden than those that using imported inputs.[60]

Poor policy implementation in tariff and capacity controls also fueled tension among segments, especially between fiber producers and spinners. Government efforts to overcome differences through negotiations with the Thai Synthetic Fibre Manufacturers Association and the TTMA generally led to the following dynamic:[61] (1) large spinning and weaving firms imported fiber, especially polyester, from Taiwan; (2) complaints by local fiber producers about market gluts due to cheap imports led to temporary, government-imposed surcharges on imported fibers; (3) the surcharges led to complaints from spinners that protection weakened their own export competitiveness; (4) the government ended or reduced protection for fibers; (5) in anticipation of a new surcharge, spinners and weavers stocked up on fiber and yarn; (6) this in turn prompted the fiber producers to plead for and often receive a further surcharge extension; (7) the larger spinners, especially those that integrated spinning and weaving, responded by raising yarn prices charged to (typically smaller) weavers who themselves were attempting to expand exports.

Poor policy implementation also discouraged the use of modern equipment: Because producers, especially spinners and weavers, could never be sure whether surcharges or capacity controls would be re-imposed, most responded to market openings by expanding capacity rather than investing in expensive equipment. Compounding this dynamic were high tariffs on new equipment. In principle, tariffs on equipment for export production were to be rebated, but rebates often took months, tying up scarce capital and further discouraging expensive investments for an uncertain market.[62]

These problems were not the result of ignorance. Firms and government officials were well aware of the industry's weaknesses and interested in combining export promotion with innovation and linkages.[63] The problem

[59] *Business in Thailand* (June 1983, 24).

[60] IMC (1985, 109); see also Suphat (1994, 26).

[61] The rest of this account is based on interview # 42. This summary is based on *Business Review* (June 1978, 410–414); *The Investor* (September 1976, 41); *Business in Thailand* (June 1978, 34–39); *Prachachaart Thurakit* (November 27 1982, 10–11); *Prahchachaart Thurakit* (August 28, 1982, 1–2); and articles in *Prachachaart Thurakit* (April 20, 1983: 13; June 18, 1983: 1, 15); Orsini (1978).

[62] *Prachachaart Thurakit* (September 2, 1982, 9; May 25, 1983, 11).

[63] *The Investor* (Bangkok) (July 1978, 47); Juanjai and Suvit (1985, 88).

lay in institutional weaknesses. As early as 1972, the MOI established a Textile Industry Division (TID) to develop and implement technology improvement in the upstream and midstream sectors. This division was staffed by six Thais sent by the Ministry to institutions such as North Carolina State and Georgia Tech for graduate training in textile technology. On returning and finding key positions dominated by foreigners, these returnees set up a BA curriculum in textile engineering at a local technology institute, as well as pilot plants and laboratories for quality control and research.[64] But within a decade, the TID "had lost its dynamism;" its equipment was outdated, and many of its technical staff jumped to the expanding private sector, which paid little attention to the agency.[65] In 1975, the MOI established the Committee to Assist Textile Manu-facturers.[66] Designed *both* to expand exports and to promote greater incorporation of domestic inputs, this group also had little impact and was superseded in 1977 by the TIDC. The TIDC lacked not only the credibility to sanction defectors, as noted earlier, but also the ability to monitor and help the industry to address technological problems in response to over-production or protectionism. The committee's response to stricter U.S. quotas in the second MFA (1978) was limited to support for export market diversification. Nor was the TIDC, working through the relevant associa-tions, able to promote agreement on prices between upstream and mid-stream producers.[67] The industry was organized into associations representing fiber producers, spinners, weavers, and garment producers. Often internally fragmented, these groups were incapable of industry-wide collective action, especially on tariffs.[68] Concern with this fragmentation led to the establishment of a peak National Federation of Thai Textile Industries (NFTTI) in 1979, but the Federation, too, was largely impotent on upgrading issues, as the following section will show.

D. Explaining Outcomes

The textile industry's impressive growth in this period owed much to the ways in which the country's competitive clientelism, fragmented bureau-cracy, insulated macroeconomic agencies, and multisectoral commercial banks encouraged secure property rights, kept entry barriers low, and

---

[64] Interviews # 4, 99.
[65] Juanjai and Suvit (1985, 22).
[66] *The Investor* (September 1976, 35–36).
[67] *Prachachat Thurakit* (April 20, 1983).
[68] Ibid.

socialized risks. These same arrangements were partially successful in addressing overcapacity problems through exports, but they were distinctly unsuccessful in promoting linkages and innovation.

Industry-specific considerations as well as national factors discouraged institutional arrangements designed to promote innovation and linkages. Effective governance in textiles involved the coordination of a large number of industry segments relative to sugar or autos, each of which could thrive on its own during this period. Also, because the more protected upstream sectors were more capital-intensive, they comprised fewer firms and had greater capacity for collective action relative to the more export-oriented garment producers.[69] And finally, despite its problems, the textile industry ran trade surpluses.

Broader political factors also inhibited reform. As discussed in Chapter 4, democratization in the mid-1970s had led to the balkanization and politicization of the ministries responsible for textiles (Commerce and Industry). Even with the return to authoritarian rule, the 1978 constitution enlarged the cabinet, expanding opportunities for political influence in the Commerce, Industry, and Agriculture ministries. According to one industry executive, despite ostensible capacity limits, Industry ministers received around 50 baht for each additional spindle approved.[70] Finally, technocratic control over budgets and borrowing deteriorated in the face of political influence, with the Prime Minister acting as his own finance minister for almost a year in 1979 and 1980.[71]

The industry grew during this period in part due to these very weaknesses. But the debt crisis and U.S. protectionism in the early-to-mid-1980s stimulated both a greater interest in textile industry restructuring and broader institutional strengthening that would seem to augur well for upgrading.

III. MARKET DIVERSIFICATION WITHOUT UPGRADING: 1985–1997

In the early 1980s, Thailand's debt crisis and subsequent austerity measures threw the textile industry into a slump: many small mills closed, larger firms ran at partial capacity, and the industry overall suffered annual losses of 1–2 billion baht during the early-to-mid-1980s.[72] Exports slowed and faced

---

[69] JICA (1989: II-176, I-14).
[70] Interview # 52.
[71] Doner and Laothamatas (1994, 418–419).
[72] "The Textile Industry" (1987).

further threats from U.S. protectionism.[73] The U.S. imposed an embargo in response to Thai exports' having exceeded group limits. But by 1986, the industry began an export-led rebound (Table 6.3), and the 1986–1988 period became known as the industry's "golden years."[74] Much of this initial resurgence involved exports to new, less-demanding, non-MFA markets (Table 6.3). These included sales to border areas (reportedly 13% of total production) and to Middle East markets, driven initially by the large Thai workforce in the region.[75] Subsequent growth involved garment exports to quota-free Japan, often handled by Taiwan and Hong Kong investors anxious to take advantage of currency shifts. Rising labor costs, however, cut Thai exports to some traditional, low-end markets, such as Indonesia, China, and Bangladesh, and producers from these same countries were beginning to compete successfully with Thailand in other markets.[76] Thai producers gained new access to the U.S. market in 1994 after Washington cut quotas for Thailand's competitors and U.S. rules of origins discouraged Hong Kong garment exports.[77]

Currency and trade factors thus encouraged a shift of garment production from Northeast to Southeast Asian countries, including Thailand, as part of the triangle manufacturing system noted earlier. Thailand's ability to take advantage of this arrangement owed much to the country's smart macroeconomic management, including its 1984 devaluation, and the hard budget constraints reviewed earlier in this book. As discussed later, there were also some important successes in breaking up oligopolistic structures that encouraged the industry's flexibility.

Yet industry leaders worried that this growth – based largely on weakened competition, external demand, a devalued currency, and cheap labor – was not sustainable.[78] Garment exports were growing, but the industry's export ratio was low relative to its total production, and upstream and midstream production could not meet the needs of downstream producers. Concern with these problems, especially in the context of the country's debt-induced vulnerability, stimulated public–private consultations, studies of the industry, and requests for textile legislation to provide information

[73] Textile growth rates were 37.3% in 1980, 44.2% in 1981, 11.1% in 1983, 38.4% in 1984, 19.6% in 1985, 35.3% in 1986, and 76.4% in 1987 (JICA 1989: Table II-1–3).
[74] Sung (1991, 32).
[75] Hill and Suphachalasai (1992, 326).
[76] *The Nation* (December 28, 1991, B8); Pavinee (1994, 24).
[77] *Bangkok Post* (December 30, 1994, 31–32).
[78] "The Textile Industry" (1987, 46).

on and coordinate industry reform.[79] These in turn prompted efforts to address weaknesses in local linkages, technical personnel, equipment, and foreign market management.

A. Linkages

The growing reliance of local garment producers on imported fabrics reflected the weaknesses of Thailand's domestic-oriented upstream and midstream sectors.[80] In response, government and industry leaders attempted to expand the local supply of synthetic and cotton inputs and to rectify weaknesses in local dyeing and printing capacity.[81]

Synthetic Inputs: Thailand initiated two sets of strategies to improve the supply of synthetic fibers, yarns, and fabrics. The first, more successful measure, initiated in 1987, involved ending the government's prohibition on investment in new capacity in spinning and weaving. Promotional privileges for new facilities were conditioned on export goals and on plans to use new equipment.[82] These measures broke the oligopolistic power of large fiber makers and spinners; stimulated a significant growth in more efficient foreign producers, especially from Taiwan;[83] and opened the way for increases in the numbers of Thai-based producers in all segments (Table 6.5). The success of this effort reflected the relatively small number of actors required to end the ban and a key set of distributional considerations: the increased influence of weaving and garment producers whose continued growth required improved access to inputs; and the reduced influence of textile interests in the Chart Thai Party, which had helped to impose the ban in the first place.[84] On the other hand, the government's efforts at conditioning incentives on the use of *new* equipment lacked credibility. State officials could not monitor equipment usage (see later); they also weakened this condition in 1988 out of fear that new equipment requirements would deter foreign investment.[85]

---

[79] Studies include Ajanant (1983); Ajanant and Suvit (1985); Suehiro (1983); UNIDO (1984). On proposals for legislation and the NESDB's active role, see *The Nation Review* (January 31, 1985, 26). On increased activity by industry associations, see *The Nation* and *The Bangkok Post* (1983–1986).

[80] *Textile Asia* (September 1991, 30).

[81] JICA (1989, I-109).

[82] *Textile Asia*, (June 1987).

[83] Nikorn et al. (1997, 11); interview # 43.

[84] *Textile Asia*, (June 1987).

[85] *Textile Asia* (July 1988, 106).

TABLE 6.5 *Number of Thai Textile Firms (1987–1993)*

Year	Manmade (Synthetic) Fibers	Spinning	Weaving	Garments
1987	7	65	694	1,168
1988	7	76	778	1,350
1989	8	80	915	1,574
1990	9	96	1,038	1,796
1991	11	115	1,202	2,029
1992	13	126	1,255	2,211
1993	16	131	1,356	2,530

Sources: Suphat (1992, 5); Ministry of Commerce cited in Nikorn et al. (1997, 7).

The second strategy, tariff liberalization to increase competitive pressure on local producers, was partially successful. The effort began in 1985 when Thai officials initiated a Restructuring Committee (RESCOM) to improve the country's industrial competitiveness. RESCOM engaged MOI officials with the associations through the creation of a National Textile Policy Committee to promote apparel exports with higher local value added, lower prices, and higher quality in upstream and midstream products.[86] These negotiations led to a fall in overall protection rates and surcharges by the late 1980s.[87] But tariffs on upstream and midstream products actually *rose* during the 1980s (Table 6.6), and they remained higher than those of other Asian countries.[88] Tariff rebates provided some relief but suffered from administrative delays that reduced their utility, especially for smaller firms.[89] As seen in Table 6.6, further liberalization occurred in the early-to-mid-1990s during Prime Minister Anand's push for an ASEAN Free Trade Agreement. Anand's Ministry of Finance assigned the NFTTI, the peak textile association, to explore ways in which the industry could prepare for AFTA's liberalization.[90] But distributional tensions limited reform: the protectionist demands of Thailand's newly established petrochemical industry collided with the needs of petroleum-dependent fiber producers for greater competitiveness.[91] Government plans called for an overall tariff

[86] *Prachachaart Thurakit*, (November 16, 1983, 1, 10); IMC (1985).
[87] Robinson, Byeon, and Teja. (1991, 28).
[88] JICA (1989, I-9; II-183).
[89] Interviews # 10, 14; see also JICA (1989: II-67), and TTIS (1993, 2).
[90] See, e.g., TTIS (1993, 4; 27); *Bangkok Post* (November 30, 1991, 22); and *The Nation* (November 30, 1991, B20).
[91] The following discussions draws on: *The Nation*. (May 19, 1992, 24; November 11, 1992; December 20, 1991, B1). On NESDB restructuring efforts, see Wisan and Grewe (1994).

TABLE 6.6 *Tariffs and Surcharges in Thai Textiles*

	1974	1978	1982	1992	1995	1997
Synthetic fiber	20(30)	20 (30)	20(15)	30	20	10
Synthetic yarn	20	20	22	30	20	10
Cotton yarn	25	25	27	30	20	10
Fabrics	60	80	66	60	40	20
Clothing	60	100	66	60	45	30

Source: Textile Intelligence Unit, Textiles Industry Division, Ministry of Industry, cited in Suphat (1998).
Note: Figures in parentheses refer to surcharges as % of c.i.f. import price.

restructuring while also placing petrochemicals on AFTA's "fast track" liberalization, under which an industry would have 5–7 years, rather than the customary 15, to reduce protection. However, petrochemical interests lobbied successfully to block this fast-track provision.

Cotton Inputs: The country experienced even greater difficulties in promoting local production of cotton to meet downstream demand. As garment exports rose, Thailand's self-sufficiency ratio in raw cotton fell from 40% in 1980 to around 15 in 1990 and under 10 at the end of the decade.[92] A series of efforts at expanding local cotton production faltered as fragmented agricultural institutions proved incapable of coordinating multiple interests, providing farmers with new information, and overcoming distributional tensions.

In the late 1970s, the TTMA and the MOA promoted cultivation of high-quality cotton by providing inputs and financing to farmers in exchange for guaranteed purchases by TTMA members. But the MOA lacked technical expertise, warehouses, and close ties with cotton growers, who ended up selling their product to local middlemen rather than to the textile association.[93] Due to numerous pest infestations that discouraged cotton production, subsequent efforts focused on integrated pest management (IPM). But disputes between research and extension services within the Department of Agriculture resulted in an information gap between state agencies and farmers. Also, the need for cotton to supply the country's growing textile industry resulted in a tariff policy that encouraged cotton imports, undermined the competitiveness of domestic cotton, and raised the risks to local producers. These factors, along with pressures from pesticide

[92] *Textile Asia* (February 1990, 93); Castella et al. (1999, figure 7).
[93] *Business Review* (June 1978, 404–405); *Business in Thailand* (January 1985, 38).

producers, impeded efforts to reconcile the needs of farmers with ginners and with the middlemen who constitute key sources of finance and information. Crop protection problems prompted conflicting approaches among stakeholders depending on their goals and their relationships with growers. The result was a gradual adaptation to cotton shortages. With domestic producers meeting less than 10% of industry needs, importing cotton became easier and safer than a large-scale IPM program that would have expanded and stabilized domestic supply.[94]

Dyeing and Printing: In the mid-1990s, Thailand lacked the dyeing and printing capacity necessary to produce finished fabrics with export-level quality and variety, especially compared to regional competitors. As a result, Thai garment exporters were increasing imports of finished fabric, while half of local fabric exports involved low-priced, untreated "gray cloth."[95] The lack of capacity resulted from several factors, most importantly tariffs on dyestuffs – the raw materials for dyeing and printing – and wastewater treatment facilities that could not meet European environmental restrictions.

Dyestuffs, which require heavy petrochemical inputs, make up over 40% of dyers' costs. Until the late 1980s, Thailand had only two dyestuff firms, neither capable of providing the volumes or quality required by garment exporters.[96] In order to promote local petrochemical production, the Thai government provided extensive tariff protection for dyestuff producers. But by the mid-1990s, duties on dyestuffs had been significantly reduced, despite opposition from dyestuff producers and their political supporters. This success was due in part to support from the Finance Ministry, which, prior to the (1992) VAT, had opposed liberalization due to short-term revenue losses. It was also the result of a general political opening that reduced the influence over textiles of one party, Chart Thai, which had significant interests in existing dyestuff firms A final factor was the cross-industry consultation promoted by the MOI's Textile Industry Division. In 1992, prompted by both Anand's liberalization push and pressure from downstream producers, TID officials coordinated the creation of the Association of Thai Textile Bleaching, Dyeing Printing and Finishing Industries (ATDP). The TID/ATDP alliance organized working groups to provide evidence that the dyestuff producers were themselves starting to

---

[94] Castella et al. (1999).
[95] JICA (1989, I-109); Arthit (1994).
[96] Information in this paragraph is drawn from Arthit (1994); and interviews # 11, 13, 26, 28, 31, 33, 35, 36, 39.

export and no longer needed much protection, and that an important competitor, Indonesia, had cut its duties on dyestuffs to 5% in July 1994. Finally, the ATDP began developing linkages with local dyestuff producers by offering to increase local dyestuff purchases provided that local producers demonstrated higher quality.

The water issue was more difficult to resolve. Expanding dyeing and printing capacity required reducing water usage and improving wastewater treatment.[97] This issue became especially compelling in the early 1990s as the EU threatened to close its markets to producers with poor environmental standards. Two sets of government responses to this challenge failed. One involved creating industrial estates in which dyers and printers could share water treatment facilities. But the difficulties involved – the provision of large volumes of water, the new technologies, and the need to organize numerous firms with often different kinds of operations – were well beyond state institutional capacities and deterred potential investors.[98] A second strategy – new, strict, government-mandated standards for industrial effluents – was pursued largely without consultation with the dyers and printers themselves.[99] That such an effort lacked cohesion is not surprising in light of what one study labeled "institutional stress": Thailand had "some 30 department-level agencies under seven different ministries" managing its water.[100]

An increasingly organized private sector responded with efforts to obtain information about new water treatment technologies and to monitor standards enforcement.[101] The head of the TTMA initiated a three-year process in which dyers and printers worked with foreign experts to learn about alternative standards and pollution prevention and treatment. The ATDP helped to enforce the new pollution standards by developing in-house environmental expertise, monitoring member practices, and threatening to report firms to the MOI that failed to improve wastewater practices. This marked a significant shift away from the past practice of simply paying off the MOI's environmental inspectors; it was predicated on the desire to stop firms unwilling or unable to pay for environmental equipment and modifications from free riding on those who did so.

---

[97] Prasert (2001).
[98] *The Nation* (July 2, 1992, B10); *Textile Asia*, (January 1990, 82, and October 1991, 68–69).
[99] *Bangkok Post* (January 8 1990, 28); *Bangkok Post* (April 17, 1990, 19); *Bangkok Post* (July 17, 1991, 1).
[100] *The Nation* (September 17, 1993, B3).
[101] This analysis is based on interviews # 23, 106; Prasert (2001).

These efforts helped to expand midstream capacity. Several new dyeing/printing firms entered the industry, while existing spinning/weaving operations expanded into dyeing/printing, resulting in a total of some 400 firms, of which 200 could reportedly meet global standards.[102] But the middle segment remained weak, in part due to persistent shortages of fresh water and wastewater treatment facilities.[103]

B. Technical Personnel

In 1987, in the midst of the Thai textile industry's "golden years," the head of the NFTTI warned that sustained growth required an expansion of textile-related technical personnel.[104] He noted that whereas textile production in Thailand and Taiwan had begun at roughly the same time, Taiwan far surpassed Thailand in textile-specific educational institutions and trained individuals (Table 6.7). Thai firms relied heavily on foreign technical personnel, often from Hong Kong or Taiwan. As Thai labor costs increased and the industry faced new market pressures in the 1990s, firms began to need not only engineers and technicians but also designers and chemists able to help textile producers shift from the large lot orders required by lower-value Middle East markets to the small-batch production demanded by U.S. and buyers.[105]

These problems were most pressing for garment producers for whom labor was a significant percentage of costs and who were most directly

TABLE 6.7 *Textile Graduates: Thailand and Taiwan (1987)*

	Taiwan	Thailand
Vocational	8,862	1,091
Diploma (vocational education)	24,172	550
Diploma (technical education)	0	77
Bachelors	2,753	405
Masters	183	0
Ph.D.	4	0
Total with textile degrees	35,974	2,123

Source: "The Textile Industry" (1987, 47).

[102] Interview # 64.
[103] Pavinee (1994, 28).
[104] "The Textile Industry" (1987).
[105] Information on technical labor shortages from *Bangkok Post* (July 17 1993, 15); interviews # 3, 5, 6, 7; Pavinee (1994) 28.

exposed to foreign market pressures for better quality and delivery times. The principal and most successful human resource effort therefore came from large garment exporters in the Thai Garment Manufacturers Association (TGMA): the Thai Garment Development Fund (TGDF). Initiated in 1991 by TGMA members and a local university, the effort began by drawing on U.S. consultants and Hong Kong's Clothing Industry Training Authority (CITA) to train industry instructors across the country to improve the efficiency of sewing machine operators.[106] The instability of TGDF funding, which relied on the Commerce Minister's releasing MFA quotas for auction, imposed limits on TGDF activities, but even this limited effort stands out as a success relative to the industry's negligible achievements in the training prior to 1997.[107]

C. Equipment Modernization

A 1991 Bangkok Bank report concluded that inferior technology was still the industry's main weakness and that most equipment had been in use for at least 20 years.[108] The government, in consultation with the associations, adopted two responses to this problem. One, noted earlier, involved conditioning privileges for new facilities on plans to use new equipment. The other was to lower duties on new equipment if used for exports.

While useful, this shift had limited effects due to problems within the state.[109] One problem involved the Thai Customs Department, whose agents were more interested in revenue generation than in technological improvement and who arbitrarily classified industrial goods as consumer goods. Haggling over these issues consumed time and money and impeded equipment upgrading. A second problem was a lack of data on productivity-related issues, such as the state of equipment.[110] Only in 1989, when a Japanese aid organization conducted a large-scale study,[111] did such data become available, and even this effort was not continued in the 1990s. The TID and the MOC both attempted to collect data, but firms were reluctant to share information for fear of tax ramifications. Without effective monitoring capacities, state efforts to encourage equipment upgrading lacked

---

[106] Information on the TGDF based on interviews # 19, 96, 101, 101.
[107] Brimble and Doner (2007).
[108] *Bangkok Post Weekly Review* (June 7, 1991, 11).
[109] *Bangkok Post* (July 17, 1993, 15); interview # 15; *The Nation.* (May 19, 1992, 24).
[110] *Textile Asia* (February 1987, 48); JICA (1989); interviews # 5, 38, 39; *Lok Thurakit Naew Naa,* February 28, 1, 7).
[111] JICA (1989).

credibility. Although the textile associations expressed concern about productivity, their focus was largely on ensuring foreign market access

D. Managing Foreign Trade

Since its inception in 1975, the MFA provided Thailand with key export markets by limiting the exports of the "Big 3" textile producers: Hong Kong, South Korea, and Taiwan. Thailand's MFA markets, covered by quotas, remained critical to the industry during most of the 1990s . Allocating these quotas among industry segments and between large and small firms preoccupied both public and private sectors, particularly in the mid-1980s, when Washington, having discovered that Thailand had exceeded group limits stipulated in the 1982 agreement between the two countries, threatened to embargo Thai textiles.[112] Thailand's response to this market saturation problem emphasized market diversification, not upgrading: garments shifted to nonquota markets, including Singapore, Japan, Panama, and the Gulf.[113]

Key features of Thailand's quota system help to explain this outcome. The system was jointly managed by the industry associations and the Commerce Ministry's Department of Foreign Trade (DFT).[114] Basic or principal quotas, 80% of the total, were allocated to exporters based on past performance, while the remaining 20%, known as central or residual quotas, were based on unfilled basic quotas and/or the Commerce Ministry's decision to reserve a percentage of total quotas for this category. Most of the residual quota was allocated to new producers based largely on their utilization of domestic inputs, price per unit, and domestic value-added. The system thus allocated basic quotas to large exporters with strong sales histories. This arrangement had two important strengths: it ensured that available quotas were filled, and it encouraged smaller exporters, who had difficulty obtaining quotas, to become resourceful in penetrating nonquota markets.

There were also serious flaws: Finding it easier to capitalize on rents from past performance, established producers had little incentive to move into higher value-added products or more demanding markets.[115] In principle,

---

[112] *Lok Thruakit Naewnaa (Progressive Business World)*, (August–November 1985).

[113] Paopongsakorn and Pawadee (1998, 315).

[114] The following summary excludes details on frequent modifications to the system. It is based on (Suphat 1994, 57–64); Kaewjai (1989). There were actually two systems – one for yarn and fabrics, the larger one for garments. Our focus here is on the garment system.

[115] Paopongsakorn and Pawadee (1998, 315).

the value-added and local input criteria of residual quota allocation should have promoted upgrading, but only around 15% of total quotas were based on such criteria, and small firms were typically unable to fulfill them.[116] Without improvements in midstream and upstream inputs, the system's very success in encouraging large, modern garment producers to fulfill quotas actually impeded local sourcing. *Specifically, under triangle manufacturing, Thai garment producers received consigned orders from overseas buyers, which they were encouraged to fill using foreign fabrics. This allowed garment exports to grow without linkages to upstream suppliers.*[117] Because nonquota markets were characterized by unstable orders for low-priced, simple products, the newer firms that focused on such markets could not afford to invest in modern equipment or even to hire regular workers; rather, they used small, unregistered subcontractors.[118] This dualistic structure was plagued by conflicts, most involving protests by smaller firms over its domination by the larger, established firms who ran the TGMA.[119] Finally, some firms operated solely to set up quotas and did no actual production.[120]

Thailand's diversification-without-upgrading response to market saturation reflected a particular set of institutional capacities, as well as underlying political forces. The Ministry of Commerce's Department of Export Promotion, working with the TGMA, constituted a mini-corporatist pocket of excellence in the development of new markets. But Commerce lacked the capacity to gather and monitor basic data. Indeed, its Department of Foreign Trade (DFT) was unaware of the overshipments that prompted the U.S. embargo.[121] Dominated by the Social Action Party (SAP), the MOC also politicized quota allocation, limiting the potential for using quota rents to promote competitiveness. The ministry had the power to vary the percentage of quota reserved for the residual category, to keep those percentages secret, and to allocate quotas in return for bribes. Such bribes enriched ministers and financed SAP electoral campaigns. This system encouraged firms to engage in lobbying and bribing.[122] The Anand governments did make allocations more transparent and set aside a small

---

[116] Suphat (1994, 60).

[117] JICA 1989, (II-2).

[118] Paopongsakorn and Pawadee (1998, 315).

[119] For example, *Lok Thurakit Naew Naa*, (various issues, February–December 1985); *Textile Asia*, (May 1985, 15)

[120] "Garment makers set up marketing firm." *The Nation* (December 7, 2004).

[121] *Textile Asia* Dec. (1985, 119–120).

[122] Kaewjai (1989, 274–275).

portion of basic quotas to reward firms exporting to new markets, but by injecting new uncertainties into the system, these changes also reduced government credibility in the industry.

E. Explaining Outcomes

The textile industry's uneven performance in this period can be attributed to the impact of a growing number of veto players and to initially intense but overall moderate systemic pressures. Recall that the 1985–1996 period encompassed Prem's quasi-democracy (until 1988) followed by a succession of unstable democratic regimes. Under the policy side of Prem's "pork-policy compromise," a small number of veto players in the macroeconomic agencies implemented exchange rate and fiscal reforms that allowed Thai firms to take advantage of regional producers searching for low-cost production sites with available quotas. The pork side, in which increasingly diverse parties dominated line ministries, lowered entry barriers for new, often smaller entrants by reducing the power of traditionally dominant interests, especially those under the Chart Thai Party.[123] Increased political competition after 1988 gave a further boost to this process. The combination of early macroeconomic reforms with increasing political competition was highly beneficial with regard to *market opening* in fibers, spinning, and dyestuffs. In addition, the industry's weaknesses, in the context of Thailand's debt crisis, stimulated intense associational activities and an impressive set of upgrading initiatives in tariffs, equipment, and training.

But these same factors limited the results of upgrading initiatives. Intensified party competition resulted in coalitional instability whose most obvious impact was to delay the creation of what was to be the institutional anchor of textile upgrading: the Thai Textile Institute (ThTI). The ThTI was proposed in 1985 by MOI technocrats. Despite strong support from the TID and many sectors of the industry, it was not established until 1996, and its role was minimal until almost a decade later.[124] The delay was due in part to splits among the industry's diverse segments and conflicts between government and industry over financing and control – the same distributional tensions that undermined the National Cane and Sugar Research Institute (Chapter 5). Final approval of the ThTI was also blocked by the short tenure of Thailand's post-Prem governments. That the ThTI did

---

[123] *Textile Asia,* (January 1985, 106–107; July 1988).
[124] The most comprehensive review of the ThTI is Arthit (1996). This analysis also draws on interviews # 8, 20, 26.

finally see the light of day reflected a growing fear that exports would slump. This concern intensified when over 1,000 workers at Thai Durable, a large, integrated producer, went on strike for two weeks to protest the firm's layoff of 376 workers from the firm's weaving department, ostensibly to make room for modern, labor-saving equipment.[125] In response, Thai officials rushed the ThTI's official approval just before the fall of the Banharn government in 1997, but without clarifying the degree to which the state vs. industry would finance the institute.[126]

Political competition further encouraged parties to use ministerial positions as sources of party financing. Fragmentation even limited the benefits of market opening: while applauding the end of the government ban on new fiber and yarn producers, observers anticipated that without an equivalent expansion of dyeing and printing activities, upstream growth would overload the midstream and perpetuate the industry's imbalance.[127] And multiple veto players inhibited institutional strengthening. In the absence of credible initiatives to improve productivity, state officials discouraged associational cohesion and public–private consultation, except on tariff issues.

This expansion of veto players and institutional weakening occurred as vulnerability pressures eased. With the improvement in Thailand's overall debt situation, RESCOM's activities ended at partial tariff liberalization. An export boom in textiles allowed for increasing politicization of the MOI and an end to industry-wide coordination. But the particular nature of the textile recovery was especially injurious to intersectoral linkages: because garment firms under triangle manufacturing had the opportunity to obtain high-quality inputs from foreign sources, downstream pressure on local fiber and fabric suppliers was moderate. The latter, meanwhile, could sell unprocessed or low-quality goods to non-MFA markets.

IV. AMBITIOUS, TRUNCATED REFORMS: 1997–2007

Upgrading efforts were especially prominent in the 1997–2007 period. The precipitous fall in textile exports just before the 1997 crisis confirmed fears about the industry's weaknesses. With upstream segments still unable to satisfy the demands of garment producers for quality and variety, and with labor costs rising, textiles was becoming known as a "sunset industry" that was "coming apart at the seams."[128] This prediction proved premature, as

---

[125] Eckardt (1993); *Bangkok Post* (July 17, 1993, 15).
[126] Interview # 47.
[127] *Textile Asia* (October 1987, 90–91).
[128] "Teijin Polyester" (1998).

exports rebounded somewhat in subsequent years (Figure 6.2). But Thailand's share of global textile trade had fallen from 2.3% in 1996 to 1.8% in 2004.[129] And with some exceptions, the rebound was based largely on a combination of weak currency, market diversification, and U.S. and EU limits on Chinese imports, not on upgrading.[130]

These weaknesses were especially troubling in light of three sets of pressures. First, the industry's reliance on imported cloth translated into yearly foreign exchange losses of 40 billion baht at a time when foreign exchange was a major concern.[131] Second, the industry was facing increased competition. Under AFTA, Thailand was committed to cut duties on textiles to 5% or lower in 2000. The MFA was scheduled to expire in 2005, thus ending Thailand's guaranteed access to quota markets. China, Vietnam, and other countries with lower labor costs, improving skills, and increasing FDI flows were lowering textile prices by as much as 30% and cutting into Thailand's lower end markets in the Middle East and Eastern Europe.[132] By 2005, the baht's appreciation was wiping out the industry's exchange rate advantages. Finally, pressures for deeper local sourcing were growing. These included FTA "yarn forward" provisions that required Thai-made garments to use local fabrics,[133] as well as global buyers' demands for lower prices, better quality, and quick response.[134] This combination of pressures was expected to result in the closing of more than 20% of textile and garment factories and layoffs of over 101,000 workers as global buyers sourced from larger, more integrated producers.[135]

Thai officials and business leaders responded to these problems with an unprecedented number of policy proposals and initiatives focused on upgrading and emphasizing public–private engagement by the governments of both Chuan Leekpai (1997–2000) and Thaksin Shinawatra 2001–2006). Textiles were a key focus of the Chuan government's IRP, under which the ThTI was responsible for developing a productivity index and implementing a (1997–2001) Master Plan for textiles. Thaksin's emphasis on upgrading was especially ambitious: through 66 ThTI-administered projects, he aimed

---

[129] *The Nation.* (May 22 2004).

[130] IFCT (2003, 2); *Financial Times Information.* (December 20, 2006).

[131] "Textile agencies ready for progress." *The Nation* (May 11, 19991).

[132] IFCT (2003, 42); *The Nation* (September 10, 2007); Suwanee (1998).

[133] Tait (2005).

[134] "Textile exporters urged to focus on supply chain." *The Nation* (May 28, 1999). interviews # 109, 114.

[135] "End of quotas will see winners, losers in Thailand's textile industry." *Bangkok Post.* (December 20, 2004, 1).

to make Thailand Asia's fashion hub. By developing Thai designs and brands, the industry aimed to produce high-fashion garments, in which China was not specializing.[136] Initiatives under both Chuan and Thaksin focused on equipment modernization, technical training, and supply chain development. Some aspects of the supply chain effort, especially market liberalization, yielded real benefits, while others, especially private sector integration and alliance moves, held significant potential. But most efforts aimed at upgrading delivered only limited benefits. By 2006, Thailand's major hope for sustained textile growth was access to foreign markets.

A. Equipment Modernization

In the mid-to-late 1990s, most dyeing and printing equipment in Thailand was 20–30- years old;[137] spinning and weaving equipment was equally outdated, and computerized cutting, pattern and grading, and conveyor equipment machines were in short supply. To encourage the purchase of new equipment, the government established a loan fund in 1997 to be administered by the ThTI with TGMA support. It attracted few applicants.[138] Firms were reluctant to invest in new equipment during a slump, and devaluation raised the cost of imported machines. Furthermore, the loan program required firms to provide land guarantees as collateral; to scrap, not sell, old equipment to avoid overcapacity; and to provide evidence of productivity improvement strategies. Firms opposed the first condition as overly burdensome, reflecting the lack of consultation that had gone into the policy's design. And while the second two requirements were linked to upgrading, the ThTI had neither the data nor the political clout to enforce them. The traditional source of data, the TID, had been weakened by staff shortages. Japanese suppliers were the only reliable sources of information about equipment.

Despite a lack of credible government support, there was some growth in bank lending to the sector. In addition, a large garment maker with an engineering background invested in the adaptation of computerized conveyors – precisely the kind of equipment required for quick response.[139] But

---

[136] Tait (2005, 6); Chalumporn (2004, 44–52).

[137] Bangkok Post (May 21, 1999).

[138] TTIS Textile Digest (September–October 1998). The rest of this paragraph is based on Textile Digest (September–October 1998); Textile Digest. 4:50 (June 1997, 21); Bangkok Post (May 21, 1999); and interviews # 45, 47, 51, 52, 53.

[139] "Getting those garments on the go." The Nation. (July 5, 2004); "Garment makers set up marketing firm." The Nation. (December 7, 2004).

exports to low-value markets were still possible without new equipment, especially if garment producers shifted operations to rural/border areas with low-cost labor.[140] Further, there is no evidence of public or industry-wide incentives to diffuse local initiatives or of collective equipment acquisition. As a result, the impact of bank loans and private sector innovations remained unclear. In 2001, for example, Thailand was "nearly at the bottom" of 15 major textile-exporting countries in its ratio of shuttleless machines.[141]

B. Linkages

Thai officials and textile firms were well aware that the industry's tradition of sectoral fragmentation was impractical in the face of buyers' growing demands.[142] The principal approaches to supply chain development focused on tax and tariff reform, the use and treatment of water, and firm-driven internalization of midstream activities.

The problem with *domestic taxes* was that the imposition of the VAT on all transactions not leading to 101% exports rewarded garment exporters for using imported, not local, inputs.[143] More progress was made in *tariff liberalization* on key upstream inputs. In 1997, the government reduced rates on fibers, yarns, and fabric by half and on garments by 15% (Table 6.6). Further restructuring proceeded slowly in the face of opposition from petrochemical interests and national elections in 2000.[144] As a result, in 2003 Thailand's downstream producers were still suffering from more protected input suppliers than was the case for their key competitors (Table 6.8). By 2007, however, the government was moving toward a "three-rate system" for 75% of all tariff lines, including petrochemicals (1% on primary raw materials, 5% on intermediates, and 10% on finished products).[145]

Progress reflected both the relatively low information costs of tariff reform and reduced distributional tensions. With garment producers increasingly influential, and with growth reducing the Finance Ministry's concern with revenue losses from tariff reduction, the gains from liberalization offset the costs. Greater consultation was also possible between a cohesive TGMA and

---

[140] "Garment-makers shift plants from Bangkok. *The Nation*. (December 1, 2003).

[141] Chalumporn (2004, 34).

[142] For example, Interview # 104.

[143] *TTIS Textile Digest* (January 2002, 33).

[144] For example, *TTIS Textile Digest*. (January 2002, 33); Leary (1998, 95); interview # 46.

[145] *Thailand Economic Monitor* (2007, 43); interview # 76; personal communication, Prof. Paopongsakorn, (May 9, 2007).

TABLE 6.8 *Import Tariffs on Upstream Products 2003*

Product	Import Tariff (%)			
	Thailand	Indonesia	Taiwan	South Korea
Petrochemicals	1–5 (lowered from 5–7 in 2000)	0–5	1	1
Manmade fiber	10	2.5–5	1.25	3–8
Chemicals and dyeing agents	1–10	0–5	2.5–5	6–8

Source: Chalumporn (2004, 35)

a stable and supportive Finance Ministry than was the case on domestic tax issues.[146] Still, protection remains "exceptionally high" for Thai garment producers, ranging from 30% to 60%.[147] These levels reflect both the TGMA's significant political influence and the garment firms' perceived strengths in medium-end products on the one hand, and their vulnerabilities to both low-end and high-end imports on the other.[148] In sum, Thai garment producers suffered from higher input costs than their rivals but enjoyed high levels of protection.

Water, its cost and postproduction treatment, remained a problem for dyers and printers. At least two sets of solutions emerged under Thaksin.[149] One was to establish clusters in which dyers and printers could share water and treatment facilities. But the government offered land that lacked water and was owned by Prime Minister Thaksin's allies who stood to benefit from their involvement. A second proposal involved state-mandated installation of remote sensing mechanisms to identify and regulate plant discharges. In addition to challenging the efficacy of such mechanisms, the dyers and printers argued that a Thaksin ally would monopolize their import and repair. These problems of private rents were exacerbated by the bureaucratic weakening engineered by Thaksin's administrative reforms. The weakened NESDB was in no position to oversee water treatment efforts, and while the (2002) creation of a new Ministry of Natural Resources and Environment

---

[146] Interviews # 55, 56, 65.
[147] Personal communication from Prof. Paopongsakorn, (May 9, 2007), based on Fiscal Policy Office data [www.e-tax.fpo.go.th] provided by researchers at the Thailand Development Research Institute).
[148] Personal communication, Prof. Suphat Supachalasai, (May 13, 2007).
[149] The following discussion is based on interviews # 118, 119.

out of the Industry Ministry would have seemed ideal for such a role, the new agency lacked expertise and coordination.

A final response to new competitive pressures involved *vertical integration and horizontal alliances.* To internalize intersegment linkages, some large dyers and printers expanded upstream into spinning and weaving, while weavers moved downstream into dyeing and printing.[150] In addition, the Department of Export Promotion initiated pilot projects in which small groups of firms were organized to adopt new technology and to improve branding, and supply chain coordination.[151] Finally, several large garment firms, comprising some 10,000 workers, initiated a manufacturing alliance designed to help provide "integrated services starting from the sourcing of raw materials to design through to the finished product."[152] Although this initiative was private, members benefited from state marketing support and the ThTI's program on supply chain management.[153]

C. Technical Training

Textile trade associations participating in the Industrial Restructuring Project stressed the primacy of technical training: better textile equipment was of limited use without a larger pool of skilled personnel.[154] The crisis prompted large firms to increase in-house training and to initiate cooperative education programs with local universities and technical institutes.[155] The TGMA's TGDF expanded its short courses and, by 2005, had trained some 6,000 operators.[156] TGDF also worked with universities to develop special MBA programs, provided in-house courses for TGMA members, and conducted benchmarking exercises and plant visits (e.g., ThTI 2005). Despite these efforts, Thailand's supply of operators and engineers remained weak by the time Thaksin was overthrown in the fall of 2006, especially when compared to regional rivals.[157]

Perhaps the greatest disappointment involved an effort to train experts in marketing, branding, design, and material sourcing. To this end, in

[150] Tait (2005, 7); interview # 44.
[151] Tait (2005).
[152] Tait (2005, 6); interviews # 96, 104.
[153] "Business Chain Management" (n.d.).
[154] Interview # 48.
[155] For example, Interview # 44.
[156] Discussion of the TGDF is based on interviews # 51, 101, 101.
[157] Chalumporn (2004); "Textiles and Garment/Capacities and Economies of Scale." *Bangkok Post* (July 3, 2006).

May 2003 the Thaksin government proposed the Bangkok Fashion City (BFC) project with the aim of making Bangkok a fashion hub by 2005. Led by the Ministry of Industry, the BFC was allocated almost $45 million to undertake nine projects, all of which were to involve the private sector and most of which were to integrate textiles, gems and jewelry, and footwear. Five of these projects were devoted to training in fashion design, technology, and management.[158] But problems emerged quickly.[159] The MOI lacked the staff and independence to coordinate the numerous businesses and politicians bidding for BFC contracts. To satisfy multiple interests, the ministry carved up the projects into smaller, less efficient programs. Even so, rejected bidders accused the MOI of favoritism. Others, including the ThTI, criticized the BFC for its lack of cohesion, its emphasis on design over production efficiency, and its neglect of small and medium enterprises. These problems undermined industry support for the project, and in October 2006, following Thaksin's ouster, the new government suspended the effort.

D. Explaining Outcomes

Among the upgrading initiatives undertaken in this period, only tariff liberalization efforts achieved some degree of clear success. This reflected the relatively small number of actors involved in trade policy reform, the limited information required, and the shifting balance of power between winners and losers. The Finance Ministry had softened its opposition to tariff cuts in light of exchange-rate-fueled growth revenues and ThTI arguments that long-term growth in state revenues could only come from a more complete and efficient local supply chain. In addition, party and factional rivalries under Chuan and Thaksin provided openings for pressure from the highly organized TGMA and from large garment firms responding to new, challenging market pressures. But politics – especially the large number of veto players under Thaksin – also limited the country's achievements in more demanding policy areas, including wastewater treatment, equipment upgrading, and technical training.

The ability to reconcile the interests of multiple actors in information-intensive areas was undermined by political control of the Industry and Commerce Ministries, by growth in the number of agencies and ministries, and by the weakening of the nonpartisan NESDB. By impeding a merger of

---

[158] www.BangkokFashionCity.com.
[159] This assessment is based on Tait (2005); *Financial Times Information.* (December 20, 2006); interviews # 100, 101, 99, 114, 118, 119.

the Commerce and Industry ministries, political rivalries blocked efforts to integrate state export and industrial promotion. Changing ministerial leadership undermined the credibility of state initiatives by encouraging policy changes and by destabilizing departmental responsibilities within the MOI.[160] Fragmented and politicized agencies also limited the effectiveness of private and public–private arrangements. The associations had to focus on the immediate goal of complying with new ministers' policies as opposed to pursuing long-term goals, such as strengthening the ThTI.[161] This reinforced the problem of financial uncertainty evident at the ThTI's creation. With subsequent ministerial shifts and changes in ThTI leadership, textile firms were uncertain as to their actual voice in the institute.[162]

The prominence of explicit upgrading efforts in this period reflected both industry awareness of the dangers posed by new competitive challenges and political leaders' recognition of textiles' significance for the overall economy. But the relatively modest results of these efforts revealed not only the persistent complexity of Thai politics but a more permissive context: cheap labor options and the improving situation of both textiles and the broader economy within which those politics evolved. This context reveals textiles to be a mirror image of broader development strategies under Thaksin: ambitious, nationalist desires to expand Thailand's position in global value chains on the one hand and erratic, often uninformed, implementation on the other.

V. THE PHILIPPINES AND TAIWAN

Textile development in Thailand is distinctly stronger than in the Philippines but weaker than in Taiwan. The cross-national distinctions are especially striking in upstream development and linkages. Annual growth in textile production in the Philippines was only around 1% between 1967 and 1995, compared to around 8% for Thailand.[163] And whereas Thailand became a net exporter of synthetic yarn and fabrics, the Philippines remained a net importer of all textile products. But Thai growth was dwarfed by Taiwan's performance. During the 1950s, Taiwan's cotton fabric and garment exports rose rapidly enough to trigger U.S. protectionism in the early 1960s; in the mid-1960s, synthetic fiber production began, increasing *16,900-fold*

---

[160] Interviews # 53, 55.

[161] Interviews # 53, 113.

[162] For example, Interview # 114. We address post-Thaksin initiatives by the ThTI in Chapter 8.

[163] Yamagata (1998, 39–40).

between 1958 and 1987; and exports of synthetic textiles and apparel increased during the 1960s and into the 1970s. Taiwan became the world's fourth largest fiber producer in 1981 and second largest in 1989.[164]

Variation in upstream capacities translated into linkage differences. From 1969 to 1990, the ratios of imported intermediate inputs to the Philippine textile and apparel industries were at least twice those of Thailand.[165] But again, Taiwan was way ahead, in part because of the link between upstream and downstream development. In the Philippines, there was essentially no upstream growth. In Thailand, upstream production developed prior to and largely independent of garments. In Taiwan the process was one of downstream-led, backward integration. The growth of synthetic textile and apparel exports in Taiwan, beginning in the 1960s, generated demand for synthetic fibers and, in turn, petrochemicals,[166] as well as for textile equipment. Upstream producers enjoyed subsidies and protection, but the fact that they were explicitly designed as inputs to downstream exports imposed effective pressure to meet global price and quality standards.[167] A similar dynamic seems to have occurred for textile production equipment. Whereas Thailand lacks any capacity for such equipment, Taiwan became the world's fourth largest producer of textile machinery in 2004.[168]

These differences in linkages and efficiency had important consequences for each country's response to the evolving global system of quotas. Even in its relatively successful garment sector, the Philippines failed to fill its allocated quota. In fact, of all major Asian garment exporters, it had the lowest utilization rates of U.S. and European market quotas.[169] Thailand typically used all its quotas, but the Thai response to quota limits was, as noted earlier, market diversification rather than upgrading. In contrast, Taiwan consistently responded to protectionism by "upgrading existing products, expanding synthetic production," and generally developing a complete supply chain.[170]

This hierarchy of industry performance is the inverse of cross-national differences in length of experience in modern textile production and in post-World War II textile industry strength. As Kuo notes, the Philippines had a

[164] Chen, Chen and Chu (2001, 285, 300); Wade (1990, 91); Yamagata (1993, 95–96).
[165] Yamagata (1998, 42–43).
[166] Chen, Chen, Chu (2001, 297–300).
[167] Chu (1994).
[168] http://hirecruit.nat.gov/tw/english/htm/taiwan_04.asp, (accessed May 15, 2007).
[169] Austria (1996, 21).
[170] Yoffie (1983, 114); Chen, Chen, Chu 2001, 284).

distinct "head start over Taiwan" in terms of production capacity.[171] In the late 1950s, visiting Japanese technicians found the quality of Philippine textiles comparable to Japanese products,[172] and even in 1960, Taiwan exported far fewer textiles than did the Philippines.[173] Accounting for variation in textile growth requires an understanding of how each country responded to policy tasks and how those responses reflected institutional capacities, political competition, and systemic pressures.

A. The Philippines

Policy Tasks: Part of the explanation for the Philippines' weak textile performance lies in the country's poor responses to several policy tasks.[174] Consider first *risk socialization.* During the 1950s, textiles – especially spinning and weaving – was a central component of the Philippine industrialization drive. As such, it benefited from extensive state support. Through tax exemptions, special exchange allocations for equipment and raw materials, and import controls and tariff protection, the industry's entire financial structure was "directly or indirectly furnished by the government."[175] In addition, discriminatory legislation pushed ethnic Chinese out of importing into fledgling textile production. But risks were "over-socialized" for these new entrants and "under-socialized" for others. Enjoying high levels of protection in the 1960s and 1970s – higher than in Thailand – large spinners and weavers focused not on exporting, but on protecting domestic market share, preventing garment firms from smuggling cheaper inputs, and obtaining dollar allocations.[176] Because increased dollar allocations yielded greater profits than operating efficiency, textile groups "considered effort at the Central Bank as important as at their plants".[177]

Fiber production, meanwhile, was "super-socialized" under Marcos: Filipino Synthetic Fiber (Filsyn) gained a monopoly over fiber sales by virtue of the fact that the firm was controlled by Marcos cronies. There was no Philippine equivalent of a Thai central bank to complement risk socialization

---

[171] Kuo (1995, 88); see also Yamagata (1998, 35); Nordhaug (1997, 201).

[172] Kuo (1995, 91).

[173] Yoffie (1983, 113).

[174] Our analysis of the Philippines extends only through the end of the Marcos regime. As reflected in performance data noted earlier in this chapter, the industry's trajectory has not differed from that established in the period covered.

[175] Stifel (1963, 184).

[176] Kuo (1995, 112); Yamagata (1998).

[177] Stifel (1963, 104).

with hard budget constraints, much less an agency capable of enforcing performance criteria.[178] The Filsyn case also illustrates the fact that risks were under-socialized for others, including not only small producers, who were often denied foreign exchange, but also large Japanese upstream producers. Teijin, for example, was a founder of Filsyn in 1968 but left the company some 15 years later out of frustration with its poor sales record and low tariffs on fibers (to help large Filipino spinners).[179] Most Japanese firms simply stayed out of the Philippines due to these factors, resulting in a loss of managerial and technical expertise (Yamagata 1998). The extensive privileges enjoyed by large mills and Filsyn discouraged any *upstream–downstream linkages.* Textile firms could raise prices without improving quality, forcing garment producers to import or smuggle in their inputs. Many apparel producers found it more profitable to sell their products on the domestic market than to attempt to export (Kuo 1995, 113). The country's system of *quota management* further discouraged exports. Beginning in the 1960s, the government limited the supply of imported inputs by issuing only a small number of import licenses. It also reduced the number of export quota holders in the early 1980s until only two, politically influential firms held the large, profitable quotas to the U.S. and Canada (Ibid., 122).

Institutional Capacities: These policy failures reflected institutional weaknesses in both public and private sectors. Consultation was undermined by a combination of fragmentation, clientelism, and technocratic arrogance. Beginning in the 1950s, contention ruled relations among the agencies with influence over textiles: the Central Bank, Budget Commission, the National Economic Commission, the Customs Bureau, and the board responsible for import licenses under the Finance Ministry.[180] These rivalries impeded effective auditing and thus any serious industrial planning, even by the Central Bank. In principle, of course, a laissez-faire approach could promote competition and exports, but in the Philippines, rivalries were focused on capturing rents, whether from dollar allocations, import licenses, or customs procedures. These rents impeded competition by significantly raising the costs of doing business. Business–government links in textiles, then, were largely clientelist. Rivalries also undermined private sector collective action. The major textile group, the Textile Mills Association of the Philippines (TMAP), included only around 10% of all mills and operated almost solely to fight for protection.

---

[178] Hutchcroft (1998; 2000).
[179] Kuo (1995, 114).
[180] On general weaknesses, see Stifel (1963, 43, 65–66); Hutchcroft 2000, 227; and Kuo (1995, 116–117).

The bright spot with regard to collective action was in garments, where the Garment Business Association of the Philippines (GBAP) expanded during the 1970s to represent a third of all firms (90% of capacity) and facilitated export quota utilization and technology transfer.[181] GBAP's growth coincided with the growth of state-supported consultation in the early 1970s. This took the form of a tripartite dialogue among the state, producers, and labor that, in 1977, morphed into the Garment and Textile Export Board (GTEB). But the GTEB never promoted an overall vision of textile development; its decisions were often arbitrary, reflecting a mixture of technocratic haughtiness *vis-a-vis* nonfavored firms and subservience to Marcos cronies; and its focus, prompted by a foreign exchange crisis, was only on garments, thus leaving the textile segment inefficient.[182]

The benefits of even limited consultation were undermined by the state's general lack of information and monitoring capacity. Writing in 1963, Stifel emphasized the almost total absence of aggregate industry statistics. Textile producers (and some firms without factories at all) took advantage of these weaknesses to exaggerate production capacities and thereby get higher allocations of foreign exchange. Data collection did improve under the garment association, GBAP, working with the GTEB in the 1980s. But this data does not seem to have included textiles, and GTEB data were used as much to support Marcos cronies as to promote exports. Indeed, the best-informed agency was probably the highly corrupt Philippines Customs Bureau, which tracked textile imports most needed by firms and would thus yield the highest bribes when seized.[183] In light of these conditions, the few textile policies in place "tended to be inconsistent over time, in conflict with one another or simply not implemented."[184] Government plans were generally "meaningless to the textile industry."[185] Only the largest producers could trust state commitments. The safer options were to circumvent official regulations, and avoid involvement in official programs.[186]

Elite Political Competition: As in the case of sugar, the Philippines' weak performance in textiles illustrates the potential for both gridlock with even a moderate number of veto players and noncredible decisiveness with few veto players. Prior to Marcos' 1972 imposition of martial law, the country's

---

[181] Kuo (1995, 121).
[182] Ibid., (123).
[183] Kuo (1995, 117).
[184] Ibid., (116).
[185] Stifel (1963, 65).
[186] Kuo (1995, 120).

combination of presidential system and bicameral legislature allowed textile interests to use the bureaucracy as sources of rents, not policy initiatives. The potential advantages of a single veto player were evident under martial law when, in the early 1970s, Marcos shifted from coddling inward-oriented textile firms to promoting export-oriented fabric producers as the government's "new star." Marcos allowed new garment firms to open and made it easier for them to import materials. By 1977, garments had become the country's largest export item.[187] Marcos also used his authority to shift the state away from rent-seeking to a more activist, purposive "rent allocation"[188] in order to create a Philippine version of the developmental conglomerates seen in South Korea and Japan. Instead, as in sugar, what emerged in the form of Filsyn was a highly concentrated clientelism in which cronies were free to operate without pressure for productive efficiency.

Systemic Pressures: Permissive conditions are key to explaining the Philippines' weaknesses in textiles. U.S. aid played a central role in this story. Approximately a third of U.S. aid to the Philippines in the 1950s went to the textile industry,[189] funding new Philippine textile mills and textile consultants.[190] Through the Public Law 480 of the U.S.–Philippines Mutual Security Act, Washington provided low-cost American cotton, which took the pressure off domestic cotton development for an industry heavily reliant on such raw materials.[191] In the 1960s, the Philippines benefited from the World Bank's emphasis on textiles as a key element in industrial modernization.[192] And the Philippines enjoyed preferential access to the U.S. market. Kuo concluded in 1995 that in its entire history, "protectionism or export quotas have never been a series concern" for Philippine textiles.[193] The importance of such enabling conditions is illustrated by an instance in which pressures intensified but subsequently abated. The industry's initial promotion was itself a response to a combination of foreign exchange shortages and growing rural poverty that threatened to result in political disorder.[194] Under these conditions, local textile production held great potential for saving precious foreign exchange and for generating employment. But as U.S. aid helped to reduce foreign exchange problems in the 1950s, the industry lapsed into protected inefficiency.

[187] Kuo (1995, 123).
[188] Hutchcroft (2000, 227).
[189] Stifel (1963, 184).
[190] Kuo (1995, 91).
[191] Stifel (1963, 48).
[192] de Vries and Brakel (1983).
[193] Kuo (1995, 92).
[194] Stifel (1963, 11).

B. Taiwan

Policy Tasks: Taiwan's Kuomintang (KMT)-led government undertook a range of *risk socialization* policies in textiles corresponding to different stages of the industry's evolution. In the late 1940s, with production capacity limited and the industry dominated by small enterprises, the government succeeded in attracting local investment into production for the domestic market by using exchange controls, import licensing, multiple exchange rates, and protective tariffs that, for some fibers and yarns, exceeded 101%.[195] Because much of the industry's initial development involved cotton products, the government supplied cotton to the mills and weavers, advanced them required capital, and bought up all production.[196] A decade later, prompted by export limits on cotton textiles in the 1962 LTA with the U.S., the government encouraged a shift to synthetic products by creating public enterprises (often subsequently handing them to private interests).[197] By 1971 there were 15 local, private synthetic fiber producers, and by the early 1980s, Taiwan was a global leader in synthetic fiber production.

This enthusiastic supply response resulted in self-sufficiency in cloth and yarn by mid-1953, but market saturation by the end of the decade. To address this *overcapacity* problem, the government encouraged exports. For local producers, the competitive export market was risky and offered less attractive prices than domestic sales. Such concerns could only be addressed collectively.[198] The solution was a Contract of Cooperation, established in 1961 and renewed throughout the decade, which required firms to sell only 40% of their goods in the domestic market and export the rest.[199] Implemented by the Taiwan Cotton Spinners' Association (TCSA) with state backing, the contract was supplemented by a series of rewards and punishments designed to push firms to join the association, to meet export quotas, and to expand exports to nonquota countries.[200] These measures succeeded but triggered an "entry rush" and, in the early 1970s, another overcapacity crisis as synthetic fiber production outstripped the capacity of downstream spinning and weaving mills. The problem was exacerbated in 1971 when the U.S. compelled Taiwan to limit exports, including fibers, and in 1973 when the first oil crisis raised the price of the key raw material

---

[195] Chen, Chen, Chu (2001, 292–293).
[196] Wade (1990, 79); Yamagata (1993, 101).
[197] Chen, Chen, Chu (2001, 312).
[198] Kuo (1995, 101).
[199] Ibid. (101); Wade (1990, 143).
[200] Kuo (1995, 101, 108); Wade (1990, 143).

for synthetic fibers, causing recessions in the industry's major export markets.[201] In response, the government encouraged mergers, stabilized domestic prices, and subsidized synthetic fiber purchases.[202]

Taiwan's export-led response to overcapacity was supplemented by two sets of measures that, unlike the Thai case, contributed to upgrading. One involved *linkage development*. The LTA-inspired growth in synthetic fibers prompted state officials to encourage domestic production of upstream inputs of chemical intermediates and basic chemicals. The availability of such inputs helped Taiwan to move into higher-value products when faced with LTA and (1974) MFA limits on lower value-added exports. But downstream users sometimes preferred imported inputs for price or quality reasons. It was in managing such upstream–downstream tensions that Taiwan's institutional capacities were especially impressive.[203] To expand exports, the use of domestic inputs had to be coupled with improvement in product quality, and that required pressure and support for *technology acquisition*. To this end, the government made entry and expansion conditional on firms agreeing to minimum scale economies and the use of latest technology; provided special quota incentives to exporters of higher technology products; and provided financial incentives for producers to replace old equipment with new machines and technology.[204] These measures in turn encouraged firms to access foreign technology. Between 1957 and 1976, 38 Taiwanese fiber firms were obtaining foreign technology, almost all through licensing agreements.[205] By 1980, Taiwanese firms were starting their own R&D operations and developing their own technologies. These efforts were complemented by an association-led textile technology college in 1972[206] and by a government-sponsored research institution beginning in 1959, whose training, incubator, and independent research activities dwarf anything seen in Thailand, much less the Philippines.

Institutional Capacities: Active state agencies and textile associations were key to Taiwan's successful upgrading.[207] This was not, however, a static or always harmonious process. The state was clearly dominant in the 1950s, and its links to private actors were largely particularistic ties to "a few influential mainlander firms."[208] But the state, through agencies such as the

---

[201] Yamagata (1993, 96).
[202] Chen, Chen, Chu (2001, 313).
[203] Wade (1990, 204); Kuo (1995, 108).
[204] Kuo (1995, 108).
[205] Chen, Chen, Chu (2001, 310–311).
[206] Kuo (1995, 101).
[207] Yoffie (1983, 118–119).
[208] Nordhaug (1997, 204).

Bank of Taiwan, the Central Trust of China, and government laboratories, was clearly able to monitor the performance of favored clients; it was credible in withdrawing support, whether for nonperformance or because basic objectives had been met. These capacities prevented Taiwan's import substitution-oriented clientelism from becoming the unproductive, "rent-seeking coalitions" more common to in the developing world.[209] These clientelist links gave way to more clearly corporatist relations in the 1960s and 1970s as stronger associations emerged to address problems of over-capacity and protectionism. Despite numerous cases of disagreement within and between the state and private industry during this period,[210] differences were often resolved through intensive, public–private consultation. The relative cohesion of the state was key in this process. Unlike in Thailand, industrial development and trade promotion functions in Taiwan were handled by one agency, the Industrial Development Bureau that was in turn able to encourage private sector coordination.[211] The information-gathering capacities of this institutional network were impressive.[212]

Even after the 1970s, when public–private linkages loosened considerably, the industry remained highly organized. Some 18 associations, led by the peak Taiwan Textile Federation, continued to play important roles in data gathering and policy development,[213] and the state has maintained an active role in supporting textile research. This contribution, and those that preceded it, constituted the basis for the industry's gradual overseas shift, first by garments in the 1980s and subsequently by knitting and dyeing operations in the 1990s. Unlike the incipient movement of Thai garment firms to cheaper labor locations, Taiwan's textile firms have remained in control of this overseas network. Using sophisticated information technology to manage complex supply chains, they have been able to "combine relocation with upgrading," maintaining an advantage over their competitors.[214]

Elite Political Competition: The institutional capacities governing Taiwan's textile industry developed within a one-party state. The KMT ruled Taiwan under martial law from 1949 until 1987, when a new party, the Democratic Progressive party, was permitted to contest national elections. After 1987, there were differences between economic liberals and proponents of state-led

---

[209] Ibid. (205).
[210] Kuo (1995, 108–109).
[211] Wade (1990, 204); Kuo (1995).
[212] Yamagata (1993, 106); Wade (1990, 138).
[213] Wade (1990, 283, 271).
[214] Thun (2001, 13).

industrial policies,[215] but these were typically a focus of negotiated compromises within the party-led state apparatus. Factions also played an important role in the predemocratic period; but these were *local* factions that did not undermine policy coherence, in contrast to the impact of factions in Thailand. For our purposes, the puzzle is why, unlike Marcos, the KMT became what Atul Kohli (2004) labels a "cohesive capitalist" state, one able to balance the decisiveness of a single veto player with the credibility necessary to induce upgrading-related investments. An important part of the answer lies in the combination of centralized authority with the active participation of a wide cross-section of private interests in policy formation, implementation, monitoring and evaluation. These constituted the functional equivalent of additional veto players.

Systemic Pressures: But these participatory arrangements themselves reflected variation in vulnerability. Taiwan faced challenges, including a credible threat from China, whose intensity and duration exceeded those seen in both the Philippines and Thailand.[216] Beginning in the late 1940s, the KMT-led government viewed the textile industry as a way to generate needed employment, to meet growing domestic demand, and to earn needed foreign exchange without relying on scarce agricultural exports. Institutional strengthening, through more corporatist linkages, began in the late 1950s when, in the face of a looming trade deficit, overcapacity, and uncertain U.S. aid, public and private interests acknowledged that a free market and clientelism could not save the textile industry.[217] Strengthening continued in response to further protectionism and the first oil crisis.

CONCLUSION

As in our analysis of sugar, the three textile cases constitute a performance hierarchy reflecting different institutional capacities. Two contrasts illustrate the variations in capacities. One involves trade administration: customs officials in the Philippines were fairly efficient, but their competence was devoted largely to obtaining bribes. Thai customs exhibited less corruption but little competence with regard to both product/segment-specific differences and tariff rebates. Taiwan was exceptionally proficient not only in such rebates but also in ensuring the quality of its exports.[218] A second difference involved the promotion of technological spillovers from foreign

---

[215] For example, Nordhaug (1997, 207).
[216] On Taiwan and systemic vulnerability, see Doner, Ritchie and Slater (2005).
[217] Kuo (1995, 105).
[218] Wade (1990, 54).

producers. Consider the case of Teijin: The giant Japanese fiber producer entered each of the three countries, with very different results. The firm quit the Philippines after several years, thus depriving the country of important technological expertise. It entered and remained an important part of Thailand's textile industry, but its operations have not been well integrated with downstream production, and Thai producers have remained dependent on its technology and networks. In Taiwan, Teijin was invited to help resolve operational and technical difficulties in 1957.[219] Taiwan producers absorbed Japanese, as well as western, fiber technology and went on to become independent, global producers. This contrast in the capacity to absorb foreign technology is further reflected in the vastly different strengths of the Philippines Textile Research Institute, the Thai Textile Institute, and the Taiwan Textile Research Institute.

These institutional differences are themselves a function of very different pressures on political leaders. The influence of these pressures is reflected by variations within each national case. In Thailand, institutional capacities were most developed in that sector – garments – most exposed to external competition and in periods, such as the debt crisis of the 1980s and the 1997 financial crisis, when the industry's weaknesses were especially problematic for national revenues and employment. A similar dynamic is apparent in Marcos' early 1970s move toward more corporatist support for garments in the Philippines. These pressures were strongest in the case of Taiwan, a country for whom textile exports were especially important given its lack of exchange, its lack of recourse to natural resource exports, and the uncertainty of foreign military aid in the face of significant security threats.

Finally, the textile cases provide further evidence for the relative weakness of regime type and, to some degree, veto players, as explanations for institutional capacity and economic performance. Martial law under Marcos and the KMT had profoundly different consequences for textiles. Veto player arguments seemed more helpful: In the Thai case, large numbers of veto players seriously impeded policy changes and institutional innovation, as reflected in the decade-long odyssey of the Thai Textile Institute. In the Philippines, the shift to a single player resulted in both decisiveness and a lack of credibility. But Taiwan's single veto player system provided both flexibility and credibility. Our explanation for such an anomaly rests in part on the extensive consultation that resulted in an effective increase in veto players. But that arrangement itself ultimately resulted from political leaders' need to address serious challenges to growth and legitimacy.

---

[219] Chen, Chen, Chu (2001, 207).

7

Automobiles

In 1995, *Business Week* identified Thailand as "Asia's New Car Capital," and Thai leaders began describing their country as the "Detroit of Asia."[1] Thai automobile production had risen from around 100,000 units per year since the mid-1980s to a million units in 2005, despite a slump following the 1997 crisis (Figure 7.1). Exports, especially of the 1-ton pickup trucks for which Thailand became the second largest market in the world and a major production site for Japanese carmakers, figured as a key part of this growth (Figure 7.2). Those exports were based in part on well-developed automotive clusters housing large numbers of global producers (Figures 7.3 and 7.4). Their growth made the industry an important part of the Thai economy: by 2005 the industry accounted for 8% of the workforce and 15% of GDP, and it was the country's second largest source of export revenues.[2]

The Thai automotive industry is, then, a clear example of successful structural change. Indonesia's auto industrialization efforts and large population (216 million vs. Thailand's 63 million in 2006) also had drawn foreign producers, but it was Thailand, not Indonesia, that became "a major base for vehicle assemblers from advanced industrial economies."[3] But Thailand's automotive record has been weaker than South Korea's

---

[1] *Business Week-International Edition* (November 20, 1995).

[2] Thai Press Reports. (November 7, 2005); *The Nation*. (September 5, 2005); "Thailand Automotive Industry Update: 2005. Business-in-Asia.com. (htttp://www.business-in-asia. com/auto)article2.html) accessed May 25, 2007.

[3] Takayasu and Mori (2004, 211). On Indonesia's export weakness and inconsistent growth, see Okamoto and Sjoholm (2000). In 1995, there were roughly 1,000 firms in the Thai auto industry compared to 287 in Malaysia, 279 in Indonesia, and 184 in the Philippines (Lecler

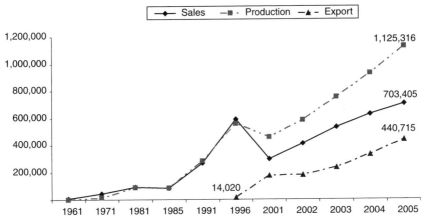

FIGURE 7.1 Thailand Production, Sales, and Exports of Automobiles (1961–2005)
Source: Federation of Thai Industries and the Thai Automotive Industry Association; cited in Paopongsakorn and Kriengkrai (2007).

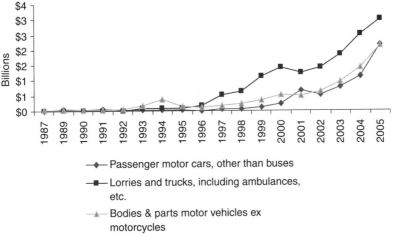

FIGURE 7.2 Thai Auto Exports in US$ Billions
Source: UN Comtrade Data

(Figures 7.5 and 7.6). As of 2006, Korea was East Asia's only mass exporter of passenger vehicles, ranking fourth in the world in vehicle production and exporting half of its output. By 1999, Korean parts exports reached

2002, 802). By 1999, Thailand had attracted 215 Japanese parts firms compared to 88 in Indonesia, 62 in Malaysia, and 54 in the Philippines (Lecler 2002, 802).

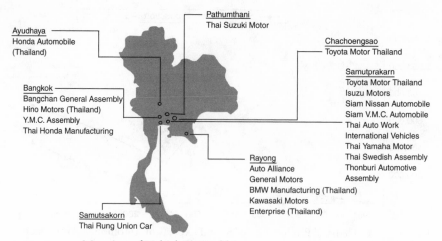

FIGURE 7.3 Mapping of Vehicle Assemblers

Source: Thai Automotive Institute, in Asia Policy Research 2005:4.

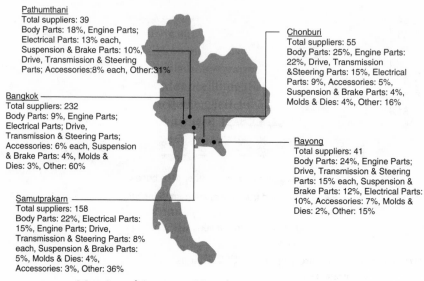

FIGURE 7.4 Mapping of Auto-part Manufacturers

Source: Thai Automotive Institute, in Asia Policy Research 2005:5.

$4 billion, compared with Thai levels of under $1.5 billion. While Korea's precrisis assembly output came from five domestically owned firms,[4] the Thai assembly sector had become foreign-dominated, largely by Japanese

---

[4] Ravenhill (2002, 111).

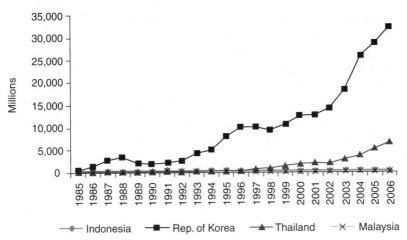

FIGURE 7.5 Comparative Automotive Vehicle Exports
Source: UN Comtrade Dataset

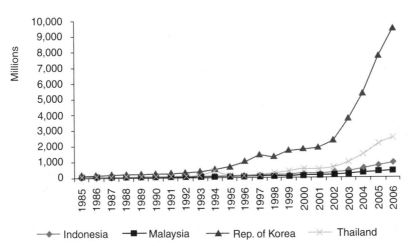

FIGURE 7.6 Comparative Autoparts Exports
Source: UN Comtrade Data

assemblers, who accounted for almost 80% of sales in 2001.[5] Also, the Thai parts sector was weaker than statistics suggest. After over two decades of promotion, Thai parts firms had not managed to develop the "base of indigenous knowledge" needed for them to develop autonomously.[6] The

[5] Takayasu and Mori (2004, table 5.4).
[6] Veloso, Romero, and Amsden (1998, 17).

1997 crisis pushed many of these weak firms toward bankruptcy or take-over by foreign partners, a process facilitated by the government's lifting of a 49% ceiling on foreign ownership.[7] Actual local content, that is, the real value added of vehicles assembled in Thailand, was closer to 20% than the official 54–70%.[8] And while automakers expanded local sourcing to reduce delivery times and foreign exchange risks, in Thailand that expansion often involved greater reliance on foreign suppliers. Reflecting differences in linkages, Korea's auto parts sector ran a trade surplus of $1.8 billion in 1999 compared to Thailand's and Indonesia's deficits of almost $200 and $128 million, respectively.[9]

None of this is to deny weaknesses in Korea's auto industry. As described later in this chapter, Korean auto producers lost significant ground to foreign capital in the latter 1990s as a result of overcapacity, debt, low margins, and perceptions of low quality.[10] Korean parts firms were neither price competitive with low-end products from China or Taiwan nor capable of challenging first-tier multinational suppliers. Yet even after the 1997 crisis, Korea surpassed Thailand not just in terms of production and export volumes, but also in the strength of local producers[11] and the competitiveness of its products as reflected in its relatively low tariff levels.[12] This superior performance occurred in a country with a smaller population (48 million) that launched its auto industry at roughly the same time as Thailand.[13]

Thailand's uneven performance reflects the country's institutional capacities and the political factors influencing those capacities. Thailand was well equipped to benefit from early opportunities to build local demand, to attract foreign assemblers, and to develop a local supply base. The country also moved more quickly than its neighbors to take advantage of the automakers' interest in exports, putting in place smart macroeconomic policies, focusing

---

[7] Information is incomplete on the precise number of Thai-owned parts producers. Estimates range from 374 (JICA 1995, cited in Kennedy 1997, 358) to 1,200 prior to the crisis (see sources cited in Doner, Noble, and Ravenhill [DNR]2004: 191) to 1,800 (Vallop 2003). Based on interviews # 77, 78, 79, 81, 82, 83, 102, and a review of auto-related newspaper reports, the TAI estimate seems highly exaggerated. Thai-owned, first-tier firms seem to number no more than a dozen or so. Further evidence of a weakened local parts base comes from a 1999 survey of Toyota suppliers (Peera (2001), and a study finding that roughly a half of all local parts firms produced imitation and fake spare parts (Wattanasiritham (2000).

[8] Brooker (1997, IV-6).

[9] DNR (2004, table 4.1, 163); see also Amsden (2001, 155).

[10] Ravenhill (2002).

[11] DNR 2004, (178).

[12] Ibid. (178; 164).

[13] Doner (1991).

on scale economies, and supporting clusters. Thailand fared less well in strengthening local producers and linkages, despite numerous "master plans" to do so in the 1990s. Officials launched these efforts under pressure from Thailand's trade liberalization commitments, which would soon end their capacity to protect the industry. As of 2006, efforts to upgrade parts producers fell short in part because overall market expansion reduced pressure, and in part because persistent political instability undermined the kinds of capacities needed to implement them. I begin to make this argument in Section I by identifying the shifting industry "drivers" within which Thailand has promoted its auto industry. Sections II–V examine the policies, institutions, and politics characterizing key periods in the development of the Thai industry, while Section VI compares the Thai case to the Indonesian and South Korean cases.

I. THE AUTOMOTIVE VALUE CHAIN: OPPORTUNITIES AND DANGERS

Developing countries have viewed the auto industry as a growth driver: a source of employment, technological expertise, and a stimulus to other sectors. But automotive industrialization has become more difficult over the past 40 years. From the 1960s through the 1980s, countries such as Thailand could produce vehicles and parts as relatively isolated national markets. Global trade rules allowed protection and trade-related investment measures, such as local content and export requirements.[14] These rules were consistent with the interests of multinational automakers who focused primarily on developing regionally integrated production systems in the larger "Triad" markets of North America, Western Europe, and Japan. In the developing world, by contrast, the automakers were content to provide the limited investment needed to support the early stages of mass production in small, fragmented, stand-alone markets. Such investments were typically concentrated in the automakers' regional backyards, with East Asia dominated by Japanese assemblers.[15] These arrangements permitted the growth of locally owned parts firms and, in some cases, assembly operations. They allowed, as in the South Korean case, the creation of relatively efficient local producers through scale economies and the acquisition of foreign technology. But they also encouraged fragmented markets and local firms unable to meet global standards.

---

[14] Humphrey and Memedovic (2003); DNR (2004); and Vickery (1996).
[15] Doner (1991).

Beginning in the 1990s, these inefficiencies became less tenable. Global trade agreements required phasing out the import substitution policies previously used to nurture domestic production and drove developing countries toward greater openness,[16] while flat Triad markets and growth in developing markets pushed the automakers to spread vehicle development costs, to establish low-cost sites for the production of selected products, and to access new markets for high-end vehicles still produced in Triad countries.[17] In East Asia, China loomed large, but even the smaller ASEAN markets attracted Western and Japanese automakers.[18] The influx of global producers intensified market fragmentation and overcapacity. In response, automakers merged and developed strategic alliances to gain access to markets, innovations, and competencies.[19] They also sought to improve scale economies by encouraging exports from developing countries, often through trade liberalization schemes that drew developing countries into extra-national production networks. The precise type and amount of vehicles and parts produced from any particular country varied with preexisting production facilities in other locales, product and process variables, and location-specific factors such as local demand characteristics and market size, human resources, supplier base, and state policies.[20]

The automakers' challenge was to reconcile scale economies with national market-specific requirements.[21] Their response has been "mass customization," an effort to achieve differentiation at minimal cost in areas visible to the consumer. Automakers have also encouraged national specialization of components to achieve scale economies. Furthermore, automakers have begun to view the supply chain itself as a source of innovation and cost reduction, relying on suppliers not only to improve productivity and to reduce delivery times at lower costs, but even to design core components to fit common platforms. This combination of specialization, localization, and devolution of responsibilities has, in theory, opened up significant opportunities for developing country producers, especially parts firms, to gain new markets and new technologies. In fact, however, it has raised entry barriers and encouraged denationalization.

---

[16] Humphrey and Memedovic (2003, 29).

[17] Ibid. (5).

[18] Veloso (2000).

[19] DNR (2004, 170).

[20] In Southeast Asia, a Brand-to-Brand Complementation in the 1980s was succeeded in 1996 by the ASEAN Industrial Cooperation program and, more recently the ASEAN Free Trade Arrangement – AFTA.

[21] The following review draws on Peera (2001); DNR 2004); and Humphrey (2003).

As a result, automakers have begun to rely on a smaller number of core suppliers. The parts sector has experienced consolidation in parallel with assembly mergers. "Mega suppliers" are responsible for selecting first-tier producers who in turn help organize the rest of a hierarchical value chain. Because developing country firms are typically limited in technical, managerial, and financial resources, automakers in developing markets have begun turning to "follow source" firms, that is, large firms already supplying the automakers elsewhere. Transnational, first-tier firms such as Denso or Delphi ensure the acceptability of standards among the lower tiers. The success of even lower-tier firms, however, requires engineering, design, and drawing capacities scarce in Thailand. Thai-based automakers thus favored Japanese joint ventures over local suppliers.[22]

How then do we explain Thai success in developing a domestically oriented automotive industry and transforming that industry into an efficient component of regional and global supply chains while losing the industry's indigenous supply base and potential linkages in the process? The short answer is that Thailand has been successful at combining open, competitive markets with scale economies, but much less adept at nurturing the competitiveness of local entrants. The following analysis outlines the institutional and political sources of these outcomes.

II. INDUSTRIAL PROMOTION AND MARKET FRAGMENTATION: 1961–1977

Thailand's early auto industrialization efforts exhibited some of the key features of both its impressive growth and the persistent weaknesses of local producers. Effective risk socialization measures encouraged an influx of assemblers and parts firms and a rapid rise in production, but efforts to improve scale economies through market rationalization foundered due to a clientelist authoritarian political system.

A. Risk Socialization

The auto industry was one of the first targets of Thailand's move toward private-sector-led industrial promotion. In 1961, the government invited producers to set up assembly plants. To lower investment risks, it ended limits on foreign land ownership, allowed capital and profit remittances, reduced business taxes, and cut tariffs on completely knocked-down (CKD)

[22] Peera (2001, 108).

vehicles to 40% compared to 80% for completely built-up (CBU) vehicles. These policies, especially the tariff adjustments, "served as an implicit guarantee to the foreign assemblers" and resulted in the establishment of nine assembly plants between 1961 and 1969.[23] The assemblers, except Toyota, entered the market via ties to large local conglomerates eager to shift from import and distribution into manufacture. As in the sugar and textile cases, Thailand's commercial banks, a part of patron–client networks, were important financial sources for these groups.[24] But problems soon emerged. The tax incentives reduced public revenues, and the openness to new entrants resulted in a proliferation of inefficient assembly operations whose import-dependence contributed to serious balance of payments and trade deficits. These problems prompted policy changes to promote localization and industry rationalization backed up by institutional reform.

B. Localization

Ministry of Industry officials sought to reduce the industry's dependence on imported components by encouraging assemblers to purchase locally produced goods. To this end, they raised tariffs on CKD kits to 50% and imposed a minimum local content requirement of 25%.[25] Despite opposition from the Commerce and Finance ministries, these measures were backed by support from aspiring local producers, from rising nationalist sentiment reflected in a student-led boycott of Japanese goods in 1972, and from the activities of a public–private coordinating body, the Automobile Development Committee (ADC) established by the MOI's Department of Industrial Economics.

C. Rationalization

There was broad consensus that localization was not feasible without efficiency, that efficiency required scale economies, and that scale economies required rationalization, that is, limits on the number of assemblers, makes and models, and engine sizes. This consensus emerged out of ADC-organized meetings in which the peak Association of Thai Industries (ATI) chastised the government for its liberal policy of unrestricted entry. With

---

[23] Paopongsakorn (1999, 1); Monsakul (2000, 43–44).
[24] Doner (1991, 191).
[25] Paopongsakorn (1999, 1–2); The analyses of localization and rationalization are based on Doner (1991, 190–195).

this support, the MOI announced a comprehensive reform of the industry in July 1971 that mandated minimum levels of investment and capacity for assemblers and limited models and engine sizes.

U.S. firms feared that limits on engine sizes would place them at a disadvantage, but the more dominant Japanese supported the strategy. The most vehement opponent of the measures was a new entrant, Bangchan General Assembly, who hoped to assemble multiple models of several different makes, well in excess of the proposed allowable limits. The firm's strenuous appeal for a relaxation of the limits was denied by the MOI, but this decision was reversed in February 1972 following the military's dissolution of the legislature and the formation of a new cabinet. The political shift allowed Bangchan to appeal directly to a top political leader, who ordered the MOI to rescind the model restrictions. The other assemblers had begun to comply with the limits but rapidly jumped on the bandwagon and expanded their models.

D. Explaining Outcomes

At one level, these contrasting outcomes reflect different distributional challenges. Although local contents requirements were burdensome for assemblers, causing GM and Ford to exit Thailand by 1980, the Japanese were anxious to expand their presence in the Thai market and responded by establishing affiliates to assemble components.[26] There was also strong support for localization from Thai capital as represented in the ATI, as well as from the broader nationalist movement. Finally, the costs of localization were offset by tariff hikes. Rationalization, on the other hand, posed challenges akin to capacity reduction (see Chapter 3). Successful consolidation would require credibility to resist the protests of firms like Bangchan and/or to provide side payments to offset such firms' losses. The institutions responsible for the auto industry seemed to have such credibility in the late 1960s and early 1970s. Policy emerged out of extensive public–private consultations led by the MOI and the ADC.[27] But credibility also depended on consistent support from political elites, support that deteriorated in the factional disputes triggering the 1971 coup.[28] In effect, the corporatist-like auto policy network was a temporary pocket of efficiency, one overwhelmed by the factionalized political elite's tendency to balkanize policy

[26] Monsakul (2000, 49).
[27] Doner (1991, 194).
[28] Morell (1972).

making. Thai factions represented veto players able to block any rationalization that had the potential to reduce available pork. Such veto players
operated not out of parties with clear programmatic preferences, but rather
as parts of clientelist networks. This stage of automotive development thus
illustrates the Janus-faced nature of Thai clientelism as a facilitator of
market entry and competition and an obstacle to scale economies and
efficiency.

These ambiguous consequences were evident through the rest of the
decade. The market-expanding aspect of clientelism was illustrated by an
influx of both assemblers and parts producers. In addition to Bangchan,
seven new assembly plants opened in the 1970s, producing some 13 different brands.[29] Encouraged by this growth, the range of locally produced
parts and components also expanded. Some of this investment came from
Japanese firms drawn to Thailand by their customers, some came from
roughly 180 Thai firms, and some came from Western automakers in the
1990s.[30] Because the Japanese transplants tended to locate close to their
customers, they helped to establish the first of what was to become a key
source of Thai strength: agglomerations or clusters. The growing number of
Thai parts producers would result in a powerful lobby for industry deepening and reform. On the negative side, there was much to reform. With the
influx of assembly plants, the industry's capacity was six times greater than
annual vehicle sales, and brands and models proliferated. This limited scale
economies, resulting in high costs, low quality, and few opportunities for
learning by local producers. There was growing demand as the economy
expanded during the mid-1970s, but high costs pushed consumers toward
CBU imports. In 1977, auto sales reached 101,000 units, but domestic
production amounted to only 65,875, further reducing scale economies and
increasing the trade deficit.[31]

Official efforts to address these problems were stymied by institutional
weaknesses and political fragmentation. Enforcement of localization targets
was undermined by a local contents formula that allowed assemblers to
inflate the value of locally sourced parts, and a lack of coordination
between the MOI and the Customs Department weakened the capacity to
monitor whether imported CKD kits had complied with regulations to
"delete" parts scheduled for localization.[32] ADC efforts to increase local

[29] Monsakul (2000, 50).
[30] Doner (1991, 198).
[31] Paopongsakorn (1999, 2).
[32] Doner (1991, 196–197) from which the rest of this discussion is drawn.

production by banning CBUs and raising tariffs on CKDs were blocked by Finance Ministry fears of revenue losses. The MOI (through the ADC) had developed the expertise and experience to rationalize a sector widely viewed as chaotic, but state efforts to promote localization and scale economies through rationalization were undermined by assembler belief that model restrictions would undermine market share and by organizational fragmentation among parts producers. This fragmentation was in part a reflection of the political volatility of the period (see Chapter 4). In this context, it is not surprising that MOI suggestions for efficient automotive localization were simply ignored.

III. LOCAL CONTENT AND THE SEEDS OF EXPORT GROWTH: 1978–1988

Industry reform efforts fared significantly better in the 1980s. Localization increased, accelerated by the emergence of an automotive cluster near Bangkok, state limits on the creation of new assembly plants, and state encouragement of the production of specific components. Absent from this picture was any systematic attention to other elements of competitiveness, since the main assumption driving reform efforts was that scale economies would be a sufficient condition for industrial deepening and local productivity improvement. The mixed outcomes of this strategy reflected the expanded but still limited institutional capacities of a moderately nationalist-industrializing network of state officials and local firms whose localization thrust was tempered by the need for scale economies and foreign exchange.

A. The Search for Efficient Localization

Local Content: A renewed push for local automotive production was in part a response to the industry's growing trade deficit and fragmentation. In 1978, state officials banned the import of small CBU vehicles and raised tariffs on both small CBUs and CKD kits.[33] They subsequently raised local content (LC) requirements for passenger vehicles and various types of commercial vehicles. They designed the LC policy to encourage production of components whose technical features were both compatible with and challenging to local firm capacities, and whose potential for standardization and scale economies increased learning opportunities. They did so by

---

[33] Ibid. (199). Unless otherwise noted, the rest of the localization discussion is drawn from Ibid. (199–218).

computing LC by assigning points for parts based on these priorities, and by mandating the deletion from imported CKD kits of parts that met these conditions, thus requiring local production. The adoption of the mandatory deletion requirement was the result of particularly effective pressure by MOI officials and Siam Nawaloha Foundry (SNF), a subsidiary of one of Thailand's largest business groups, Siam Cement, itself a part of the Crown Property Bureau (discussed in Chapter 3). SNF had expanded its machining and casting capacity and was eager to move into automotive products; it established an automotive-oriented subsidiary, Thai Engineering Products, in 1985.[34]

These policies encountered some opposition. Protests against the import ban by smaller assemblers proved ineffective in the face of backing from the larger Japanese firms that had increased local investments in anticipation of the ban. Opposition to raising local content levels to 50% was initially more effective: The Japanese balked at the investments required to move beyond 40%, and resistance also came from more export-oriented state officials, especially in the NESDB. To address the country's debt crisis, these officials had pushed to restructure 10 excessively protected industries, including automobiles. Backed by the World Bank, they argued for *cutting* local content requirements and ending the ban on CBU imports in exchange for a commitment by global automakers to use Thailand as an export base for auto parts. With the Japanese and export-promoters both opposing *further* localization, the MOI froze LC at 45% in 1983.

The freeze was temporary, however. A new Industry Minister, Ob Varusatna, a businessman-politician with close ties to the parts producers, mandated an increase in LC to 70% by 1988, based on a list of specific components available in Thailand. This move was strenuously opposed by both assemblers and state advocates of efficient export promotion. The latter were represented by Ob's replacement as Industry Minister, Chirayu (see Chapter 5). Under pressure to promote exports, a newly formed Industrial Policy Committee urged an end to localization policies. This move was blocked by both local parts firms and Japanese firms with significant investments in local components production. In 1986 and 1987, after extensive consultations among the ADC, the automakers and parts firms, local content was set at 54% for passenger cars, 61% for gasoline pickups, 72% for diesel pickups, and 45% for other commercial vehicles.[35] This proved insufficient for the parts firms who, in 1987, argued that higher

---

[34] Terdudomtham (1996, 25).
[35] Ibid. (8).

localization levels were possible if the assemblers would agree to slow down vehicle changes and place long-term orders. Assemblers rejected the proposal, insisting on their need to make new models available. The parts firms responded by agreeing to maintain the freeze in exchange for a long-term commitment to localization by the automakers. To reconcile these positions, the MOI further revised the LC formula. Instead of compelling assemblers to localize all parts locally available, the new formula required the localization of a gradually increasing number of parts, with mandatory localization of a small number of major components.

Implementing this strategy required greater scale economies than were possible in the already crowded passenger car market. State officials responded by considering the possibility of special incentives for 1-ton pickup trucks, whose sales volume already totaled half of the entire market in 1983. Because large volume production of such a relatively standardized vehicle could provide scale economies for major functional components, the focus on pickup trucks provided support for another major thrust of Thailand's effort to reconcile localization with efficiency: diesel engine production.

Diesel Engines:[36] In 1978, the BOI proposed that Thailand produce diesel engines, stemming in part from Thailand's interest in heading off an ASEAN complementarity scheme that had allocated diesel engine production to Singapore and Indonesia. But initial efforts stumbled; no significant investments had occurred as of 1981. The assemblers delayed, and the BOI lacked the technical experience to design a clear, feasible project. To achieve scale economies, the BOI staff pressed to approve only one manufacturer, but the board, composed of top economic ministers and association representatives, proved less cohesive and more vulnerable to pressures from diverse interests anxious to avoid exclusion from such a large project.

The project was resurrected in 1985, with the BOI intending to approve only one or two operations. Faced with strong pressure from several firms, however, the BOI accepted bids from four groups in 1987. These groups agreed to include motorcycle as well as automobile engines, to raise actual local content from 20% to 80% over five years, to localize the production of certain specific parts, and to pursue exports. They also agreed to two other BOI conditions that promised significant scale economies and learning opportunities: a division of labor in which three of the firms would supply specific components to each other by the mid-1990s, and participation by

---

[36] Unless noted, information on the diesel program is drawn from Doner (1991, 200–201; 215–218).

SNF in three of the projects.[37] These policy initiatives attracted increased numbers of Japanese auto parts producers and encouraged cluster development; helped generate "a group of domestic supplier firms ... as potential clients for linkage and supplier development initiatives;"[38] encouraged investments in products with large potential scale economies; provided the basis for the emergence of SNF as a de facto "national champion" firm; and obtained initial support for automotive exports from the Japanese automakers. On the other hand, there was no significant attention to improving local firms' technology absorption capacity or access to new equipment. Local linkages remained limited, and the industry's expansion resulted in greater import reliance and trade deficits.[39] Even a large engineering firm such as SNF was limited in its capacity to upgrade simply through new market opportunities.

B. Explaining Outcomes

The positive outcomes of growing localization tempered with scale economies were in part the results of Thailand's strong macroeconomic institutions. The country's impressive response to the debt crisis, including its 1984 devaluation (Chapter 4), helped to attract Japanese parts firms seeking to escape Japan's high yen and labor costs. But the emergence of new actors and institutions were also central to this period's achievements. In the private sector, the parts firms became more organized and influential. Most Thai suppliers were SMEs that attempted to influence policy within the assembler-influenced Automotive Parts Industry Club of the peak ATI. By 1978, frustrated with assembler resistance to LC increases, these firms established a separate group, the Thai Automotive Parts Manufacturers' Association. TAPMA, along with SNF, became a powerful voice for localization.

The influence of firms manufacturing auto parts was bolstered by state efforts at industrial deepening. Temporary support came from Ob as the Minister of Industry, but the more durable backing came from career bureaucrats, often with engineering backgrounds. MOI officials promoting mandatory deletion and BOI staff backing diesel engine production were part of a broader group, some of whose members were involved in the Eastern Seaboard infrastructural projects, concerned with reducing the

---

[37] Terdudomtham (1996).
[38] Lauridsen (2004, 570).
[39] Ibid. (572).

country's internal and external imbalances. This group was not monolithic. Some members advocated industrial deepening to shape Thailand's comparative advantage.[40] Others advocated ending LC and focusing solely on exports in line with World Bank recommendations. Nevertheless, a year after the 1987 localization levels were set, the MOI announced its intention to produce a "master policy on car exports."[41] The institutional strengths of this network in autos exceeded anything seen previously. The gradual increases in localization reflected extensive consultations among the assemblers, TAPMA, and state officials. The officials helped to provide information and political support for mandatory deletion.[42] As members of a BOI subcommittee on diesel engines, SNF officials successfully argued that their experience in producing agricultural diesels justified local production of automotive diesels.[43] All of these fora constituted opportunities for learning and for increasing the credibility of Thai automotive policy.

These strengths pose a puzzle: how do we account for the existence of a network promoting efficient localization given the fact that key components, especially the MOI, were part of the clientelist "pork" component of the "pork-policy compromise" of the Prem period reviewed in Chapter 4? Part of the answer lies in the fact that, given the country's overall debt crisis, MOI as well as BOI officials were painfully aware of the need for macroeconomic discipline. Projects involving inappropriate technology and excessive costs were typically considered but dropped.[44] As one official noted, Thailand did not "want to become another Philippines."[45] The importance of this concern was reflected in Ob's replacement by the economist Chirayu in the mid-1980s. And if the sectoral ministries were forced to contend with efficiency concerns, technocrats such as Chirayu were forced to extend their competence from macroeconomic stability to sectoral development.[46]

But the strengths of the institutions associated with this network were limited. Monitoring capacities were hampered by the technological weaknesses of both state actors and most of the parts firms. The institutions governing the Thai auto industry were generally hard pressed to coordinate the actions of numerous actors, some of whom would incur significant

[40] Unger (1998, 143–144).
[41] *Bangkok Post* (March 30, 1988).
[42] Interview # 60.
[43] Doner (1991, 215).
[44] Muscat (1994, 180; 215).
[45] Cited in Unger (1998, 149).
[46] Unger (1998, 179).

losses, in areas requiring specific types of expertise. As a result, they focused on broad localization objectives and big projects, paying little attention to problems such as upstream–downstream tariff reconciliation and technological upgrading of local producers. These outcomes are not surprising in light of political constraints and changing economic conditions. Politically, this is a period in which the ministerial capacities for coordination remained inhibited by coalitional and thus ministerial shifts, problems that intensified with Prem's replacement by Chartchai in 1988. Thai technocrats may have been pushed to address sectoral issues, but the political space in which they could do so remained constrained. Vulnerability pressure for automotive upgrading abated in the latter 1980s, moreover, as investment flooded in, the economy boomed, external balances improved, and automobile sales and production tripled.

IV. LIBERALIZATION AND INTERNATIONALIZATION, 1988–1997

It is tempting to view Thailand's post-1997 surge in automotive exports (Figure 7.2) simply as the automakers' smart response to the crisis-induced fall in domestic demand. In fact, a series of liberalization and export-promotion policies, beginning in 1988, made that response possible. The 1988–1997 period is thus one in which state officials, building on the localization gains of the 1980s, sowed the seeds for Thailand's move toward automotive exports. The formal beginning of this effort was the MOI's introduction of a "master plan on car exports." The "master plan" never constituted a coherent set of guidelines, but it did help to trigger subsequent, successful export promotion efforts.

If moderately successful localization efforts in the 1980s seemed puzzling in light of the "pork-policy" compromise during the Prem period, effective export promotion in the subsequent period might seem even more bewildering. After all, Prem was succeeded by corrupt "buffet cabinets" of the Chartchai government, an authoritarian interlude in 1991–1992, and then several unstable coalition governments (Chapter 4). Part of the explanation for this disjuncture between bureaucratic pathologies and policy achievements lies in the autonomy and technocratic efficiency of the Anand government (though Anand took up efforts initiated by his less autonomous predecessor, and Anand's achievements were extended by his less efficient successors). Another part of the explanation involves the overlap between the state's awareness of global trade liberalization and the resulting need to promote competition and exports on the one hand, and competition-induced export moves by the automakers on the other. Consistent with Robert Wade's concept of "big followership,"[47] Thai officials assisted the automakers "significantly to extend their investments" in Thailand as an automotive export base through sporadic consultation with the automakers and moderate interagency coordination. These institutional capacities proved useful for liberalizing the auto market, providing export incentives, and attracting new entrants, but they were much less conducive to developing linkages and nurturing productivity improvement in local suppliers. In other words, Thai institutions set the stage for the denationalized automotive expansion of the postcrisis period.

A. Promoting Competition and Exports

During the first half of the 1990s, Thai governments adopted an impressive range of measures designed to reform what had become a large, inefficient auto industry. By 1991, 12 firms were producing 16 brands and 42 models in a market of only 304,000 units. Although sales rose at around 30% a year from 1987 to 1991, further market growth was threatened by rising car prices,[48] and Thailand's commitments to reduce tariffs under AFTA and to end local content under the GATT Uruguay Round made liberalization an urgent goal. As seen in Table 7.1, government measures included allowing imports of smaller CBUs, ending model restrictions, providing special tax incentives for pickup trucks and tariff/tax incentives for exporters, promising an end to local ownership requirements, reducing tariffs on both CBUs and CKDs, and reducing the tariff gap between CBUs and CKDs. By making CBUs available and/or cheaper, CKD assemblers would be forced to reduce their costs through internal efficiencies and through cost pressures on local suppliers. With lower profits, parts firms would themselves be forced to export. The export incentives, combined with the existing supplier base and increased support for clusters in industrial estates,[49] stimulated an inflow of new automotive investments. The value of BOI-approved investments in both assembly and parts production from 1994 to 1997 was four times greater than in 1990–1993 and well in excess of those elsewhere in ASEAN.[50] These new arrivals, most of whom would be involved in exports, fueled the development of a new state-promoted cluster.

---

[47] Wade (1990, 28).
[48] Handley (1991, 34).
[49] Paopongsakorn and Kriengkrai (2007).
[50] Paopongsakorn (1999, 7–8).

TABLE 7.1 *Automotive Reform Measures, 1991–1994*

Import Bans
- End ban on imports of CBUs under 2.3 liters (1990)

Model Limits
- End restrictions on series and models (1990)

Tariffs
- CBUs over 2.3 liters from 300% to 100% (1991)
- CBUs under 2.3 liters from 180% to 60% (1991)
- CKDs for cars, pickups and vans from 112% to 20% (1991)
- Testing equipment and machine tools reduce tariffs

Taxes
- Exempt pickup trucks from excise tax (1992)
- Business tax replaced by VAT (1992)

Export Incentives (for firms exporting over 1000 units)
- Exempt tariffs on equipment (1994)
- Exempt corporate tax for eight years (1994)
- Refund import duties on raw materials (1994)
- Cut CKD tariffs from 20% to 2% (1995)
- 0–5% tariffs on inputs for AICO participation (1996)

Ownership
- Commit to ending local ownership requirement (announced 1993; implemented 1997)

Local Content
- 54% for passenger cars; 60% for gasoline pickups; 72% for diesel pickups; divided into List A- required, and List B-chosen by assembler (1989)
- Required use of locally produced diesel engines for 1-ton pickups (1991)

Sources: Bangkok Post (July 3, 4, 1991); Paopongsakorn (1999); Handley (1991, 34); *Bangkok Post* (April 15, 19, 1994); EIU (1994); *Nation* (August 26, 1995); interviews # 29, 24.

B. Linkages: Input Tariffs

One risk of the government strategy was that independent, Thai-owned parts firms would be unable to meet new demands by assemblers forced to compete and export. Highly protected local firms found it more profitable to produce for the domestic market than to export.[51] In principle, tariff reductions on CKD and an end to local content, mandated by the 1993 Uruguay Round, would increase competitive pressures on parts producers. In addition, the replacement of the business tax with VAT was designed to encourage vertical disintegration and thus closer links between assemblers and suppliers.[52]

---

[51] Ibid. (17).
[52] For example, Lauridsen (2005, 72).

Suppliers also suffered from high costs of raw materials and intermediate inputs. As early as 1988, the MOI was concerned about this issue and commissioned studies that led to tariff cuts on testing equipment and machine tools.[53]

Yet as of 1997, tariffs on inputs, especially raw materials such as plastics and steel, stayed high.[54] Since almost all raw materials used in locally made components had to be imported, only a limited number of parts could be made in Thailand in a cost-effective way.[55] Duty drawbacks for raw materials tariffs were available for exporters, but these involved paying interest on working capital tied up while firms endured long administrative procedures. Although tariffs were automatically reduced for involvement in ASEAN Brand-to-Brand and ASEAN Industrial Cooperation (AICO) arrangements, the technical capacities required to participate in these exchanges typically excluded Thai firms from these arrangements.

C. Linkages: Supplier Development

Thai officials were concerned that, owing to these weaknesses, rising local content would involve increased linkages to foreign input producers. In response, the MOI and BOI launched two initiatives designed to help local firms improve their productivity and quality by matching them with foreign assemblers: the BOI Unit for Industrial Linkage Development (BUILD), initiated in 1991, and the National Supplier Development Program, launched in 1994. Having reviewed the general problems of these two programs in Chapter 4, we note here some additional points specific to the auto industry. Budget allocations for BUILD and the NSDP were quite small. This may have reflected officials' hope that the assemblers would become the key drivers.[56] The assemblers were in fact willing to host groups of suppliers, but they never viewed the programs as all that useful. If anything, they conflicted with Japanese assemblers' in-house "cooperation clubs," which aimed to improve suppliers' productivity but have functioned more to create trust and to help suppliers improve their management systems than to diffuse technology. The new government programs were supplemented by at least two other initiatives. One, the MOI's Master Plan for the Development of Supporting Industries (1995) was designed to strengthen firms in activities such as mold and die production. The plan was to be

[53] Interview # 29.
[54] Brooker (1997b, V-10).
[55] Ibid. (V-8, V-3).
[56] This review is based on interviews # 32, 37, 57, 123, and Lauridsen (2005, 31).

implemented by the Metal Industries Development Agency, an agency within the MOI established in the early 1990s, with Japanese technical support. Yet, by the end of 1996, the government had failed to set a budget for the plan.[57]

D. Explaining Outcomes

Thailand made significant progress at liberalizing the auto industry, promoting auto exports, and attracting new firms in this period. Nonetheless, its efforts at strengthening the capacities of independent Thai firms to contend with more open markets fell short. Officials in the MOI and BOI were highly concerned with Thai participation in the auto industry, particularly in the face of Thailand's AFTA and GATT commitments to cut tariffs and to end local contents by 2000, which left the country with a rapidly closing window of opportunity to prepare local producers for full-scale competition.[58] The problem was that these efforts were largely undertaken by career officials, not political leaders, in a broader context of agency fragmentation and associational weakness. Successes occurred in policy areas whose resolution did not require overcoming protests from losers, complex, technical information, or the coordination of multiple actors.

Consider first the Anand government's liberalization measures. A prevalent view is that Anand's success in cutting tariffs and ending the ban on CBU imports was his ability to move without consulting the private sector, including the Japanese automakers.[59] The counterfactual assumption is that predecision consultation would have triggered effective resistance, including from assemblers whose investments in local production came under pressure from more affordable, imported vehicles. There is some truth in this perspective. The assemblers did lodge protests, and the credibility of Anand's military backing was useful. But the protests were over the pace and magnitude of liberalization, not the plan itself.[60] The relatively muted response reflected the fact that the firms had begun to prepare for a more open, export-oriented strategy in 1988, when a strong yen and initiatives by

---

[57] Lauridsen (2004, 576–577).

[58] In addition to BUILD and NSDP efforts, these concerns were reflected in the MOI's 1988 "master plan on car exports," its 1996 "Auto Industry Export Promotion Project," and its 1996 "Master Plan for Supporting Industries."

[59] Author interviews # 22, 30; *Bangkok Post* (June 21, 1991).

[60] *The Nation* (June 19, 1991). On pressure to expand the gap between CKD and CBU tariffs, see *The Nation* (June 6, 1991).

Mitsubishi to use Thailand as an export base had triggered a series of export initiatives by Japanese producers that in turn stimulated export-supporting moves by Thai officials.[61] The reforms thus did not require major new investments and are best understood as a revival of an earlier administration's proposals to cut tariffs.[62] The fact that these reforms were limited to CKDs and CBUs also limited the actors involved and information requirements, so that extensive consultation and monitoring were not required.

What of Thailand's success in promoting automotive clusters on industrial estates? After all, creating industrial estates involves potential distributional conflicts over land rights as well as the need to coordinate multiple actors for the supply of industry-specific goods. As Unger (1998) shows, several of these challenges did in fact delay the estates' development, but opposition by landowners was dampened by the collective action problems of organizing many small owners and by officials' ability to work through powerful, local political interests.[63] The informational challenges were moderated by the fact that automotive firms had already begun to agglomerate to produce large volumes for regional and global export,[64] by the state's decision to provide only general infrastructure and by its decision to leave a number of key functions, such as human resource and technology diffusion, to private property developers. The government's failure to implement its commitment to create an automotive training institute, designed to lure GM, illustrated the low priority of human resource issues for the state. Finally, successful estate development owed much to coordination by the Industrial Estates Authority of Thailand, which existed to promote foreign capital-based exports.[65]

The challenges of linkage promotion, through upstream–downstream tariff adjustment and supplier development, were much greater. Reducing tariffs on raw material and intermediate inputs threatened both state revenues and long-protected firms in petrochemicals, steel, and plastics.[66]

---

[61] "SCG-Toyota Venture Aimed at Reverse Engine Exports" (*The Nation*, May 19, 1988); "Car Exporter Urges Clearance for Auto Parts Exchange Plan." (*Bangkok Post*, February 15, 1988); "Toyota Diesel Engines Head for Portugal" (*Bangkok Post*, February 28, 1989);" Reduction Sought on Auto-Part Duties for Export Assemblers" (The Nation, March 15, 1988); "Panel to Facilitate Export Process" (*Bangkok Post*, May 30, 1988); "Duty Cut Sought to Support Car Exports" (*The Nation*, November 29, 1988).

[62] *Bangkok Post* (March 4, 1992).

[63] Shatkin (2004).

[64] Economist Intelligence Unit (1994, 39, 49).

[65] Glassman (2004a, 127).

[66] *The Nation* (December 13, 1993); Handley (1991, 35).

Because of their variety, reducing tariffs on inputs also involved managing voluminous and complex information. Coordinating these multiple interests, overcoming the losers' opposition, and managing relevant information would have required at least the cohesion and credibility of Anand's military-backed government, and Anand reportedly intended to address the input tariff issue before losing power in 1992.[67] Institutional arrangements under succeeding coalitional governments were even less appropriate for addressing these difficulties.

One problem was simply that politician-ministers did not understand the issues to be dealt with and, given the distributional challenges, had little impetus to address them.[68] Bureaucratic conflicts and fragmentation were also obstacles. The MOI's commitment to reducing upstream tariffs to promote linkages sometimes ran up against the Ministry of Finance's (MOF's) concern with the need for tariff-based revenues. More generally, the two ministries "spoke different languages" and had different views of the private sector.[69] Compared to the engineer-dominated MOI, the MOF, dominated by neoclassical economists, had little knowledge of sector-specific needs or patience for industrialists' appeals. And while the MOI generated research demonstrating the need for cuts on input tariffs, it was the MOF that controlled the overall tariff structure – and even this power was limited. The BOI could and often did grant special tariff treatment for firms as export incentives or for special, one-year exemptions.[70] Responsibility for tariff changes within the MOF was itself divided among multiple committees.[71] The MOF also struggled to define tariffs' role in revenue generation vs. protection, an issue it eventually resolved by adopting a VAT for revenue purposes.[72] When the MOF did attempt more extensive tariff changes, their implementation was often slow due to the inefficiency and outright corruption in the Customs Department and the difficulties of specifying the function of different products within value chains.

Implementation problems were also a function of weaknesses in private sector organization and in public–private consultation. With multiple associations and foreign assemblers often operating individually, the automotive industry lacked an effective unified voice. The activism of the larger, often foreign, parts producers, was further discouraged by their

---

[67] Interview # 21.
[68] Interview # 21.
[69] Interview # 24.
[70] Interview # 25.
[71] Interview # 27.
[72] Interview # 27, from which the rest of this paragraph is drawn.

membership in the "cooperation clubs" organized by each Japanese assembler. Further, linkages between auto firms and officials, especially the MOF, were sporadic at best. Parts firms viewed themselves as particularly excluded from tariff deliberations. While the auto associations mainly operated through the MOI's ADC, their participation in the MOI's principal effort to encourage local upgrading as well as export growth – the 1996 Automotive Industry Export Promotion Project – was negligible.[73] Finally, the promotion of "supporting industries" required significant financial and institutional resources, but the effort relied on a minor agency within the MOI that "lacked political backing."[74]

There was, in sum, "no specific policy" for improving auto industry productivity.[75] Public and private sector institutions were incapable of developing and implementing productivity-related initiatives by the MOI and BOI. The resulting de facto policy presumed that productivity improvement for local firms would result naturally from liberalization and increased scale economies.[76]

V. POSTCRISIS EXPORT SHIFT: TOWARD DENATIONALIZED INDUSTRIALIZATION

The 1997 crisis hit the auto industry hard. Domestic sales, which accounted for 90% of production, dropped from almost 590,000 units in 1996 to 144,000 in 1998 (Table 7.2). This was especially damaging given the industry's excess capacity: capacity utilization, only 48.5% in 1996, dropped to 24% in 1998.[77] But by 2003, sales rebounded to over 500,000 units, and, combined with growing exports, resulted in production exceeding 1 million in 2005).[78] Exports were especially impressive, growing from almost nothing to 235,000 units ($2.4 billion), roughly a third of production (Figure 7.7). Parts exports rose as well, from roughly $23 million in 1996 to $568 million in 2003.[79] At the same time, the industry became more efficient, as reflected in labor productivity, falling prices, and trade balances.[80]

---

[73] Interview # 41.
[74] Lauridsen (2005, 50).
[75] Terdudomtham (1996, 15).
[76] Manuavee (2000, 97).
[77] Paopongsakorn (1999, 9).
[78] Thailand Automotive Institute (http://www.thaiauto.or.th/Records/eng/vehicleproduction_eng.asp).
[79] Asia Policy Research (2005, 10).
[80] Paopongsakorn and Kriengkrai (2007, 29).

TABLE 7.2 *Automotive Sales in Thai Domestic Market (1990–2004)*

Year	Total (Unit)	Passenger Car	Total Commercial Vehicle	Commercial Vehicle					
				Van & Micro Bus	1 Ton Pick Up	2–4 Ton Truck	Truck Over 4 Ton	Less Than 1 Ton	OPV
1990	304,062	65,864	238,198	6,980	167,613	15,920	32,126	11,960	3,599
1991	268,560	66,779	201,781	7,670	155,366	10,312	15,895	10,200	2,338
1992	362,987	121,441	241,546	9,924	182,958	12,465	17,549	14,490	4,160
1993	456,468	174,169	282,299	11,727	224,388	12,717	15,573	14,207	3,687
1994	485,678	155,670	330,008	12,672	258,091	14,139	22,312	19,564	3,230
1995	571,580	163,371	408,209	12,425	323,813	16,383	31,766	16,402	4,720
1996	589,126	172,730	416,396	12,633	327,663	16,683	31,814	15,018	12,585
1997	363,156	132,060	231,096	8,353	188,324	9,021	11,275	5,642	8,481
1998	144,065	46,300	97,765	2,792	81,263	2,838	3,756	2,841	4,275
1999	218,330	66,858	151,472	4,167	129,904	3,750	3,434	3,018	7,199
2000	262,189	83,106	179,083	6,492	151,703	4,655	4,804	3,780	7,649
2001	296,985	104,502	192,483	6,582	168,639	3,807	4,398	2,686	6,371
2002	409,362	126,353	283,009	8,335	241,266	4,564	5,560	1,664	21,620
2003	533,176	179,005	354,171	8,489	309,144	7,366	1,216	1,478	16,492
2004	552,775	184,047	368,728	8,841	326,192	7,853	12,958	806	9,908

Source: Thai Automotive Institute 2005 – in Asia Policy Research (2005, 7)

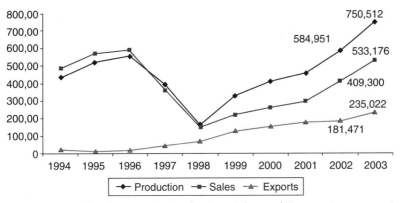

FIGURE 7.7 Thai Automotive Production, Sales, and Exports (1994–2003)
Source: Thai Automotive Institute http://www.thaiauto.or.th/Records/eng/vehicle-production_eng.asp

Serious linkage problems remained, however. The industry was still heavily dependent on imported raw materials and intermediates,[81] and independent Thai producers lost ground. As noted, many went bankrupt; those that survived followed the "partner or perish" strategy of becoming joint ventures with foreign firms. Several years after the crisis, local producers remained technologically weak and uncompetitive in export markets.[82] In 2005, a Japanese report summarized the "ambiguity" of Thailand's export-led automotive growth: "If Thai firms grow healthily along with foreign firms, all is well. But if local firms are eliminated and the industrial base continues to be dominated by foreign firms due to the lack of competitiveness or ineffective policy, will Thailand still be satisfied?"[83]

These uneven outcomes are puzzling in light of efforts to promote both exports and local inputs, which occurred within a more systematic and consultative industrial planning effort than had ever been the case in Thailand. This process began with the Industrial Restructuring Project in 1998 and intensified under a detailed "master plan" (2002–2006) during the Thaksin governments.[84] The plan's contents and goals emerged from the business community, while its "design, implementation and adjustment" were a cooperative effort of business and government.[85] These arrangements achieved uneven results:

[81] Asia Policy Research (2005, 17).
[82] Ibid. (19); and "Liberalisation Looms for Inefficient Sector." Bangkok Post (February 18, 1999).
[83] Ohno (2005, 3).
[84] Thailand Automotive Institute (2002).
[85] Ohno (2005, 5).

their strengths reflected the political elite's acute sensitivity to crisis- and liberalization-induced vulnerabilities, while their weaknesses reflected not only the gradual moderation of those pressures but also the fragmenting impact of multiple veto players, even under Thaksin's one-party rule.

A. Tariff and Tax Reform

Committed to ending local content requirements by January 2000, the government shifted to trade and tax policy as *the* key mechanisms for promoting both export expansion and local producers.[86] In 1999, the MOF raised tariffs on CKD parts from 20% to 30–35%, while maintaining high duties on raw materials and intermediates. This protectionist move was offset by a number of other measures. To cushion the impact of higher duties on consumers, the Ministry cut excise taxes. To sustain competitive pressure on parts producers and to gain access to regional markets, it negotiated FTAs with Australia and Japan and moved toward an integrated regional market by approving AICO applications and agreeing to implement AFTA commitments to lower tariffs on automotive products traded within the region to 0–5% by 2003. To ensure that these agreements would not discourage local production (since firms could use AFTA or FTAs to import rather than produce components in Thailand), governments continued to lure new investors with special incentives. Especially important was easy access to otherwise-protected raw materials and intermediates for direct exporters or where suitable local products were not available.[87] Because foreign firms dominated the export sector, they, not local producers, benefited from such incentives. Thai trade policy was thus a de facto strategy of FDI promotion that provided only superficial support for local producers of parts or upstream inputs. Absent was reciprocity of the sort practiced in South Korea, where the state extended protection to upstream firms in exchange for productivity improvements (Amsden 1989).

B. The Search for Niche Products

Eco-Cars: With roughly 70% of Thai production devoted to a limited market for pickups, industry officials and firms discussed the need for a "2nd product champion" to help sustain exports and scale economies for

---

[86] Unless noted, this review is drawn from 1998. "Auto Tariff Reforms a Priority." *Bangkok Post.* (January 9, 1998); "Automobiles – Buyers Will not be Affected as Hike Offset by Excise Cut." *Bangkok Post.* (January 24, 1999); OIE (2002); and Ohno (2005, 15).

[87] Interview # 79.

domestic parts production. In 2004, the government proposed promoting small, energy-efficient passenger vehicles known as "city cars" or "eco cars."[88] The project was the focus of extensive consultation with the automakers who, while favorable, raised concerns that the eco-car would undermine sales of pickup trucks, that demand for the vehicle was uncertain and might not justify large investments, and that state-specified criteria for promoted vehicles might preclude necessary flexibility in vehicle design. These problems, combined with cabinet changes, resulted in vacillation that fed assembler skepticism.[89]

But the need for a new export channel became especially important in late 2006, when political instability shook the domestic market. In response, the caretaker government that had overthrown Thaksin revived the project and approved a set of incentives, including a preferential excise tax rate and eight-year exemptions from corporate taxes and equipment tariffs regardless of production location in Thailand. To qualify, the cars would have to be energy-efficient and environmentally friendly, and assemblers would have to invest at least $145 million, produce at least 100,000 vehicles a year within five years, and produce at least 80% of parts domestically.[90] Production would not begin until 2009, but the decision seems a clear instance of bureaucratic initiative in the face of assembler concerns and political changes.

Replacement Parts: Production of spare parts for the replacement market (REM) emerged as an alternative for the large numbers of "non-tier" Thai firms unable to participate in assembler-led OEM networks. Institutionalized support became especially important as Thai REM producers feared losing market share to Chinese producers.[91] The program, which builds on an earlier clustering initiative by spare parts producers, involves the creation of the Cluster of Thai Automotive Parts (CTAP). With support from the MOC (especially the Commerce Ministry's Department of Export Promotion), CTAP signed agreements with a consortium of U.S. parts importers and established an auto re-export facility in the United Arab Emirates to service Middle East customers. Although the results of these initiatives were

---

[88] "Eco-friendly cars to qualify for tax breaks." *Bangkok Post* (June 15, 2004).

[89] Pichaya (2005).

[90] "BOI drives the eco-car forward," *Thailand Investment Review* (July 2007); and *The Economist.* (June 21, 2007).

[91] The rest of this discussion is drawn from interview # 110; and from *Financial Times Information.* (March 20, 2003); Thai Press Reports. (November 16, 2005; and Bangkok Post (November 7, 2005); Nation. (June 25, 2002).

not clear as of this writing, we can identify two significant institutional features. CTAP has been built on close, long-standing ties between smaller parts firms, represented by TAPMA and the Department of Export Promotion. These linkages are not yet integrated, however, with more assembler-based networks focused on expanding the pool of skilled personnel and local R&D capacities.

C. Technical Training

Like other Thai manufacturing sectors, the auto industry lacks technical personnel.[92] The skill shortage prompted assembler initiatives at improving automotive training in Thai educational institutions prior to the crisis[93] and Japan-financed training efforts under the IRP after 1997.[94] Neither of these efforts achieved much, and with the problem worsening as the industry recovered, the MOI and Thai Automotive Institute (TAI) worked with Japanese firms and aid agencies to create an Automotive Human Resources Development Project (AHRDP), initiated in 2006. The AHRDP is essentially a "train the trainer" program in which firms agree on skill-specific certification standards and help run an automotive "academy" focused on specific competencies. Graduates of this institution in turn staff technical institutions to train others. What makes this program especially significant is its base in collaboration among four global auto firms, each of which will specialize in a particular competency. This is the first significant case of industry-based collaboration on production issues since the diesel engine project.

The AHRDP will, in principle, strengthen the entire industry, including the small number of large, independent Thai producers. Smaller Thai producers are concerned, however, that the program will be a weak add-on to in-house training efforts and that it will largely exclude "non-tier" producers. Such firms had little input into the program's development, and their ability to make use of new competencies is constrained by their inability to afford modern equipment. The principal area of potential overlap between the AHRDP and small, independent firms involves the program's intention to provide training for mold and die producers. These "supporting

---

[92] In 1997, only 3% of those employed in the Thai auto industry were engineers (Paopongsakorn 1999, 22–23). See also "Auto workers: It's dog eat dog." *The Nation.* (May 20, 2004).

[93] Brimble and Doner (2007).

[94] Unless noted, information in this section is based on interviews # 83, 117, 115, 121; Lauridsen (2005, 52–67); and Thai Automotive Institute (2005, 12).

industries" constitute a critical upstream step for locally produced plastic and metal auto parts. This is an area in which past LC requirements have generated around 500 local producers with experience and potential comparative advantage.[95] With the collapse of the auto industry and assemblers' demand for higher grade quality, the mold and die firms' need for support intensified. The official response was a set of Master Plans under the Industrial Restructuring Project, the creation of the Thai–German Institute to provide training in production technology, and the establishment of a National Institute of Molds and Dies. Despite the impressive resulting range of technology transfer activities, the ability of local mold and die producers to benefit and survive remains questionable in light of assembler moves to procure molds and dies from transplants or produce them in-house.

D. Product Standards and Testing

If local firms were to survive as second- or third-tier producers, or even as REM producers, they needed to test and certify the quality of their products. In 2002, TAPMA and the TAI proposed the creation of an independent testing facility to be part of a broader effort to develop a university-based automotive engineering program.[96] At the time, parts producers spent large sums of money and time to have their products tested overseas, usually paying the assemblers in Japan for these services. Without a testing center, small Thai manufacturers seemed likely to lose parts manufacturing to multinational corporations or major-brand-controlled suppliers.[97] But the proposal garnered little support from either the assemblers or top officials.[98] In 2005, the Industry Minister, the head of a large Thai parts firm, questioned the idea on the grounds that the assemblers had their own facilities and that it would be difficult to know if the products tested actually had export potential.[99] He subsequently backed the proposal for the facility, but the Budget Bureau refused to fund the center on the grounds that suppliers could use assembler facilities.[100]

---

[95] Lauridsen (2005, 64–67).
[96] Interview # 121.
[97] "Research and Testing Centre Revived After Three Years on Hold." *Bangkok Post.* (December 31, 2005).
[98] *Financial Times Information.* (August 20, 2004).
[99] *Bangkok Post* (October 10, 2005.
[100] Interview # 117; interview # 121.

E. Explaining Outcomes

The initiatives reviewed above were undertaken in the context of extensive consultation, first through the IRP and subsequently under Thaksin's Master Plan. The plan was not an exercise in Northeast Asian-style sectoral intervention but rather a combination of "top-down liberalization with general support measures."[101] The 300-page document drew on a series of meetings organized by the TAI, including some 400 industry participants and led by prominent industry figures, that generated surveys, SWOT analysis, vision plans, and action plans.[102] Many questioned Thailand's capacity for implementing and monitoring the action plans, and with good reason.[103] The preceding analyses of specific policy tasks, as well as statements by Thai officials themselves, indicate a much more jagged set of capacities than implied by the presence of a master plan and a top-level Automotive Strategy Committee. What emerges from my analysis are three tiers, sometimes overlapping, with different foci and capacities.

At the top were the Finance Ministry, the Industrial Estates Authority, the BOI, and the foreign assemblers represented within the FTI. Dominated on the state side by economists, this network effectively addressed issues influencing the volume, nature, and location of automotive investment: trade policy and investment incentives. This tier's success is due in part to its extensive formal and informal coordination, as well as to the small number of actors involved (i.e., major producers and top-level officials), the low information requirements of most trade and investment issues (especially those unconnected to technology), and the relatively minor distributional differences among the major players. Significantly, the main area in which these actors made little progress involved upstream tariffs, which requires multiple actors (including Customs), potentially creates domestic losers, and has high information requirements. It is also an area in which loopholes could allow foreign producers a virtual free trade regime.

At the second tier was the MOI, especially its Office of Industrial Economics, the TAI, and the assemblers and key suppliers. Influenced by engineers, this network focused largely on productivity issues, such as standards, skills development, and product benchmarking.[104] The speed of its activities has been slower and its impact less clear than those of the

---

[101] Ohno (2005, 3).
[102] Interview # 67.
[103] Ohno (2005, 2). Concerns were also reflected in NESDB calls for a "national auto committee on auto industry" (*Financial Times Information*. March 20, 2003).
[104] Thai Automotive Institute (2005); OIE (2005).

first-tier network, in part because it deals with more technologically complex issues that and involve coordinating many players. In principle, the distributional difficulties are not significant, but because the group may address productivity issues in-house or through more vertical arrangements, assemblers and "follow source" suppliers have less incentive to devote significant resources to them. In the face of such challenges, Thai institutions are only moderately strong. The parts associations are divided between large, often foreign suppliers and smaller local producers.[105] There is little expertise within the state on these issues, with the minor exception of MOI agencies. These conditions leave the TAI heavily reliant on the interests and resources of foreign producers.

The third tier is occupied by the Departments of Export Promotion and Industrial Promotion on the one hand, and independent Thai firms, often operating within TAPMA and the mold and die associations on the other. This tier focuses on market development and technological improvement, especially for SMEs, which are more information- and coordination-intensive than the issues addressed by the top two tiers. Success in these areas does not involve losses. Technology absorption and development is difficult for firms that are simply trying to get product out the door and often lack funds for new machinery and training. The level of consultation at this tier is extensive, but as noted, the coordinating agencies and firms at this tier are often divided, and the relevant state agencies are not strong enough to manage successful collaboration. Lacking support from the first tier, this network had little credibility to impose sanctions or grant significant rewards. The result was "a weak linkage policy and the lack of a coherent supplier development policy".[106]

Our explanation for this variation itself hinges on the political fragmentation of the period and on the shifting pressures facing political elites. The coalitional struggles under Chuan and interfactional fight under Thaksin affected the auto industry, albeit unevenly. Cabinet shifts may have delayed tariff and tax reform, but they did not block them, especially when it came to expanding investment and exports. Political shifts were more deleterious to productivity-related initiatives, especially those affecting independent Thai firms: ministerial turnover offered new interests the chance to block policy initiatives or ushered in leaders ignorant of important challenges.

---

[105] Interview # 102.
[106] Lauridsen (2005, 73).

The policy activism and uneven institutional capacities of this period are themselves best understood as responses to two sets of pressures.[107] The most important, of course, was the need to recover after the 1997 crash and to prepare for Thailand's commitment to end local content and reduce tariffs. Facing a five-year window of opportunity, political elites supported (or at least did not block) investment and market development incentives. In addition, the crisis and subsequent partisan competition raised the political importance of local SMEs.[108] Concern with the fate of Thai producers contributed to the impressive frenzy of consultation in the IRP and fed into the efforts of mid-level officials in the MOI to improve indigenous productivity. But the pressures abated. As noted in Chapter 4, Thaksin's concern with manufacturing SMEs was short-lived, diluted by his political success, his focus on services, and his tendency to cede manufacturing issues to foreign producers, especially following the auto industry's recovery, which blinded top officials to the need to strengthen the local supply base. Their main focus was on expansion through new product promotion and market access via AFTA and FTAs.[109]

This is not to detract from Thailand's impressive macro, trade and investment policies and related institutions. With these policies, relatively rare in the developing world, the auto industry could "take care of itself." Just as Thailand's general economic recovery defused efforts to combine export and industrial promotion by creating a Japanese-style Ministry of International Trade and Industry (MITI), the automotive recovery weakened efforts to strengthen the position of local firms in the industry. Now, the industry's dominant feature is the presence of foreign-dominated production enclaves, with ambiguous implications for upgrading. This arrangement may well alleviate foreign exchange constraints; it may anchor foreign enterprises more firmly to Thailand; and it may lead to certain spillovers to domestic firms. But it does not solve the underlying problem of weak linkages and value-added leakage.

VI. INDONESIA AND SOUTH KOREA

In terms of production, sales, exports, trade balances, and strength of local firms, Thailand's auto industry is more developed than Indonesia's but less than South Korea's. This lineup suggests that despite potential scale

---

[107] Monsakul (2000, 98–127).
[108] Lauridsen (2004, 577); see also Chapter 4.
[109] Interview # 117.

economies, large populations are no guarantee of automotive success. Nor is performance correlated with the presence of foreign firms, local owner-ship, or the timing of auto industrialization efforts.[110] In the following analyses, we trace cross-national variation in auto industrialization to capacities for overcoming key development tasks and the factors underlying those capacities.

A. Indonesia

Like Thailand, Indonesia has achieved impressive growth and structural change. From the beginning of President Suharto's New Order in 1966 to the 1977 crisis, real GDP in Indonesia grew at 5% annually, poverty rates declined significantly, and the economy shifted from reliance on a small number of agricultural products and natural resources to a more balanced structure.[111] With the growth of manufactures (from 10% of GDP in 1966 to 25% in 1996) and manufactured exports (from 0% in 1966 to 53% of total exports in 1996), Indonesia's export profile became more diverse than expected for a country with its level of development and resource endow-ment. The auto industry has contributed to Indonesia's impressive perfor-mance. From under 10,000 units in 1970, production rose to roughly 389,000 in 1997. The industry's share of total manufacturing also grew, from 1.6% in 1975 to 5.3% in 1990.[112] Sales and production fell dra-matically in 1988 but rebounded by 2003. Local parts production rose as well, from 30% to 40% share of the industry's value added between the 1980s and 1990s.[113] Components exports rose from almost nothing in

---

[110] On numbers of local firms and Japanese suppliers in Thailand vs. Indonesia, see fn. 2, this chapter. Until the 1997 crisis, the foreign presence in Korea was small. The crisis triggered the bankruptcy of four of the five assemblers: Kia, Daewoo, Samsung Motors, and Ssangyong. Hyundai, the only viable locally owned firm, took over Kia and a dominant (70%) share of the domestic market. GM acquired Daewoo, Renault took over Samsung, and Ssangyong was sold to a Chinese firm. The crisis also weakened local parts firms and ushered in an influx of foreign firms, of which some 100 either entered the Korean parts industry or expanded their presence. All global first-tier suppliers now operate in Korea. (See Ravenhill 2002; DNR 2007). Foreign ownership was limited in all three countries (relative to Latin America, but most limited in Korea, less so in Indonesia, and still less in Thailand (Amsden 2001, 212). Thailand and Korea both began auto industrialization efforts in the early 1960s, whereas Indonesia began in 1970s (Doner 1991, Ch. 6). For arguments that national ownership is a necessary but insufficient basis for success, see DNR (2004, 197).

[111] Rock (2003, 2–4).

[112] Ito (2003, 8).

[113] Aswicahyono, Basri and Hill [ABH] (2000, 225–226); Okamoto and Sjoholm (2000, 62).

1989 to over $1 billion in 1993.[114] And by 2003, Japanese assemblers had moved to make Indonesia an export base for "multipurpose vehicles" with over 50% local content.[115]

This progress is relatively recent, however, and if Indonesia's auto industry has grown, its performance has been inferior to Thailand's. According to a 2000 study, Indonesia's "very disappointing" automotive development record resulted in the country missing "the opportunity to become Southeast Asia's leading automotive nation" – an opportunity seized by Thailand.[116] Indonesia's relative weakness is all the more interesting because the country's officials viewed the industry as a key stimulus for technological modernization, giving more attention to automobile policy than to that of any other manufacturing industry. Moreover, Indonesian auto development was undertaken under a single veto player authoritarian regime, as was Korea's. The contrasting outcomes reflect the impact of two factors that differentiate Indonesia from Thailand and Korea: ethnic divisions and petroleum revenues.

Policy Tasks: Whereas Thailand's initiation of local auto assembly was a response to balance of payments problems, Indonesia's move into the industry reflected a marriage of state-led developmentalism and emerging private interests. After a short, free import regime in the latter 1960s, officials in the Department of Industry mandated local assembly and restricted the import of CBUs in 1969.[117] These measures were the first step in a series of localization and rationalization efforts undertaken by a group of "bureaucratic nationalist"[118] officials who viewed autos as part of an integrated industrial base that could contribute to national resilience.[119] They were followed by a ban on foreign control of the assembly sector and calibrated tariffs to encourage sales of commercial vehicles in 1972; a ban on CBU imports in 1974; mandatory localization of specific commercial vehicle components in 1976; and localization of diesel engines and major components in 1983. Localization requirements were loosened somewhat after a mid-1980s recession, but significant liberalization measures came only in the early 1990s.[120]

---

[114] UN Comtrade Data, cited in DNR (2006).
[115] "Auto Industry Analysis Report"(2004).
[116] ABH (2000, 210).
[117] This review of localization measures is drawn from Sato (1996); Doner (1992, Ch. 6); ABH (2000).
[118] Robison (1986, 149).
[119] Rock (2003).
[120] For a review of Indonesia's liberalization, see Doner, Noble, and Ravenhill (2007).

Private sector compliance with state goals was far from complete, but increasingly costly investments were made, as reflected in growing numbers of locally assembled vehicles and parts. How were the *risks of these investments socialized?* For local capital, especially Indonesian–Chinese firms, auto investments offered access to state protection and to new, state-sponsored market opportunities. Indeed, even before the 1969 directive, Astra, a then little-known Indonesian–Chinese group, joined the Department of Industry in an assembly venture.[121] Astra's investments, as well as others by well-placed local interests, triggered high levels of protection and generated a great deal of rent-seeking activity in the industry.[122]

Other factors also helped to reduce the risks for foreign (mostly Japanese) automakers and components firms. The automakers were under pressure from local partners, such as Astra, to comply with the state's developmental nationalism. Given the country's sometimes explicit anti-Japanese (and anti-ethnic Chinese) feelings, Japanese firms needed local partners. In addition, the Japanese were unwilling to cede a potentially large market to each other The possibility of large volume production of commercial vehicles, favored by the government with low taxes, was especially compelling.[123]

The Japanese managed to limit costs by keeping production in-house and by adapting flexible production methods to small volumes.[124] Finally, the domestic market was relatively strong, buoyed by government purchases; until the early 1980s, state enterprises, funded by oil revenues, were major buyers of the industry's output.[125]

As in Thailand, Indonesia's success in attracting investors resulted in market fragmentation. But Indonesia's record on *rationalizing* this industry was worse than Thailand's. Numerous efforts to encourage scale economies by limiting models and encouraging firms to share production of standardized parts achieved little. As late as 2002, there were still some 20 major assembly operations, none of which had significant scale economies. The situation was better in commercial than in passenger vehicles, but even in the former, the three dominant producers operated at under 100,000 units a year.[126] The root of this problem was the industry's politically based organization. Until the late 1990s, the assembly of various brands came under the purview of only four Indonesian business groups functioning as

---

[121] Sato (1996).
[122] Aswicahyono and Feridhanusetyawan (2004, 17); see also ABH (2000, 223).
[123] Doner, (1991, 305, fn. 23).
[124] Doner (1991, 83, 135).
[125] ABH (2000, 216).
[126] Ibid. (219); see also Okamoto and Sjoholm (2000, 68).

"brand holder sole agents." Most of these were selected for their political influence rather than their manufacturing capacities, and prior to 1999, they were authorized by the government to import, produce, sell, or export cars, as well as to produce major components. This arrangement discouraged *linkage development,* beginning with local parts production. Because brand holders controlled multiple brands and assembly operations, there was "little apparent synergy in the production activities of these groups, even at the firm level."[127] Weak brand synergy, combined with high protection, discouraged Japanese parts producers from developing close ties with joint venture partners or fostering local input suppliers. Nor was there much incentive to use a key local intermediate – steel. Officials did have plans to develop a government-owned operation, Krakatau Steel, into an integrated metals complex to serve auto parts, but Krakatau was a notoriously inefficient money loser funded largely by rising state oil revenues. The poor quality of its product undermined government pressure on foreign producers for full localization of even simple parts, such as cabins and frames.[128] Owing to this combination of factors, the component industry itself was largely an assembly operation relying on imported, semifinished products.[129]

Conditions were even less propitious for improving the technological capacities of local firms. The weakness of joint ventures between foreign and local parts firms, as well as the lack of subcontracting ties, deprived local firms of key technology sources. Nor was there much state support for technology absorption. Indonesian officials tended to share their Thai counterparts' assumption that scale economies were a sufficient condition for learning. More broadly, Indonesia's poor record in secondary and tertiary education, combined with the country's lack of manufacturing support services or R&D centers, provided little support for firms attempting to upgrade their productivity.[130] Indonesia's principal bright spot involved Astra, the "model proponent of the government's policies."[131] In the early-mid 1980s, the group created a Technology Development Division to

---

[127] ABH (2000, 219).

[128] Doner (1991, 154).

[129] ABH (2000, 219).

[130] Whereas Rock correctly emphasizes Indonesia's achievements in primary education (2003, 4), our emphasis here is on the latter years. According to World Bank figures cited in Thee (2006, 351), Indonesia ranked lowest on education expenditure as a percentage of total government spending and on percentage of relevant age group in secondary and tertiary education. On the weakness of government support and research institutions, see Rasiah (2004, 23); and Dhanani (2000, 9–10).

[131] Sato (1996, 257).

support its move into components production.[132] But Astra never came anywhere near to attaining Hyundai's technology level and was compelled to sell the majority share of its manufacturing operations to Toyota and Daihatsu after the Asian crisis.

Institutional Capacities: Indonesia's auto industrialization efforts were led by a relatively small group of "bureaucratic nationalists" in the Ministry of Trade and the Department of Industry's Directorate of Basic Industries.[133] With relatively long tenures in office, backing from the President, and a solid sense of the need for scale economies, these officials would seem to have been well equipped to implement their national industrialization project. In fact, their achievements were largely limited to the creation of an assembly industry, albeit one whose focus on multipurpose vehicles provided the basis for industrial expansion after liberalization. This record reflected uneven institutional capacities. Success in promulgating early localization measures hinged on extensive consultations with local auto industrialists as a collective body. In the early 1970s the architects of the early measures engineered a merger between the two existing associations to create GAAKINDO, the Indonesian Association of Automobile Sole Agents and Assemblers. This merger not only facilitated information flows necessary for the new policies, it also crystallized an alliance between *pribumi* (ethnic Indonesian) and *non-pribumi* (ethnic Chinese) entrepreneurs. Unfortunately, this alliance proved somewhat fragile. As localization efforts expanded, *pribumi* interests resisted, whereas the stronger Chinese groups complied. The result was a splintering of earlier, more cohesive arrangements. GAAKINDO fragmented in the late 1970s as higher localization pitted "weak" (*pribumi*) against "strong" (*non-pribumi*) brothers. State officials increasingly sought to bypass *pribumi* firms and GAAKINDO by developing bilateral, often clientelist links with the more compliant Chinese firms. This strategy may have helped pressure foreign firms into greater local production. But it triggered *pribumi* resistance to localization efforts. This in turn posed challenges of monitoring and sanctions beyond the capacities of state officials.[134]

Veto Players: When compared to the stagnation of auto policy in the previous, highly fragmented Sukarno governments, the advantages of Suharto's single veto player regime are clear.[135] Under the New Order, officials acted

---

[132] Doner (1991, 154–155); Sato (1996, 262).

[133] This discussion is based on Doner (1992, Chs. 6, 9).

[134] Doner (1991, 152).

[135] See MacIntyre (2003), Hansen (1971).

decisively to promote local auto production. Yet the New Order's credibility in auto industrialization was limited. These limits stemmed from two factors. One was the regime's need to balance developmental and ethnic objectives. Going full tilt for localization would have meant weeding out weaker players, which would have undermined support from *pribumi* business interests. But even if it had elected to push harder for localization and rationalization, the state still had to deal with the lack of institutional capacities to implement its plans. It lacked these capacities, we believe, because there was no pressure to develop them. This lack of pressure also helps to explain the even more basic puzzle of why Indonesia did not turn to export promotion earlier.

Systemic Pressures: Indonesia's automotive development efforts were undertaken in a context of much greater financial security than was the case in Thailand. The growth of petroleum revenues in the 1970s made possible the pursuit of national resilience through industrialization, of which auto policy was a part. Pertamina funds were used to stimulate demand for locally assembled vehicles and as a source of subsidized credit for or direct investment in local auto producers. The firms used these funds to expand manufacturing activities and to move into new economic activities. In contrast to the Thai case, petroleum revenues delayed the move to automotive exports, even in the face of recession and a decline in revenues in the 1980s. The fall in oil prices pushed Suharto to liberalize the trade and investment regimes, but not to act on the scale of Anand's reforms, and the liberalization move did not extend to an export push in autos. In contrast to the Korean case, Indonesia's revenues encouraged a move to industrial deepening without any real pressure to be competitive.

B. South Korea

Although South Korea is the only country since Japan to create a successful, indigenous assembly industry, it has not succeeded in developing a technologically sophisticated components sector.[136] The industry also has significant overcapacity problems which, when combined with high levels of debt, contributed to the bankruptcy of four assemblers and control by foreign automakers in the wake of the 1997 Asian crisis.[137] "Decades of meandering policies, failed directives, and bureaucratic squabbling" in

---

[136] For background, see Biggart and Guillen (1999, 730). The one possible exception is the Hyundai spinoff, Mobis. I am grateful to John Ravenhill for comments on this point.

[137] Ravenhill (2002).

Korea's auto industry help to account for its problems.[138] Nonetheless, Korea has performed comparatively very well, especially in addressing upgrading-related policy challenges.

Policy Tasks: Beginning in 1962, when a military coup established Park Chung Hee as president, the Korean government launched a series of *risk socialization* measures to attract local investment in auto manufacturing. These plans had more to do with "lobbying and bribing of government officials" than with automotive development, however.[139] The Long-Term Development Plan of 1973, adopted after Park's tightening of authoritarian control under the Yushin Constitution (1971), was the true beginning of systematic state efforts to draw local investment in auto assembly and eventually exports. These efforts included subsidized loans, limits on entry of foreign producers, tariff exemptions for inputs, bans or tariffs on imports, LC requirements, infrastructure development, domestic demand stimulus, accelerated capital depreciation, and designation of specific parts firms as affiliates of particular assemblers.[140] Although many of these measures resemble those adopted by Indonesia and Thailand, Korea's approach was distinctive in its strong preference for local firms, its systematic and early encouragement of auto exports, and its linking auto exports to Korea's second-stage import substitution effort, the country's Heavy and Chemical Industrialization project (HCI). Put differently, Korea aimed to socialize the risks of upgrading – to encourage Korean firms to produce export-level quality using local inputs. Korea is also distinctive in the government's "capacity push" strategy of encouraging investment ahead of demand.[141] This approach was designed to accelerate learning by increasing scale economies.

This strategy quickly led to overcrowded markets.[142] That the problem became more serious after the 1997 crisis testifies to the difficulties of industry *rationalization,* despite numerous efforts by Korean officials to address it.[143] Yet gauged by the growth of Korean producers, Korea managed these problems better than other developing countries. It did so, first, by repeated efforts to restrict market entry for assemblers. Although never fully successful, these measures did reduce some industry crowding.[144] Entry limitations were supplemented by at least two other measures designed to

---

[138] Ibid. (116).
[139] Lew (1992, 145).
[140] Lew (1992; Ravenhill 2002).
[141] Lautier (2001).
[142] Ravenhill (2002, 118–122).
[143] Ibid.; Lew 1992).
[144] Huang (2002, 556–557); Doner (1991, 410–412).

encourage scale economies and learning: the state's imposition of pressure to export and the combination of localization requirements with severe model limits. Both of these limitations were imposed earlier in Korea than in the other two cases. In 1973, the government directed assemblers to reduce the number of models and to produce a "people's car," a small vehicle whose low costs would stimulate demand and whose relative simplicity would encourage standardization.[145] This was the basis of Hyundai's highly successful Pony.[146] Finally, the government encouraged the clustering of parts producers by establishing an industrial district in Changwon.[147]

South Korea was also relatively successful with regard to *linkage development*. Although weaker than the assembly sector, the parts sector was strengthened by a series of localization policies in the 1980s designed to reduce the industry's trade deficit with Japan and to stabilize parts delivery from local firms experiencing labor unrest.[148] As part of the HCI program, the auto industry was also designed to stimulate and make use of locally produced intermediates and capital equipment.[149] As such, it constituted a downstream customer for steel produced by the state-owned Pohang Iron and Steel Company.[150] As a user of capital goods, the industry also became an important producer of machine tools. Prompted by the rapid growth in auto demand, especially exports, car assemblers signed technology license agreements in the 1980s to produce machine tools; by the 1990s, Hyundai initiated its own designs for such equipment. In fact, "the technological learning and investment" of industries like auto producers became "the springboard for the development of the Korean capital goods industry."[151]

The *technological learning* of automotive user firms was indeed impressive, as Korean companies rapidly adopted and improved imported technologies.[152] This technological development was in part a result of the state's early efforts to encourage technology acquisition by indirect means, such as capital imports and technology licensing, rather than FDI.[153]

---

[145] Lew (1992, 172–173).
[146] Doner (1991, 412).
[147] Markusen and Park (1993).
[148] See Lew (1992, 304–308, 191).
[149] Ibid. (173–174).
[150] Specific data on this is unavailable. Our assumption that such use was extensive is based on the fact that POSCO had become one of the world's most efficient producers and largest exporters by the mid-1980s (Amsden 1989, Ch. 12), and that it was also one of the largest producers of automotive steel sheet (e.g., Fujimoto and Oh 2006).
[151] Lew (1992), 184).
[152] Ravenhill (2002, 127).
[153] Kim (2001, 301).

Indeed, Korea went well beyond our other two cases in enforcing guidelines on technology transfer, ownership, and raw materials provision.[154] In auto parts, the government acted in the early 1980s to supplement these guidelines with subsidized financing for parts producers and support for assembler–supplier linkages as sources of technological learning.[155] The promotion of technological development in the assemblers was less direct, involving measures such as industrial standards, incentives for in-house training, support for movement into capital equipment production, and the provision of opportunities for technological learning through scale economies, such as via the "people's car." The government assumed that the assemblers themselves, and the business groups or *chaebol* to which they belonged, were the best mechanisms for technology absorption and development. In fact, the government's promotion of the *chaebol* can be considered a form of technology policy. As productivity weaknesses in Thai and Indonesian business groups suggest, however, size is far from a sufficient, or even necessary condition for technological progress.

The intensity with which the *chaebol* absorbed technology was the result of crises.[156] First, export promotion policies both created opportunities and "imposed externally evoked crises," forcing firms to compete in the external market through "reverse engineering, importing, and rapidly assimilating production technology."[157] The state also imposed a crisis on firms by the rapid adoption of the HCI projects without adequate technological preparation. Lacking capability, the *chaebol* had to assimilate technology quickly and upgrade capacity utilization to survive. Firms encountered these crises without being able to rely on foreign partners. And many firms, including those in autos, actually constructed crises to increase the intensity of organizational and individual effort.

As Ravenhill has noted, technology acquisition strategies varied by firms, with Hyundai distinguishing itself by an insistence on maintaining managerial and technological autonomy through its own R&D.[158] Why was it Hyundai and not Daewoo that reorganized its planning department and established its own R&D center in 1979 to obtain and apply foreign technologies at the lowest price for the Pony?[159] Why was it Hyundai that was able to draw on the manufacturing expertise of other group affiliates,

---

[154] Mardon (1990).
[155] Amsden (1989, 184–188;) see also Lew (1992, 304–305).
[156] This argument draws on Kim (2001, 300–301).
[157] Ibid. (300).
[158] Ravenhill (2002, 127); Amsden (1989, Ch. 7).
[159] Amsden and Kim (1985).

such as Hyundai Cement?[160] One answer hinges on industrial origins: Hyundai's origins lay in construction and cement, activities with more "technomanagerial spinoffs" than the more commercial origins of Daewoo.[161] But despite its origins in Siam *Cement* and its engineering focus, Thailand's Siam Nawaloha, the indigenous core of Thailand's diesel engine project, never attained the manufacturing capacity of Hyundai. And while Astra's origins lay in trade, its technological ambitions and auto industrializing goals rivaled Hyundai's.

Institutional Capacities: Korea's performance hinged on impressive institutional capacities and supportive organizational arrangements. There is no question that the state under President Park in the 1970s was the driving force behind Korea's auto industrialization. While state officials and leaders took aggressive, autonomous action, they did not do so alone and uninformed. The tremendous concentration of power in the executive was combined with close government–business collaboration that excluded other interest groups.[162] In autos, close consultation between state officials and the *chaebol* informed and sometimes even transformed key state initiatives.[163] By the 1980s, such consultation incorporated parts firms as well.

Successful implementation of consultation-based initiatives involved reciprocal control mechanisms that included "conditionalities and performance standards."[164] Such mechanisms presumed that the state could both monitor firms' performance and credibly offer sanctions as well as rewards. To some degree, monitoring was facilitated by the clarity of export figures. But state officials not only kept close track of such figures, they also monitored whether car prices were within prescribed limits and whether firms were using locally made inputs when available.[165]

The state's ability to enforce directives by reward or punishment was far from absolute, as reflected, for example, in the failed merger attempt of 1980. Indeed, observers have rightly noted that the Korean state's capacity to discipline firms weakened in the 1980s as the *chaebol* became more financially independent and the political system opened up.[166] This changing capacity was mirrored by a shift in state strategy from a promotional and developmental role

---

[160] Amsden (1989, 424).

[161] Ibid. (Ch. 7).

[162] Kohli (2004, 109).

[163] See Doner (1992, 412); Back (1990; Lew (1992).

[164] Amsden (2001, 141).

[165] Amsden (2001, 157); and Amsden (personal communication, June 2007).

[166] Ravenhill (2002, 120).

focused on supply management in the 1970s to a regulatory role focused on demand management in the 1980s.[167] Acknowledging these limits does not obviate the point that Korean officials, backed by political leaders, had significant capacity to allocate resources in exchange for market performance.

This capacity was in part a function of relatively cohesive organizational arrangements. At a general level, Korea's advantage lay in a "cohesive and purposeful" state, not in the bureaucracy, which was fragmented.[168] For autos, this meant politically directed bureaucratic changes in the early 1970s involving greater influence for the Ministry of Trade and Industry (MTI), the creation of a new division responsible for the auto industry within MTI, and leadership shifts – all reflecting the industry's importance to the state.[169] This was not a static situation: the MTI's policy dominance in the 1970s gradually gave way to greater influence by the more efficiency-minded Economic Planning Board and intrabureaucratic rivalry at the end of the decade. Nor, as suggested earlier, did state agencies operate on their own, although bilateral links to the assemblers dominated relations with parts firms. Only in the 1980s, did the state re-establish support for Korea's major association of parts producers.[170]

Veto Players: The Korean auto case suggests the possibility of different performance outcomes under the same number of veto players. Korean politics involved a single veto player, Park Chung Hee, for almost two decades (1961–1979). Yet the policy outcomes and institutional arrangements of the 1960s and 1970s exhibit significant differences. As noted earlier, auto policy in the 1960s was driven more by rent seeking than by disciplined industrialization efforts of the sort seen in the 1970s. This is consistent with an understanding of the Park regime as shifting from an initial focus on ensuring political legitimacy through broad dispersal of largesse to a more consciously developmentalist policy based on an alliance with and reliance on the *chaebol*.[171] How do we account for the developmentalist shift in the regime's automotive policies and institutions?

Systemic Pressures: Our answer involves the challenges prompting the Park regime to undertake deliberate and rapid industrialization in the early 1970s. As Soek-Jin Lew argues, several factors undermined the regime's existing strategy for financing economic growth – growth critical to Park's

---

[167] Lew (1992, 333).
[168] Kohli (2004, 91; Kang (2002).
[169] Lew (1992, 172).
[170] Ibid. (130–133); Doner (1992, 420).
[171] Haggard (1990, 74); Waldner (1999, 134–135).

legitimacy: the IMF's cancellation of 61 loans to South Korea; the return of Korean troops from Vietnam; resulting in a fall in remittances; the with-drawal of one-third of U.S. army troops from Korea and the resulting loss of $100 million in annual revenues; and the imposition of textile quotas by the U.S. Security concerns were also mounting. The Nixon Doctrine hinted at the total withdrawal of U.S. forces even as North Korea localized its weapons industry and South Korean officials worried about the state of their defenses. Added to this were factional disputes within the ruling party fueled by the exhaustion of export-led growth based on light industry.[172] These pressures were well beyond the challenges facing Thai or Indonesian political elites. Indeed, the Park regime's sense of crisis led to its ultimately productive imposition of "constructed crises" on Korean auto firms.

CONCLUSION

The three auto industries analyzed in this chapter occupy different positions on a hierarchy running from structural change to upgrading. The Indonesian industry has been a component, but a weak one, in the economy's overall diversification. Its vehicle output levels have risen since the beginning of local assembly in the late 1960s, but its production, exports, and local value-added levels have not reached those of Thailand. The Thai industry has been a van-guard of the country's diversification, having grown to manufacture over 1 million vehicles a year and to become a leading employer and source of manufactured exports. But the industry has become denationalized. Inde-pendent Thai producers, plentiful and profitable under import substitution, have not developed the managerial and technological capacities necessary to meet the export requirements of Thai-based foreign assemblers and compo-nents producers. Nor has Thailand developed intermediate, capital goods, or supporting industries capable of supplying automotive producers. South Korea has achieved much in all these areas. Its production volumes and exports are the highest of any developing country except China. Despite the increasing role of foreign producers, local firms have absorbed and developed technology, and the auto industry uses locally produced steel and capital equipment.

Our explanation for these differences focuses on the degree to which external and domestic pressures prompt political leaders to promote insti-tutional capacities appropriate for different kinds of development tasks. We can appreciate the utility of this approach through the weaknesses of alternative explanations, one of which is the presence of ambitious,

---

[172] Lew (1992, 148–149; 168–169).

industrializing entrepreneurs. Hyundai was not, as we have noted, all that different from Thailand's Siam Nawaloha. Significant financial resources, independent technology development, and ambitious automotive industrialization goals were also characteristic of Astra.[173] Nor does high-level political support account for these differences. Hyundai received significant backing from President Park, although it had to contend with other *chaebols*. Thailand's SNF, while confronting challenges from firms backed by influential politicians, enjoyed the financial and political support of its royally based parent group, Siam Cement.[174] Astra's backing from President Suharto was also quite strong. The three cases also do not vary much with regard to the expertise and developmentalist orientations of their bureaucracies. Korea's officials were not significantly better trained and organized than their Southeast Asian counterparts,[175] while key movers behind both Thai and Indonesian auto efforts were engineers committed to localization and rationalization.[176]

What did distinguish these three cases were institutional capacities. To illustrate, consider the contrasting experiences of Hyundai and Aapico – a rare, locally developed, successful OEM producers of sophisticated automotive components.[177] Although internal initiatives and resources were obviously core to Hyundai's success, the firm was the object of close attention, monitoring, encouragement, and resources, all provided on a basis of "reciprocal exchange" by officials and political leaders.[178] Aapico, on the other hand, was simply not noticed.[179] Despite its success, including being the first developing country firm to provide assembly jigs for the Mercedes S Class vehicles, Thai officials did not, as of 2007, visit the firm or use Aapico's experience as a case study for the diffusion of best practices. These differences are further reflected in the lack of technical institutions supporting Thai (as well as Indonesian) producers.[180]

Aapico may have been ignored because Thailand's fragmented democratic regimes impeded policies designed to promote and diffuse local firms' capacity for technology absorption. Yet it would be incorrect to conclude

---

[173] On Astra's origins, see Robison (1986). For an account of Astra's technology objectives, see Butler (2002).
[174] See, e.g., Handley (2006, 329–330).
[175] Kang (2002).
[176] On the developmentalist ideologies of Indonesian officials, see Thee (2003).
[177] Deyo and Doner (2000b).
[178] Amsden (1989; 2001).
[179] Interview # 87.
[180] On Indonesia's weaknesses, see Dhanani (2000).

that multiple veto player arrangements are inherently bad or that single veto player arrangements are inherently good for automotive development. Even under fragmented regimes, Thai leaders successfully implemented key policy and infrastructural reforms that put Thailand on the road to export success. Conversely, rent seeking, protection, and neglect of productivity issues characterized the authoritarian regimes of Suharto's New Order and the pre-Yushin years of Park's regime.

These capacity differences were instead, a function of varying degrees of pressures – external security, financial resources, and domestic unrest – on political leaders to pursue a "tough love" industrial policy in which local firms would be pushed hard to improve market position *and* supported in doing so. To illustrate: A top Astra official recounted a meeting in South Korea at which the head of Hyundai Motors emphasized that his company was given no choice but to develop the internal capacities necessary for exporting automotive products with high levels of local value added. By contrast, until the 1990s Indonesia's clientelist politics, its large domestic market, and its extensive protection, (itself facilitated by commodity exports), allowed Astra lots of "freedom" to avoid exports while depriving the firm of the support required to improve its internal technical capacities.[181]

---

[181] Interview # 124.

8

Conclusion

This book has addressed the institutional and political bases of two key growth transitions: structural change – the move from an economy based on a small number of traditional sectors to a more diversified structure of multiple, nontraditional activities; and upgrading – the efficient production of higher value added goods based on local inputs. The first transition is difficult: the identification of and mobilization of resources for risky new activities pose significant coordination and information challenges. My principal focus, however, has been on the even more challenging obstacles of upgrading: Why have some countries that succeeded in diversifying their economies had a much more difficult time at upgrading?

Although this set of questions has received little attention from scholars and policy makers, it lies at the heart of differences between the East Asian NICs and the "little tigers" of Southeast Asia. I have addressed these questions through comparative analyses of one "little tiger" – Thailand – a country that has transitioned from low-income to middle-income status within just a few decades and has continued to grow on the basis of impressive diversification. Yet Thailand faces "a real challenge of sustaining its growth and transitioning into a higher income country ..." With more intense global competition, Thailand needs to improve its productivity and competitiveness "if it ... (is) ... to avoid being stuck in a middle-income trap in which many Latin America (sic) countries have been in for several decades."[1] Such improvements require not only progress in skills and knowledge, areas in which Thailand has continued to decline relative to

---

[1] World Bank (2008, 5). Thai growth rates remain impressive (4.8% from 2005–2007), but they lag behind developing East Asia's overall rate (9.7%) for the same period (Ibid).

competitors such as China and Vietnam, but also in the creation of technologically competent indigenous final producers and suppliers. Despite the country's participation in global value chains, foreign investment in Thailand "has transferred amazingly little tacit knowledge and technology through vertical or horizontal spillovers."[2] The problems of uneven growth motivating this book has thus persisted.

In this concluding chapter, I suggest refinements of my core explanation for these problems in light of the book's evidence. I begin with a brief review and assessment of my arguments. I then address the implications of these findings for three key development issues: How can these findings enrich our understanding of innovation, a key ingredient in upgrading? Does this book's evidence for *structural* (i.e., vulnerability) pressures on economic performance preclude upgrading by developing countries not faced with such pressures? And finally, is diversification-without-upgrading as unsustainable as argued in Chapter 1 of this book?

I. EXPLAINING THE MIDDLE-INCOME TRAP

In Chapter 2, I critically reviewed existing approaches to uneven growth, including economic (investment and human capital), sociological (entrepreneurship, ethnicity, social capital), and political (regime type) arguments. By identifying the weakness of each approach in light of empirical evidence from Northeast and Southeast Asia, I highlighted the need for a framework that specifies (1) the availability of institutional capacities appropriate for specific development tasks, and (2) the political factors accounting for the supply of such capacities.

This framework, elaborated in Chapter 3, begins with an emphasis on the need to distinguish among development stages and tasks within those stages. More specifically, information, large numbers, and distributional challenges inherent in nuts and bolts upgrading policies (e.g., technology diffusion, reconciliation of upstream–downstream interests, investment

---

[2] NESDB (2008b, xi). On the absence of Thai firms as "important and innovative producers of electronic components ... ," see Ibid. (18). Local ownership of final producers/exporters is not coterminous with upgrading. But the fact that locally owned and managed firms are largely absent from the ranks of final producers and suppliers in Thailand (as well as most of Thailand's neighbors), does indicate weak upgrading. On the lack of globally competent, local firms in the ASEAN-4 relative to the NICs, see "The Tigers That Lost Their Roar," *The Economist* (February 28, 2008). Exceptions to this generalization are, for reasons consistent with this book's argument, the presence of world-class suppliers in Singapore and Penang (Malaysia). See the discussion of these cases in Chapter 3 and in McKendrick et al. (2000).

screening for technology spillovers, agricultural extension), are particularly challenging.[3] As a result, upgrading performance will reflect the capacity of public and private actors to address these challenges through institutional capacities for consultation, monitoring, and credible commitments. The political side of the framework predicts that such capacities are more likely to emerge only when political leaders feel compelled by the external and domestic pressures identified in this book to promote them. Finally, the argument predicts that while institution-building efforts must operate through existing structures of political competition, i.e. veto players, such structures will themselves shift in the face of external and domestic pressures.

At least two kinds of evidence can challenge this argument. One is successful diversification in the absence of active engagement by public and private institutions to address the problems inherent in risky shifts to new sectors (or unsuccessful diversification in the presence of such factors). In the empirical chapters, I found no such disconfirming evidence. Rather, the establishment of large, export-oriented sugar, textile and auto sectors in Thailand resulted from sector-specific promotion efforts to address information, coordination, and related risk problems. These findings are consistent with Dani Rodrik's contention that scratching the surface of any nontraditional export success story will reveal a range of institution-based interventions "lurking beneath the surface."[4]

A second type of disconfirming evidence is successful upgrading in the absence of not only significant consultation, monitoring and credible commitments, but also heavy pressures on political leaders to encourage the creation of such capacities (or unsuccessful upgrading in the presence of such factors). Again, the empirical evidence largely supports my arguments. Despite awareness of declining competitiveness, Thai officials and managers undertook few serious efforts to encourage expansion of indigenous technological capacity in the sectors reviewed in Chapters 5–7. The efforts they did make came during "tough times" – on the heels of the 1980s debt crisis and the 1997 financial crisis – and these initiatives faded as conditions improved. Further support for the book's arguments comes from the cross-national comparisons in which sustained, successful sectoral upgrading in

---

[3] Robert Wade's otherwise insightful discussion of viable strategies for developing countries fails to recognize such distinctions: "It is not obvious that a state that can ... (enforce patents and copyrights) ... would not be able to implement effective protection and other forms of industrial policy" (Wade 2003, 634–635). The cases reviewed in this book, especially Thailand, indicates the frequent gap between the capacities for patent enforcement on the one hand, and for policies designed to generate patentable innovations on the other.

[4] Rodrik (2007, 109).

Brazil, Taiwan, and South Korea reflected both the institutional capacities and vulnerability pressures anticipated by my arguments. Conversely, poor performances by the Philippines and Indonesia were associated with weak capacities and low vulnerability.

The preceding discussion might suggest that vulnerability is key for upgrading but irrelevant for diversification. Yet Thailand's intermediate position *between* high and low performers belies this implication and suggests the importance of disaggregating structural change. Relative to the Philippines and Indonesia, the Thais did more than just diversify. They did so *efficiently* and for reasons consistent with this book's core arguments: In addition to lacking Indonesia's petroleum rents or the Philippines' military assistance and special U.S. quota access, Thailand faced intermittent security threats.[5] The Thais were thus under moderate but consistent pressure to earn foreign exchange. They responded with constant efforts to improve exports. In sugar, for example, this took the form of ongoing efforts at price stabilization and coordination between farmers and millers. In textiles, Thailand's system of quota management, while never serving as the kind of productivity-improvement mechanism seen in Taiwan, encouraged new entrants and market diversification rather than the kind of inefficient monopoly seen in the Philippines. And while the Thai auto industry has lacked the indigenous technology strengths seen in South Korea, Thai officials implemented tariff, taxes, and investment incentives to promote export-oriented automotive clusters that have been absent in Indonesia. Thailand's experience thus suggests the need to append to Rodrik's argument about interventions lurking beneath the surface of nontraditional export successes: Lurking beneath the surface of such interventions themselves are pressures on political elites to promote efficient outcomes.

But if structural pressures, defined here as systemic vulnerability, influence leaders' willingness to promote developmental institutions, I also noted the potential role of more proximate political factors – veto players – as intervening variables: veto players influence leaders' ability to translate willingness into institutional reality while in turn reflecting vulnerability pressures. The material reviewed in this book provides confirmation of the hypothesized *effect* of many veto players. Thailand's frequently fragmented party systems, reflecting what Cox and McCubbins label "separation of

---

[5] On resource access in Indonesia and the Philippines, see Unger (1998, 74), who also quotes a Thai official reluctant to proceed with expensive infrastructure projects because "We don't want to become another Philippines" (Ibid., 149).

purpose,"[6] translated into fragmentation in those ministries with sectoral responsibilities. This undermined both the credibility of upgrading-related initiatives, such as skills development, and the capacity for decisive policy changes. On the other hand, single or small numbers of veto players, as under Prem in the 1980s, Anand in the early 1990s, and Thaksin in the first few years after assuming power in 2001, were associated with significant reform efforts, some of which involved sectoral upgrading.

But the effects of small vs. large numbers of veto players are far from uniform. Thailand's "pork-policy" compromise demonstrated how, even under fragmented political structures, leaders enhanced credibility in one key area, macroeconomic policy, by tying their hands through delegation of responsibility to agencies, the Finance Ministry and Bank of Thailand, which were both insulated and engaged in consultation with key private parties. The shadow cases, on the other hand, demonstrate the indeterminate impact of single veto players. Relatively cohesive authoritarian rule was associated with successful upgrading based on decisiveness and credibility in Taiwan, South Korea, and Brazil, but not in the Philippines and Indonesia. These outcomes suggest that to achieve both the decisiveness and credibility required for upgrading, governments must reduce the effective number of veto players *and* create institutions that tie the hands of the veto players, through mechanisms such as delegation, and consultation. Such mechanisms can mitigate the inherent weaknesses of large vs. small numbers of effective veto players.

The challenge is to account for the emergence of mitigation mechanisms as well as shifts in numbers of veto players.[7] Our shadow cases, consistent with the Israel and Singapore cases noted in Chapter 3, suggest that mechanisms are established where systemic vulnerability is high and sustained. In countries where vulnerability pressures are much lower and less sustained, as in Thailand, such arrangements emerge during times of crisis, but are not institutionalized sufficiently to last as the crisis abates. Prior to the financial crisis of 1997–1998, the Thai government was indecisive on issues of both upgrading and financial management. As the crisis intensified, both the actual number of veto players declined and their interests and preferences converged. This led to a rapid increase in decisiveness in policy making, while institutions such as the IRP were created to aid in policy credibility through delegation and consultation.

---

[6] Cox and McCubbins (2000, 26).
[7] The rest of this discussion draws on Doner, Hicken, and Ritchie (forthcoming 2009).

This process culminated with Thaksin's rise to power, representing both a decline in the number of veto players *and* an explicit commitment to the promotion of indigenous innovation capacity. At no other time in Thai history had there been a prime minister who explicitly promoted innovation while seeming to have the political leverage and institutional capacity to make good on his commitments. With the new government's emphasis on consultation-based master plans and bureaucratic reform, the country seemed to be on the verge of significant progress in upgrading. In the event, Thailand utterly failed to realize this potential. The vulnerability pressures were neither sustained enough nor perhaps sufficiently severe to result in the entrenchment of these new institutions. The new government proved unwilling to tie its hands via consultation. The IRP fell apart. In the areas not directly in the interest of Thaksin's ruling party and its supporters, political reform stalled and economic policy initiatives languished. With the easing of the crisis, resources were again available to feed disparate parties and factions operating within the bureaucracy. The number of veto players again began to proliferate without mitigation mechanisms, leading to less and less reform. And by 2008, the World Bank, as noted, continued to warn of Thailand's "middle-income trap."

II. IMPLICATIONS FOR INNOVATION THEORY

Thailand's potential to escape this trap depends in no small part on its capacity for innovation, a process key to upgrading.[8] But the now-voluminous innovation literature is of limited use. These writings have highlighted the role of institutions, such as corporate governance rules, financial institutions, property rights, public–private consultation, R&D organizations, university–industry ties, interfirm collaboration systems, and rules to ensure competitive market structures.[9] But with some exceptions, they devote insufficient attention to issues of task specificity, institutional capacities, and politics. What follows are some suggestions for addressing these gaps in light of this book's findings.

Innovation Tasks: The literature on innovation delineates numerous areas of upgrading in which innovation is important: (1) process improvement (e.g., inventory reduction), (2) introduction of new products or improvement of existing ones, (3) shifting or expanding core functions (e.g., manufacturing,

---

[8] On the link between upgrading and innovation, see Kaplinsky (2005, Ch. 4).

[9] In addition to Nelson's (1993) classic text, see, e.g., Kim and Nelson (2000). Nelson and Winter (1982); Kim (1993); and Hobday (1995). On Thailand, see Patarapong (2004).

design, logistics, quality control), and (4) shifting to different value chains.[10] The literature further differentiates these dimensions by levels of technology development: imitation of existing technology; internal firm development of products or processes superior to foreign inputs; and local capacities to introduce state-of-the-art core technologies and market-leading products.[11]

But innovation writings typically fail to assess the nuts and bolts challenges of tasks such as technical and vocational training. They also lack a metric through which to distinguish among the challenges of different types of innovation at different stages of technological development. This weakness is compounded by a level-of-analysis problem: The literature's useful focus on firm-level organizational routines tends to either neglect the question of how firm-level strengths, themselves often derived through engagement with other firms and institutions, are diffused to the overall sector, or to assume that this process occurs through a natural process of competitive emulation.[12] This invisible-hand assumption is rarely justified. High-performing firms often constitute "pockets of vitality" that fail to become actual innovation systems.[13] This is in part because the process of scaling up from firm to sector is most often characterized by "uncertainty and long gestation periods ..."[14] This book's taxonomy of development tasks can be helpful in illuminating the ways in which such a process requires new types of information, the participation of many actors, both private and public, and short-term losses for some as well as overall, longer-term gains. Together, these kinds of challenges require "detailed discretion in implementation."[15]

Institutional Capacities and Institutional Design(s): The need for such implementation bears on what institutions actually do and how they are designed. As noted, innovation writings stress the importance of organizational structures, such as R&D consortia, technical training institutes, and university–industry arrangements. Other scholars stress the ways in which upgrading is inherently a mutual discovery process in which "firms and the government learn about underlying costs and opportunities and

---

[10] Kaplinsky (2005, Ch. 4).
[11] Lee Won-Young (2000, 270).
[12] See the review in Chapter 2; and Breznitz (2007, 26).
[13] Kuznetsov and Sabel (2005, 4). See also the discussion of the Thai firm Aapico in Chapter 7. The issue of scaling up from firm to sector is more typically addressed in the developmental state literature (e.g., Wade 1990; Evans 1995). For a useful, eclectic approach to these issues that draws on but goes beyond innovation theories, see Breznitz (2007).
[14] Hill (2004, 355).
[15] Lindauer and Pritchett (2002, 27).

engage in strategic coordination."[16] These observers usefully note the lack of any one-size-fits-all institutional design and the importance of crafting institutions appropriate to specific sectoral, national, and temporal conditions.[17]

Three important issues get less attention. One is the need to specify the kinds of capacities appropriate for different kinds of innovation-related tasks. Why, for example, might we expect programs encouraging high-level R&D to require quite different arrangements than those supporting vocational training, SME-assembler linkages, testing facilities, or standard setting? How do different tasks involve interactions among multiple agencies and issue areas? Does the "mutual discovery process" involve different numbers and sets of actors at the formulation vs. the implementation stage? By disaggregating capacities into consultation, monitoring and credible commitments, I have attempted to provide the basis for such specification.

This bears on the question of institutional design. This book's findings suggest that we can go beyond recognizing the pitfalls of a one-size-fits-all approach in at least three ways. One, as noted in Chapter 3, is to acknowledge the benefits of corporatist (as opposed to more pluralist) structures. A second is to specify institutional dimensions along which all states, including corproratist ones, vary (e.g., porousness, influence of macroeconomic vs. sectoral agencies, recruitment and retention rules), and how such variation might result in different outcomes.[18] Finally, the innovation literature will be strengthened by an explicit focus on the institutions of private actors, especially the impact of different kinds of selective incentives on the strength of business associations or unions. Ben Schneider has argued that, compared to compulsory membership or individual benefits, delegated public functions, such as training or marketing, are superior for encouraging greater associational participation, representativeness, and less vulnerability to capture. Such associational strength in turn improves associations' potential for coordination helpful to economic development.[19] This book's findings, such as the existence of extensive upgrading-related activities and extensive membership involvement seen in Taiwan's textile association, especially relative to their Thai counterparts, support Schneider's arguments.

Finally, just as upgrading is an iterative discovery process, so is the identification and development of appropriate institutions – appropriate both for the task at hand and for the local/national context. Successful

---

[16] Rodrik (2007, 101).
[17] Ibid.
[18] A useful illustration is Breznitz (2007, 32–33).
[19] Schneider (2004, 55; 239)

institutions are rarely importable; they are best viewed as reflecting tacit kinds of knowledge that emerge "locally, relying on hands-on experience, local knowledge, and experimentation."[20] Upgrading thus involves willingness – on the part of political elites who help create the context in which firms operate – to learn about appropriate institutions. Indeed, a striking feature of successful upgrading is not unalloyed success but rather an ongoing process of difficulties, experimentation, and tinkering by leaders attempting to craft incentives and institutions encouraging firms, in turn, to tinker with and absorb new technology.

Politics: Political leaders are central to this process of experimentation and learning, yet the innovation literature is largely silent on the factors influencing their behavior. In some cases there is simply no mention of politics; in others, the issue is relegated to a residual category of "political will"; and in still others equate politics with policy.[21] What kinds of political analysis might innovation writings usefully incorporate?

First, they would explicitly acknowledge and assess the seriousness of political challenges inherent in institutional creation and the implementation of upgrading-related policies.[22] Distributional questions would loom large in this analysis. For example, in Thailand, political leaders found it difficult to resolve such problems as: upstream producers resisting trade reforms designed to improve inputs for end users; less efficient firms undermining capacity reduction efforts; and public universities dragging their feet on reforms to promote linkages with industry. Second, writings on innovation would identify factors influencing leaders' will and capacity to address such problems. This discussion would, at a minimum, draw attention to the pressures identified in the systemic vulnerability argument and the ways in which more proximate political institutions reflect and mediate those pressures. But it would also raise the question of precisely how deterministic such conditions are.

III THE LIMITS OF STRUCTURAL PRESSURES

Can political leaders encourage growth-promoting policies and institutions despite not facing external threats, resource constraints, and popular pressures? This book's findings, along with other evidence, suggest a

---

[20] Rodrik (2007, 164).
[21] See works cited in fn. 9. A partial exception is Breznitz (2007).
[22] Features such as uncertainty "immediately underline the links between innovation and a country's political and institutional structures" (Hill 2004, 355).

qualified "yes," qualified because it emphasizes room for maneuver under moderate levels of vulnerability. This position thus presumes that vulnerability is not a dichotomous variable. With three components, the vulnerability condition can be considered moderate if any of the three is absent or very weak and/or if all three are present but weak. Countries and sectors explored in this book often came under moderate levels of vulnerability that prompted upgrading efforts. Thai leaders, for example, reacted promptly to rural unrest and external threats in the 1970s, resource constraints (external debt) in the 1980s, and resource constraints (financial crisis) in the late 1990s.[23]

Whether leaders take advantage of more limited vulnerability in turn depends on other factors. One involves the nature of their coalitions. As noted in Chapter 4, the fact that Thaksin's most influential supporters came from service sectors likely weakened his commitment to upgrading in textiles and autos, and even in the more mobilized sugar industry. In Brazil, on the other hand, sugar's role as solution to energy problems was enhanced by the political influence of the industry, especially the "modernized, large-scale, and capital intensive sugar sector in the Center-South ... (which) ... embodied the developmental values of the military regime."[24] Brazil's "developmental values" highlight the potential impact of a second set of factors: ideas and ideology. Brazil's tradition of developmentalist thinking, combined with the belief in its regional leadership and what Emmanuel Adler called a "quest for technological autonomy," encouraged the military's active support for an upgrading response in sugar and other sectors.[25]

Finally, economic and/or political institutions operating prior to shifts in structural pressures can influence the reaction to such pressures. Chile constitutes a positive illustration of this point: Chile's recent success in agro-industrial is not simply the result of trade liberalization and a public–private institution (Fundacion Chile) established under Pinochet in response to a combination of debt and rural opposition in the 1980s. Chile's success was also "the fruition of government efforts initiated in the 1960s in the fishing, agricultural and forestry sectors, along with the efforts of local private

[23] In addition to degree, vulnerability pressures can vary by sector. Brazilian sugar, e.g., became a primary focus of upgrading efforts as a result of both its key position as a foreign exchange earner and the decline in export prices for raw sugar exports.

[24] Barzelay (1986, 137–138). It is, of course, difficult to state whether the sugar industry's political influence would have been as significant without the crises that elevated sugar's role in the country's overall development. My assumption above is that coalitional interests are one dimensional. But complex coalitions of multiple partners can allow leaders' options to expand (Slater 2008). Note also that coalitional interests and pressures can vary by locale (e.g., Tendler 1997; McDermott 2005).

[25] Adler (1987).

firms."[26] On the negative side, Thailand's tradition of cross- and intraministerial fragmentation (departmental autonomy) impeded efforts to sustain upgrading policies by, for example, merging the Industry and Commerce Ministries.

The cases covered in this study thus suggest that whereas very high (low) levels of vulnerability are necessary and sufficient to explain successful (unsuccessful) upgrading efforts, moderate levels of vulnerability are necessary but *not* sufficient to explain concomitant levels of upgrading. Under moderate levels, leaders have the incentive to initiate upgrading policies and institutions; but they also have the latitude to undertake *or* to avoid such difficult efforts. Whether they respond to vulnerability pressures will depend on the interests of their coalitional bases, their ideas and ideologies, and their preexisting institutional capacities.

This set of conclusions is open to at least two challenges. One is that my argument – especially the contention that very high levels of vulnerability are necessary and sufficient to stimulate upgrading – is overly deterministic. What of the possibility that extreme vulnerability leads not to upgrading responses but to economic and political implosion? Is not some preexisting level of political coherence and bureaucratic capacity necessary for an upgrading response to tough times? While this view is indeed plausible, the cases covered in this book do not provide the empirical basis to assess it. What I do provide is a falsifiable set of propositions and thus the basis to assess whether my argument is "typological," that is, that it covers only those states with a modicum of preexisting capacity, or whether it also applies to possibilities even for states with no such capacity. And to the extent that my argument fails to account for certain outcomes, it encourages identification of other variables offsetting vulnerability pressures. Furthermore, my argument encourages attention to puzzling but positive outcomes, whether in the form of upgrading, diversification, or strong, static efficiency-based growth rates.[27] In sum, my argument is designed both to explain an

---

[26] Perez-Aleman (2005, 659). The key institution was the Corporacion de Fomento (CORFO). The same dynamic is seen in Brazil with institutions initiated under Vargas in the 1940s and 1950s. On Fundacion Chile, see Meissner (1988).

[27] Consider Botswana, a country Acemoglu, Johnson, and Robinson. (2001) label "An African Success Story." Botswana's per capita growth rate was the highest in the world over the last three decades of the twentieth century. Although Botswana's economy exhibits little structural change, much less upgrading, its impressive growth merits examination, especially since this performance has been strongly influenced, or at least not impeded, by a fairly interventionist state in a country rich with natural resources (diamonds) (Ibid., 84). In my view, Botswana represents not an inexplicable outlier but an additional empirical example of state institutions being strengthened by ruling elites' need to satisfy broad

important set of otherwise successful, middle-income cases and to stimulate research on the growth performances of lower-income countries.

A second potential challenge to my conclusion is that it neglects the value of recent work on policy choice and institutional selection. Proponents of "growth diagnostics," for example, provide useful criteria for deciding which distortions are most important and feasible to target; and "new industrial policy" advocates identify sectoral policies based not on picking winners but on institutional design providing incentives to stimulate private discovery and risk taking.[28] My intent is not to minimize the importance of such guidelines. I wish rather to emphasize that the willingness and ability of political leaders to engage in diagnostics and discovery processes reflect a particular set of endogenous pressures not easily manipulated by external, much less domestic actors.[29]

IV THE LIMITS OF DIVERSIFICATION: DISARTICULATION POLITICS

I conclude by revisiting one of the justifications for my emphasis on upgrading: the assumption that diversification without increased, efficient value added based on local linkages cannot sustain growth in middle-income developing countries. Thailand's continued (GDP) growth suggests the need for a partial revision of this argument based on the role of exports. Not all diversifiers are equal. Thailand's pursuit of *export-based*

---

coalitional needs in a context of relative resource constraints. Since gaining independence in 1965, Botswana's ruling Democratic Party was prompted by the threat of electoral defeat to make extensive investments in rural infrastructure, as well as in educational and health systems. Many of these measures were redistributive in nature, but such "redistribution took a basically efficient form" (Ibid., 98). I ascribe such efficiency to the hard budget constraints initially facing state elites, who built state institutions a full decade *before* income from diamonds began to accrue in the mid-1970s. This explanation contrasts with Acemoglu et al.'s argument that the relatively "light" weight of colonialism allowed precolonial institutions to survive as key bases for subsequent institutional strengths (Ibid., 96). Note that these two accounts may not be mutually exclusive. At the very least, my emphasis on vulnerability pressures constitutes a temporally proximate account of why a historical legacy of institutional strength was used for growth-promoting ends.

[28] On growth diagnostics, see Rodrik (2007, Ch. 2). On "new industrial policy," see Kuznetsov and Sabel 2005.

[29] "Even if one were to discover stable empirical associations, this still leaves the difficulty of deriving policy advice from growth regressions. The specifications embody other fundamental problems, in that the stuff on the right-hand side is almost never policy. *Instead, much of the right hand stuff is structural, including variables that are not under anyone's direct control and thus cannot have direct policy implication*" (Lindauer and Pritchett 2002, 21; emphasis added).

diversification has made the country a highly efficient diversifier that has continually reduced the costs of promoted but protected industries.

Yet there remain important challenges to this strategy's long-term viability. Demand for Thailand's resource-based commodities (e.g., rice, rubber) will likely grow; but manufactured exports will encounter volatile demand, growing competition from lower-cost producers, and eroding labor cost advantages due to the probable appreciation of the baht.[30] The strategy's economic viability is also threatened by Thailand's ever-increasing reliance on imports of intermediate and capital goods reflecting the economy's disarticulation, that is, its lack of domestic linkages to the export sectors.[31] The ability to finance such imports will depend on continued growth in exports of final goods, yet such export growth is, as noted above, far from certain. Such constraints, along with insufficient technological capacities, might even limit the country's ability to diversify into new product areas.[32]

These economic flaws have societal and political consequences. As suggested in Chapter 1,[33] heavy reliance on exports and thin input–output linkages between sectors undermine the kinds of robust coalitions between capitalists and workers that both stabilize demand and encourage productivity-oriented labor market policies. Further, with over 40% of the labor force still employed in the primary sector, continued growth will require further shifts from rural to more productive jobs in the urban sectors; yet growth in this source of employment is declining, thus sustaining if not aggravating the rural–urban gap.[34] These problems have grown as Thailand has deepened its global exposure. Internal integration has not kept up with external integration.

Robert Wade suggests that by limiting the creation of class alliances, such a "socially and sectorally unintegrated ... (production) ... structure ... handicaps democratic regimes."[35] His implication – that production politics gets reflected in state politics – applies to the Thai case. As of this writing (summer 2008), Thai politics continued to fragment. Parties and groups were not only contesting pork. They were also struggling to compete for

---

[30] NESDB (2008).

[31] Ibid. (16).

[32] Ibid. (xiv).

[33] See also Wade (2003, 635).

[34] NESDB (2003, vi). On the persistence of rural–urban problems and inequality in Thailand, see Krongkaew and Zin (2007, 20).

[35] Wade (2003, 635). A related, promising line of research explores the ways in which social fragmentation undermines the presumed public goods benefits of democratic political regimes (Keefer 2003).

mass allegiance, especially in the countryside. And underlying these conflicts were differences over fundamental questions of sovereignty and
equality under globalization.[36] For Thailand, then, the "middle-income
trap" has a disturbing political expression. With the country risking a
further constitutional revision and its 19th coup since the end of the
absolute monarchy in 1932, *The Economists* warned that Thailand could
become "one of those perenially unstable, tragi-comic countries, such as the
Philippines ..."[37]

[36] For a useful review of key divisions, see Tejapira (2002).
[37] "Protests and coup rumors return." *The Economist* (May 31, 2008, 46).

APPENDIX

List of Interviews

With one exception (#124), the interviews listed below were conducted in and around Bangkok. Most of the interviewees were conducted on the basis of anonymity. I have thus opted to list only the positions of the interviewee.

Number	Date	Sector	Title	Organization
1	6/22/1989	Sugar	Assistant Director-General	Industrial Promotion Department, Ministry of Industry
2	6/26/1989	Sugar	Secretary-General	Office of the Cane and Sugar Board, Ministry of Industry
3	7/11/1989	Textiles	Official	Textile Industry Division, Department of Industrial Promotion, MOI
4	7/24/1989	Textiles	Official	Textile Industry Division, Department of Industrial Promotion, MOI
5	7/28/1989	Textiles	Manager	Thai Iryo Garments / Thai Blanket Industry
6	7/31/1989	Textiles	Manager	Luckytex
7	8/2/1989	Textiles	Director	Uthai Product Company
8	8/3/1989	Textiles	Director	Textile Industry Division, Department of Industrial Promotion, MOI

(continued)

Number	Date	Sector	Title	Organization
9	8/3/1989	Sugar	Deputy General Manager	Thai Sugar Trading Corp, Ltd.
10	8/7/1989	Textiles	Manager	Luckytex
11	6/10/1991	Textiles	Official	Teijin Polyester
12	6/26/1991	Textiles	Director	Saha Union Corporation
13	6/28/1991	Textiles	Researcher	Textile Industry Division, Department of Industrial Promotion, MOI
14	7/15/1991	Textiles	Official	TGMA
15	7/22/1992	Textile	Official/ Owner	Thai Weavers Association/ Jong Stit. Co.
16	7/23/1992	Sugar	Assistant Director- General	Industrial Promotion Department, Ministry of Industry
17	7/24/1992	Sugar	Secretary- General	Office of the Cane and Sugar Board, Ministry of Industry
18	7/27/1992	Sugar	Deputy General Manager	Thai Sugar Trading Corp, Ltd.
19	1/25/1993	Textiles	Professor	NIDA
20	1/26/1993	Textiles	Director	Textile Industry Division, Department of Industrial Promotion, MOI
21	1/28/1993	Auto	Manager	Toyota Motor Thailand
22	2/2/1993	Auto	Researcher	TDRI
23	2/4/1993	Textiles	Officers	Association of Thai Textile Bleaching Dyeing Printing and Finishing Industries
24	2/5/1993	General	Researcher	Thailand Development Research Institute
25	3/27/1994	Auto	Manager	Automotive Resource Asia
26	6/1/1994	Textiles	Researcher	Textile Industry Division, Department of Industrial Promotion, MOI
27	6/6/1994	Trade/ Finance	Official	Fiscal Policy Office, Ministry of Finance

Number	Date	Sector	Title	Organization
28	6/8/1994	Textiles	Vice Chair	Association of Thai Dyers and Printers
29	7/1995	Auto	Officer	Metal Industries Development Institute, Dept of Industrial Promotion, MoI
30	7/14/1995	Auto	Director	Automotive Resources Asia
31	7/18/1995	Textiles	Researcher	Textile Industry Division, Department of Industrial Promotion, MOI
32	7/20/1995	Manager	Director	Thai Engineering Products Co.
33	7/25/1995	Textiles	Director	Association of Thai Textile Printers and Dyers/ United Textile Mills Co.
34	7/25/1995	Auto	Official	Office of Industrial Econ, MOI
35	7/3/1996	Textiles	Researcher	Textile Industry Division, Department of Industrial Promotion, MOI
36	7/3/1996	Textiles	Director	Association of Thai Textile Printers and Dyers/ United Textile Mills Co.
37	7/8/1996	Auto	Director	Siam Motors; TAPMA; Parts club
38	7/9/1996	Textiles	Researcher	Faculty of Economics, Thammasat University
39	7/11/1996	Textiles	Researcher	Textile Industry Division, Department of Industrial Promotion, MOI
40	7/17/1996	Textiles	President	Oriental Fibre Co.
41	7/17/1996	Auto	Official	Office of Industrial Econ, MOI
42	7/19/1996	Textiles	Manager	Thai Textile Manufacturer's Association
43	6/4/1998	Textiles	President	Oriental Fibre Co.

(continued)

Number	Date	Sector	Title	Organization
44	6/4/1998	Textiles	President	Jong Stit Co.
45	6/8/1998	Textiles	Director	Export Development Trading Company
46	6/14/1998	Textiles	Editor	Technology Consulting Editor, Textile Asia
47	6/14/1998	Textiles	Managing Director	TTIS Co., LTD.
48	6/16/1998	Textiles	Official/ Director	Ministry of Industry/ Industrial Restructuring Committee
49	7/1998	Sugar	Managing Director	KSL Export Trading Co.
50	7/29/1999	Sugar	Managing Director	KSL Export Trading Co.
51	7/30/1999	Textiles	Exec. Director	TGMA
52	7/31/1999	Textiles	President	Oriental Fibre Co.
53	8/2/1999	Textiles	President	Oriental Fibre Co.
54	6/6/2001	Auto	Director	Auto Parts Industry Club, FTI/S&L Commercial Co.
55	5/24/2002	Textiles	Professor	Thammasat University, Office of Industrial Economics
56	5/24/2002	Textiles	Manager	Thailand Textile Institute
57	5/28/2002	Auto	Manager	AAPICO
58	5/29/2002	Textiles	Professor	Thammasat University, Faculty of Economics
59	5/31/2002	General	Official	MOI
60	6/2/2002	Auto	Official	MOI
61	6/3/2002	Auto, Textile	Professor	Faculty of Engineering/ SVI, Thammasat University
62	6/3/2002	General	Professor	Thammsat University
63	6/4/2002	General	Researcher	TDRI
64	6/6/2002	Textiles	Director	United Textile Mills; ADTP
65	6/6/2002	Textiles	President	TGMA
66	6/6/2002	Auto	Director	Auto Parts Industry Club, FTI/S&L Commercial Co.

Number	Date	Sector	Title	Organization
67	6/11/2002	Auto	Manager	Thailand Automotive Institute
68	6/11/2002	Textiles	Professor	Faculty of Economics, Thammasat University
69	6/12/2002	General	former official	Ministry of Finance
70	12/31/2004	Textiles	Director	THTI
71	1/4/2005	Textiles	Researcher	Faculty of Economics, Thammasat University
72	1/4/2005	Textiles	Exec. Director	Textile Digest Magazine
73	1/5/2005	Textiles	Researcher	Faculty of Economics, Thammasat University
74	1/5/2005	Textiles	Chairman	Bobae Export Service Center, Bobae Garment Association
75	1/5/2005	Textiles	Director	PASAYA
76	1/6/2005	Textiles	Professor	Faculty of Economics, Thammasat University
77	1/6/2005	Auto	Professor	Faculty of Economics, Thammasat University
78	1/6/2005	General	Official	MOI
79	1/6/2005	Auto	Professor	Faculty of Economics, Thammasat University
80	1/7/2005	Sugar	Director	KSL Export Trading Co.
81	1/7/2005	General	Professor	Faculty of Engineering/ SVI, Thammasat University
82	1/7/2005	Auto	Official	Dept. of Industrial Promotion, MOI
83	1/7/2005	Auto	Director	Thai Automotive Institute
84	1/7/2005	Textiles	Exec. Director	Thai Garment Manufacturer's Association
85	1/10/2005	General	Official	Department of Industrial Promotion, MOI
86	1/10/2005	Textiles	Manager	Federation of Thai Industries
87	1/10/2005	Auto	Manager	AAPICO

(continued)

Number	Date	Sector	Title	Organization
88	1/10/2005	Textiles	Product Design Officer	Product Development Center
89	1/10/2005	Textiles	Editor	TTIS Co., LTD.
90	1/11/2005	General	Official	NTSDA
91	1/11/2005	General	Official	MOI
92	1/11/2005	Finance	former official	Ministry of Finance
93	1/11/2005	Textiles	President/ Chair	Asia Fiber Co/Thai Synthetic Fiber Mfgs Assoc
94	1/11/2005	Textiles	Senior Trade Officer	Department of Export Promotion
95	1/11/2005	Sugar	Researcher	Mitr Pol Sugarcane Research Center
96	1/12/2005	Textiles	President	TGMA
97	1/12/2005	Textiles	Director	Thai Textile Manufacturer's Association
98	1/12/2005	Textiles	Manager	Association of Thai Textile Dyeing and Printing
99	1/13/2005	Textiles	Exec. Director	Thailand Textile Institute
100	1/19/2005	Textiles	President	TGMA
101	1/19/2005	Textiles	Director	TGMA
102	1/19/2005	Auto	Manager	Auto Parts Industry Club, FTI/S&L Commercial Co.
103	1/20/2005	Education	Official	Thai Research Fund
104	1/20/2005	Textiles	Director/ Director	Gold Mine Garment Co/ TGMA
105	5/23/2005	Textiles	Editor	TTIS Co., LTD.
106	8/15/2005	Textiles	Official	United States Environmental Protection Agency
107	5/27/2006	Education	Consultant	Box Hill Institute
108	6/2006	Auto	Official	Dept. of Industrial Promotion, MOI
109	6/6/2006	Textiles	Official	TGMA
110	6/6/2006	Auto	Official	TAPMA

Number	Date	Sector	Title	Organization
111	6/9/2006	General	Professor	Faculty of Political Science, Chulalongkorn University
112	6/12/2006	Auto	Professor	Faculty of Engineering/ SVI, Thammasat University
113	6/12/2006	Textiles	President	TGMA
114	6/13/2006	Textiles	Exec. Director	TGMA
115	6/13/2006	Auto	Official	Department of Industrial Promotion, MOI
116	6/13/2006	Textiles	Exec. Director	TGMA
117	6/14/2006	Auto	President/ Former Pres.	Wichien Dynamic Industry/TAMPA
118	6/15/2006	Textile	MD	United Textile Mills; ADTP
119	6/15/2006	Textile	Exec. Director	PN Textiles
120	6/2006	Sugar	Managing Director	KSL Export Trading Co.
121	6/16/2006	Auto	Vice Chairman/ Director	Auto Parts Industry Club, FTI/S&L Commercial Co.
122	11/11/2006	General	Official	NSTDA
123	6/7/2007	Auto	Consultant	Private consulting firm
124	6/10/2007	Auto	former official	Astra (Indonesia)
125	7/17/2007	General	Professor	Faculty of Economics, Thammasat University
126	7/17/2007	General	Official	National Science and Tec
127	7/18/2007	General	Official	Office of Industrial Economics, MOI
128	7/18/2007	General	Professor/ Consultant	Faculty of Engineering, Chulalongkorn University/SVI International

Bibliography

Abonyi, George. 2005. "Policy Reform in Thailand and the Asian Development Bank's Agricultural Sector Program Loan." Report prepared for the Asian Development Bank (April).

Acemoglu, Daron, Simon Johnson, and James A. Robinson. 2001. "An African Success Story: Botswana." In Dani Rodrik, ed., *In Search of Prosperity: Analytic Narratives on Economic Growth*. Princeton: Princeton University Press, pp. 80–122.

Adler, Emmanuel. 1987. *The Power of Ideology: the Quest for Technological Autonomy in Argentina and Brazil*. Berkeley: University of California Press.

Ahmad, Ali and Somporn Isvilanonda. 2003. "Rural Poverty and Agricultural Diversification in Thailand." Paper presented at the Second Annual Swedish School of Advanced Asia and Pacific Studies, October 24–26, Lund.

Ahrens, Joachim. 2002. *Governance and Economic Development: A Comparative Institutional Approach*. Northampton: Edward Elgar.

Amsden, Alice. 1989. *Asia's Next Giant*. New York: Oxford University Press.

1994. Why Isn't the Whole World Experimenting with the East Asian Model to Develop? *World Development* 22:4, pp. 627–633.

2001. *The Rise of the Rest: Challenges to the West from Late-Industrializing Economies*. New York: Oxford University Press.

Amsden, Alice and Wan-Wen Chu. 2003. *Beyond Late Development: Taiwan's Upgrading Policies*. Cambridge: MIT Press.

Amsden, Alice and Linsu Kim. 1985. "The Role of Transnational Corporations in the Production and Exports of the Korean Automobile Industry." Harvard Business School Working Paper.

Anderson, Bendict. 1977. "Withdrawal Symptoms: Social and Cultural Aspects of the October 6 Coup." *Bulletin of Concerned Asian Scholars*. 9:3, pp. 13–30.

1988. "Cacique Democracy and the Philippines: Origins and Dreams." *New Left Review*. 169, pp. 3–33.

Apichat, Satitniramai. 1992. "The Formation of Labor Unions in Textile Industry (sic)." M.A. Thesis, English Language Program, Faculty of Economics, Thammasat University.

Apinya, Feungfuskul. 1984. "Japanese Transnational Corporations in Thailand: A Case Study of the Textile Industry." M.A. Thesis, Dept. of International Relations, Chulalongkorn University.

Archanun, Kohpaiboon. 1995. "Policy Distortion and Competitiveness of Thai Textile Industries." M.A. Thesis, Thammasat University, Dept. of Economics.

Arnold, Erik, Martin Bell, John Bessant, and Peter Brimble. 2000a. *Enhancing Policy and Institutional Support for Industrial Technology Development in Thailand Vol 1: The Overall Policy Framework and the Development of the Industrial Innovation System.* Report for the National Science and Technology Development Agency of Thailand (NSTDA) (December). Bangkok.

Aron, Janine. 2000. "Growth and Institutions: A Review of the Evidence." *The World Bank Research Observer.* 15:1 (February), pp. 99–135.

Arthit, Wuthikaro. 1994. "A Study of the Tariff Structure Adjustment in Chemicals Used in Dyestuff Production and Textile Printing, Dyeing and Finishing Industries." Bangkok: Textile Intelligence Unit, Textile Industry Division, Department of Industrial Promotion, Ministry of Industry.

    1996. "Sataaban Sing Thaw: Ch'an Raw Ma Naan Lew Na" – Textile Institute: I've Been Waiting So Long." *Colourworld.*

Asia Policy Research Co. 2005. "Automotive Industry Investment Opportunity Profile." Bangkok.

Asian Development Bank (ADB). 1996. *Thailand Update.* Manila: IN.250–96 (November).

    2000. *Asian Development Outlook.* Manila: ADB.

    2001. *Asian Development Outlook.* Manila: ADB.

Aswicayhono, Haryo M., Chatib Basri, and Hall Hill. 2000. "How Not to Industrialize? Indonesia's Automotive Industry." *Bulletin of Indonesian Economic Studies* 36:1 (April), pp. 209–241.

Aswicayhono, Haryo M. and Tubagus Feridhanusetyawan. 2004. "The Evolution and Upgrading of Indonesia's Industry." Jakarto: CSIS, Economics Working Paper Series, http:wwww.csis.or.id/papers/wpe73.

Austria, Myrna S. 1996. "The Effects of the MFA Phase Out on the Philippines Garments and Textiles Industries." Philippines Institute for Development Studies, Discussion Paper Series No. 96–07, Makati City, Philippines.

"Auto Industry Analysis Report." 2004. Automotive Information Platform, www.marklines.com/en/amreport/rep279, (June 7). Accessed June 28, 2007.

Babbie, Earl. 2004. *The Practice of Social Research.* 10th ed., Belmont: Wadsworth/ Thompson Learning.

Back, Jong Gook. 1990. "Politics of Late Industrialization: The Origins and Processes of Automobile Industry Policies in Mexico and South Korea." Ph.D. diss., University of California, Los Angeles.

Bair, Jennifer and Gary Gereffi. 2002. "NAFTA and the Apparel Commodity Chain: Corporate Strategies, Interfirm Networks and Industrial Upgrading." In Gary Gereffi, David Spener, and Jennifer Bair, eds., *Free Trade and Uneven Development: The North American Apparel Industry After NAFTA,* Philadelphia: Temple University Press, pp. 23–52.

Baker, Chris and Pasuk Phongpaichit. 2005. *A History of Thailand.* New York: Cambridge University Press.

Barnes, Justin, Raphael Kaplinsky, and Mike Morris. 2004. "Industrial Policy in Developing Economies: Developing Dynamic Comparative Advantage in the South African Auto Sector." *Competition and Change.* 8:2, pp. 153–172.

Barzelay, Michael. 1986. *The Politicized Market Economy: Alcohol in Brazil's Energy Strategy.* Berkeley: University of California Press.

Bates, Robert H. 1988. "Contra Contractarianism: Some Reflections on the New Institutionalism." *Politics and Society.* 16, pp. 387–401.

___ 1995. "Social Dilemmas and Rational Individuals: An Assessment of the New Institutionalism." In John Harris, Janet Hunter, and Colin Lewis, eds., *The New Institutional Economics.* New York: Routledge, pp. 27–48.

Bell, Martin. 2003. "Knowledge Resources, Innovation Capabilities and Sustained Competitiveness in Thailand: Transforming the Policy Process." Bangkok: University of Sussex – SPRU / Brooker Group.

Bello, Walden and S. Rosenfeld. 1990. *Dragons in Distress: Asia's Miracle Economies in Crisis.* London: Penguin.

Bennett, Andrew. 2000. "Causal Inference in Case Studies: From Mill's Methods to Causal Mechanisms." Unpublished ms.

Berger, Martin and Javier Revilla Diez. 2006. "Technological Capabilities and Innovation in Southeast Asia – Empirical Evidence From Singapore, Penang (Malaysia) and Singapore." *Science, Technology and Society.* 11, pp. 109–148.

Bertrand, J. 1998. "Growth and Democracy in Southeast Asia." *Comparative Politics.* 30:3, pp. 355–375.

Bhanupong, Nidhiprabha. 2005. "Dynamism of Thai Agriculture." *East Asian Economic Perspectives.* 16:2 (August), pp. 22–45.

Bidhya, Bowornwathana.1995. "Responses of Public Administration of Thailand to Global Challenges." In Sirajuddin Salleh and Ledvina Carino, eds., *Globalisation and the ASEAN Public Sector.* Kuala Lumpur: Asian and Pacific Development Centre, pp. 365–430

___ 2001. "Thailand: Bureaucracy under Coalition Governments." In John Burns and Bidhya Bowornwathana, eds., *Civil Service Systems in Asia.* Cheltenham: Edward Elgar, pp. 281–318.

Biggart, Nicole Woolsey and Muaro Guillen. 1999. "Developing Difference: Social Organization and the Rise of the Auto Industries of South Korea, Taiwan, Spain, and Argentina." *American Sociological Review.* 64:5 (October), pp. 722–747.

Biggs, Tyler and Brian D. Levy. 1991. "Strategic Interventions and the Political Economy of Industrial Policy in Developing Countries." In Dwight H. Perkins and Michael Roemer, eds., *Reforming Economic Systems in Developing Countries.* Cambridge: Harvard University Press, for the Harvard Institute for International Development, pp. 366–401.

Billig, Michael S. 1993. "Syrup in the Wheels of Progress: The Inefficient Organization of the Philippine Sugar Industry." *Journal of Southeast Asian Studies.* 24, pp.122–147.

___ 1994. "The Death and Rebirth of Entrepreneurism on Negros Island, Philippines: A Critique of Cultural Theories of Enterprise." *Journal of Economic Issues.* 28 (September), pp. 659–678.

2003. *Barons, Brokers, and Buyers: The Institutions and Cultures of Philippine Sugar*. Honolulu: University of Hawai'i Press.

Birdsall, Nancy, Thomas Pinckney, and Richard Sabot. 2000. "Natural Resources, Human Capital, and Growth." Carnegie Endowment for International Peace, Global Policy Program Working Papers, No. 9.

Birdsall, Nancy, David Ross, and Richard Sabot. 1997. "Education, Growth and Inequality." In Nancy Birdsall and Frederick Jaspersen, eds., *Pathways to Growth: Comparing East Asia and Latin America*. Washington, DC: The Johns Hopkins University Press, pp. 93–130.

Book Club Finance and Securities. 1976. *The Textile Industry in Thailand*. Bangkok.

Booth, Alison L. and Dennis J. Snower. 1996. "Introduction: Does the Free Market Produce Enough Skills?" In Booth and Snower, eds., *Acquiring Skills: Markets Failures, Their Symptoms and Policy Responses*. Cambridge: Cambridge University Press, pp. 1–16.

Booth, Ann. 1999. "Initial Conditions and Miraculous Growth: Why is Southeast Asia Different from Taiwan and South Korea?" *World Development*. 27:2, pp. 301–321.

Borrell, Brent and Ronald C. Duncan. 1992. "A Survey of the Costs of World Sugar Policies," *The World Bank Research Observer*. 7:2 (July), pp. 171–194.

Brady, Henry E. and David Collier, eds. 2004. *Rethinking Social Inquiry: Diverse Tools, Shared Standards*. Landham: Rowman and Littlefield.

Bratton, Michael. 1989. "Beyond the State: Civil Society and Associational Life in Africa." *World Politics*. 41:3 (April), pp. 407–430.

"Brazil Semi-Annual Sugar 2005." www.fas.usda.gov/gainfiles

"Brazilian Sugar." 2003. www.fas.usda.gov/htp/sugar/2003/Brazilsugar03.pdf.

Breznitz, Dan. 2007. *Innovation and the State: Political Choice and Strategies for Growth in Israel, Taiwan and Ireland*. New Haven: Yale University Press.

Brimble, Peter and Richard Doner. 2007. "University-Industry Linkages and Economic Development: The Case of Thailand." *World Development*. 35:6 (June), pp. 1021–1036.

Brooker Group. 1997a. "BoI Investment Vision Support Document." Bangkok: Prepared for the Thailand Board of Investment.

1997b. "Automotive Industry Export Promotion Project: Thailand Industry Overview (January 26).

2001. "International Competitiveness of Asian Economies: A Cross Country Study – Thailand Background Paper." Bangkok.

Brunetti, Aymo and Beatrice Weder. 1994. "Political Credibility and Economic Growth in Less Developed Countries." *Constitutional Political Economy* 5:1, pp. 23–43.

Brunetti, Aymo and Beatrice Weder and Beatrice Weder. 1995. "Political Sources of Growth: A Critical Note on Assessment." *Public Choice*. 82, pp. 125–134.

Bueno de Mesquita, Bruce, Alastair Smith, Randolph M. Siverson, and James D. Morrow. 2003. *The Logic of Political Survival*. Cambridge: MIT Press.

Burki, Shahik Javed and Guillermo E. Perry. 1998. *Institutions Matter: Beyond the Washington Consensus*. Washington, DC: World Bank Latin American and Caribbean Studies.

Butler, Charlotte. 2002. *Dare to Do: The Story of William Soeryadjaya and PT Astra International*. Singapore: McGraw Hill 2002.

Campos, Jose Edgardo and Hilton L. Root. 1996. *The Key to the Asian Miracle.* Washington: Brookings.

Careaga, Maite and Barry R. Weingast. 2003. "Fiscal Federalism, Good Governance, and Economic Growth in Mexico." In Dani Rodrik, ed., *In Search of Prosperity: Analytic Narratives on Economic Growth.* Princeton: Princeton University Press, pp. 399–438.

Castella, Jean-Christophe, Damien Jourdain, Guy Trebuil, and Banpot Napompeth. 1999. "A Systems Approach to Understanding Obstacles to Effective Implementation of IPM for the Cotton Industry." *Agriculture, Ecosystems and Environment.* 72:1 (January 12), pp. 17–34.

Chalumporn Lotharukpong. 2004. "The Future of Thailand's Textile and Garment Industry: The Challenge, Opportunity and Threats in the Post-quota Period." Bangkok: International Chamber of Commerce

Chambers, Paul. 2003. "Cabinet Coalitions and the Durability of Parties and Factions: 1979–2001. Ph.D. diss., University of Northern Illinois.

2006. Factions, Parties, and the Durability of Parliaments, Coalitions, and Cabinets: The Case of Thailand (1979–2001). Unpublished ms.

Chang Ha-Joon. 2002. "The East Asian Model of Economic Policy." In Evelyn Huber, ed., *Models of Capitalism: Lessons for Latin America.* University Park: Pennsylvania State University Press, pp. 197–236.

Chen Been-Lon, Tain-Jy Chen, and Yun Peng Chu. 2001. "The Role of Textiles and Man-made Fiber in the Process of Industrialization: The Case of Taiwan." In Poh-Kam Wong and Chee-Yuen Ng, eds., *Industrial Policy, Innovation and Economic Growth.* Singapore: Singapore University Press, pp. 283–322.

Chen Goh Pek. 1999. "The Semiconductor Industry in Malaysia." In K. S Jomo., Greg Felker, and Rajah Rasiah, eds., *Industrial Technology Development in Malaysia: Industry and Firm Studies.* New York: Routledge, pp. 125–149.

Cheng Lu-lin. 2001. "Footwear in Taiwan" In Frederick Deyo, Richard Doner, and Eric Hershberg, eds., *Economic Governance and The Challenge of Flexibility in East Asia.* Boulder: Rowman and Littleifield, pp. 13–54.

Chiu, Stephen W. K. and Tai-Lok Lui, 2001. "Hong Kong: Garment and Electronics Industry Case Studies." In Poh-Kam Wong and Chee-Yuen Ng, eds., *Industrial Policy, Innovation and Economic Growth.* Singapore: Singapore University Press, pp. 460–502.

Christensen, Scott. 1992. "Between the Farmers and the State: Towards a Policy Analysis of the Role of Agribusiness in Thai Agriculture." Background paper for the Year-End Conference on Thailand's Economic Structure: Towards Balanced Development? Bangkok: Thailand Development Research Institute, December 12–13.

1993. "Coalitions and Collective Choice: The Politics of Institutional Change in Thai Agriculture." Ph.D. diss., University of Wisconsin-Madison.

1995. "Fashioning a Visible Hand: The State, Institutions, and Agricultural Policy in Thailand." Unpublished ms, Pacific Basin Research Center, Kennedy School of Government.

Christensen, Scott, David Dollar, Ammar Siamwalla, and Pakorn Vichyanond. 1993. "Institutional and Political Bases of Growth-Inducing Policies in

Thailand." Draft prepared for "Legacies and Lessons," World Bank project on East Asian development. Bangkok: Thailand Development Research Institute.

Christensen, Scott and Akin Rabibhadana. 1994. "Exit, Voice and the Depletion of Open Access Resources: The Political Bases of Property Rights in Thailand." *Law and Society Review* (November), 28:3, pp. 639–655.

Christensen, Scott and Amar Siamwalla. 1993. "Beyond Patronage: Tasks for the Thai State." Paper presented at 1993 Year-end Conference: Who Gets What and How? Challenges for the Future." Thailand Development Research Institute, December 10–11.

Chu Wan-Wen. 1994. "Import Substitution and Export-Led Growth: A Study of Taiwan's Petrochemical Industry." *World Development.* 22:4, pp. 781–794.

Chularat Saengpassa. 2006. "Unis (sic), Vocational Schools Get Poor Progress Report." *The Nation.* (November 2).

Clague, Christopher. 1997. "The New Institutional Economics and Economic Development." In Clague, ed., *Institutions and Economic Development.* Baltimore: Johns Hopkins University Press, 1997, pp. 1–13.

Cohen, W. M. and D. A. Levinthal. 1990. "Absorptive Capacity: A New Perspective on Learning and Innovation. *Administrative Science Quarterly.* 35, pp. 128–152.

Collier, David and James Mahoney. 1996. "Insights and Pitfalls: Selection Bias in Qualitative Research." *World Politics.* 49 (October), pp. 56–91.

Collier, Paul. 2007. *The Bottom Billion: Why the Poorest Countries are Failing and What Can be Done About It.* New York: Oxford University Press.

Coloco, Francis X. 1998. "Thailand's International Competitiveness: A Framework for Increased Productivity." Paper presented at the Conference on Thailand's Dynamic Economic Recovery and Competitiveness, Bangkok, May 20–21.

Connors, Michael Kelly. 2004. "Thaksin's Thailand – To Have and To Hold: Thai Politics in 2003–2004. Paper presented to the Thai Update Conference, Macquarie University, April 20–21.

Corden, W. M. 1967. "The Exchange Rate System and the Taxation of Trade." In T. H. Silcock, ed., *Thailand: Social and Economic Studies in Development.* Singapore: Donald Moore.

Cox, Gary and Mathew McCubbins. 2001. "The Institutional Determinants of Economic Policy Outcomes." In Stephen Haggard and Mathew D. McCubbins, eds., *Presidents, Parliaments and Policy.* New York: Cambridge University Press, pp. 21–63.

Crispin, Shawn and G. Pierre Goad. 2000. "Thai Cornucopia." Far Eastern Economic Review. (July 13), pp. 58–59.

Crouch, Colin. 2005. "Models of Capitalism." *New Political Economy.* 10:4 (December), pp. 439–456.

Culpepper, Pepper. 2001. "Employers, Public Policy, and the Politics of Decentralized Cooperation in Germany and France." In Peter A. Hall and David Soskice, eds., *Varieties of Capitalism.* New York: Cambridge University Press, pp. 275–304.

Cypher, James M. and James L. Dietz. 1997. *The Process of Economic Development.* New York: Routledge.

D'Costa, Anthony P. 1999. *The Global Restructureing of the Steel Industry: Innovations, Institutions and Industrial Change*. New York: Routledge.

de Vries, Brand and Willem Brakel. 1983. "Restructuring the Manufacturing Industry: The Experience of the Textile Industry in Pakistan, Philippines, Portugal and Turkey." *World Bank Staff Working Papers #558*. Washington: World Bank.

Demsetz, Harold. 2000. "Dogs and Tails in the Economic Development Story." In Claude Menard, ed., *Institutions, Contracts and Organizations: Perspectives from New Institutional Economics*. Northampton: Edward Elgar, pp. 69–87.

Deyo, Frederick and Richard F. Doner. 2000a. "Dynamic Flexibility and Sectoral Governance in the Thai Auto Industry: The Enclave Problem." In Fredrick Deyo, Richard Doner, and Eric Hershberg, eds., *The Challenge of Flexible Production in East Asia*. Boulder: Rowman and Littlefield, pp. 107–136.

Deyo, Frederick and Richard F. Doner. 2000b. "Introduction: The Political Economy of Flexible Production in East Asia." In Fredrick Deyo, Richard Doner, and Eric Hershberg, eds., *The Challenge of Flexible Production in East Asia*. Boulder: Rowman and Littleifield.

Dhanani, Shafiq. 2000. "Indonesia: Strategy for Manufacturing Competitiveness/ Vol. II. Main Report." Jakarta: UNDP/UNIDO Project No. NC/INS/99/004 (November).

Dhanani, Shafiq and Philippe Scholtes. (July) 2002. "Thailand's Manufacturing Competitiveness: Promoting Technology, Productivity and Linkages." Vienna: UNIDO, SME Technical Working Paper.

Diaz-Alejandro, Carlos. 1983. "Some aspects of the 1982–83 Brazilian Payments Crisis." Brookings Papers on Economic Activity. 2, pp. 515–552.

Dixit, Avinash. 1998. *The Making of Economic Policy: A Transaction Cost Politics Perspective*. Cambridge: MIT Press.

Dixon, Chris. 1999. *Uneven Development and Internationalization*. London: Routledge.

Dollar, David and Mary Hallward-Driemeir. 1999. "Crisis, Adjustment and Reform: Results from the Thailand Industrial Survey." Unpublished paper, Development Research Group, World Bank.

Doner, Richard F. 1991. *Driving a Bargain: Automobile Industrialization and Japanese Firms in Southeast Asia*. Berkeley: University of California Press.

1992. "Limits of State Strength: Toward an Institutionalist Approach to Economic Development." *World Politics*. 44:3 (April), pp. 398–431.

2006. "Automotive Industry Development in East Asia: Performance, Politics and Institutions." Paper presented at the 2006 meeting of the International Studies Association, San Diego, CA, March 22–27.

2007. "Industrial Competitiveness of the Auto Parts Industries in Four Large Asian Countries: The Role of Government Policy in a Challenging International Environment." Unpublished ms, World Bank Policy Research Report #4106.

Doner, Richard F. and Gary Hawes. 1995. "The Political Economy of Growth in Southeast and Northeast Asia." In Manocher Dorraj, ed., *The Changing Political Economy of the Third World*. Boulder: Lynne Reiner, pp. 145–186.

Doner, Richard F., Allen Hicken, and Bryan Ritchie. Forthcoming. "The Political Challenge of Innovation in the Developing World." *Review of Research Policy*.

Doner, Richard F. and Anek Laothamatas. 1994. "Thailand: Economic and Political Gradualism." In Stephan Haggard and Steven B. Webb, eds., *Voting for Reform: Democracy, Political Liberalization and Economic Adjustment*. Washington, DC: Oxford University Press for the World Bank, pp. 411–452.

Doner, Richard F., Gregory Noble, and John Ravenhil. 2004. "Production Networks in East Asia's Automobile Parts Industry." In Shahid Yusuf, M. Anjum Altaf, and Kaoru Naveshima, eds., *Global Production Networking and Technological Change in East Asia*. Washington, DC: Oxford University Press / World Bank, pp. 159–208.

Doner, Richard F. and Ansil Ramsay. 1997. "Competitive Clientelism and Economic Governance: The Case of Thailand." In Sylvia Maxfield, and Ben Schneider, eds., *Business and the State in Developing Countries*. Ithaca: Cornell University Press.

Doner, Richard F. and Ansil Ramsay. 2000. "Rent-Seeking and Economic Development in Thailand." In Mushtaq Khan and K. S. Jomo, eds., *Rents, Rent-Seeking and Economic Development: Theory and Evidence in Asia* Cambridge: Cambridge University Press, pp. 145–181.

Doner, Richard F. and Bryan Ritchie. 2003. "Economic Crisis and Technological Trajectories: Hard Disk Drive Production in Southeast Asia." In William W. Keller and Richard J. Samuels, eds., *Crisis and Innovation in Asian Technology*. New York: Cambridge University Press, pp. 187–225.

Doner, Richard F., Bryan Ritchie, and Dan Slater. 2005. "Systemic Vulnerability and the Origins of Developmental States: Northeast and Southeast Asia in Comparative Perspective." *International Organization* 59:2 (Spring), pp. 327–362.

Doner, Richard F. and Ben Schneider. 2000. "Business Associations and Economic Development." *Business and Politics*. 2:3, pp. 261–288.

Dong Quan. 2006. "Intel Signing in HCMC Glimpse of the Future." VietNamNet. (March 2). Accessed online.

Easterly, William. 2002. *The Elusive Quest for Growth: Economists' Adventures and Misadventures in the Tropics*. Cambridge: MIT Press.

Eckardt, James. 1993. "High-Tech Shake-Out." *Manager* (October), pp. 44–48.

Eden, Lorraine and Fen Osler Hampson. 1997. "Clubs are Trump: The Formation of International Regimes in the Absence of a Hegemon." In J. Rogers Hollingsworth and Robert Boyer, eds., *Contemporary Capitalism: The Embeddedness of Institutions*. New York: Cambridge University Press, pp. 360–394.

Eggertsson, Thrainn. 1996. "A Note on the Economics of Institutions." In Lee J. Alston, Thrainn Eggertsson, and Douglass C. North, eds., *Empirical Studies in Institutional Change*. New York: Cambridge University Press, pp. 6–24.

Ernst, Dieter. 2000. "What Permits David to Grow in the Shadow of Goliath? The Taiwanese Model in the Computer Industry." In Michael Borrus, Dieter Ernst, and Stephan Haggard.eds., *International Production Network: Rivalry or Riches*. New York: Routledge, pp. 110–140.

2004. "Global Production Networks in East Asia's Electronics Industry and Upgrading Perspectives in Malaysia." In Shahid Yusuf, M. Anjum Altaf, and Kaoru Nabeshima, eds., *Global Production Networking and Technological Change in East Asia*. New York: Oxford University Press and the World Bank, pp. 89–158.

Ernst, Dieter, Tom Ganiatsos, and Lynn Mytelka., *Technological Capabilities and Export Success in Asia*. New York: Routledge.

Etzkowitz, Henry. 2002. "Networks of Innovation: Science, Technology and Development in the Triple Helix Era." *International Journal of Technology Management and Sustainable Development*. 1:1, pp. 7–20.

Evans, Peter. 1995. *Embedded Autonomy: States and Industrial Transformation*. Princeton: Princeton University Press.

——— 1997. "Government Action, Social Capital and Development: Reviewing the Evidence of Synergy." In Peter Evans, ed., *State-Society Synergy: Government and Social Capital in Development*. Berkeley: University of California, International and Area Studies, Research Series no. 94.

Feeny, David. 1998. "Thailand versus Japan: Why was Japan First?" In Yujiro Hayami and Masahiko Aoki, eds., *The Institutional Foundations of East Asian Economic Development*. New York: St. Martin's Press.

Felker, Greg B. 1998. "Upwardly Global? The State, Business and MNCs in Malaysia and Thailand's Technological Transformation." Ph.D. diss., Princeton University.

——— 2001. "Politics of Industrial Investment Policy Reform in Malaysia and Thailand." In K. S. Jomo ed., *Southeast Asia's Industrialization: Capabiities and Sustainability*. Houndmills: Palgrave.

Felker, Greg B. and K. S. Jomo 2003. "New Approaches to Investment Policy in the ASEAN-4." In K. S. Jomo, ed., *Southeast Asian Paper Tigers?* London: Routledge, pp. 81–135.

Fields, Karl. 1995. *Enterprise and the State in Korea and Taiwan*. Ithaca: Cornell University Press.

Fry, Gerald W. 2002. "Synthesis Report: From Crisis to Opportunity, the Challenges of Educational Reform in Thailand." Study prepared for the Office of the National Education Commission and the Asian Development Bank, August 8.

Fry, James 1999. "International Productivity Comparisons." International Society of Sugar Cane Technolgists (ISSCT) 23rd Congress, New Delhi, India, February 22–26.

Frye, Timothy. 2000. *Brokers and Bureaucrats: Building Market Institutions in Russia*. Ann Arbor: University of Michigan Press.

Fuglie, Keith. 2001. "Thailand." In Carl Pray and Keith Fuglie, eds., *Private Investment in Agricultural Research and International Technology Transfer in Asia*. U.S. Dept. of Agriculture, Economic Research Service, Agricultural Economic Report No. 805, accessed at www.ers.usda.gov.

Fujimoto, Takahiro and Oh Jewheon. 2006. "Competition and Cooperation in Automotive Steel Sheet Production in East Asia. MMRC Discussion Paper No. 73, University of Tokyo.

Geddes, Barbara. 1994. *Politicians' Dilemma*. Berkeley: University of California Press.

Geertz, Clifford. 1963. *Peddlers and Princes*. Chicago: University of Chicago Press.

——— 2004. "The Global Economy: Organization, Governance, and Development." In Neil Smelser and Richard Swedberg, eds., *Handbook of Economic Sociology*. Princeton: Princeton University Press.

Gereffi, Gary. 2005. "The Global Economy: Organization, Governance, and Development: In Neil Smelser and Richard Swedberg, eds., *Handbook of Economic Sociology*, Princeton: Princeton University Press.

Gereffi, Gary and Olga Memedovic. 2003. "The Global Apparel Value Chain: What Prospects for Upgrading by Developing Countries." Vienna: UNIDO.

Gerring, John. 2007. *Case Study Research: Principles and Practices.* New York: Cambridge University Press.

Gershenkron, Alexander. 1962. *Economic Backwardness in Historical Perspective.* Cambridge: Harvard University Press.

Gibbon, Peter. 2001. "Upgrading Primary Production: A Global Commodity Chain Approach." *World Development.* 29:2, 345–363.

Gill, Indermit and Homi Kharas. 2006. *An East Asian Renaissance: Ideas for Economic Growth.* Washington DC: World Bank.

Glassman, Jim. 2004a. *Thailand at the Margins: Internationalization of the State and the Transformation of Labour.* New York: Oxford University Press.

2004b. "Economic 'Nationalism' in a Post-Nationalist Era: The Political Economy of Economic Policy in Post-Crisis Thailand." *Critical Asian Studies.* 36:1, pp. 37–64.

"Golden Years Over for Garment Industry." 1994. Bangkok Journal (April 5–18), p. 9.

Gore, Charles. 2000. "The Rise and Fall of the Washington Consensus as a Paradigm for Developing Countries." *World Development.* 28:5, pp. 789–804.

Goss, Jasper and David Burch. 2001. "From Agricultural Modernisation to Agrifood Globalisation: the Waning of National Development in Thailand." *Third World Quarterly.* 22:6, pp. 969–986.

Grief, Avner. 1993. "Contract Enforceability and Economics Institutions in Early Trade: The Maghribi Traders Coalition." *American Economic Review* 83:3, pp. 525–548.

Grindle, Merilee. 2001. "In Quest of the Political: The Political Economy of Development Policymaking." In Gerald Meier and Joseph Stiglitz, eds., Meier, *Frontiers of Development Economics.* Washington, DC: World Bank and Oxford University Press, pp. 345–380.

2004. *Despite the Odds: The Contentious Politics of Education Reform.* Princeton: Princeton University Press.

Haggard, Stephan. 1990. *Pathways from the Periphery.* Ithaca: Cornell University Press.

1997. "Democratic Institutions, Economic Policy, and Development." In Christopher Clague, ed., *Institutions and Economic Development: Growth and Governance in Less-Developed and Post-Socialist Countries.* Baltimore: Johns Hopkins University Press, pp. 121–152.

2003. "Institutions and Growth in East Asia." SCID draft.

Haggard, Stephan and Euysung Kim. 1997. "The Sources of East Asia's Economic Growth." *Access Asia Review* (Summer), pp. 31–63.

Haggard, Stephan and Steven B. Webb. 1994. "Introduction." In Haggard and Webb, eds., *Voting for Reform: Democracy, Political Liberalization and Economic Adjustment.* Washington, DC: Oxford University Press for the World Bank.

Hagopian, Francis. 1994. "Traditional Politics Against State Transformation in Brazil." In Joel Migdal, Atul Kohli, and Vivienne Shue, eds., *State Power and Social Forces: Domination and Transformation in the Third World.* New York: Cambridge University Press, pp. 36–64.

Hall, Peter and David Soskice. 2000. *Varieties of Capitalism: The Institutional Foundations of Comparative Advantage*. New York: Oxford University Press.

Hallerberg, Mark. 2002. "Veto Players and the Choice of Monetary Institutions." *International Organization*. (November) 56, pp. 775–802

Hamilton-Hart, Natasha. 2002. *Asian States, Asian Bankers: Central Banking in Southeast Asia*. Ithaca: Cornell University Press.

Handley, Paul. 1991. "Cutting Edge." *Far Eastern Economic Review*. (August 29), pp. 34–35.

1997. "More of the Same? Politics and Business." In Kevin Hewison, ed., *Political Change in Thailand: Democracy and Participation*. New York: Routledge, pp. 94–113.

2006. *The King Never Smiles: A Biography of Thailand's King Bumibol Adulyadej*. New Haven: Yale University Press.

Hansen, J. F. 1971. "The Motor Vehicle Industry." *Bulletin of Indonesian Economic Studies*. 7:2 (July), pp. 38–69.

Harris, John, Janet Hunter, and Colin M. Lewis, eds. 1995. *The New Institutional Economics and Third World Development*. New York: Routledge.

Hawes, Gary. 1987. *The Philippine State and the Marcos Regime: The Politics of Export*. Ithaca: Cornell University Press.

Hefner, Robert W. 1998. *Market Cultures: Society and Morality in the New Asian Capitalisms*. Boulder,: Westview Press.

Helfand, Steven M. 1999. "The Political Economy of Agricultural Policy in Brazil: Decision Making and Influence from 1964 to 1992." *Latin American Research Review*. 34:2, pp. 3–41.

Herderschee, Han. 1993. "Incentives for Exports: The Case of Thailand." *ASEAN Economic Bulletin*. 9:3 (March), pp. 348–364.

Hewison, Kevin H. 1985. "The State and Capitalist Development in Thailand." In Richard Higgott and Richard Robison, eds., *Southeast Asia: Essays in Political Change*. London: Routledge, pp. 266–294.

1986. "Capital in the Countryside: The Sugar Industry." *Journal of Contemporary Asia*. 16:1, pp. 3–17.

1989. *Bankers and Bureaucrats: Capital and the Role of the State in Thailand*. New Haven: Yale University Center for International and Area Studies, Monograph Series #34.

2003. "The Politics of Neo-Liberalism: Class and Capitalism in Contemporary Thailand." Southeast Asia Research Centre, City University of Hong Kong.

Hicken, Allen. 2004. "The Politics of Economic Reform in Thailand: Crisis and Compromise." William Davidson Institute Working Paper #638, University of Michigan Business School.

2006a. "Politics of Economic Recovery in Thailand and the Philippines." In Andrew MacIntyre, T. J. Pempel, and John Ravenhill, eds., *East Asia Ten Years After the Crisis*. New York: Cambridge University Press.

2006b. "Party Fabrication: Constitutional Reform and the Rise of Thai Rak Thai." *Journal of East Asian Studies*. 6:3, pp. 381–408.

Hicken, Allen and Bryan Ritchie. 2002. "The Origin of Credibility Enhancing Institutions in Southeast Asia." Presented at the annual APSA Meeting, August 29–31, 2002, Boston.

308   *Bibliography*

Hill, Hal. 2004. "Technology and Innovation in East Asia." In Shahid Yusuf, Anjum Altaf, and Kaoru Nabeshina, eds., *Global Production Networking and Technological Change in East Asia*. New York: Oxford University Press for the World Bank, pp. 353–394.

Hill, Hal and Suphat Suphachalasai. 1992. "The Myth of Export Pessimism (even) under the MFA: Evidence from Indonesia and Thailand." *Weltwirtschaftliches Archiv/Review of World Economics*. 128:2, pp. 310–329.

Hirschman, Albert A. 1958. *The Strategy of Economic Development*. New Haven: Yale University Press.

Hobday, Michael. 2000. "East versus Southeast Asia Innovation Systems: Comparing OEM and TNC-Led Growth in Electronics." In Linsu Kim and Richard Nelson, eds., *Technology, Learning, and Innovation: Experiences of Newly Industrializing Economies*. Cambridge: Cambridge University Press, pp. 129–169.

Hobsbawm, Eric. 1968. *Industry and Empire*. Middlesex, England: Penguin Books.

Hoff, Karla and Joseph E. Stiglitz. 2001. "Modern Economic Theory and Development." In Gerald M. Meier, eds., *Frontiers of Development Economics: The Future in Perspective*. New York: World Bank and Oxford University Press, pp. 389–459.

House, Maurice W. 2000. "Thailand Sugar Annual – Revised." United States Department of Agriculture. GAIN Report #TH0032 (April 7).

Huang Yasheng. 2002. "Between Two Coordination Failures: Automotive Industrial Policy in China with a Comparison to Korea." *Review of International Political Economy*. 9:3(August), pp. 538–573.

Humphrey, John. 1998. "Assembler–Supplier Relations in the Auto Industry: Globalisation and National Development." Sussex: IDS, University of Sussex.

2002. "How Does Insertion in Global Value Chains Affect Upgrading in Industrial Clusters." *Regional Studies*. 36:9, pp. 1017–1027.

Humphrey, John and Olga Memedovic. 2003. "The Global Automotive Industry Value Chain: What Prospects for Upgrading by Developing Countries?" Vienna: UNIDO

Humphrey, John and Hubert Schmitz. 2002. "How Does Insertion in Global Value Chains Affect Upgrading in Industrial Clusters?" *Regional Studies* (December), 36:9, pp. 1017–1027.

Hutchcroft, Paul. 1994. "Booty Capitalism: Business–Government Relations in the Philippines." In Andrew MacIntyre, ed., *Business and Government in Industrializing Asia*. Ithaca: Cornell University Press, pp. 216–267.

1998. *Booty Capitalism: The Politics of Banking in the Philippines*. Ithaca: Cornell University Press.

2000. "Obstructive Corruption: The Politics of Privilege in the Philippines." In Mushtaq H. Khan and K. S. Jomo, eds., *Rents, Rent-Seeking and Economic Development: Theory and Evidence in Asia*. New York: Cambridge University Press, 2000, pp. 207–247.

Imbs, J. and R. Wacziarg. 2003. "Stages of Diversification." *American Economic Review*. 93:1 (March), pp. 63–86.

Industrial Finance Corporation of Thailand. 2003. "Textiles." IFCT Research Division. Bangkok

Industrial Management Company (IMC). 1984. *Comparative Advantage of Textile and Cement Industries in Thailand*. Bangkok.

1985. *Industrial Restructuring Study: Technology Development and Promotion for the Engineering Industries.* Bangkok.

1985. *Tax System for Industrial Restructuring – Industrial Restructuring Study, Final Report, Vol 1.* (September).

Ingram, James. 1955. *Economic Change in Thailand Since 1850.* Stanford: Stanford University Press.

Intarakumnerd, Patarapong. 2004. "Thailand's National Innovation System in Transition." Bangkok: Thai National Science and Technology Development Agency.

Intarakumnerd, Patarapong. 2005. "Foreign Direct Investment in R&D in Thailand: Evolution and Challenges." Paper presented at ASEAN-UNCTAD Seminar on Key Issues of FDI: Attracting Quality FDI, Bangkok, May 5–6.

James, William E. and Eric D. Ramstetter. 2005. "Trade, Foreign Firms, and Economic Policy in Indonesian and Thai Manufacturing." Kitakyushi: International Center for the Study of East Asian Development, Working Paper Series Vol. 2005–01 (April).

Jansen, Karel. 1997a. "The Macroeconomic Effects of Direct Foreign Investment: The Case of Thailand." *World Development.* 23:2, pp. 193–210.

1997b. *External Finance in Thailand's Development: An Interpretation of Thailand's Growth Boom.* New York: St. Martin's Press.

JICA (Japan International Cooperation Agency). 1989. *A Study on Industrial Sector Development in the Kingdom of Thailand: Second Year Final Report Draft.* Bangkok.

Jeong, Insook and Michael J. Armer. 1994. "State Class and Expansion of Education in South Korea." *Comparative Education Review.* 38, pp. 531–545.

Johnson, Chalmers. 1982. *MITI and the Japanese Miracle: The Growth of Industrial Policy, 1925–19 75.* Stanford: Stanford University Press.

1999. "The Developmental State: Odyssey of a Concept." In Meredith Woo-Cumings, ed., *The Developmental State.* Ithaca: Cornell University Press, pp. 32–60.

Juanjai Ajanant, 1983. "Export Promotion in Processed Foods and Textile Products." UNDP/UNIDO-NESDB (June).

Juanjai Ajanant, and Suvit Thaniyavarn. 1985. *Industrial Restructuring in Textile Industries: Final Report* (April 30). Bangkok: Industrial Management Co. for UNDP, UNIDO-NESDB Industrial Restructuring Project.

Jutting, Johannes. 2003. "Institutions and Development: A Critical Review." Paris: OECD Development Centre, Working Paper No. 210. (July).

Kaewjai Siriwatpatara. 1989. "A Study of the MFA and Bilateral Agreements and the Effects of Quota Restrictions on Thai Textile Exports." M.A. Thesis, Faculty of Economics, Thammasat University.

Kahler, Miles. 1990."Orthodoxy and Its Alternatives: Explaining Approaches to Stabilization and Adjustment." In Joan Nelson, ed., *Economic Crisis and Policy Choice: The Politics of Adjustment in the Third World* Princeton: Princeton University Press, pp. 33–62.

Kang, David. 2002. *Crony Capitalism: Corruption and Development in South Korea and the Philippines.* New York: Cambridge University Press.

Kanitha Srisilpavongse. 1985. "Textiles: Restructuring is the Name of the Game." *Bangkok Bank Monthly Review.* 26:1 (January), pp. 24–33.

Kaplinsky, Raphael. 2000. "Globalisation and Unequalisation: What Can Be Learned from Value Chain Analysis." *Journal of Development Studies.* 37:2, pp. 118–146.
  2005. *Globalization, Poverty and Inequality.* Malden: Polity Press.
Karndee Prichanont, Seeronk Prichanont,and Nuanpan Buansri. 2005. "Improvement Guidelines for Sugar Cane Delivery Systems." Paper presented to 35th International Conference on Computers and Industrial Engineering.
Keefer, Phillip. 2003. "Does Democracy Help?" *Economic Growth in the 1990s: Learning from a Decade of Reform.* Washington: World Bank, pp. 313–333.
  2004. "Clientelism, Credibility and Democracy." Unpublished ms, World Bank (March 2004).
Kennedy, Julia. 1997. "The Future of the Automotive Industry in Thailand: Quantifying Exports Till 2010." Bangkok: Thailand Development Research Institute.
Kesavatana, Wiworn. 1989. "Political Economy of Direct Foreign Investment in Thailand: A Case Study of the Automobile Industry." Ph.D. diss., Dept. of Political Science. University of Michigan.
Kim Jong-Il and Lawrence Lau. 1994. "The Sources of Economic Growth of the East Asian Newly Industrialized Countries." *Journal of the Japanese and International Economies.* 8:3, pp. 235–271.
Kim Khee-Young. 1984. "American Technology and Korea's Technological Developments." In Karl Moskowitz, ed., *From Patron to Partner: The Development of U.S.-Korean Business and Trade Relations.* Lexington: D. C. Heath, pp. 90–94.
Kim, Linsu. 2001. "The Dynamics of Technological Learning in Industrialization." *International Social Science Journal.* (December) 53:168, pp. 297–308.
  1993. "National System of Industrial Innovation: Dynamics of Capability Building in Korea." In Richard Nelson, ed., *National Innovation Systems: A Comparative Analysis.* New York: Oxford University Press, pp. 357–383.
Kim, Linsu and Richard R. Nelson. 2000. "Introduction." In Linsu Kim and Richard R. Nelson, eds., *Technology, Learning and Innovation: Experiences of Newly Industrializing Economies.* New York: Cambridge University Press, pp. 1–13.
Kim Youngsoo. 2000. "Technological Capabilities and the Samsung Electronics Network." In Michael Borrus, Dieter Ernst, and Stephan Haggard, eds., *International Production Networks in Asia.* London and New York: Routledge, pp. 141–175.
Kitschelt, Herbert. 1991. "Industrial Governance Structures, Innovation Strategies, and the Case of Japan: Sectoral or Cross-National Comparative Analysis?" *International Organization.* 45:4 (Autumn), pp. 453–494.
Knight, Jack. 1992. *Institutions and Social Conflict.* New York: Cambridge University Press.
Kohli, Atul. 2004. *State-Directed Development: Political Power and Industrialization in the Global Periphery.* Princeton: Princeton University Press.
Krirrkiat Phiphatseritham and Kunio Yoshihara. 1983. *Business Groups in Thailand.* Singapore: Institute of Southeast Asian Studies.
Krongkaew, Medhi and Ragayah Haji Mat Zin. 2007. "Income Distribution and Sustainable Economic Development in East Asia: A Comparative Analysis." IDEAs Working Paper Series # 02/2007.

Krugman, Paul. 1994. "The Myth of Asia's Miracle." *Foreign Affairs*. 83:6, pp. 62–78.

Kuo Cheng-Tian. 1995. *Global Competitiveness and Industrial Growth in Taiwan and the Philippines*. Pittsburgh: University of Pittsburgh Press.

Kuznetsov, Yevgeny. 2004. "Chile: Towards a Pragmatic Innovation Agenda." Presentation to the Development Policy Review Workshop, World Bank Institute, Santiago, November 29.

Kuznetsov, Yevgeny and Charles Sabel. 2005. "New Industrial Policy: Solving Economic Development Problems without Picking Winners." (June 13). Washington: World Bank Institute.

Lall, Sanjaya. 1994. "'The East Asian Miracle' Study: Does the Bell Toll for Industrial Strategy?" *World Development* 22:4, pp. 645–654.

  1998. "Thailand's Manufacturing Sector: The Current Crisis and Export Competitiveness." Paper presented at the conference on Thailand's Dynamic Economic Recovery and Competitiveness. Bangkok, May 20–21.

  2000. "Technological Change and Industrialization in the Asian Newly Industrializing Economies: Achievements and Challenges. " In Linsu Kim and Richard R. Nelson, eds., *Technology, Learning and Innovation: Experiences of Newly Industrializing Countries.*. Cambridge: Cambridge University Press, p. xxx.

Landa, Janet. 1991. "Culture and Entrepreneurship in Less-Developed Countries: Ethnic Trading Networks as Economic Organizations." In Brigitte Berger, ed., *The Culture of Entrepreneurship*. San Francisco: ICS Press.

Laothamatas, Anek. 1991. *Business Associations and the New Political Economy of Thailand*. Boulder: Westview Press.

  2007. *Thaksin – Prachaniyom (Thaksin – Populism)*. Bangkok: Matichon Publishing House.

Larkin, John A. 1993. *Sugar and the Origins of Modern Philippine Society*. Berkeley: University of California Press.

Larson, Donald F. and Brent Borrell. 2001 "Sugar Policy and Reform." World Bank. www.worldbank.org/files.1724_wps.2602.pdf

Lauridsen, Laurids S. 2000. "Industrial Policies, Political Institutions and Industrial Development in Thailand 1959–1991." Roskilde University: International Development Studies Working Paper No. 21.

  2002a "Coping with the Triple Challenge of Globalisation, Liberalisation and Crisis: The Role of Industrial Technology Policies and Technology Institutions in Thailand." *European Journal of Development Research*. 41:2 (June), pp. 101–125.

  2002b. "Struggling with globalization in Thailand: Accumulation, Learning, or Market Competition." *South East Asia Research*. 10:2 (July), pp. 155–183(29).

  2004. "FDI, Linkage Formation and Supplier Development in Thailand During the 1990s – the Role of State Governance." *European Journal of Development Research*. 16:3 (Autumn), pp. 581–586.

  2005. "Industrial Deepening and Upgrading Policy – Supplier Development in Downstream Plastic Parts and Mould Industries in Thailand." November 24.

Lautier, Marc. 2001. "The International Development of the Korean Auto Industry." In Frederique Sachwald, ed., *Going Multinational: The Korean Experience*. New York: Routledge.

Leary, R. H. 1998. "Thailand: Down But Not Out." *Textile Asia.* (January), p. 95.

Lecler, Yveline. 2002. "The Cluster Role in the Development of Thai Car Industry." *International Journal of Urban and Regional Research.* 24:4 (December), pp. 799–814.

Lee Won-Young. 2000. "The Role of Science and Technology Policy in Korea's Industrial Development." In Linsu Kim and Richard Nelson, eds., *Technology, Learning and Innovation.* New York: Cambridge University Press, pp. 269–290.

Leff, Nathaniel. 1978. "Industrial Organization and Entrepreneurship in the Developing Countries: The Economic Groups." *Economic Development and Cultural Change* 26 (July), pp. 661–675.

Lew Seok-Jin. 1992. "Bringing Capital Back In: A Case Study of the South Korean Automobile Industrialization." Ph.D. diss. Yale University. November.

Liebenstein, Harvey. 1968. "Entrepreneurship and Development." *American Economic Review.* 58:2 (May), pp. 72–83.

Lim, Linda. 1983. "Singapore's Success: The Myth of the Free Market Economy." *Asian Survey.* 23:6 (June), pp. 752–764.

Lin, Justin Yifu. 1999. "An Economic Theory of Institutional Change." In Colin Barlow, ed., *Institutions and Economic Change in Southeast Asia: The Context of Development from the 1960s to the 1990s.* Northampton: Edward Elgar, pp. 8–24.

MacIntyre, Andrew. 1994. "Business, Government and Development: Northeast and Southeast Asian Comparisons." In Andrew MacIntyre, ed., *Business and Government in Industrializing Asia.* Sydney: Allen and Unwin, pp. 1–128.

 2003. *The Power of Institutions: Political Architecture and Governance.* Ithaca: Cornell University Press.

Mahoney, James and Gary Goertz. 2004. "The Possibility Principle: Choosing Negative Cases in Comparative Research." *American Political Science Review.* 98:4 (November), pp. 653–669.

Mardon, Rusell. 1990. "The State and the Effective Control of Foreign Capital: The Case of South Korea." *World Politics.* 43:1 (October), pp. 111–137.

Markusen, Ann and Sam Ock Park. 1993. "The State as Industrial Locator and District Builder: The Case of Changwon, South Korea." *Economic Geography.* 69:2 (April), pp. 157–181.

Martines-Filho, Joaoa Burnquist, and Carlos Vian. 2006. "Bioenergy and the Rise of Sugarcane-Based Ethanol in Brazil." *Choices.* 21:2, pp. 91–96.

Matthews, John, and Dong-Sung Cho. 2000. *Tiger Technology: The Creation of a Semiconductor Industry in East Asia.* Cambridge, U. K.: Cambridge University Press.

McCargo, Duncan. 2002a. "Democracy Under Stress in Thaksin's Thailand." *Journal of Democracy.* 13:4 (October), pp. 112–126.

Mccargo, Duncan, ed. 2002b. *Reforming Thai Politics.* Copenhagen: Nordic Institute of Asian Studies.

 2002c. "Introduction." In McCargo, ed., *Reforming Thai Politics.* Copenhagen: Nordic Institute of Asian Studies, pp. 1–21.

 2002d. "Thailand's January 2001 General Election: Vindicating Reforms." In McCargo, ed., *Reforming Thai Politics.* Copenhagen: Nordic Institute of Asian Studies, pp. 247–259.

McCoy, Alfred. 1983. "In Extreme Unction: The Philippine Sugar Industry under Martial Law." In R. S. David ed., *The Political Economy of Philippines Commodities*. Quezon City: Third World Studies Program, University of the Philippines.

McDermott, Gerald A. 2005. "The Politics of Institutional Renovation and Competitive Upgrading: Lessons from the Transformation of the Argentine Wine Industry." Paper presented at the 17th Annual SASE Meetings on Socio-Economics, Budapest, June 29–July 3.

McKean, Cressida, Kiert Toh, and William Fisher. 1994. "Export and Investment Promotion in Thailand." Washington, DC: USAID Technical Report No. 17 (April).

McKendrick, David, Richard F. Doner, and Stephan Haggard. 2000. *From Silicon Valley to Singapore: The Competitive Advantage of Location in the Hard Disk Drive Industry*. Stanford: Stanford University Press.

McVey, Ruth. 2000. *Money and Power in Provincial Thailand*. Chiang Mai: Silkworm Books.

Meier, Gerald. 2001. "The Old Generation of Development Economists and the New." In Gerald Meier and Joseph Stiglitz, eds., *Frontiers of Development Economics*. Washington, DC: World Bank and Oxford University Press, pp. 13–50.

Meissner, Frank. 1988. *Technology Transfer in the Developing World: The Case of the Chile Foundation*. New York: Praeger.

Milanovic, Branko. 2005. *Worlds Apart: Measuring International and Global Inequality*. Princeton: Princeton University Press.

Mingsarn Santikarn Kaosa-Ard. 1992a. "Manufacturing Growth: A Blessing for All," In *Thailand's Economic Structure: Towards Balanced Development?* Chon Buri: Thailand Development Research Institute, pp. II-1–II-24.

   1992b. "Priorities for Thai Tourism Development in the 1990s." In *Thailand's Economic Structure: Towards Balanced Development?* Chon Buri: Thailand Development Research Institute, pp. III-1–III-27.

Monsakul, Manusavee. 2000. "Policy Networks and Thai Industrial Policy During the Economic Crisis: A Case Study of the Thai Automobile Industry." M.A. Thesis, University of Auckland..

Montobbio, Fabio and Franceso Rampa. 2005. "The Impact of Technology and Structural Change on Export Performance in Nine Developing Countries." *World Development*. 33:4, pp. 527–547.

Motonishi, Taizo. 2003. "Why Has Income Inequality in Thailand Increased? An Analysis Using 1975–1998 Surveys." Manila: Asian Development Bank, ERD Working Paper No. 43 (June).

Moon Chung-in and Rashemi Prasad. 1998. "Networks, Politics and Institutions." In Steve Chan, Cal Clark, and Danny Lam, eds., *Beyond the Developmental State: East Asia's Political Economies Reconsidered*. New York: St. Martin's Press, pp. 9–24.

Moran, Theodore H. 1998. *Foreign Direct Investment and Development*. Washington, DC: Institute for International Economics.

Morawetz, David. 1981. *Why The Emperor's New Clothes Are Not Made in Colombia: A Case Study in Latin American and East Asian Manufcatured Exports*. Boulder: Oxford University Press for the World Bank.

Morell, David. 1972. "Thailand: Military Checkmate." *Asian Survey.* 12:2 (February), pp. 156–167.

1974. "Power and Parliament in Thailand: The Futile Challenge." Ph.D. diss., Woodrow Wilson School, Princeton University.

Muscat, Robert. 1994. *The Fifth Tiger: A Study of Thai Development Policy.* Armonk: M.E. Sharpe.

Mutebi, Alex. 2006. "Thailand's Independent Agencies under Thaksin: Relentless Gridlock and Uncertainty." *Southeast Asian Affairs.* (January), pp. 303–321.

National Industrial Development Committee (NIDC). 1998. "Khrongkan Pai Dai Padthipat Kan Phea Kan Prab Prung Khrong Sang Utsahaakam" (Projects Under the Industrial Restructuring Plan). Bangkok.

Nelson, Joan. 1999. *Reforming Health and Education: The World Bank, The IDB, and Complex Institutional Change.* Washington, DC: Overseas Development Council.

Nelson, Richard F., 1993. *National Innovation Systems: A Comparative Analysis.* New York: Oxford University Press.

Nelson, Richard F. and S. J. Winter. 1982. *An Evolutionary Theory of Economic Change.* Cambridge: Belknap Press.

NESDB. 2008. Office of the National Economic and Social Development Board, with the World Bank. "Towards a Knowledge Economy in Thailand." Bangkok: NESDB.

Nexus Associates Inc. 2000. "Evaluation of Industry Technical Institutes in Thailand." Report submitted to the Royal Thai Government and the World Bank. Belmont.

Nikorn Wattanapanom, Philippe de Lombaerde, Pradit Withisuphakorn, and Pradit Wanarat. 1997. "The Relocation of the garment industry as an instrument for regional development in the Northeastern region of Thailand." Bangkok: Centre for ASEAN Studies-CAS Discussion paper No. 11 (April).

Noble, Gregory. 1998. *Collective Action in East Asia: How Ruling Parties Shape Industrial Policy.* Ithaca Cornell University Press.

Noland, Marcus and Howard Pack. 2003. *Industrial Policy in an Era of Globalization: Lessons from East Asia.* Washington: Institute for International Economics.

Nordhaug, Kristen. 1997. "State and U.S. Hegemony in Taiwan's Economic Transformation." Ph.D. diss., Roskilde University Centre. Oslo: Centre for Development and the Environment, University of Oslo, Dissertations and Thesis No. 3/97.

North, Douglass and Robert Paul Thomas. 1970. "An Economic Theory of the Growth of the Western World," *The Economic History Review,* 2nd series. 23:1, pp. 1–17.

Nunberg, Barbara. 1986. "Structural Change and State Policy: The Politics of Sugar in Brazil Since 1964." *Latin American Research Review.* 21:2, pp. 53–92.

Ockey, James. 1992. *Business Leaders, Gangsters and the Middle Class.* Ph.D. diss., Dept. of Government, Cornell University.

2004a. *Making Democracy: Leadership, Class, Gender, and Political Participation in Thailand.* Bangkok: Silkworm Books for University of Hawaii Press.

2004b. "State, Bureaucracy and Polity in Modern Thai Politics." *Journal of Contemporary Asia.* 34:2, pp. 143–160.

OECD. 1999. "Industrial Restructuring in the Asian Economies." Paris: Directorate for Science, Technology and Industry, OECD (February).

Office of the Cane and Sugar Board. 2006. "Sugarcane and Sugar Industry and Renewable Energy Production (sic)." (March). http://www.ocsb.go.th – accessed 12/7/06.

Office of Industrial Economics (OIE). 2002. "Automotive Industry in Thailand." (March). Bangkok: Ministry of Industry.

Ohno, Kenichi. 2005. "Ministry of Industry – Vietnam Development Forum Joint Mission on Industrial Policy Formulation in Thailand" (March).

Okamoto, Yumiko and Fredrik Sjoholm. 2000. "Productivity in the Indonesian Automotive Industry." *ASEAN Economic Bulletin.* 17:1 (April), pp. 60–73.

Olson, Mancur. 1965. *The Logic of Collective Action.* Cambridge: Harvard University Press.

Orsini, Kay. 1978. "Thai Synthetic Manufacturers' Association: Thai Government Help Wanted." *Business in Thailand.* 9:6 (June), pp. 42–45.

Ostrom, Eleanor. 1990. *Governing the Commons: The Evolution of Institutions for Collective Action.* Cambridge: Cambridge University Press.

Overholt, William. 1999. "Thailand's Financial and Political Systems: Crisis and Rejuvenation." *Asian Survey.* 39:6 (December), pp. 1009–1035.

Pack, Howard. 2000a "Industrial Policy: Growth Elixir or Poison?" *The World Bank Research Observer.* 15:1 (February), pp. 47–67.

2000b. "Research and Develpment in the Industrial Development Process." In Linsu Kim and Richard R. Nelson, eds., *Technology, Learning and Innoation: Experiences of the Newly Industrializing Economies.* New York: Cambridge University Press, pp. 69–94.

Page, John M. 1994. "The East Asian Miracle: An Introduction." *World Development.* 22:4, pp. 615–625.

Painter, Martin. 2005. "Thaksinocracy or Managerialization? Reforming the Thai Bureaucracy." Working Paper Series No. 76, Southeast Asia Research Centre, City University of Hong Kong (May).

Paitoon Chettamonarongchai, Arroon Auansakul, and Decha Supawan. 2001. "Assessing the Transportation Problems of the Sugar Cane Industry in Thailand." *Transport and Communications.* 70, pp. 31–40.

Pakorn, Abdulbhan and Khubbol Suksupha. 1976. "Growth and Structure of the Sugar Industry in Thailand." *International Sugar Journal.* 78, pp. 266–299.

Palpacuer, Florence, Peter Gibbon, and Lotte Thomsen. 2004. "New Challenges for Developing Country Suppliers in Global Clothing Chains: A Comparative European Perspective." *World Development.* 33:3, pp. 409–430.

Pansak Vinyaratn. 2004. *21st Century Thailand: Facing the Challenge – Economic Policy and Strategy.* Hong Kong: CSLA Books.

Paopongsakorn Nipon. 1999. "Thailand Automotive Industry (Part I)." Thailand Development Research Institute, Bangkok. Processed.

Paopongsakorn Nipon and Belinda Fuller. 1997. "Thailand's Development Experience from the Economic System Perspective: Open Politics and Industrial Activism." In Toru Yanagihara and Susumu Sambommatsu, eds., *East Asian Development Experience: Economic System Approach and Its Applicability.* Tokyo: IDE, pp. 466–518.

Paopongsakorn Nipon and Somkiat Tangkitvanich. 2001. "Industrial Restructuring in Thailand: A Critical Assessment." In Seichi Masuyama, Donna Vandenbrink, and Chia Siow Yue, eds., *Industrial Restructuring in East Asia: Towards the 21st Century.* Tokyo: Nomura Research Institute, pp. 108–138.

Paopongsakorn Nipon and Kriengkrai Techakanont. 2007. "The Development of Automotive Industry Clusters and Production Networks in Thailand." Unpublished ms, Thammasat University, Faculty of Economics (May).

Paopongsakorn Nipon and Pawadee Tonguthai. 1998. "Technological Capability Building and the Sustainability of Export Success in Thailand's Textile and Electronics Industries." In Dieter Ernst, Tom Ganiatsos, and Lynn Mytelka., eds., *Technological Capabilities and Export Success in Asia.* New York: Routledge.

Paopongsakorn Nipon and Viroj Na Ranong. 2000. *Khrongkanwichai utsahakam oi lae namtansai: lu thang kankkayai kanphalit phua phoem kansongawk. lem thi 1(A study of the sugarcane and refined sugar industry: toward increasing productivity to expand exports.* vol 1). Bangkok: Thailand Development Research Institute Foundation.

Pasuk Pongpaichit. 1995. *Thailand: Economy and Politics.* Kuala Lumpur: Oxford University Press.

    1997. "Power in Transition: Thailand in the 1990s." In Kevin Hewison, ed., *Political Change in Thailand: Democracy and Participation.* New York: Routledge, pp. 21–41.

Pasuk Pongpaichit and Chris Baker. 1996. *Thailand's Boom.* Chiang Mai: Silkworm Books.

    1998. *Thailand's Boom and Bust.*

    2000. *Thailand's Crisis.* Bangkok: Silkworm Books.

    2002. " 'The Only Good Populist is a Rich Populist': Thaksin Shinawatra and Thailand's Democracy." Murdoch University, Southeast Asia Research Centre Working Paper, No. 36.

    2004a. "Thailand Under Thaksin: Another Malaysia?" Murdoch Asia Research Centre, Working Paper No. 109.

    2004b. *Thaksin: The Business of Politics in Thailand.* Chiang Mai: Silworm Books.

Pasuk Pongpaichit and Sungsidh Priyiarangsan. 1994. *Corruption and Democracy in Thailand.* Bangkok: Silworm Books.

Pavinee Kiatchaipipat. 1994. "Ready-Made Garments." *Bangkok Bank Monthly Review.* 35:9 (September), pp. 24–28.

Peera Charoenporn. 2001. "Automotive Parts Procurement System in Thailand: A Comparison of American and Japanese Companies." M.A. Thesis, Dept. of Economics, Thammasat University.

Perez-Aleman, Paola. 2005, "Cluster Formation, Institutions and Learning: the Emergence of Clusters and Development in Chile." *Industrial and Corporate Change.* 14:4 (June), pp. 651–677.

Perkins, Dwight. 1994. "There Are At Least Three Models of East Asian Development." *World Development.* 22:4, pp. 655–661.

Petchanet Pratruangkrai. 2006. "Govenrment Bounces Rubber Plan." *Nation* (July 27).

Phillips, Herbert P. 1976. "Some Premises of American Scholarship on Thailand." In Clark Neher, ed., *Modern Thai Politics*. Cambridge: Schenkman, pp. 446–466.

Phitsanes Jessadachatr.1977. *A History of Sugar Policies in Thailand: 1937–75.* Bangkok: Faculty of Economics, Thammasat University.

Pichai Kanivichaporn. 1999. "Outlook for the Thai Sugar Industry." Paper prepared for The 5th Annual Asia International Sugar Conference, Cebu Island, The Philippines, 13–16 July.

Pichaya Changsorn. 2005." 'Detroit of Asia': Extra Push Needed for Auto Goal." *The Nation*. September 5..

Pierson, Paul. 2000. "Increasing Returns, Path Dependence, and the Study of Politics." *American Political Science Review*. 94 (June), pp. 251–267.

Porter, Michael E. 2003. "Thailand's Competitiveness: Creating the Foundations for Higher Productivity." (May 4). Institute for Strategy and Competitiveness, Harvard Business School.

Prasert Tapaneeyangkul. 2001. "Thailand – Country Profile." In *Green Production in Selected Industry Sectors*. Tokyo: Asian Productivity Organization.

Prasertkul, Seksan. 1989. "The Transformation of the Thai State and Economic Change (1855–1945)." Ph. D. diss., Cornell University.

Prayong, Netayarak.1988. *Kankamnot nayobai sethakit kankaset: karani tuayang Kankamnot rakha oi* [Setting agricultural economic policy: the case of sugarcane Pricing]. Bangkok: Faculty of Economics, Thammasat University.

Pritchett, Lant. 1997."Divergence, Big Time." *Journal of Economic Perspectives*. 11:3 (Summer), pp. 3–17.

2003. "A Toy Collection, A Socialist Start, and a Democratic Dud? Growth Theory, Vietnam, and the Philippines." In Dani Rodrik, ed., *In Search of Prosperity*. Princeton: Princeton University Press, pp. 124–151.

2004. Does Learning to Add Up Add Up? The Returns to Schooling in Aggregate Data," BREAD Working Paper #053.

Pritchett, Lant and Michael Woolcock. 2004. "When the Solution is the Problem: Arraying the Disarray in Development." *World Development*. 32:2, pp. 191–212.

Przeworski, Adam and Fernando Limongi. 1993. "Political Regimes and Economic Growth." *Journal of Economic Perspectives*. 7:2 (Summer), pp. 51–69.

Przeworski, Adam, Michael E. Alvarez, Jose Antonio Cheibub, and Fernando Limongi. 2000. *Democracy and Development: Political Institutions and Well-Being in the World 1950–1990*. New York: Cambridge University Press.

Radosevic, S. 1999. "International Technology Transfer Policy: From 'Contract Bargaining' to 'Sourcing'." *Technovation*. 19, pp. 433–444.

Ramsay, Ansil. 1987. "The Political Economy of Sugar in Thailand," *Pacific Affairs*. 60:2, pp. 248–270.

Rasiah, Rajah. 2000. "Politics, Institutions and Flexibility: Microelectronics Transnationals and Machine Tool Linkages in Malaysia." In Frederick Deyo, Richard Doner, and Eric Hershberg, eds., *Economic Governance and the Challenge of Flexibility in East Asia*. Boulder: Rowman and Littlefield.

2003." Manufacturing Export Growth in Indonesia, Malaysia and Thailand." In K. S. Jomo, ed., *Southeast Asian Paper Tigers? From Miracle to Debacle and Beyond*. London: Routledge Curzon, pp. 19–80.

2004. "Technological Intensity and Export Incidence: A Study of Foreign and Local Auto-Parts, Electronics and Garment Firms in Indonesia." Maastricht: United Nations University/INTECH, Discussion Paper #2004-5.

Ravenhill, John. 2002. "From National Champions to Global Partners: Crisis, Globalization, and the Korean Auto Industry." In William Keller and Richard Samuels, eds., *Crisis and Innovation in Asian Technology*. New York: Cambridge University Press, pp. 108–136.

Riker, William H. 1962. *The Theory of Political Coalitions*. New Haven: Yale University Press.

Ritchie, Bryan. 2005. "Progress through Setback or Mired in Mediocrity? Crisis and Institutional Change in Southeast Asia." *Journal of East Asian Studies*. 5:2 (June), pp. 273–314.

Robinson, David, Yangho Byeon, and Ranjit Teja. 1991. "Thailand: Adjusting to Success – Current Policy Issues." Occasional Paper 85. Washington: IMF.

Robison, Richard. 1986. *Indonesia: The Rice of Capital*. London: Allen and Unwin.

Rock, Michael. 1995. "Thai Industrial Policy: How Irrelevant Was It to Export Success? *Journal of International Development*. 7:5, pp. 745–757.

2000. "Thailand's Old Bureaucratic Polity and Its New Semi-Democracy." In K. S. Jomo and Mushtaq Khan, eds., *Rents, Rent-Seeking and Economic Development*. Kuala Lumpur: Cambridge University Press, pp. 182–206.

2003. "The Politics of Development Policy and Development Policy Reform in New Order Indonesia." Ann Arbor: William Davidson Institute Working Paper #632, University of Michigan Business School.

Rodrik, Dani. 2003. "Introduction: What Do We Learn from Country Narratives?" In Rodrik, ed., *In Search of Prosperity: Analytic Narratives on Economic Growth*. Princeton: Princeton University Press, pp. 1–22.

2004. "Industrial Policy for the Twenty-First Century." Harvard University, Kennedy School of Government.

2007. *One Economics, Many Recipes: Globalization, Institutions and Economic Growth*. Princeton: Princeton University Press.

Romer, Paul. 1990. "Endogenous Technological Change." *Journal of Political Economy*. 98:5, S71–S102.

1994. "The Origins of Endogenous Growth." *Journal of Economic Perspectives*. 8:1, pp. 3–22.

Ross, Michael. 1999. "The Political Economy of the Resource Curse." *World Politics*. 51:2, pp. 297–322.

Sabel, Charles. 1994. "Learning by Monitoring: The Institutions of Economic Development." In Neil Smelser and Richard Swedberg, eds., *The Handbook of Economic Sociology.*. Princeton: Princeton University Press.

Saint, William. 1982. "Farming for Energy: Social Options under Brazil's National Alcohol Programme." *World Development*. 10:3, pp. 223–238.

Sakkarin Niyomsilpa. 2000. *The Political Economy of Telecommunications Reforms in Thailand*. London: Pinter.

Sandler, Todd. 1992. *Collective Action: Theory and Applications.* Ann Arbor: University of Michigan Press.

Sato, Yuri. 1996. "The Astra Group: A Pioneer of Management Modernisation in Indonesia." *The Developing Economies.* XXXIV:3 (September), pp. 251–267.

Satyanath, Shanker. 2006. *Globalization, Politics, and Financial Turmoil: Asia's Banking Crisis.* New York: Cambridge University Press.

Sayon Inson. 1987. "Anachak Thai Rung Ruang" [The Thai Rung Ruang Kingdom], *Phuchatkan* [Manager]. 5:51 (December), pp. 113–132.

Scharpf, Fritz. 1997. *Games Real Actors Play: Actor-Centered Institutionalism in Policy Research.* Boulder: Westview.

Schein, Edgar H. 1996. *Strategic Pragmatism: The Case of Singapore's Economic Development Board.* Cambridge, MA: MIT Press.

Schiller, Daniel. 2006a. "Higher Education Funding Reform and University–Industry Links in Developing Countries: The Case of Thailand." *Higher Education.* 54:3 (October), pp. 543–556.

2006b. "The Emerging Role of Public Universities in Upgrading the Thai Innovation System." Paper presented at 3rd Asialics International Conference, Shanghai, April 1–19.

Schleifer, Andrei and Robert W. Vishny. 1993. "Corruption." *Quarterly Journal of Economics.* 108 (August), pp. 599–617.

Schmitz, Hubert. 2005. *Value Chain Analysis for Policy Makers and Practitioners.* Geneva: International Labor Office.

Schneider, Ben Ross. 1991. *Politics within the State: Elite Bureaucrats and Industrial Policy in Authoritarian Brazil.* Pittsburgh: University of Pittsburgh Press.

1999. "The *Desorllista* State in Brazil and Mexico." In Meredith Woo-Cumings, ed., *The Developmental State.* Ithaca: Cornell University Press, pp. 276–305.

2004. *Business Politics and the State in Twentieth-Century Latin America.* New York: Cambridge University Press.

Schneider, Ben Ross and Sylvia Maxfield. 1997. "Business, the State, and Economic Performance in Developing Countries." In Maxfield and Schneider, eds., *Business and the State in Developing Countries.* Ithaca: Cornell University Press, pp. 3–35.

Schrank, Andrew. 2004. "Ready-to-Wear Development? Foreign Investment, Technology Transfer, and Learning by Watching in the Apparel Trade." *Social Forces.* 83:1 (September), pp. 123–156.

Shafer, Michael. 1994. *Winners and Losers: How Sectors Shape the Developmental Prospects of States.* Ithaca: Cornell University Press.

Shatkin, Gavin. 2004. "Globalization and Local Leadership: Growth, Power and Politics in Thailand's Eastern Seaboard." *International Journal of Urban and Regional Research.* 28:1 (March), pp. 11–26.

Sheales, T., S. Gordon, and C. Toyne. 1999. "Sugar: International Policies Affecting Market Expansion." Australian Bureau of Agricultural and Resource Economics, Research Report 99.14. Canberra, Australia.

Siamwalla, Ammar. 1975. "Stability, Growth and Distribution in the Thai Economy." In Prateep Sondysuvan, ed., *Finance, Trade and Economic Development in Thailand.* Bangkok: Sompong Press.

1991a. "Why do Voters Elect Corrupt Politicians? Towards a Theory of Representative Kleptocracy." Unpublished ms, Thailand Development Research Institute.

1991b. "Land-Abundant Agricultural Growth and Some of Its Consequences: The Case of Thailand." Bangkok: Thailand Development Research Institute.

1992a. "Myths, Demons, and the Future of Thai Agriculture." In *Thailand's Economic Structure: Towards Balanced Development?* Chon Buri: Thailand Development Research Institute, pp. I-1– I-37.

1992b. "Liberalization: What For?" Unpublished ms, Thailand Development Research Institute. (March).

1996. "Thai Agriculture: From Engine of Growth to Sunset Status." *TDRI Quarterly Review.* 11:4 (December), pp. 3–10.

1997a. "The Thai Economy: Fifty Years of Thai Expansion." In Ammar Siamwalla, ed., *Thailand's Boom and Bust.* Bangkok: Thailand Development Research Institute, pp. 1–20.

1997b. "Can a Democracy Manage its Macroeconomy? The Case of Thailand." In *Thailand's Boom and Bust.* Bangkok: Thailand Development Research Institute. Presented as the Gibson Lecture at Queen's University, Ontario.

2000. "Anatomy of the Thai Crisis." Unpublished ms, Thailand Development Research Institute.

2001. "Roles and Actors in the Provision of Rural Goods and Services." In Ammar Siamwalla, ed., *The Evolving Roles of State, Private and Local Actors in Rural Asia.* New York: Oxford University Press, for the Asian Development Bank, pp. 23–82.

Siamwalla, Ammar and Andrew MacIntyre. 2001. "The Political Economy of Food Grain and Fertilizer Distribution." In Ammar, ed., *The Evolving Roles of State, Private, and Local Actors in Rural Asia.* Manila: Asian Development Bank, pp. 213–270.

Siamwalla, Ammar and Suthad Setboonsarng. 1987. *Agricultural Pricing Policies In Thailand: 1960–1985.* Bangkok: Thailand Development Research Institute.

Siamwalla, Ammar, Paitoon Wiboonchutikula, and Surakiart Sathirathai. 1989. "Fun and Games with Quotas: Thailand and the VERs on Cassava and Garments." Paper prepared for the International Conference on Voluntary Export Restraints, Trade Policy Research Center, Washington DC, June 5–8.

Skinner, G. William. 1957. *Chinese Society in Thailand: An Analytical History.* Ithaca: Cornell University Press.

1958. *Leadership and Power in the Chinese Community of Thailand.* Ithaca: Cornell University Press.

Silcock, T. H. 1967. *Thailand: Social and Economic Studies.* Singapore: Donald Moore.

Singh, Dukhpal. 2005. "Role of the State in Contract Farming in Thailand: Experience and Lessons." ASEAN Economic Bulletin. 22:2, pp. 217–228.

Slater, Dan. 2006. *Ordering Power: Contentious Politics, State Building, and Authoritarian Durability in Southeast Asia.* Ph.D., diss., Department of Political Science, Emory University.

2008. "Altering Authoritarianism: Institutional Complexity and Autocratic Agency in Indonesia." Unpublished ms, University of Chicago.

Snyder, Richard. 2001. "Scaling Down: The Subnational Comparative Method." *Studies in Comparative International Development.* 36:1, pp. 93–110.

Sombat Chmpathong. 1998. "The Textile Industry." 1998. *Bangkok Bank Monthly Review* (http://www.bbl.co.th/research/junindust1.htm – accessed January 1, 2006).

Somboon Siriprachai. 1998. *Control and Rent-Seeking: The Role of the State in the Thai Cassava Industry*. Lund, Sweden: Lund University Press.

——— 2008. "Thailand." In Anis Chawdhury and Iyanatul Islam, eds., *Handbook on the Northeast And Southeast Asian Economies*. Edward Elgar, pp. 129–148.

Somporn Thapanachai. 2004. "Some Signs of Progress." *Bangkok Post Mid-year Economic Review*.

Solow, Robert. 1957. "Technical Change and the Aggregate Production Function." *Review of Economics and Statistics*. 39, pp. 312–320.

Stifel, Lawrence. 1963. *The Textile Industry: A Case Study of Industrial Development in the Philippines*. Ithaca: Cornell University Press.

Stiglitz, Joseph E. 2000. "Contributions of the Economics of Information to Twentieth Century Economics." *Quarterly Journal of Economics*. (November), pp. 1441–1478.

Streeck, Wolfgang, eds. 2001. *The Origins of Non-Liberal Capitalism: Germany and Japan in Comparison*. Ithaca: Cornell University Press.

Subramanian, Arvind and Devesh Roy. 2003. "Who Can Explain the Mauritian Miracle?" In Dani Rodrik, ed., *In Search of Prosperity: Analytic Narratives on Economic Growth*. Princeton: Princeton University Press, pp. 203–243.

Suehiro, Akira. 1982. "Textile Industry." In *Comparative Advantage of Manufacturing Industries in Asian Countries*. Tokyo: Institute of Developing Economies.

——— 1983. *Development and Structure of Textile Industry in Thailand 1946–80*. Bangkok: National Research Council of Thailand (September).

——— 1989. *Capital Accumulation in Thailand: 1885–1985*. Tokyo: Center for East Asian Cultural Studies.

——— 1992. "Capitalist Development in Postwar Thailand: Commercial Bankers, Industrial Elite, and Agribusiness Groups." In Ruth McVey, ed., *Southeast Asian Capitalists*. Ithaca: Cornell University Southeast Asia Program, pp. 35–65.

Sung, Kayser. 1991. "Thailand's Success and Bottleneck." *Textile Asia*. (September), pp. 28–32, 50.

Suphat Suphachalasai. 1989. "Export Growth of Thai Clothing and Textiles." *Working Paper 89/4*. Canberra: National Center for Development Studies, Australian National University.

——— 1990. "Export Growth of Thai Clothing and Textiles." *The World Economy*. 13:1 (March), pp. 51–73.

——— 1992. *The Structure of the Textile Industry and Government Policy in Thailand. Background Report*. Bangkok: Thailand Development Research Institute.

——— 1994. *Thailand's Clothing and Textile Exports*. Singapore: Institute of East Asian Studies.

——— 1998. "Textiles Industry in Thailand." Singapore: APEC Studies Centre Network, Monash University (November).

Suwanee Ruangwithaychote. 1998. "Thai Textiles Meets the Third Wave" (in Thai). *Textile Digest*. 6:58 (September–October), pp. 22–25.

Tait, Niki. 2005. *An Overview of Thailand's Clothing Industry: Management Briefing*. Worcestershire, UK: Aroq Limited / Just-style.com

Takayasu, Ken'ichi and Minako Mori. 2002. *East Asia's Automobile Industries in the Global Strategies of Vehicle Assemblers.* Tokyo: Center for Pacific Business Studies, Japan Research Institute (January).

2004. "The Global Strategies of Japanese Vehicle Assmeblers and the Implications for the Thai Automobile Industry." In Shahid Yusuf, M. Anjum Altaf, and Kaoru Naveshima, eds., *Global Production Networking and Technological Change in East Asia.* Washington, DC: Oxford University Press/World Bank, pp. 209–254.

Tambunlertchai, Somsak and Ippei Yamazawa. 1983. *Manufactured Export Promotion: The Case of Thailand.* Tokyo: Institute of Developing Economies.

"Teijin Polyester (Thailand)." 1998. Siam Future Development Co., http://www.siamfuture.com/WorldInThai/teijin.asp (accessed April 27, 2007).

Tejapira, Kasian. 2002. "Post-Crisis Economic Impasse and Political Recovery in Thailand: The Resurgence of Economic Nationalism." *Critical Asian Studies.* 34:3, pp. 323–356.

2006. "Toppling Thaksin." *New Left Review.* 39 (May–June), pp. 5–37.

Temple, Jonathan. 1999. "The New Growth Evidence." *Journal of Economic Literature.* (March), pp. 112–156.

2001. "Generalizations That Aren't? Evidence on Education and Growth." *European Economic Review.* 45:4–6, pp. 905–918.

Tendler, Judith. 1997. *Good Government in the Tropics.* Baltimore: Johns Hopkins University Press..

Terdudomtham, Thamavit. 1996. "The Automobile Industry in Thailand." Bangkok: Thailand Development Research Institute.

Tewari, Meenu. 2006. "Is Price and Cost Competitiveness Enough for Apparel Firms to Gain Market Share in the World After Quotas? A Review." *Global Economy Journal* 6:4, pp. 1–46.

Thai Automotive Institute. 2002. *The Master Plan for Thai Automotive Industry 2002–2006, Proposed to the Office of Industrial Economics, Ministry of Industry.* (September).

2005. *Annual Report.*

"Thai Sugar, and Sugarcane, 2006: Higher Production Costs, Falling Outputs." *Thai News Service* (November 20).

"Thailand." 1997. Proceedings of the Fiji/FAO 1997 Asia Pacific Sugar Conference. http://www.fao.org/DOCREP/005X0513E/x0513224.htm (accessed 12/4/06).

"Thailand: Agriculture and Cooperatives Ministry Aims to Increase Amount of Sugar." *Thai News Service* (October 20).

"Thailand Sugar Semi-Annual 2005." GAIM Report Number TH5099, (September 30). www.fas.usda.gov

"Thailand Sugar: Sugar Shortage Situation 2006." GAIN Report #TH6011, January 1, 2. www.fas.usda.gov.

Thaksin Shinawatra. 2001. *Rethinking Recovery.* Singapore: Institute of Southeast Asian Studies.

"The Textile Industry." 1987. *Business in Thailand.*18:7, pp. 42–50.

Thee Kian Wie. 2003. *Recollections – The Indonesian Economy, 1950s–1960s.* Singapore: Institute of Southeast Asian Studies.

2006. "Policies Affecting Indonesia's Industrial Technology Development." *ASEAN Economic Bulletin.* 22:3, pp. 341–359.

Thelen, Kathleen. 2003. "How Institutions Evolve: Insights from Comparative Historical Analysis." In James Mahoney and Dietrich Rueschemeyer, eds., *Comparative Historical Analysis in the Social Sciences.* New York: Cambridge University Press.

Thippawal Srijantr, François Molle, and Chatchom Chompadist. 1999. "Profitability and Yield Gap of Sugar Cane Cultivation in the Mae Klong Region." *Kasetsart Journal of Agricultural Economics.*

Thitinan Pongsudhirak. 2001. "Crisis from Within: The Politics of Macroeconomic Management in Thailand, 1947–1997." Ph.D. diss., London School of Economics.

Thun, Eric. 2001. "Growing Up and Moving Out: Globalization of 'Traditional' Industries in Taiwan," Industrial Performance Center, MIT IPC Globalization Working Paper 00–004, MIT [available at Google Scholar].

Todaro, Michael P. 2000. *Economic Development.* Reading: Addison-Wesley.

Tsebelis, George. 2002. *Veto Players: How Political Institutions Work.* Princeton: Princeton University Press.

TTIS. 1993. "Effect of AFTA on Textile Competitiveness" (Final Report). Bangkok: Report for the National Federation of Thai Textile Industries (August).

UNIDO (United Nations Industrial Development Organization). 1984. *Interim Report on Restructuring of the Textile Industry* Bangkok (August).

1988. *Industrial Restructuring Policies in Developing Asian Countries with Particular Attention to the Textile and Garment Industry.* Geneva. (December 29).

2002. *Industrial Development Report 2002–2003: Innovation and Learning to Drive Industrial Development.* Geneva: UNIDO.

Unger, Danny. 1998. *Building Social Capital in Thailand: Fibres, Finance and Infrastructure.* New York: Cambridge University Press.

Uriu, Robert. 1996. *Troubled Industries: Confronting Industrial Change in Japan.* Ithaca: Cornell University Press.

Vallop Tiasiri. 2003. "Key Success Factors of Thai automotive Industry." Bangkok: Thailand Automotive Institute.

Vartiainen, Juhana. 1999. "The Economics of Successful State Intervention in Industrial Transformation." In Meredith Woo-Cumings, ed., *The Developmental State.* Ithaca: Cornell University Press, pp. 200–235.

Veloso, Francisco. 2000. "The Automotive Supply Chain: Global Trends and Asian Perspectives." Background paper for project on international competitiveness of Asian economies. Massachusetts Institute of Technology. Processed.

Veloso, Francisco and Erica Fuchs. 2004. "The Future of the Asian Auto Industry: Regional Integration, Alternative Designs, and Chinese Leadership." *International Journal of Vehicle Design.* 35:1/2, pp. 111–136.

Veloso, Francisco, Jorge Soto Romero, and Alice Amsden. 1998. "A Comparative Assessment of the Auto Parts Industry in Taiwan and Mexico: Policy Implications for Thailand." Massachusetts Institute of Technology, Cambridge, MA, Processed.

Vickery, Graham. 1996. "Globalization in the Automobile Industry." *Globalization of Industry.* Paris: OECD, pp. 153–205.

Virat Tandaechanurat. 2007. "Coping with Restrictive Policies and Maintaining Competitiveness: Thailand." Presentation to Regional Dialogue on Restrictive Policies
on the Textile and Clothing Trade in Asia and the Pacific, Shanghai, April 9–10.

Viroj NaRanong. 2000 "The Thai Sugar Industry: Crisis and Opportunities," *TDRI
Quarterly Review.* 15:3 (September), pp. 8–16.

Wade, Robert. 1982. *Irrigation and Agricultural Politics in South Korea.* Boulder:
Westview.

    1990. *Governing the Market.* Princeton: Princeton University Press.

    1992. "East Asian Economic Success: Conflicting Paradigms, Partial Insights,
Shaky Evidence." *World Politics.* 44:2, pp. 270–320.

    2003. "What Strategies are Viable for Developing Countries Today? The World
Trade Organization and the Shrinking of 'Developmental Space." *Review of
International Political Economy.* 10:4 (November), pp. 621–644.

    2005. "Escaping the Squeeze: Lessons from East Asia on How Middle-Income
Countries Can Grow Faster." In Blandine Laperche, ed., *John Kenneth
Galbraith and the Future of Economics.* Basingstoke: Palgrave Macmillan.

    2006. "The Case for 'Open-Economy Industrial Policy'." Paper presented at the
World Bank, April 25–26, Washington, DC.

Waldner, David. 1999. *State Building and Late Development.* Ithaca: Cornell
University press.

Warin Wonghanchao. 1986. "The Relationship between the Business Elites, Sugarcane Planters, and the Bureaucracy in the Thai Sugar Industry." Paper prepared for the Social Science Research Council-Joint Council for Southeast Asia,
Sukhothai, Thailand, December 9–12.

Warr, Peter. 1993a. *The Thai Economy in Transition.* New York: Cambridge
University Press.

    1993b. "The Thai Economy." In Warr, ed., *The Thai Economy in Transition.*
New York: Cambridge University Press, pp. 1–80.

    1997. "The Thai Economy: From Boom to Gloom?" *Southeast Asian Affairs
1997.* Singapore: Institute of Southeast Asian Studies, pp. 317–333.

    1998. "Thailand." In Ross H. McLeod and Ross Garnaut, eds., *East Asia in Crisis:
From Being in a Miracle to Needing One?* London and New York: Routledge,
pp. 49–65.

Wattanasiritham, Supawan. 2000. "The Impact of Local Content Requirement
Policy on the Development of Thai Auto-parts Industry: Case of Engine
Industry." M.A. Thesis, Graduate School for International Development and
Cooperation, Hiroshima University.

Weiss, Linda. 1998. *The Myth of the Powerless State.* Ithaca: Cornell University Press.

Weerayut Chokchaimadon. 2006. "Thaksinization or Managerialism? Reforming the
Thai Bureaucracy 1." *Journal of Contemporary Asia.* (March) 36:1, pp. 26–47.

Whitley, Richard. 1992. *Business Systems in East Asia: Firms, Markets, and Soci-
eties.* London: Sage.

Williamson, Oliver. 1985. *The Economic Institutions of Capitalism.* New York:
Free Press.

    1995. "The Institutions and Governance of Economic Development and Reform."
In Michael Bruno and Boris Pleskovic, eds., *Proceedings of the World Bank
Annual Conference on Development Economics 1994 (sic),* Washington, DC:
The World Bank, pp. 71–197.

Wingfield, Tom 2002. "Democratization and Economic Crisis in Thailand: Political Business and the Changing Dynamic of the Thai State." In Edmund Terence Gomez, ed., *Political Business in East Asia*. New York: Routledge, pp. 250–300.

Wisan Puppavesa and Maureen Grewe. 1994. "Enhancing Thailand's Trade Policy through AFTA." *TDRI Quarterly Review*. 9:2 (June), pp. 7–14.

Wong Poh-kam and Chee-yuen Ng. 2001. "Rethinking the Development Paradigm: Lessons from Japan and the Four Asian NIEs." In Poh-Kam Wong and Chee-Yuen Ng, eds., *Industrial Policy, Innovation and Economic Growth*. Singapore: Singapore University Press, pp. 1–55.

Woo, Wing The. 1990. "The Art of Economic Development: Markets, Politics and Externalities." *International Organization*. 44:3 (Summer), pp. 403–429.

Woo-Cumings, Meredith. 1998. "National Security and the Rise of the Developmental State in South Korea and Taiwan." In Henry Rowen, ed., *Behind East Asian Growth: The Political and Social Foundations of Prosperity*. New York: Routledge, pp. 319–337.

1999. "Introduction: Chalmers Johnson and the Politics of Nationalism and Development." In Woo-Cumings, ed., *The Developmental State*. Ithaca: Cornell University Press, pp. 1–32.

Worawan Cahndoevwit. 2005. "Financing Universal Health-care Coverage. TDRI *Quarterly Review*. 20:3, pp. 14–19.

World Bank. 1983. *Managing Public Resources for Structural Adjustment*. Washington, DC.

1993. *The East Asian Miracle: Economic Growth and Public Policy*. New York: Oxford University Press.

2005a. "Thailand: Investment Climate, Firm Competitiveness, and Growth." Bangkok: World Bank Draft Report (August 30).

2005b. *Thailand Economic Monitor*. Bangkok.

2006a. *Thailand Economic Monitor*. Bangkok.

2006b. *Governance Matters 2006: A Decade of Measuring the Quality of Governance*. Washington, DC: The World Bank.

2008. *Thailand Economic Monitor* (April). Bangkok: World Bank Office.

Yamagata, Tatsufumi. 1993. "Taiwan's Textile Industry: From Industry Promotion to Trade Friction." In R. Inoue H. Kohama, and S. Urata, eds., *Industrial Policy in East Asia*, Tokyo: JETRO, pp. 90–115.

1998. "Ineffective Protection, Weak Linkage and Poor performance: The Philippine and Thai Textile Industries." In Mitsuhiro Kagami, John Humphrey, and Michael Piore, eds. *Learning, Liberalization and Economic Adjustment*. Tokyo: Institute of Developing Economies, pp. 34–59.

Yoffie, David B. 1983. *Power and Protectionism: Strategies of the Newly Industrializing Countries*. New York: Columbia University Press.

Yoshihara, Kunio. 1988. *The Rise of Ersatz Capitalism in Southeast Asia*. Singapore: Oxford University Press.

Young, Alwyn. 1994. "Lessons from East Asian NICs: A Contrarian View." *European Economic Review*. 38: 3–4, pp. 964–973.

Zimmerman, Beate and Jurgen Zeddies. n.d. "International Competitiveness of Sugar Production." Department of Farm Management, University of Hohenheim, Stuttgart, Germany.

Index